KEY TO THE HA  W9-BYR-628

THE MACMILLAN

HANDBOOK OF ENGLISH

THE MACMILLAN
HANDBOOK OF
ENGLISH Sixth Edition

John M. Kierzek
Late of Oregon State University

Walker Gibson
University of Massachusetts

Revised by
Robert F. Willson, Jr.
University of Missouri–Kansas City

Macmillan Publishing Co., Inc.
New York

MACMILLAN PUBLISHING CO., INC.
866 Third Avenue, New York, New York 10022
COLLIER MACMILLAN CANADA, LTD.

Library of Congress Cataloging in Publication Data

Kierzek, John M   (date)
  The Macmillan handbook of English.

  Bibliography: p.
  Includes indexes.
    1. English language—Rhetoric.   2. English language—Grammar—1950–   I. Gibson, Walker, joint author.   II. Willson, Robert Frank, (date)
  III. Title.
  PE1408.K57   1977   808'.042   75-40376
  ISBN 0-02-363040-X

Printing: 1 2 3 4 5 6 7 8   Year: 7 8 9 0 1 2 3

ACKNOWLEDGMENTS

Stefan Kanfer, "Orwell 25 Years Later: Future Imperfect" (*Time*, March 27, 1975, pp. 77–78). Reprinted by permission from *Time*, The Weekly Newsmagazine; Copyright Time Inc.

Winston Churchill, speech to the House of Commons. From *Blood, Sweat, and Tears.* Copyright 1941 by Winston S. Churchill. Courtesy of G. P. Putnam's Sons, Cassell & Company, Ltd., and McClelland and Stewart, Limited.

Learned Hand, *The Spirit of Liberty.* Copyright 1960 by Alfred A. Knopf, Inc.

Oscar Handlin, *The Americans.* Copyright © 1963 by Oscar Handlin. From *The Americans* by Oscar Handlin, by permission of Little, Brown and Co.–Atlantic Monthly Press and The Hutchinson Publishing Group.

J. Robert Oppenheimer, *Science and the Common Understanding.* Copyright 1953, 1954 by J. Robert Oppenheimer. Reprinted by permission of Simon and Schuster, Inc. and Dr. Oppenheimer, and the Oxford University Press, London.

Alexander Eliot and the Editors of *Life, Greece.* From *Greece,* by Alexander Eliot and the Editors of *Life.* © Time Incorporated, 1963.

Marchette Chute, *Ben Jonson of Westminster.* From the book *Ben Jonson of Westminster* by Marchette Chute. Copyright 1953 by Marchette Chute. Reprinted by permission of the publishers, E. P. Dutton & Co., Inc., and Martin Secker & Warburg Limited.

Edwin Way Teale, *The Strange Lives of Familiar Insects.* Reprinted by permission of Dodd, Mead & Company from *The Strange Lives of Familiar Insects* by Edwin Way Teale. Copyright © 1962 by Edwin Way Teale.

E. B. White, "Calculating Machine." "Calculating Machine" from *The Second Tree from the Corner* (1954) by E. B. White. Copyright 1951 by E. B. White. Originally appeared in *The New Yorker* and reprinted by permission of Harper &

iv

Row, Publishers, Inc., and Hamish Hamilton Ltd.

Robert Penn Warren, *All the King's Men.* Copyright 1946 by Harcourt, Brace & Co. Reprinted by permission of Harcourt, Brace & Co., and of Eyre & Spottiswoode, Ltd., London.

Virginia Woolf, *The Death of the Moth and Other Essays.* From *The Death of the Moth and Other Essays* by Virginia Woolf, copyright, 1942, by Harcourt Brace Jovanovich, Inc., and reprinted with their permission and the permission of Leonard Woolf and the Hogarth Press Limited.

Norman Podhoretz, "My Negro Problem—and Ours." Reprinted with the permission of Farrar, Straus & Giroux, Inc. from *Doings and Undoings* by Norman Podhoretz, Copyright © 1953, 1954, 1955, 1956, 1957, 1958, 1959, 1962, 1963, 1964 by Norman Podhoretz.

The New Yorker, unsigned movie review of *The Great Gatsby* and unsigned book review of *The Toll.* Reprinted by permission; © 1974 The New Yorker Magazine, Inc.

Harold S. Ulen and Guy Larcom, Jr., *The Complete Swimmer,* 1949. Reprinted by permission of Macmillan Publishing Co., Inc.

Vilhjalmur Stefansson, *Hunters of the Great North.* From *Hunters of the Great North,* copyright 1922, 1950 by Vilhjalmur Stefansson. Reprinted by permission of Harcourt, Brace & World, Inc.

Alan B. Shepard, Jr., and Walter M. Schirra, Jr., from *We Seven* by the Astronauts Themselves. Reprinted by permission of Simon and Schuster, Inc., and Cassell and Company, Ltd. Copyright © 1962.

Norman Mailer, *Miami and the Seige of Chicago.* From *Miami and the Seige of Chicago* by Norman Mailer. Copyright © 1968 by Norman Mailer. Reprinted by arrangement with The New American Library, Inc., New York, N.Y.

Phyllis McGinley, "Ladies on the Highway." Published originally as "Women Are Better Drivers." Reprinted from *The American Weekly* © 1959 by Hearst Publishing Co., Inc.; by permission of the author.

Bob Dylan, "With God on Our Side." © 1963 Warner Bros. Inc. All Rights Reserved. Used by permission.

Bertrand Russell, *In Praise of Idleness and Other Essays.* Copyright 1935 by Bertrand Russell. Reprinted by permission of W. W. Norton & Company, Inc.

Ernest Hemingway, *In Our Time.* Reprinted with the permission of Charles Scribner's Sons from *In Our Time* (Copyright 1925 Charles Scribner's Sons; renewal copyright 1953 Ernest Hemingway) by Ernest Hemingway. Reprinted with acknowledgments to the Executors of the Ernest Hemingway Estate and to Jonathan Cape Limited, publishers.

Alfred Kazin, "The Block and Beyond." From *A Walker in the City,* copyright, 1951, by Alfred Kazin. Reprinted by permission of Harcourt Brace Jovanovich, Inc.

Ernest Hemingway, *Death in the Afternoon.* Reprinted with the permission of Charles Scribner's Sons from *Death in the Afternoon* (Copyright 1952 Charles Scribner's Sons; renewal copyright © 1960 Ernest Hemingway) by Ernest Hemingway. Reprinted with acknowledgments to the Executors of the Ernest Hemingway Estate and to Jonathan Cape, Limited, publishers.

Bertrand Russell, *Education and the Good Life.* Published by Liveright Publishing Corp., N.Y. Copyright 1926 by Boni & Liveright, Inc. Also reprinted by permission of George Allen & Unwin, Ltd., from *On Education.*

Joyce Carol Oates, "New Heaven and Earth." Reprinted by permission of the author and her agent, Blanche C. Gregory, Inc. Copyright © 1972 by Joyce Carol Oates.

John Gunther, *Inside Russia Today.* From *Inside Russia Today* by John Gunther. Harper & Brothers, 1958. Reprinted by permission.

Herbert Hoover, *The Memoirs of Herbert Hoover: Years of Adventure.* Copyright 1951 by Herbert Hoover. Reprinted by permission of Macmillan Publishing Co., Inc.

Joseph Wood Krutch, *The Great Chain of Life.* From *The Great Chain of Life* by Joseph Wood Krutch. Houghton Mifflin Co., 1956. By permission of the publisher.

Allan Nevins and Henry Steele Commager, *The Pocket History of the United States.* From *The Pocket History of the United States* by Allan Nevins and Henry Steele Commager. Copyright © 1951, 1956, 1966 by Allan Nevins and Henry Steele Commager. Reprinted by permission of Simon & Schuster, Inc., Pocket Books Division.

The New York Times Magazine, "To the Planets and Beyond." From "To the Planets and Beyond," *The New York Times Magazine,* January 11, 1959. Reprinted by permission.

Nancy Hale, "The Two Way Imagination." "The Two Way Imagination" from *The Saturday Evening Post,* April 29, 1961. Reprinted with permission from *The Saturday Evening Post* © 1961 The Curtis Publishing Company.

David S. Berkeley, examples from "An Agreement of Subject and Verb in Anticipatory *There* Clauses," *American Speech,* May, 1953. By kind permission.

Webster's New World Dictionary of the American Language, entry for the word *pull.* From *Webster's New World Dictionary of the American Language,*

ACKNOWLEDGMENTS

Second College Edition. Copyright © 1974 by William Collins and World Publishing Company, Inc.

The American College Dictionary, entry for the word *crowd.* Reprinted by permission of Random House, Inc., from *The American College Dictionary.* Copyright 1947, copyright © 1966, 1973.

Webster's New Collegiate Dictionary, entries for the words *formicary, formidable, stiff,* and *stiff-arm.* By permission. From *Webster's New Collegiate Dictionary* © 1975 by G. & C. Merriam Co., Publishers of the Merriam-Webster Dictionaries.

The American Heritage Dictionary of the English Language, entry for the word *cool.* © 1969, 1970, 1971, 1973, 1975, 1976, Houghton Mifflin Company. Reprinted by permission from *The American Heritage Dictionary of the English Language.*

Thomas Wolfe, *Of Time and the River.* Reprinted from *Of Time and the River* by Thomas Wolfe, copyright 1935 Charles Scribner's Sons. Used by permission of Charles Scribner's Sons and William Heinemann Ltd., Publishers.

Margaret Halsey, *With Malice Toward Some.* Simon & Schuster 1938. Reprinted by permission of the publisher.

John Steinbeck, *Cannery Row.* From *Cannery Row.* Copyright 1945 by John Steinbeck, Reprinted by permission of The Viking Press, Inc., and William Heinemann, Ltd.

Roy Chapman Andrews, *This Amazing Planet.* Reprinted by permission of Putman's & Coward-McCann, publishers. Copyright 1938, 1939, 1940.

Preface

THE sixth edition of *The Macmillan Handbook of English* continues the tradition of its predecessors. It is a combined rhetoric and handbook dedicated to the propagation of precise, effective writing. The rhetoric (Sections I and II) contains material useful for classroom instruction and individual study in the strategies of composition; Section III, "A Handbook of Writing and Revision," provides guides and principles for the preparation, correction, and revision of papers. Each part supplements the other, however, and information and suggestions based on one may be approached and reevaluated with fresh perspectives drawn from the other.

As a new editor I have attempted to retain as much as possible of the good instruction laid down by the *Handbook*'s earlier developers, John M. Kierzek and Walker Gibson. Their discussions of standard grammar as a tool of good writing, of constructing efficient sentences and persuasive paragraphs, and of the processes of planning, setting down, and revising various kinds of essays remain, on the whole, untouched. My primary role in these topics has been to introduce recent examples of good exposition chosen from books and magazines that represent the diverse styles of writing found in the seventies; my second, much-less-exercised privilege has been the reduction of commentary, without sacrificing detail or thoroughness, to simplify some of the discussion.

These changes I have made are designed to conform to the major aim of the previous editors: to offer a guide that gives helpful, commonsense advice on questions relating to expository writing. One former chapter, "The English Language," has been replaced by "The Task of Writing" (Section I, Chapter 1), a discussion of ways the beginner can search out models of argumentation and style. Although I believe it is important for all students of the language (and they include anyone who uses it in the act of writing) to know something of its development, such information is readily available in books designed to explain in detail matters that were only touched upon in "The English Language." Following a philosophy of practicality, I have introduced the chapter on planning and writing after "The Task of Writing" and have followed it, in turn, with chapters on the research paper and letter writing. By initiating a new and separate section, "The Elements of Structure: Sentences and Paragraphs" (Section II), to follow the first broad discussion of writing and major writing projects, I implement my belief that the best way to begin writing is immediately to confront overall questions of focus, subject selection, outlining, and revising. Specific tactics of composition come second. A new research paper, written by a student, is analyzed as a composite of all the broad issues involved in expository writing. The succeeding chapters in Section II have been pared to eliminate overlap, in the discussion of sentences and paragraphs, between the rhetorical portions of the text and the handbook of mechanics. I have greatly expanded "A Guide to Usage," now Section IV, in attempting to cover as many questions of proper usage as possible in a limited space. For a just appreciation of the book's treatment of usage, "A Guide to Usage" should be considered in conjuction with §20, "Similar Forms," in Section III, Chapter 4, "Spelling."

Among those who read early drafts of this revision and cast a beam of fresh counsel into dark corners, Rosemarie Arbur of Lehigh University and J. Chesky Taylor of Washington State University deserve my particular gratitude, not only for suggestions of numerous improvements, but for much-needed words of encouragement. For his invaluable and often witty advice on almost every phase of this revision, I want to thank Anthony English, editor at Macmillan. I am also grateful to the reference librarians at the University of Missouri–Kansas City for their expert assistance in finding books and journals that were essential to my task. To my wife Barbara, who did more than her share of organizing and typing, in addition to allowing me to use her prized dining room table, I offer deep thanks and love.

ROBERT F. WILLSON, JR.

Contents

CONTENTS

Chapter 3
The Research Paper   81

Chapter 4
The Letter   131

SECTION II
THE ELEMENTS OF STRUCTURE: SENTENCES AND PARAGRAPHS

Chapter 1
The Sentence: Grammatical Patterns   147

CONTENTS

SECTION III
A HANDBOOK OF WRITING AND REVISION

Chapter 2
Mechanics   286

Chapter 3
Punctuation

Chapter 4
Spelling

355

Chapter 5
Words and Phrases

368

Chapter 6
The Paragraph   447

SECTION IV
A GUIDE TO USAGE

THE EXPRESSION

AND

COMMUNICATION

OF THOUGHT

1 *The Task of Writing*

In his novel *Breakfast of Champions,* Kurt Vonnegut, Jr., says that many people in Midland City were insecure about using their own language because they had been told by their English teachers that

they were unworthy to speak or write their language if they couldn't love or understand incomprehensible novels and poems and plays about people long ago and far away, such as *Ivanhoe.* (p. 138)

Many of us no doubt share feelings of insecurity with the inhabitants of Vonnegut's fictional city, and probably because we were told the same thing about the indispensability of "old masters" as sources of good writing. If contemporary formal writing is supposed to echo the stylistic peculiarities of *Ivanhoe,* then it is probably better left to dead novelists and English teachers. After all, most of the rest of us have vocal chords and can shout "Fire!" to more purpose than we can pen "conflagration."

The main problem left unaddressed by that attitude is that each of us is called upon (and *not* just by English instructors) to write letters, papers, and examinations to fulfill social obligations and course requirements. Our careers too usually demand proficiency in writing letters and reports and sometimes even in correcting the writings of others. The spoken word simply will not answer many of these assignments and obligations. Nor, for that matter, will reverence for the language of one century-and-a-half-old novel. A broad acquaintance with the ways various writers at various times have put their words together is, on the other hand, invaluable. Your first step in satisfying the task of writing, then, is to develop and cultivate the habit of reading.

READING FOR BETTER WRITING

At this point it is probably clear that you need not start your reading habit by going immediately to the library in order to plunge into *Ivanhoe*. By all means begin with that work if you choose, but, if you do, you will find the language badly dated, the sentences long and burdened with adjectives, and the characters given to melodramatic and stilted musings. Such qualities are products of the time in which *Ivanhoe* was written, a century-and-a-half distant from our own. Their application to a contemporary subject for a contemporary audience is inappropriate, if not fantastic. *Ivanhoe,* moreover, is a novel, and most of the writing you will be called on to do is *expository,* or *essay,* writing, which requires proof of an assertion through carefully developed argument. The word *essay* derives from the Old French word *essai,* which meant "an attempt or trying out," in the sense of a trial balloon. Knowing the derivation of the word will help you to remember that your composition, term paper, or report will not be accepted as a work chiseled in stone but as a personal effort to convince your reader that the position taken is sound. The writer is not above question just because he writes.

THE ESSAY

To write essays you should read essays. Read them on a variety of subjects. Newsmagazines, such as *Time* and *Newsweek,* regularly feature articles on subjects ranging from cancer to culture shock written in a manner designed both to inform and to provoke the reader's thoughts. These essays are addressed to a literate and informed audience; many of the allusions found in them are to the works of literature and art commonly introduced in undergraduate survey courses. Yet the writers of these essays assume no specialized knowledge in their readers, and their work is, as a result, a useful model for students who want to instruct and entertain a wide audience. Although the styles of newsmagazine essays are sometimes marred by excessive wit and chattiness, their arguments are generally tightly constructed, with a clear sense of purpose and an easy movement

4

from the statement of a thesis to its proof. Reading essays like the following with an eye to the logic of the argument, the use of proof, and the form of the conclusion will help you understand the scope—and limitation—of the papers you will probably be called on to write.

ORWELL 25 YEARS LATER: FUTURE IMPERFECT

"Eric Blair" suits him. The crisp syllables suggest a Briton of spare style and countenance. But he despised his real name; it smacked, somehow, of Aryanism and privilege. So he cloaked his origins in a common-sounding nom de plume. His disguise became him, and at last he became his disguise. Today the world remembers him only as George Orwell, seer of the future imperfect. Neither name nor reputation is quite correct.

Now, 25 years after his death at 46, Orwell is enshrined in the language as a cliché for apocalypse. Virtually every doomsday prophecy uses "Orwellian" to describe any impingement on freedom, from imprisonment to wiretapping. Yet the word derives from Orwell's least characteristic book, *1984.* *

To remember him solely for this final volume is like recalling a life by its terminal illness. Indeed when he wrote *1984,* Orwell was in the last throes of tuberculosis. The book's pervasive slogan, "Big Brother Is Watching You"; the portmanteau words "Newspeak," "bellyfeel," "doublethink"; the inverted graffiti, "Freedom Is Slavery," "Ignorance Is Strength"—all these may be indelible. Nonetheless, if some of *1984*'s predictions have come true, most have not. If the book lives, it is more as a warning than as prophecy.

Properly, Orwell should not be commemorated for his novels, which he hoped would be enduring, but for his journalism, which he assumed to be ephemeral. It is his fugitive pieces—letters, critiques, articles—that Critic George Steiner justly calls "a place of renewal for the moral imagination."

The writer of those pieces never wasted a line. The only thing he seemed to squander was his life. The heir to a relentlessly middle-class colonial tradition, Orwell gained a scholarship to Eton, then made a

---

[1] Stefan Kanfer, "Orwell 25 Years Later: Future Imperfect" (*Time,* March 27, 1975, pp. 77–78). Reprinted by permission from *Time,* The Weekly Newsmagazine; Copyright Time Inc.

* Other writers have propelled words into the public consciousness; Orwell has done so with a figure. The 1974 World Food Conference in Rome was expected to produce a ten-year projection. Instead an eleven-year study was offered, presumably to avoid the horrific overtones of *1984.*

5

false start as a policeman in Burma. Out of that five-year catastrophe came the embittered radical who could dissect his emotions and his country with pitiless surgery.

In the classic memoir, *Shooting an Elephant,* Orwell recalls the morning a behemoth ran wild and stomped a coolie. The animal might have been saved, but the psychology of the moment demanded a kill. "Here was I," recalled the ex-official, "the white man with his gun, standing in front of the unarmed native crowd—seemingly the leading actor of the piece; but in reality I was only an absurd puppet pushed to and fro by the will of those yellow faces behind." After the ritual sacrifice, the writer confesses, "I was very glad that the coolie had been killed; it put me legally in the right and it gave me a sufficient pretext for shooting the elephant. I often wondered whether any of the others grasped that I had done it solely to avoid looking a fool." That is more than the bottom line of a 1936 article; it is the epitaph of the British imperial style.

Orwell was a master of exit lines. Yet it is his openings that remain in the mind: "As I write, highly civilized human beings are flying overhead, trying to kill me"; "Dickens is one of those writers who are well worth stealing"; "It was a bright cold day in April, and the clocks were striking thirteen." Where is the reader whose eye could rove from a page with those beginnings?

It was no wonder that even in the limited circulation of British "little magazines," Orwell attracted an international following—and a roster of rabid enemies. For though he thought of himself as a thoroughgoing leftist, he was in fact an enemy of all political movements. When other Etonians sought upward mobility, Orwell literally immersed himself in dirty water and coal dust to investigate the lives of the dishwasher and the miner. When his peers went up to London to seek careers, he went to Spain as a correspondent and stayed to fight against Franco's troops. When many fellow leftists sang the praises of the Cominform, he was rude enough to point out that "the thing for which the Communists were working was not to postpone the Spanish revolution till a more suitable time, but to make sure it never happened."

During World War II he called pacifists "fascifists"; yet later he pleaded for clemency toward German war criminals. When half the Western world referred warmly to Joseph Stalin as "Uncle Joe," Orwell in 1946 produced his Swiftian satire *Animal Farm,* with its caricature of a U.S.S.R. where leaders are pigs and their motto is "All animals are equal but some animals are more equal than others."

6

At the time, much of this seemed sheer perversity, a quixotic desire to be history's odd man out. But the truth of Orwell's observations slowly vindicated him. The writer was first characterized as a crank, then as an apostle of common sense, and at last, in V. S. Pritchett's phrase, "as the wintry conscience of a whole generation."

Still, that generation has long since passed in review. By now, Orwell's perceptions have been duly noted, even by the obtuse. The world no longer needs English journalists to inform it of the obscenities of the Stalin years; the news comes out of Russia itself. The dangers of secrecy and invasions of privacy are piously trumpeted even in Congress. By now, Orwell should be no more than a footnote to a bad time. Instead, he is more readable and more germane than the writers who once overshadowed him.

In part, Orwell's durability is due to his central obsession. It was not politics or personalities that concerned him so much as language itself. In the '30s he saw words bent; in the '40s he chronicled the result: whole governments twisted out of shape. His best work was an attempt to restore the meaning to words, to prove that "good prose is like a window pane." "One ought to recognize," he wrote, "that the present political chaos is connected with the decay of language, and that one can probably bring about some improvement by starting at the verbal end."

For most of his professional life Orwell sought to bring about that improvement. His weapons were not formidable. As Lionel Trilling observes, Orwell's pieces excel "by reason of the very plainness of his mind, his simple ability to look at things in a downright undeceived way . . . he is not a genius—what a relief! What an encouragement. For he communicates to us the sense that what he has done, any one of us could do."

Therein lies Orwell's lasting power. He holds out hope that ordinary citizens may see through systems and rhetoric, may speak and write the truth to each other, and demand the truth from their leaders. It takes little skill to imagine the furious response Orwell would have provoked on both sides of the DMZ, or what he would have said about the windy self-righteousness of the U.N., or about the excesses of Peking, Moscow, Paris and Washington. The need for an Orwell is more acute now than it was a generation ago. But the tonic power of his writings is still available to anyone who has, or appreciates, an independent mind. It is not necessarily 1984 that his writings concern; it could as well be 1975.

—Stefan Kanfer

Worth special comment in this essay is the way the writer challenges the popular belief that Orwell's greatness lies in the prophetic truth of *1984*. His *argument,* or *thesis,* is that Orwell's journalism, his "fugitive pieces," speak more urgently about social and political corruption, perversion of the language, and independent thinking than do his novels. In his conclusion the writer restates his thesis by pointing out that we read Orwell looking too often for evidence that 1984 is around the corner, when we should be noticing how his writings concern the present.

Argumentative Essays

Returning to the derivation of the word *essay,* accept the fact that most of your college writing, essays, will require the argumentative or thesis-proving attempt. Whether you set out to describe the reaction of sodium in an acid solution or to enumerate the factors that contribute to inflation, your essay will be more convincing and readable if you have formed a *point of view,* determined what you want your reader to understand and to feel, before setting about the actual writing. Writing from a point of view tests your ability to articulate an opinion, and to convince your reader that your way of looking at the question or solving the problem is the best way. Skill in consolidating your own point of view is the first step toward persuading, dissuading, motivating, or informing your reader. An essay lacking a solid point of view is no more than a communication of vague impressions.

The more methods of argument you are exposed to through reading, the better prepared you will be to solve the expository problems of particular writing assignments, especially those of *essay questions* that seem to be an indispensable part of final examinations. By analyzing the structure and style of numerous essays you will develop your knowledge of *rhetoric,* a term whose primary meaning has been distorted by activist label-makers and bureaucratic politicians alike. In its primary meaning rhetoric simply comprises the *art of discourse,* the techniques used by writers and speakers to achieve certain effects. In the following selection see if you can identify some of the means the author uses to define and illustrate the term *style* while making you believe it is a desirable thing to acquire.

Style in writing is something like style in a car, a woman, or a Greek temple—the ordinary materials of this world so poised and perfected as to stand out from the landscape and compel a second look, something that hangs in the reader's mind, like a vision. It is an idea made visible, and polished to its natural beauty. It is your own voice, with the hems and haws chipped out, speaking the common language uncommonly well. It takes a craftsman who has discovered the knots and potentials in his material, one who has learned to like words as some people like polished wood or stones, one who has learned to enjoy phrasing and syntax, and the very punctuation that keeps them straight. It is a labor of love, and like love it can bring pleasure and satisfaction. Once you have learned to enjoy the work, you will please others. You will convince and delight, and get more than one admiring look.

—SHERIDAN BAKER, *The Complete Stylist*

The author defines his term by means of *comparison*, a rather casual *simile* in the first sentence: "something like style in a car . . . ," then an *extended comparison* or *analogy* in the rest of the paragraph in which the writer is seen as an artist or craftsman, someone who respects the materials of his art and loves his work so deeply that he *compels* a second look from those who pass by. This analogy is reinforced by the carefully selected *diction* of the paragraph: a good writer "hangs" visions in our minds; he "chips" out the imperfections of spoken language; he "poises and perfects," discovers "the knots and potentials in his material." At the close of the paragraph, the author uses a *figure of speech* that could almost be classified as a cliché, "labor of love," but he rescues the remark by specifying that love rather than labor is one of the benefits of accomplished writing. These techniques, in this case wrought almost to the point of art, lead the reader almost imperceptibly to the conclusion that admiring looks are the rewards of a pleasing style. What makes this selection even more admirable is the way Baker not only defines effective style but demonstrates it in achieving his goal.

Nonargumentative Essays

Other kinds of essays provide useful models for the beginning writer. Autobiographical articles and books provide insight into how the facts of your own life might be arranged to interest readers. Even if you are not planning to pen your autobiography (although your English instructor may ask you to recall some personal incident as a subject for a theme), practice in the technique of transmitting poignant experience is invaluable, especially when you wish to insert an anecdote in an argumentative essay for emphasis or effect, as is done in the essay quoted from *Time*. Most popular magazines now use the *interview* as a way of presenting autobiographical material; you may therefore learn a good deal about question-and-answer techniques from these "in-depth" dialogues.

Essays that attempt to explain a *complicated* or *obscure process* to an uninformed audience (e.g., how a bill is passed in the legislature, how a bridge is constructed) occur in specialized magazines. *Scientific American,* for example, sometimes publishes articles written for the unscientific. In these pieces the writer must define his terminology and explain in more detail than he would for a professional reader the procedures in an experiment or survey. Newspaper articles by science editors are another source of so-called popularized writing.

Many essays are devoted almost exclusively to *description*. Such magazines as *Holiday* or *Atlantic* regularly publish articles that attempt to evoke the special atmosphere of a place. Others, like *People* and *Harper's,* feature sketches of well-known personalities. The writers of these essays give their readers not only facts and figures but also some feeling for the place or person. They emphasize some striking trait—an exotic odor, an oblique sense of humor—that distinguishes their subjects. Analysis of such articles will train you to observe, to select details necessary to the impression you wish to convey. Even *Ivanhoe* may yield some useful details of the descriptive kind.

Newspapers are gold mines of another type of writing: *narration*. Reviews of rock concerts or political demonstrations yield useful models for narrating a series of events effectively and dramatically. The sports pages are also stuffed with accounts of memorable races, histories of teams, descriptions of games, and often achieve a prose astonishing in its inventiveness and color, if not in its precision. Even the editorial pages may retrace step by step the development of some political scandal. Note the devices by which the writers achieve *transition* from incident to incident and the strategy employed to bring the story to some *climax.*

Novels and short stories are also obvious sources for narrative writing, but the reader sounding them for stylistic inspiration must guard against the attractions of the story. The more electrifying you find it, the more likely you are to overlook the deliberate tactics of the storyteller that make it so.

There is no point in studying any piece of writing without trying to understand its content. In reading essays of the kind mentioned, however, cultivate the habit of observing in what order and with what emphases the authors present their cases. Evaluate *styles* of composition for what they may contribute to your own. Try to be aware of how each writer organizes the argument, what tone he or she establishes toward you and the material, and what devices of language make the essay interesting and readable. All good essays are successful attempts to impose form and order on chaos; if you conclude that a particular essay has not overcome chaos, savor it as a model of what *not* to do.

General Reading

While reading essays of a specific kind will help you to confront the task of writing, reading of a general nature will expand your capacity for being interested. If you are not curious or adventurous in a search for knowledge, you will probably not find much use for reading, or for writing. Yet the more one reads, the more one realizes that much of what is published on such topics as politics, economics, entertainment, or the arts is subject to challenge. The act of challenging or disagreeing with an author's assertions is itself a useful exercise in the calisthenics for growing writers. Intellectual muscles once flexed by catching the flaws in an author's logic, or research, or conclusion will be better prepared to produce their own style of expression,

11

their own technique for jumping the hurdle of composition. An expanded mind and, no doubt, an expanded vocabulary are just two benefits of wide reading. Finally, although we should not need to say it, reading is an excellent source of pleasure. Whatever you are required or choose to read, however, try to concentrate on the *form* as well as the *content*, noticing the details of structure you might use in your own writing.

SPEAKING AND WRITING

To many beginners the task of writing seems elementary because they assume they need only transfer their style of speaking to the page. They notice no distinction between their performance in conversation and their performance in composition—it is all a matter of "communication." Yet beginners soon learn, usually from the comments of their English instructors, that there are major differences between talking and writing, and that beginners had better discover quickly what the differences are. The root of the differences is that we get away with errors, inconsistencies, and assumptions in speech that are not tolerated in expository writing. They are not tolerated in writing because they hinder understanding.

Perhaps the primary distinction between speech and writing is that speech depends on sound, whereas writing depends on sight and on those strange processes of the mind that translate written symbols into sound and meaning. A reader reads what *he* interprets, not what someone else says to him. There are other differences important to the linguist, of course, but the main distinction is that speech benefits from the help of certain visual and audial aids writing does not have. In speech we add to and qualify our meaning by physical gestures: by movement of the hands, by shrugs, and by facial expressions such as smiles, frowns, or even the lifted eyebrow. Our resources of sound are many—intonation, the rise and fall of the voice, the changes in pitch. We can vary the intensity or the volume of sound; we can, on occasion, whisper, shout, mumble, or even growl. All these add meaning; they are strengths written language does not have.

On the other hand, spoken language has obvious weaknesses. That collection of fleeting, ephemeral noises we call human speech is gone a moment after it is uttered. Often it is gone even before it has been heard accurately—a wonderful phenomenon for those of us with hot tempers who tend to revile the parentage of strapping truck drivers when they blow us off the road. Perhaps our words linger for a while in someone's memory, especially if they are spoken lovingly or disparagingly, but the speech itself cannot be called back to life. It may be caught and preserved on tape or on a phonograph record, but most of what has been thus saved was first worked over and shaped and set down in writing before it was recited. It is only partly spoken English, often self-consciously delivered. Written English has a longer life, a greater permanence; it will exist, in Shakespeare's words, "So long as men can breathe or eyes can see." Writing is also the more accurate communication because it can be re-read, examined, and studied. Because it is enduring and susceptible to critical review, it demands greater care in its composition. As a writer you assume a responsibility to build your sentences, to select and arrange your words, and to use or modify the rhetorical and stylistic devices that other writers have created and developed.

THE STUDENT'S CHOICE OF STYLE

A student should know something of the history of the English language, its forms and varieties, its resources and limitations, so that his attitude toward the tools of writing may be practical and humble: so that he may use words with respect for their pasts and assume the role of rebel or innovator only when he knows something of what has already been tried. The history of the language is a history of innumerable changes, many of which have occurred because of social and scientific revolutions. It is still a changing language, and many of the changes have not been for the better. In general, modern usage tends to ignore the metaphoric possibilities of the language, opting instead for words and phrases that smack of both jargon and vagueness. Think of how frequently you find words such as "interface" or "programmed" used in contexts to which their meaning is only partly apt. Many expressions will pass out of the language as quickly as they passed in. "Telling it like it is" will, it is hoped, never become a lasting substitute for "telling the truth"—or even for the less definite "telling it *as* it is". What, then, *is* the realistic attitude in the face of rapid changes in usage? The commonsense procedure is to ask, "What *is* being done at the present time by people of education, of taste, of wit, of experience, people whose opinions I value?" These are the persons who address not just an elite but the vast audience of readers and writers. Adoption of their standards is important for any writer aspiring to some degree of influence.

What these standards are you could probably discover for yourself by wide reading and by long, careful observation of the writing practices of educated persons. That is how the authors of handbooks, grammars, and dictionaries find out what current usage is. Most of us, of course, have little time or opportunity for this sort of individual research; we have to defer to the judgment of others. It is realistic to do so, but do not abandon reading and observation, for such study is rewarding. Note current usage in the magazines and books you read; listen to the literate persons you see on television; and always, when you are in doubt or in a hurry, remember that a good dictionary will provide a fairly accurate but by no means up-to-the-minute reflection of general usage.

In most of the papers you will write in college, you will make a conscious choice of style, language, and point of view. Often your choices will be determined by the situation. If your instructor asks for a discussion of the social effects of widespread unemployment, you will naturally decide to write, not a conversational, breezy sketch, but a well-planned, serious, and carefully researched essay in formal, standard English. It is hard to imagine any other decision appropriate to such an assignment, especially since recent unemployment levels have aroused so many deep and often embittered emotions.

Frequently choice lies between a *formal* and an *informal* treatment of the subject. A subject such as "TV Soap Operas" may be handled with deep seriousness or with a light, humorous touch. Tone depends on the particular aspect of the subject selected for emphasis, on the situation, and on the readers addressed. Your decision, whatever it is, should always respect writing as clear and persuasive communication. You are not merely writing; you are writing for someone to read.

Selection of a formal or an informal treatment depends on recognition of the differences between the two styles. The following section provides several examples of both kinds of writing and is therefore worth studying closely.

STANDARD ENGLISH: FORMAL AND INFORMAL

The Formal Varieties

Formal writing is not the verbal equivalent of formal dress. The tuxedo and the ball gown, the top hat and the elbow-length gloves appear only at functions of unusual starchiness. At other times, to be well dressed is to be *appropriately* dressed: jeans for painting the house, a business suit or dress for the job interview, and, for special after-dinner effect, virtually anything the traffic will bear, from prefaded denims to crushed velours. Writing or speech is also prescribed by occasion, but in each case the formal degree, unlike the formal degree of dress, is a style appropriate to the greatest number of serious uses—something, that is, a good deal more versatile than a top hat. For the writer, an occasion consists of the combined demands of subject and audience, and the professional dress of language, known as formal standard English, will suit most occasions.

The language that we call *formal*—for want of a term with less unfortunate connotations—is far from being by definition cold, reserved, or stodgy. It has warmth, strength, beauty, and an infinite range and variety. It is not confined to a few scientific and scholarly treatises. The great body of our literature, from Shakespeare and Bacon down to the latest book on the international crisis, is written in formal English. It is the language striven for by authors of most books of history, sociology, political science, botany, chemistry—every textbook that you use in college. It is the language of the professions, such as law, medicine, teaching. It is the language of all serious essays, of a good part of all novels and poems. Most business letters are written in formal English. As a matter of fact, a good share of the nation's private and public daily work is carried on with the help of formal English.

Examine a few examples of the formal style and try to learn from this study what are the distinguishing marks of standard English in its more serious and dignified uses. The first three examples are from public speeches. The occasions were as solemn and formal as any in the history of mankind.

I expect that the Battle of Britain is about to begin. Upon this battle depends the survival of Christian civilization. Upon it depends all our British life, and the long continuity of our institutions and our Empire. The whole fury and might of the enemy must very soon be turned on us. Hitler knows that he will have to break us in this Island or lose the war. If we can stand up to him, all Europe may be free and the life of the world may move forward into broad, sunlit uplands. But if we fail, then the whole world, including the United States, including all that we have known and cared for, will sink into the abyss of a new Dark Age made more sinister, and perhaps more protracted, by the lights of perverted science. Let us therefore brace ourselves to our duties, and so bear ourselves that, if the British Empire and its Commonwealth last for a thousand years, men will say, "This was their finest hour."

—WINSTON CHURCHILL, speech to the House of Commons, June 18, 1940

I see a book kissed which I suppose to be the Bible, or at least the New Testament, which teaches me that all things whatsoever I would that men should do unto me, I should do even so to them. It teaches me further to remember them that are in bonds as bound with them. I endeavored to act up to that instruction. I say I am yet too young to understand that God is any respector of persons. I believe that to have interfered as I have done, as I have always freely admitted I have done in behalf of His despised poor, I did no wrong, but right. Now, if it is deemed necessary that I should forfeit my life for the furtherance of the ends of justice and mingle my blood further with the blood of my children and with the blood of millions in this slave country whose rights are disregarded by wicked, cruel, and unjust enactments, I say, let it be done.

—JOHN BROWN, last speech

16

With malice toward none, with charity for all, with firmness in the right as God gives us to see the right, let us finish the work we are in, to bind up the nation's wounds, to care for him who shall have borne the battle, and for his widow and his orphans, to do all which may achieve and cherish a just and lasting peace among ourselves and with all nations.

—ABRAHAM LINCOLN, *Second Inaugural Address*

Obviously these selections are not brief portions of run-of-the-mill prose. There would be no point in using ordinary, pedestrian prose in a book devoted to the encouragement of better-than-average composition. In these three samples, note how the speaker's sincerity and earnestness inspire through what are, for the most part, simple, homely, everyday words. Monosyllables are frequent, even predominant, as in this sentence: "Hitler knows that he will have to break us in this Island or lose the war." Note in all three the rhythms of spoken prose, the balance of phrase against phrase, and the dramatic climax in the Churchill selection. The single sentence quoted from Lincoln's address is in itself a fine example of climax. The style of the speech by John Brown is strongly influenced by his knowledge of the King James Bible. All three selections should be read aloud.

Now look at two other examples of serious prose, this time the work of two of our most distinguished jurists, Oliver Wendell Holmes and Learned Hand. Both writers are discussing an aspect of law; in a way they are saying the same thing—that the knowledge of law, the interpretation of law, and the making of law depend on our knowledge of the past. Their vocabularies combine the commonplace and the erudite. Both depend for their style on balanced elements—phrases, clauses, words—Judge Holmes more so than Judge Hand. Judge Holmes makes use of *antithesis*, which is a form of balance, as you may observe in almost every sentence of the paragraph, notably in this one: "The life of the law has not been logic; it has been experience." In the paragraph by Judge Hand we have interesting examples of complex sentences, of clause piled on clause, each succeeding clause helping to clarify, illustrate, and strengthen the author's central idea.

17

The object of this book is to present a general view of the Common Law. To accomplish the task, other tools are needed besides logic. It is something to show that the consistency of a system requires a particular result, but it is not all. The life of the law has not been logic: it has been experience. The felt necessities of the time, the prevalent moral and political theories, intuitions of public policy, avowed or unconscious, even the prejudices which judges share with their fellow-men, have had a good deal more to do than the syllogism in determining the rules by which men should be governed. The law embodies the story of a nation's development through many centuries, and it cannot be dealt with as if it contained only the axioms and corollaries of a book of mathematics. In order to know what it is, we must know what it has been, and what it tends to become. We must alternately consult history and existing theories of legislation. But the most difficult labor will be to understand the combination of the two into new products at every stage. The substance of the law at any given time pretty nearly corresponds, so far as it goes, with what is then understood to be convenient; but its form and machinery, and the degree to which it is able to work out desired results, depend very much upon its past.

—OLIVER WENDELL HOLMES, JR., *The Common Law*

A constitution, a statute, a regulation, a rule—in short, a "law" of any kind—is at once a prophecy and a choice. It is a prophecy because it attempts to forecast what will be its effects: whom it will benefit and in what ways; on whom its impact will prove a burden; how much friction and discontent will arise from the adjustments that conformity to it will require; how completely it can be enforced; what enforcement will cost; how far it will interfere with other projects or existing activities; and in general, the whole manifold of its indirect consequences. A thoroughgoing and dependable knowledge of these is obviously impossible. For example, although we can anticipate with some degree of assurance who will pay a steeply graded income tax and in what amounts, there is no way to tell what its indirect effects will be: what activities of the taxpayers in the higher brackets it will depress; if they do not work so hard, in what way will they occupy their newly acquired leisure; how any new activities they may substitute will affect others; whether this will be offset by a loss of the mellowed maturity and the wisdom of those who withdraw. Such prophecies infest law of every sort, the more deeply as it is far-reaching; and it is an illusion to suppose that there are formulas or statistics that will help in making them. They can rest upon no more than enlightened guesses; but these are likely to be successful as they are made by those whose horizons have been widened, and whose outlook has been clarified, by knowledge of what men have striven to do, and how far their hopes and fears have been realized. There is no substitute for an open mind enriched by reading and the arts.

—LEARNED HAND, *The Spirit of Liberty*

And here is formal standard English as a historian uses it. His vocabulary, as in the preceding selections, is a mixture of homely words and scholarly words. His sentences show the effects of care, a regard for structure, for an easy rhythmical flow of sounds—all contribute to qualities of a pleasing style in good formal writing.

For the mass of men in 1600, the ocean still held the terrors of the past. That a succession of adventurers had reached the outer shores of these uncharted wastes did not in the least allay the fears of the earthbound. Nothing in the chronicles or in the tales that passed by word of mouth gave a friendlier aspect to the waters of the Atlantic.

Yet soon, in their scores, in their hundreds and thousands, and later in their millions, the earthbound men and women of Europe passed across the unfriendly sea. In their coming they created a nation.

Tiny vessels, sixty to two hundred tons in the main, bore the voyagers westward. Riding at anchor in the sheltered bays of the homeland, the ships seemed substantial enough. Their sturdy timber and looming masts, their cabins that rose like castles several stories high in the stern, were impressive in comparison with the harbor craft that flitted about them. At sea, it would be another matter. All became precarious as the isolated specks, buffeted by the elements, beat their way into the unknown immensity before them; and the men below huddled fearfully in the cramped space that set their condition of life.

—OSCAR HANDLIN, *The Americans*

A scientist aware of the need to make a point clear to the nonscientist may write as the nuclear physicist J. Robert Oppenheimer writes:

Each of us knows from his own life how much even a casual and limited association of men goes beyond him in knowledge, in understanding, in humanity, and in power. Each of us, from a friend or a book or by concerting of the little we know with what others know, has broken the iron circle of his frustration. Each of us has asked help and been given it, and within our measure each of us has offered it. Each of us knows the great new freedom sensed almost as a miracle, that men banded together for some finite purpose experience from the power of their common effort. We are likely to remember the times of the last war, where the common danger brought forth in soldier, in worker, in scientist, and engineer a host of new experiences of the power and the comfort in even bleak undertakings, of common, concerted, co-operative life. Each of us knows how much he has been transcended by the group of which he has been or is a part; each of us has felt the solace of other men's knowledge to stay his own ignorance, of other men's wisdom to stay his folly, of other men's courage to answer his doubts or his weakness.

—J. Robert Oppenheimer, *Science and the Common Understanding*

Finally, as an example of formal, serious writing that is aimed at a very wide reading public, here is a quotation from one of a series of "interpretations in depth" of modern nations—this one of Greece.

An immortal tale tells of a "Clear Land" where colors are purer and the forms of things are finer than on earth. At first the Clear Land seems only a radiant reflection of earthbound countries. The trees, houses and mountains known to everyday experience are all outlined there with dazzling clarity upon the shining air. "Then comes the strange part. When you are perfectly at home there you see again that it is very like our lower world!" Such conditions seem to come true in Greece. Even the Greek battle cry has unlooked-for resonance. *Aera!* the fighting men sing out, meaning "Air!" Greece is a Clear Land, where the sun caresses the mountains and where life itself has a clearer shape. It does not seem surprising that Greece was the setting, some 2,500 years ago, for one of man's best efforts to define the nature and purposes of life on earth.

Awakening in this Clear Land is often an especially keen delight. The roosters which are everywhere about help you to it at an early hour. With luck you may see the first pale rosy rays spiking out from behind a dark mountain. This is the hand of "rosy fingered Dawn," the same that Homer, the first and greatest of the poets of western civilization, knew so many dewy mornings ago. And once again the god Apollo's golden chariot comes winging up over the steep countryside, making the bare peaks shine like crystal above the cold violet valleys and the still dark sea.

The roosters crow the louder; in this country nothing quiets them. But the nightingales fall silent now, or rather their rich silver improvisations vanish like light into light. The thrilling shriek of Athena's silent-winged owl too is stilled. The owl huddles deep in a plane tree by a bubbling spring; it fears the ravens whose black-suited flocks are flapping heavily to their larcenous work in the sun-swept fields. Sarcastically the black robbers light on a breeze-teased scarecrow, a tattered coat upon a stick, while cawing up the sudden warmth of day.

The village innkeeper puts out a single table and chair, tentatively, like a tortoise thrusting out a foot. Sparrows peck and chitter on the cobblestones of the village's steep and winding street. Now they fly up like brown leaves in a gust as a peasant girl appears. She is all in black, but her smile and her glancing eyes gleam white as the morning. The innkeeper's mangy hound stretches out his forepaws and growls approval as the girl goes by. Her thick black hair is coiled in a single braid to signify maidenhood. She passes, straight and graceful, with a tall brown jug upon her head. The girl is on her way to the spring beneath the plane tree, where the owl dozes already and a serpent sleeps too beneath the roots.[1]

. . . .

Amongst these old mountains Pan and the nymphs are dancing still, and sometimes voiceless invisible hunger also dances. Greece as a whole resembles an improbable rock garden, fragrant with herbs and wild flowers, sea-bathed on every hand, beautifully sculptured and yet harsh in its own way. Like marble it is gleaming and lovely in the distance, hard-edged close by and chill beneath the fingers. This rocky southeast corner of Europe has given more to the world perhaps than any other place. But its fruits are of the spirit.

—ALEXANDER ELIOT AND THE EDITORS OF LIFE, *Greece*

The last two selections differ in one respect; in another they are alike. Mr. Oppenheimer has used balance and repetition to give his writing continuity and unity. By repeating the opening phrase of each sentence—"each of us knows . . . each of us has broken . . . each of us knows the great new freedom . . ."—he leads up to the climax of the last sentence—"the solace of other

---

[1] Two paragraphs of the text have been omitted here. Note that omissions of one or more paragraphs are indicated by a single typed line of spaced periods, or line of ellipsis. Refer to this for illustration when you study the use of quoted matter in Chapter 3, "The Research Paper," in this section.

men's knowledge . . . of other men's wisdom . . . of other men's courage to answer his doubts or his weakness." Mr. Eliot, on the other hand, writes in shorter and simpler sentences, and depends for his effects on color, on clarity, and on a subtle use of words, especially adjectives, that echo the epic style of Homer. Such descriptive epithets as "shining air," "pale rosy rays," "dewy mornings," "still dark sea," "silent-winged owl," are here not by accident but by most careful design. Take a look at a good translation of Homer's *Iliad* to see the classical Greek source of Mr. Eliot's inspiration.

There is one thing, above all others, we can learn from this brief analysis of formal English. It is that the writers devote care to structure. Their sentences are *built;* they are not thrown together. The various devices that writers have at their disposal are discussed more fully in Chapter 2 in this section. When you study the various devices of structure discussed there, turn back to these illustrations to observe the principles in practice.

Characteristics of the Formal Style. What are the marks of standard English in its more serious and dignified uses? First, restrictions upon vocabulary, although important, consist of no more than excluding words and expressions labeled "colloquial" or "substandard" in your desk dictionaries. Slang and obscenity are, of course, inappropriate. It is untrue that formal English demands only big words, bookish words, the cold, impersonal words of pure science, though such words are probably more common here than in very informal writing. But short, simple words are as much a part of the vocabulary of formal English as multisyllables.

In the second place, standard English on the more formal levels is characterized by orderly structure. The expression and communication of ideas are a planned process, not a spontaneous outpouring. Ideas are grouped and arranged in some logical sequence. There is a serious attempt to show the interrelationship between ideas. As a consequence, paragraphs tend to be more fully developed than in the informal varieties of English; the complexity of a sentence is usually proportionate to the maturity of its thought.

Third, those who use the language in formal situations, in the serious discussion of serious ideas, tend, as a rule, to be relatively conservative in their attitude toward matters of grammar and usage. It matters little whether the writer is a statesman like Churchill, a scientist like Oppenheimer, a historian, a sociologist, a college professor, or just an ordinary fellow who faces the problem of giving a talk before some governmental body. The deference to what is known as correct usage is strong in mind. He seeks to respect the correct forms.

And finally, standard English in the more formal situations is characterized by an impersonal or objective attitude toward the subject matter communicated and by a relatively distant, rather than intimate relation with the reader. This is not to say that the exclusion of the writer's or speaker's self is a requisite of the formal style. Indeed, some of the finest formal writing is intensely personal. But it is personal because the personal element is the vital substance of what is being said. When the personal element is not vital, subjects are usually treated objectively. In the case of research reports and college essays, a safe generalization is that an impersonal and objective treatment involves less risk of misinterpretation and scornful dismissal than a personal and emotional one.

The More Informal Varieties

Before we begin to examine the characteristics of informal English, we must recognize that the essential unity of standard English is much more important than the differences among its varieties. One does not stop writing formal English and begin writing informal English as if stepping through a door from one room to another, after having changed into something more comfortable.

Much good writing lies in an area somewhere between the intensely serious varieties we have quoted and the chatty, familiar essays, often flavored with wit and humor, that anyone would accept as informal. This intermediate kind of writing has a serious intent, but it is written for the common reader, who is expected to enjoy his reading in a relaxed mood. Here are two examples:

Every grammar school in England taught each little Elizabethan schoolboy the same thing. It taught him Latin. Sometimes an exceptional school like Westminster went a step further and taught one other subject, and in that case the subject was Greek. The explanations in the Greek grammar were of course in Latin, for the boys of Westminster School were expected to use nothing but Latin in their school hours. If anyone forgot and spoke in English it counted against him as much as three mistakes in spelling.

It might be said in general of the Tudor school system that its aim was to turn out little Roman-Christian gentlemen who could write exactly like Cicero. To this end the boys struggled through the Stoic precepts of the *Disticha* in the first form, learned elegant Latin colloquialisms from Terence in the second, and emerged on the great plateau of Cicero—"the very foundation of all"—in the third. Throughout, there was a stern emphasis on the two great principles of Tudor education: the gentlemanly Christian virtues on the one hand and a sound Latin style on the other.

The emphasis on character development was not new, and Ben Jonson started school with the same moral maxims that had been inculcated in young Geoffrey Chaucer. The teaching of Latin, however, had changed. Chaucer was taught a Latin over which the dust of centuries had been drifting; no one knew exactly what "correct" Latin was supposed to be and no one cared. But by the time Ben Jonson went to school it had been decided that "correct" Latin meant the Latin that Cicero wrote. The blurred medieval theories on vocabulary and syntax were replaced by a single standard, and the great Roman orator became the emperor of all the English schoolrooms of Queen Elizabeth's day.

Education is a curious thing. All over England the wriggling young Elizabethans sat in their classrooms and studied the classic ideal of gravity and control. They learned elegance and restraint from Horace; they learned a balanced and antithetical prose from Cicero; they learned the tight rules of dramatic construction from Terence. And then they went forth and produced the tangled, loose, barbaric magnificence of the Elizabethan drama.

—Marchette Chute, *Ben Jonson of Westminster*

Is this formal or informal writing? Although it really does not matter, it is worthwhile to point out some characteristics of Marchette Chute's style. Her sentences are built with care, but they are more relaxed than the stately rhetorical structures Judge Learned Hand builds. Since informality depends partly on situation, partly on the reader addressed, and partly on the attitude of the writer toward his reader and toward his material, note the good-natured irony that runs throughout but is permitted to surface only in the last paragraph.

A biologist writing for other scientists writes in a particular formal style, using a scientific vocabulary and perhaps a complex sentence structure; writing for the common reader, with the intention to give enjoyment as well as information, he changes his style materially, as you see in the following:

An insect walks in a manner that is unique among animals. If you possessed six legs and had to use them in walking, how would you move them? That is the problem which instinct has solved for the infinitely varied hosts of the adult insects.

The six legs are usually moved as a series of tripods, three legs at a time. The front and rear legs on one side, and the middle leg on the other, move in unison. Thus, the insect is always securely planted on the ground. It does not have to use a large number of muscles, as we do, just to maintain an erect posture. In walking, the average adult person employs a motor mechanism that weighs about eighty pounds—sixty pounds of muscle and twenty pounds of bones. Each step we take puts about 300 muscles in action. One hundred and forty-four are employed just to balance our spine and keep it upright.

Many insects use their legs in specialized ways. The common water-strider employs its forelegs to capture its prey, its oarlike middle legs to propel itself over the water, and its rear legs to guide it in the manner of a rudder. The legs of a dragonfly are held together to form a basket for scooping victims from the air. They are set so far forward on the insect's body that they are almost useless for walking. A dragonfly clings and climbs but hardly ever tries to walk. The monarch is sometimes called "the four-legged butterfly" because of a peculiarity in its use of its legs. This insect holds its forelegs against its body as a general rule and uses its middle and rear pairs of legs for walking. Male monarchs have short atrophied legs that are virtually useless.

For a cow or horse, cat or dog, legs are used almost exclusively as a means of transportation. Among the insects, however, legs have innumerable other uses. Often they are whole tool kits. The rear legs of the bumblebee and the honeybee contain spine-ringed depressions—baskets for carrying pollen home from the fields. The forelegs of the mole cricket and the seventeen-year cicada nymph are enlarged into digging shovels. The swimming legs of the diving beetle are fringed with hairs to increase their effectiveness as oars.

25

Some insects use the claws on their feet to hang themselves up for a night's sleep. The praying mantis employs its spined forelegs as a trap for catching prey. The water-strider has legs with "snowshoes" formed of hairs that help keep it from breaking through the surface film. When not in use, these hairs fold up into a slot in the insect's leg. A few moths have similar masses of hairs that open out into "powder-puffs" just below the knees on the forelegs as a means of attracting their mates. The legs of no other living creatures have as great variety in form and uses as the legs of the insects.

—EDWIN WAY TEALE, *The Strange Lives of Familiar Insects*

Note in the above selection the relatively simple sentence structure, the economy and directness of diction, and, incidentally, the scientific neatness with which the author wraps up this segment of exposition by the first and the last sentences. In a stilted carry-over from his formal style he uses *employs* instead of the more honest and more familiar *uses,* but he refrains, at least, from saying *utilizes.*

In some writing conventionally labeled informal, the actual extent of the informality consists in no more than the attitude of the writer toward the material and the reader. You may find in them the same discriminating taste in choice of words, the same respect for present-day standards in grammatical correctness and in usage, the same mature structure as in the best formal writing. The only difference is that the writer frankly and freely interprets his subject through his own personality or through his own likes and prejudices.

In the following selection note the flashes of wit that accentuate the writer's easy informality and her familiar relation with her readers.

. . . I sometimes delude myself about why I keep a notebook, imagine that some thrifty virtue derives from preserving everything observed. See enough and write it down, I tell myself, and then some morning when the world seems drained of wonder, some day when I am only going through the motions of doing what I am supposed to do, which is write—on that bankrupt morning I will simply open my notebook and there it will all be, a forgotten account with accumulated interest, paid passage back to the world out there: dialogue overheard in hotels and elevators and at the hat-check counter in Pavillon (one middle-aged man shows his hat check to another and says, "That's my old football number"); impressions of Bettina Aptheker and Benjamin Sonnenberg and Teddy ("Mr. Acapulco") Stauffer; careful *aperçus* about tennis bums and failed fashion models and Greek shipping heiresses, one of whom taught me a significant lesson (a lesson I could have learned from F. Scott Fitzgerald, but perhaps we all must meet the very rich for ourselves) by asking, when I arrived to interview her in her orchid-filled sitting room on the second day of a paralyzing New York blizzard, whether it was snowing outside.

—JOAN DIDION, *Slouching Toward Bethlehem*

The following passage, written by an acknowledged master of the informal style, is serious enough in its content; yet the tone is obviously personal and the diction is varied enough, ranging from the solemn to the disrespectful.

A publisher in Chicago has sent us a pocket calculating machine by which we may test our writing to see whether it is intelligible. The calculator was developed by General Motors, who, not satisfied with giving the world a Cadillac, now dream of bringing perfect understanding to men. The machine (it is simply a celluloid card with a dial) is called the Reading-Ease Calculator and shows four grades of "reading ease"—Very Easy, Easy, Hard, and Very Hard. You count your words and syllables, set the dial, and an indicator lets you know whether anybody is going to understand what you have written. An instruction book came with it, and after mastering the simple rules we lost no time in running a test on the instruction book itself, to see how *that* writer was doing. The poor fellow! His leading essay, the one on the front cover, tested Very Hard.

Our next step was to study the first phrase on the face of the calculator: "How to test Reading-Ease of written matter." There is, of course, no such thing as reading ease of written matter. There is the ease with which matter can be read, but that is a condition of the reader, not of the matter. Thus the inventors and distributors of this calculator get off to a poor start, with a Very Hard instruction book and a slovenly phrase. Already they have one foot caught in the brier patch of English usage.

Not only did the author of the instruction book score badly on the front cover, but inside the book he used the word "personalize" in an essay on how to improve one's writing. A man who likes the word "personalize" is entitled to his choice, but we wonder whether he should be in the business of giving advice to writers. "Whenever possi-

27

ble," he wrote, "personalize your writing by directing it to the reader." As for us, we would as lief Simonize our grandmother as personalize our writing.

In the same envelope with the calculator, we received another training aid for writers—a booklet called "How to Write Better," by Rudolph Flesch. This, too, we studied, and it quickly demonstrated the broncolike ability of the English language to throw whoever leaps cocksurely into the saddle. The language not only can toss a writer but knows a thousand tricks for tossing him, each more gay than the last. Dr. Flesch stayed in the saddle only a moment or two. Under the heading "Think Before You Write," he wrote, "The main thing to consider is your purpose in writing. Why are you sitting down to write?" And echo answered: Because, sir, it is more comfortable than standing up.

Communication by the written word is a subtler (and more beautiful) thing than Dr. Flesch and General Motors imagine. They contend that the "average reader" is capable of reading only what tests Easy, and that the writer should write at or below this level. This is a presumptuous and degrading idea. There is no average reader, and to reach down toward this mythical character is to deny that each of us is on the way up, is ascending. ("Ascending," by the way, is a word Dr. Flesch advises writers to stay away from. Too unusual.)

It is our belief that no writer can improve his work until he discards the dulcet notion that the reader is feeble-minded, for writing is an act of faith, not a trick of grammar. Ascent is at the heart of the matter. A country whose writers are following a calculating machine downstairs is not ascending—if you will pardon the expression—and a writer who questions the capacity of the person at the other end of the line is not a writer at all, merely a schemer. The movies long ago decided that a wider communication could be achieved by a deliberate descent to a lower level, and they walked proudly down until they reached the cellar. Now they are groping for the light switch, hoping to find the way out.

We have studied Dr. Flesch's instructions diligently, but we return for guidance in these matters to an earlier American, who wrote with more patience, more confidence. "I fear chiefly," he wrote, "lest my expression may not be *extra-vagant* enough, may not wander far enough beyond the narrow limits of my daily experience, so as to be adequate to the truth of which I have been convinced. . . . Why level downward to our dullest perception always, and praise that as common sense? The commonest sense is the sense of men asleep, which they express by snoring."

Run that through your calculator! It may come out Hard, it may come out Easy. But it will come out whole, and it will last forever.

—E. B. WHITE, "Calculating Machine"

More extreme varieties of informal writing are to be found everywhere in our society, where the friendly touch is often the way to riches, as in advertising. Sportswriting too has been notoriously informal for half a century and has influenced other branches of journalism. Here is an example by a professional golfer, whose prose may strike you as affected in its efforts to be pals with the reader:

Show me a really morose, down-at-the-mouth, give-up-the-game, leave-me-alone-at-the-clubhouse-bar golfer and I will show you a golfer who is having trouble with one of two clubs, the putter or the driver. We all have a way of surviving those weeks when our long irons aren't long or our sand blasts move lots of sand instead of the ball. But when our putting is sour or our driving is awful, then we are in honest, interminable, miserable trouble. Consequently, the putter and the driver are two clubs that merit some special attention, and that is what we are going to give them now. Then we will add a quick word about club selection for when you don't happen to be using the putter or the driver.

—ARNOLD PALMER, in *Sports Illustrated*

The intimate tone and calculated effect of disorganized spontaneity characteristic of the farther reaches of informal writing have found a literary home in modern fiction, particularly in modern American fiction (although the world seems quick to follow). The modern novelist strives for informality with all the diligence that was required to write the more formal nineteenth-century novel. In the following famous opening paragraph notice the consistency of the tone in vocabulary and structure, and see how the reader is constantly appealed to, so that he is forced into assuming a close contact with the narrator:

To get there you follow Highway 58, going northeast out of the city, and it is a good highway and new. Or was new, that day we went up it. You look up the highway, and it is straight for miles, coming at you, with the black line down the center coming at and at you, black and silky and tarry-shining against the white of the slab, and the heat dazzles up from the slab so that only the black line is clear, coming at you with the whine of the tires, and if you don't quit staring at that line and don't take a few deep breaths and slap yourself hard on the back of the neck you'll hypnotize yourself and you'll come to just at the moment when the right front wheel hooks over into the black dirt shoulder off the slab, and you'll try to jerk her back on but you can't because the slab is high like a curb, and maybe you'll try to reach to turn off the ignition just as she starts the dive. But you won't make it, of course.

—ROBERT PENN WARREN, *All the King's Men*

While these selections give you an idea of the range of styles you will no doubt encounter in reading, they are limited in their usefulness as models for improving style. We do not, after all, write like Winston Churchill or Abraham Lincoln, even in our formal moods. But, for most of us, some guides are necessary if we are to avoid floundering in a swamp of undisciplined informality under the assumption that it is the only alternative left to those not naturally blessed with a gift for grand style. The next chapter, "The Process of Planning and Writing," introduces practical suggestions for locating and limiting a subject, outlining an effective argument, and stating a convincing conclusion. What has been presented so far has defined the general task of writing and emphasized the relation of writing to reading and speaking. Discussion of a few nice matters of form crept in, but that couldn't be helped.

Bibliography. The following books dealing with some of the matters discussed in this chapter—the levels and varieties of English usage, the sources of its vocabulary, the relation of spoken to written English—will be found in almost every college library.

ADAMS, J. DONALD. *The Magic and Mystery of Words.* New York: Holt, Rinehart and Winston, 1963.

BLOOMFIELD, MORTON W., and LEONARD NEWMARK. *A Linguistic Introduction to the History of English.* New York: Alfred A. Knopf, 1963.

BRYANT, MARGARET M. *Modern English and Its Heritage.* 2nd ed. New York: Macmillan Publishing Co., Inc., 1962.

CARROLL, JOHN B. *The Study of Language.* Cambridge: Harvard University Press, 1958.

COPPERUD, ROY H. *American Usage: The Consensus.* New York: Van Nostrand Reinhold, 1970.

EVANS, BERGEN, and CORNELIA EVANS. *A Dictionary of Contemporary American Usage.* New York: Random House, 1957.

FOLLETT, WILSON. *Modern American Usage: A Guide.* New York: Hill and Wang, 1966.

FOWLER, H. W. *A Dictionary of Modern English Usage,* 2nd ed. Oxford: Clarendon Press, 1965.

GIBSON, WALKER, Editor. *The Limits of Language.* New York: Hill and Wang, 1962.

JESPERSEN, OTTO. *Growth and Structure of the English Language,* 9th ed. New York: Doubleday and Co., 1955.

KRAPP, GEORGE PHILIP. *The Knowledge of English.* New York: Henry Holt and Co., 1927.

NEWMAN, EDWIN. *Strictly Speaking: Will America Be the Death of English?* Indianapolis: Bobbs-Merrill, 1974.

PYLES, THOMAS. *Words and Ways of American English.* New York: Random House, 1952.

ROBERTSON, STUART. *The Development of Modern English.* New York: Random House, 1952.

SAPIR, EDWARD. *Language.* New York: Harcourt, Brace and World, Inc., 1921.

2 The Process of
Planning and Writing

PROBLEMS OF SUBJECT AND FOCUS

Selecting a Subject

One of the questions on a history examination reads: "What were the chief military and political arguments against Lincoln's issuing the Emancipation Proclamation in 1862?" A proper answer will take at least a paragraph or two of discussion, a characteristic that designates the question an *essay question.* Like any essay, the answer requires some thought and organization, but one problem is solved by the question itself: there is no doubt what is to be written about. The history instructor is playing fair. He wants you to prove you have learned a few facts. Now, by way of contrast, observe the devious mind of the English teacher: "Write a five-hundred-word theme on the subject of humor." That is not a question but an order, it has no correct answer, and where on earth do you begin? The last is the first; deciding where to begin is the preliminary step in any piece of writing. It is a crucial step when no specific information has been requested. Finding the "answer," under these circumstances, is a matter of selecting a subject.

Preliminary Planning

If the length of a paper is established in advance, it will automatically affect the paper's subject. An eight-hundred-word theme on some local custom, on a new development in science, on the author John Updike, or on any other subject is, before all other considerations, an eight-hundred-word theme. The student faced with such a theme and the professional writer paid to supply a six-thousand-word article on the commercial uses of man-made satellites have a common obligation to interest the reader in a limited space. When filling space receives more attention than interesting the reader, the temptation is to think of large subjects that promise to take up room with little effort. Subjects like "Humor," "Home and Friends," "Amusements," "Politics," or "Vacations" are not suitable subjects for short papers; they are warehouses full of random facts, opinions, and impressions.

Replace the problem of filling a blank space with that of engaging a reader's interest, however, and the task changes from a matter of *discovering* what to talk about to one of *selecting* what is most important to say.

An effective piece of writing forces the reader to notice aspects of its subject he or she has not already considered. The more general the treatment of the subject, the greater the probability is that the reader will have heard it or thought it before. When writing about something, therefore, you must be prepared to describe it in detail. Everyone can visualize a forest, but the writer describes the kinds of trees composing it, the colors and shapes of the leaves, the depth of the shade, the thickness of the undergrowth, the positions of the trunks, and the texture of the barks until it is no longer *a* forest but *the* forest. An immense subject, such as American politics, requires proportionately elaborate detail, which means more exposition. A six-thousand-word subject will not fit into an eight-hundred-word theme.

Limiting the Subject

How does one know when a subject is the right size? By thinking about it carefully before beginning to write. Let us say an eight-hundred-word theme is set with no more prescriptive reference to subject than that it should be based on an interest or hobby. A quick review of your hobbies and interests produces antiques. "Antiques" is a general subject about which many books have been written. A short paper cannot pretend to comprehend everything there is to know about it. But you know something about antiques because your mother and grandmother have several cupboards filled with early American glass, a considerably less extensive topic than "Antiques." You have, moreover, begun a glass collection of your own with a few choice pieces. By analyzing your acquaintance with "antiques," you have already begun to trim the subject down to size.

Now ask what you can tell your reader about antiques that lies within your experience and is neither trite nor general. In response to that difficult question, you may decide to focus your essay on a single idea, the theory that an amateur collector of glass develops through three stages. State this objective in the form of a thesis or summarizing sentence: "An amateur collector of early American glass develops through three stages: first, he buys everything in sight; second, as his knowledge and taste grow, he discards all except a few of his choicest pieces; third, he begins to trade in a discriminating way with other collectors." There you have a target to shoot at, a rough plan of operations, and some idea of the ammunition you are going to use. Up to this time most of your planning has been done in your head. Now jot down your main ideas on a sheet of paper (or speak them into a tape recorder), write down under each main head (e.g., "Buying Everything in Sight") a few of the details as they occur to you, and you now have a working plan.

You will probably change your plan as you proceed, but every writer must do that. Change will improve your finished product so long as you keep to your main objective and your first general plan. Your paper will have direction, purpose, organization, and clearness.

Some Types of Subject. Three fairly simple general subject categories are listed below. Under each heading are ten relatively limited subjects derived from it. Although the example does not carry the case so far, many of the limited subjects are susceptible of even further subdivision. Experiment with a few of them yourself.

GENERAL SUBJECT: HOME AND FAMILY LIFE

1. Space problems in an apartment house
2. Feeding the baby
3. I am an only child
4. Father comes home at night
5. The dinner hour in Suburbia
6. The well-planned kitchen
7. Papering a room
8. Sister falls in love
9. Nostalgia in an attic
10. Short-order cooking

GENERAL SUBJECT: HOBBIES

1. Hunting birds with a camera
2. The fascination of old guns
3. Indian relics in my community
4. The sports car club
5. Collecting antique glass
6. Keeping a journal
7. Wood carving
8. Remaking old cars
9. Photographing flowers in color
10. The rock hunter

GENERAL SUBJECT: TRAVEL

1. Bicycle trips on Cape Cod
2. Exploring in a canoe
3. A strange place I have slept in
4. Touring with a trailer
5. Glacier Park trails
6. Bus versus car travel
7. Plane versus ship travel
8. A day in Rome
9. A walking trip in England
10. The trouble with sleeping bags

Each of the categories presented is chosen for its potential relation to personal experience. To write about "Home and Family Life," one does not ordinarily rush to the encyclopedia and take copious notes. There is a time, of course, for research, and it comes soon enough for most of us. For the moment, however, the essay based on personal experience, or, at most, on sources of information more readily available than the library, is an excellent field for experiment. The various kinds of writing discussed in the following passages should reveal a bit of the raw material most writers have immediately at hand.

Autobiographical Materials. "The Story of My Life" is of course a favorite topic that our natural egotism rather enjoys. But there are dangers. Beware of writing a narrative account of your life, listing in chronological order such items as when and where you were born, who your parents are, where you went to school, and so on. Instead, try telling about the development of your interest in music, about your religious life, about your attitude toward a life work. Alternatively, isolate one aspect of your character: perseverance, sense of humor, pride, aggression. Remember that it is not you but your reader who must be interested in your exposure, and don't announce, "Self-respect is the dominant trait of my character" and expect the world to hang on your lips waiting for the next pearl. Recount instead an incident, as does the author of the following example, to show your self-respect at work.

There were many times when I had to exercise a great deal of ingenuity to keep out of trouble. It is a southern custom that all men must take off their hats when they enter an elevator. And especially did this apply to us blacks with rigid force. One day I stepped into an elevator with my arms full of packages. I was forced to ride with my hat on. Two white men stared at me coldly. Then one of them very kindly lifted my hat and placed it upon my armful of packages. Now the most accepted response for a Negro to make under such circumstances is to look at the white man out of the corner of his eye and grin. To have said: "Thank you!" would have made the white man *think* that you *thought* you were receiving from him a personal service. For such an act I have seen Negroes take a blow in the mouth. Finding the first alternative distasteful, and the second dangerous, I hit upon an acceptable course of action which fell safely between these two poles. I immediately—no sooner than my hat was lifted—pretended that my packages were about to spill, and appeared deeply distressed with keeping them in my arms. In this fashion I evaded having to acknowledge his service, and, in spite of adverse circumstances, salvaged a slender shred of personal pride.

—RICHARD WRIGHT, *The Ethics of Living Jim Crow*

A single memorable incident is often a better choice than a number of sketchily treated events in your life. And be wary of the obvious incidents everyone has talked about: the camping trip, the auto accident, the big fire downtown. Much more effective is some apparently minor incident, so developed with concrete detail that it acquires importance in the telling.

The best of learning came on the morning radio, which I learned to love. Every town of a few thousand people has its station, and it takes the place of the old local newspaper. Bargains and trades are announced, social doings, prices of commodities, messages. The records played are the same all over the country. If "Teen-Age Angel" is top of the list in Maine, it is top of the list in Montana. In the course of a day you may hear "Teen-Age Angel" thirty or forty times. But in addition to local news and chronicles, some foreign advertising creeps in. As I went farther and farther north and it got colder I was aware of more and more advertising for Florida real estate and, with the approach of the long and bitter winter, I could see why Florida is a golden word. As I went along I found that more and more people lusted toward Florida and that thousands had moved there and more thousands wanted to and would. The advertising, with a side look at Federal Communications, made few claims except for the fact that the land they were selling was in Florida. Some of them went out on a limb and promised that it was above tide level. But that didn't matter; the very name Florida carried the message of warmth and ease and comfort. It was irresistible.

—JOHN STEINBECK, *Travels with Charley*

You can always find material for descriptive or expository papers in your home life—anything from short profiles of your father or your mother to longer discussions interpreting your family life in terms of its relation to American social history. Or you can take a single brief incident out of your home life and make it interesting and significant.

First Impressions of College. The student who is not asked or tempted to record his or her first impressions of the brave new college world is lucky. Even great writers succumb to the urge or the necessity, and, when they do, the result is worth consideration.

In order to place this question fairly before you, I will describe, for memory has kept the picture bright, one of those rare but, as Queen Victoria would have put it, never-to-be-sufficiently-lamented occasions when in deference to friendship, or in a desperate attempt to acquire information about, perhaps, the French Revolution, it seemed necessary to attend a lecture. The room to begin with had a hybrid look—it was not for sitting in, nor yet for eating in. Perhaps there was a map on the wall; certainly there was a table on a platform, and several rows of rather small, rather hard, comfortless little chairs. These were occupied intermittently, as if they shunned each other's company, by people of both sexes, and some had notebooks and were tapping their fountain pens, and some had none and gazed with the vacancy and placidity of bull frogs at the ceiling. A large clock displayed its cheerless face, and when the hour struck in strode a harried-looking man, a man from whose face nervousness, vanity, or perhaps the depressing and impossible nature of his task had removed all traces of ordinary humanity. There was a momentary stir. He had written a book, and for the moment it was interesting to see people who have written books. Everybody gazed at him. He was bald and not hairy; he had a mouth and a chin; in short he was a man like another, although he had written a book. He cleared his throat and the lecture began. Now the human voice is an instrument of varied power; it can enchant and it can soothe; it can rage and it can despair; but when it lectures it almost always bores. What he said was sensible enough; there was learning in it and argument and reason; but as the voice went on attention wandered. The face of the clock seemed abnormally pale; the hands too suffered from some infirmity. Had they the gout? Were they swollen? They moved so slowly. They reminded one of the painful progress of a three-legged fly that has survived the winter. How many flies on an average survive the English winter, and what would be the thoughts of such an insect on waking to find itself being lectured on the French Revolution? The enquiry was fatal. A link had been lost—a paragraph dropped. It was useless to ask the lecturer to repeat his words; on he plodded with dogged pertinacity. The origin of the French Revolution was being sought for—also the thoughts of flies. Now there came one of those flat stretches of discourse when minute objects can be seen coming for two or three miles ahead. "Skip!" we entreated him—vainly. He did not skip. There was a joke. Then the voice went on again; then it seemed that the windows wanted washing; then a woman sneezed; then the voice quickened; then there was a peroration; and then—thank Heaven!—the lecture was over.

—VIRGINIA WOOLF, *The Death of the Moth and Other Essays*

The Narrative Incident. Have you ever found yourself in a situation where you are the victim of some random act of violence? Consider the difficulties involved in trying to recall and to narrate such an incident. Note how this writer vivifies his account through the use of concrete detail, realistic dialogue, and the present tense.

The athletic meet takes place in a city-owned stadium far from the school. It is an important event to which a whole day is given over. The winners are to get those precious little medallions stamped with the New York City emblem that can be screwed into a belt and that prove the wearer to be a distinguished personage. I am a fast runner, and so I am assigned the position of anchor man on my class's team in the relay race. There are three other seventh-grade teams in the race, two of them all Negro, as ours is all white. One of the all-Negro teams is very tall—their anchor man waiting silently next to me on the line looks years older than I am, and I do not recognize him. He is the first to get the baton and crosses the finishing line in a walk. Our team comes in second, but a few minutes later we are declared the winners, for it has been discovered that the anchor man on the first-place team is not a member of the class. We are awarded the medallions, and the following day our home-room teacher makes a speech about how proud she is of us for being superior athletes as well as superior students. We want to believe that we deserve the praise, but we know that we could not have won even if the other class had not cheated.

That afternoon, walking home, I am waylaid and surrounded by five Negroes, among whom is the anchor man of the disqualified team. "Gimme my medal, mo'f——r," he grunts. I do not have it with me and I tell him so. "Anyway, it ain't yours," I say foolishly. He calls me a liar on both counts and pushes me up against the wall on which we sometimes play handball. "Gimme my mo'f——n' medal," he says again. I repeat that I have left it home. "Le's search the li'l mo'f——r," one of them suggests, "he prolly got it *hid* in his mo'f——n' *pants.*" My panic is now unmanageable. (How many times had I been surrounded like this and asked in soft tones, "Len' me a nickle, boy." How many times had I been called a liar for pleading poverty and pushed around, or searched, or beaten up, unless there happened to be someone in the marauding gang like Carl who liked me across that enormous divide of hatred and who would therefore say, "Aaah, c'mon, le's git someone else, *this* boy ain't got no money on 'im.") I scream at them through tears of rage and self-contempt, "Keep your f——n' filthy lousy black hands offa me! I swear I'll get the cops." This is all they need to hear, and the five of them set upon me. They bang me around, mostly in the stomach and on the arms and shoulders, and when several adults loitering near the candy store down the block notice what is going on and begin to shout, they run off and away.

—Norman Podhoretz, *My Negro Problem—and Ours*

Descriptions. Description, telling what is to be seen, heard, tasted, touched, smelled, and possibly surmised, seems so straightforward a task that its chief pitfall sometimes escapes notice until it is too late. The problem is *unity,* the importance of each element relating coherently to the others. A verbal picture may be unified by a summarizing statement that ties the components together or by a dominant and consistent attitude toward the images described. A visual scene assembled on the page as through a fish-eye lens with every detail simultaneously and indiscriminately distinct is usually confusing. What is more, it is impersonal; there is nothing in it to connect writer and reader, and only a very confident, or very rash, writer throws away the bond of understanding with the reader. That bond may be preserved in a point of view. *Point of view* in general application means the writer's attitude toward the subject. In description the phrase has a more specific meaning: where the writer is sitting, standing, lying, or crouching while describing and evaluating. What does this point of view that surprisingly means exactly what it says have to do with unity? Remember that the reader is seeing through Someone Else's eyes, and, if Someone Else is admiring the blaze in the third-floor kitchen and, at the same time, noting how the fire truck takes the corner at Broad and Fremont, the reader is going to have a headache. Do not give readers headaches! A shift in point of view is permissible if the reader is given warning that a shift is coming or occurring, but the shift should be for a purpose, to contribute to a conclusion, not just because a lot of facts or impressions present themselves with the price of admission.

. . . The things I liked best about the Polo Grounds were sights and emotions so inconsequential that they will surely slide out of my recollection. A flight of pigeons flashing out of the barn-shadow of the upper stands, wheeling past the right-field foul pole, and disappearing above the inert, heat-heavy flags on the roof. The steepness of the ramp descending from the Speedway toward the upper-stand gates, which pushed your toes into your shoe tips as you approached the park, tasting sweet anticipation and getting out your change to buy a program. The unmistakable, final *"Plock!"* of a line drive hitting the green wooden barrier above the stands in deep left field. The gentle, rockerlike swing of the loop of rusty chain you rested your arm upon in a box seat, and the heat of the sun-warmed iron coming through your shirtsleeve under your elbow. At a night game, the moon rising out of the scoreboard like a spongy, day-old orange balloon and then whitening over the waves of noise and the slow, shifting clouds of floodlit cigarette smoke. All these I mourn, for their loss constitutes the death of still another neighborhood—a small landscape of distinctive and reassuring familiarity.

—ROGER ANGELL, *The Summer Game*

Sometimes an effective general description of a complex scene can be clarified by emphasizing contrasts between the present occasion and some former time more familiar to the reader. Here a journalist describes the look of a modern army camp by using this device of contrast:

From the road, the camp seemed quiet, clean, almost deserted. Gone were the tent cities, the mud roads, the steam locomotive acting as a temporary boiler plant for a new hospital. The white barracks of World War II were still there, but alongside them now were the brick barracks, built to house a whole company instead of a platoon.

And indoors things had changed. Instead of a single room filled with cots, walls now gave each set of four bunks almost the privacy of a room. Instead of bare chairs in a day room, this one had the soft chairs and the relaxed look of a recreation room at a resort hotel. Instead of long wooden tables in a drab mess hall, it had separate tables, each seating four soldiers. There were tablecloths, curtains, photomurals in color, and the word was out that china dishes would soon replace metal trays. But the new pressed meat tasted like the old Spam, and the G.I. coffee had aged, but not changed.

—RALPH G. MARTIN, *"An Old Soldier Looks at the New Army"*

Occupations. The work you have done during your vacations, the job you have while attending college, the profession you expect to enter after you leave college—all offer material for interesting discussion. The last-named topic, however, is probably the most difficult and dangerous. Most persons, even if they have determined on a future occupation, necessarily speak of it in vague terms because they have experienced so little of its details and complexities. A general rule: it's hard to write about what you don't know about.

One familiar decision that faces many students seeking a profession is whether to concentrate on the scientific and engineering side of life or on those occupations that do not involve such technical training. The relation here with immediate choices in undergraduate education is of course obvious. Anyone facing such decisions, and trying to write about them, might ponder the following defense of the humanistic side of things. It was written by a nonscientist.

> The scientist indeed may be less qualified than the nonscientist to talk outside his field, for his education is likely to have become rigorously narrow. Unless he has had the good fortune to attend an old-fashioned liberal arts college, he will have had the most superficial and hurried contact with the social sciences and humanities. If he has gone to one of the larger colleges of engineering, many of which are now turning out scientists as well as engineers, his contact may well have been nonexistent, for many such schools design special humanities and social-science courses which have been dehydrated of their most vital content. He will not know the facts and concepts of history or sociology or the ideas and values of literature or philosophy. Even if the scientist's undergraduate studies were sufficiently humane and liberal, the world he moves in makes for narrowness and, except in his own discipline, for shallowness. A physical chemist, lamenting his restricted focus, once complained to me in desperation that he can scarcely keep up with the work being done in his particular specialty, let alone in physical chemistry itself; he long ago gave up hope of keeping up with the whole of chemistry. His only reading outside chemistry since his one undergraduate course in humanities was for an inter-disciplinary honors class he was assigned to for one year.

> —MORRIS FREEDMAN, *Confessions of a Conformist*

The Profile. A profile is a short biographical sketch that depends for its effect on a few well-chosen, vivid facts and details. When you draw on autobiographical material for a subject, the aim is to isolate a single circumstance worth discussing. In a profile very nearly the opposite process is followed; you portray the whole person in terms of several selected traits or acts. The subject of a successful profile need not be famous—or notorious; as a matter of fact, the writer of a profile often takes some totally obscure person and tries to make the reader feel that that person is worth knowing. On the other hand, many profiles, like some of those in *People* or *Playboy,* are of celebrities. You may take your choice.

One possible project is to write a profile of a distinguished citizen in your community, one whom you have known fairly well. Select one you have liked and admired. Go to the library and consult some local "who's who" for background facts. Then organize your profile on the basis of a number of the following divisions.

I. An interview, in which you introduce your subject and give a quick picture of his or her appearance
II. A glimpse of the subject at work
III. A transition to the facts about this person's career, education, and so on
IV. The subject's dominant traits
V. A typical professional performance (your big scene)
VI. What others say about the subject

You need not use all of these divisions, but if you want to compress, remember that I, III, and V are essential.

If you want to do a more ambitious biographical piece, one that will take you to some of the reference books in the library, try writing a biographical sketch of (1) the author of a book you are reading; (2) a community leader; (3) the man or woman who represents you in Congress; (4) a well-known scientist who is connected with your college or university. You will find more detailed assistance for writing such papers in Chapter 3 of this section. Be careful to give all your borrowed information in your own words! To lift commentary verbatim without acknowledging the author is to commit *plagiarism,* the name for passing stolen ideas, and the penalties are usually severe.

When Senator John F. Kennedy, shortly before he became president, wrote his book about several distinguished past and present members of the Senate, he called it *Profiles in Courage,* and he was using the word *Profiles* in this more ambitious sense. Here is a passage from his profile of Senator Robert A. Taft, in which you will note the combination of incidents, quotations from others, and personal testimony from the writer's own experience that can make a persuasive piece of writing in this genre.

So Bob Taft, as his biographer has described it, was "born to integrity." He was known in the Senate as a man who never broke an agreement, who never compromised his deeply felt Republican principles, who never practiced political deception. His bitter public enemy, Harry Truman, would say when the Senator died: "He and I did not agree on public policy, but he knew where I stood and I knew where he stood. We need intellectually honest men like Senator Taft." Examples of his candor are endless and startling. The Ohioan once told a group in the heart of Republican farm territory that farm prices were too high; and he told still another farm group that "he was tired of seeing all these people riding in Cadillacs." His support of an extensive Federal housing program caused a colleague to remark: "I hear the Socialists have gotten to Bob Taft." He informed an important political associate who cherished a commendatory message signed by Taft that his assistant "sent those things out by the dozen" without the Senator ever seeing, much less signing them. And a colleague recalls that he did not reject the ideas of his friends by gentle indirection, but by coldly and unhesitatingly terming them "nonsense." "He had," as William S. White has written, "a luminous candor of purpose that was extraordinarily refreshing in a chamber not altogether devoted to candor."

It would be a mistake, however, to conclude from this that Senator Taft was cold and abrupt in his personal relationships. I recall, from my own very brief service with him in the Senate and on the Senate Labor Committee in the last months of his life, my strong impression of a surprising and unusual personal charm, and a disarming simplicity of manner. It was these qualities, combined with an unflinching courage which he exhibited throughout his entire life and most especially in his last days, that bound his adherents to him with unbreakable ties.

—JOHN F. KENNEDY, *Profiles in Courage*

The Brief, Informal Book Review. More and more in recent years, the tempo of book publication has increased to the point where no one can expect to read all the new books, even those restricted to a particular field of interest. Readers therefore must depend on the reports of others in order to select the particular books they may want to buy and read. The same is true of movies. To meet this demand for quick and ready information, there has developed in newspapers and magazines a special kind of review: a very short, informal description of a book (film), with some brief information about the author (director), and at least an implied evaluation of his or her work. You will find such brief reports in *Time,* in *The New Yorker,* and in several other magazines and newspapers that are likely to reach serious readers of books and moviegoers.

Sometimes such an informal review can be accomplished—or at least attempted—in a single paragraph. In the examples below you will note the almost breezy tone adopted by the anonymous reviewers. But beneath the informality there is much serious purpose, and much important information is presented in short and palatable form. Note how similar in style are these two reviews, one of a film, the other of a book.

THE GREAT GATSBY—F. Scott Fitzgerald's short masterpiece turned into a slow, stately, two-and-a-half-hour movie, directed by Jack Clayton and photographed by Douglas Slocombe. Overuse of tracking shots, redundant dialogue, and too many Charlestons did the mysterious lengthening trick. Daisy is finely played as a creature of beautiful, aerial selfishness and apparent simplicity by Mia Farrow, with a voice that whispers like a bird on the lawn in the Fitzgerald Long Island summer. Her best performance so far. The first-person narrative is transformed into voice-over comment by the character of the observant Nick (Sam Waterston, a good actor, wonderfully picked by Clayton); but the first-person technique works better in novels than in the movies. The small-part casting is first-rate. So is the sensibility. One mostly misses Scott Fitzgerald's terseness. Bruce Dern as Tom Buchanan is very fine, Robert Redford as the pining, mysteriously rich Gatsby a bit Ivy League. Script by Francis Ford Coppola.[1]

—The New Yorker, April 8, 1974.

THE TOLL, by Michael Mewshaw (Random House). The setting is up-country Morocco. There is a group of young, nomadic, hippie-type Americans—three men and two women—with an old VW bus emblazoned "The Gravy Train." A sixth member of the group, brother of one of the others, is being held in a small-town jail, and his friends are determined to break him free. They encounter an older American, a down-on-his-luck mercenary fresh from Biafra, and he engages, at a price (the Gravy Trainers, though ragged, have moneyed parents back home), to lend them his discipline and experience. A plan is arranged and carried out, but the Gravy Trainers are what they are—irresponsible, sentimental, off-the-pigs amateurs. The result is disaster. The survivors flee into the mountains, into the desert, and with every hour the disasters multiply. Mr. Mewshaw prefaces his novel with an epigraph from "For Whom the Bell Tolls" that seems to describe his intention: "It was as though you had thrown a stone and

[1] Reprinted by permission; © 1974 The New Yorker Magazine, Inc.

the stone made a ripple and the ripple returned roaring and toppling as a tidal wave." His theme would thus seem to be that every act—and every inertia—has its consequence, and every consequence its further consequence. His success is very considerable.[2]

—The New Yorker, April 8, 1974

In attempting such a brief review yourself, you should keep in mind at least three purposes. First, you should indicate something of the author's or director's reputation or qualifications. Second, you should summarize the contents of the book or film in a brief survey of the chief points of its argument or plot. Third, let your reader know whether you think the work good or bad. The modest reviewer also provides some reason for his judgment.

Directions, Processes, Organizations. The "how to do it" and "how it was done" literature of America is impressive in extent, and some of it, at least, is of impressive literary quality. The ability to give accurate directions is extremely important and should be cultivated just as strictly as the more creative kinds of writing. Here are a few exercises that you may find useful:

1. Take two points that lie far apart in your locality, such as your home and a distant shopping center. Draw up a short set of directions by which a total stranger might arrive at your home starting from the center. *Do not* use any of the points of the compass—North, South, East, or West—in your instructions. Depend entirely on an accurate description of landmarks and distances.

2. Explain to an unmechanical friend how to start and operate a power mower. Do not use a single technical term without explaining it in clear, untechnical language.

3. Tell one of your younger friends what he is to do to register in college. Take him from one building to another, and explain every step of the procedure in words that he cannot fail to understand.

Setting out directions is a useful exercise not only in clarity but in establishing order. All instructions have a clear beginning and a virtually unalterable sequence in which they must

---

[2] Reprinted by permission; © 1974 The New Yorker Magazine, Inc.

be given if they are to work. It's no good explaining how to change an ordinary household fuse without first telling where the fusebox is.

An explanation of a process is not necessarily a set of directions to be followed by someone. Thousands of such explanations are written merely because there are people who like to know how things work. If you try one of the following subjects, you might try making it an interesting explanation as well as a set of directions to be followed:

1. Measuring wind velocity
2. Photographing children
3. Coming about in a sailboat
4. How to use a fly rod
5. Making Christmas cards

6. Format in the school paper
7. How to model clothes
8. Operating a motorcycle
9. Transplanting wild flowers
10. Making a banana split

An explanation of an organization calls for somewhat more extensive treatment, in many cases, than an explanation of a process. It is a particularly effective device for practicing outlining techniques, for you must see to it that your divisions are coordinate, that they meet each other neatly without overlapping.

Here are a few topics that you might use:

1. A military unit
2. Your fraternity or sorority
3. The Department of State
4. An army induction center
5. A city police department
6. Camp Fire Girls or Girl Scouts

7. The 4-H clubs
8. A consumers' cooperative
9. A Junior Achievement group
10. An insurance company

One world of activity in which "how to do it" writing plays an important role is sports. The following example describes in precise, simple language the flutter kick in swimming. The author's problem is to distinguish the art of the flutter kick from the natural, instinctive motion of kicking without repelling the reader with a barrage of intricate and unfamiliar detail.

In the flutter, the water is squeezed, thrust, and kicked away, imparting a forward drive. It is most effective when the power comes from the hips and thighs, the rest of the legs controlled but relaxed, the knees slightly bent, the ankles loose. The ankles may be turned slightly inward in pigeon-toed fashion and should be completely relaxed so that they flop loosely, the toes pointed to eliminate resistance.

The kick is, of course, a series of beats, the legs moving alternately up and down. As it is lifted toward the surface, the leg is relaxed at the knee and bends slightly, the bend increasing until the leg is near the surface. The downward thrust is a whiplash motion in which the whole leg is straightened, imparting a snap to the lower leg and the ankle. The effect is to drive the water down along the thighs and snap it away; or, to look at it in another way, the legs both in the upward and in the downward beat catch hold of the water and drive the body forward.

The first rule for practicing the flutter kick is to make the thighs do the lifting and thrusting. If those big muscles in the thighs and lower back do the work, the kick will not be as tiring as it would be if it were primarily a knee kick, incorrectly used by many swimmers. By applying force from his thighs, the swimmer will give an undulating movement to his legs somewhat like that of a piece of rope when one end of it is snapped. At first there should be little, if any, bending of the knees. The swimmer can let his legs twist inward slightly, rolling the knees closer together and pointing the toes inward and downward.

—Harold S. Ulen and Guy Larcom, Jr., *The Complete Swimmer*

A good test of a "how to do it" article is this: can you, from reading it, put the process into operation yourself? Experiment with the example just given only if you have an exceptionally big bathtub, but the test of "Can you do it?" is generally appropriate in the case of an unfamiliar process. It is particularly appropriate when you are reading an account of a process that is utterly unfamiliar to you.

Here is Vilhjalmur Stefansson's explanation of the method used by Eskimos in catching fish under ice:

In getting ready to fish through ice you fasten your floats to one edge of the net and your sinkers to the other, so that one edge of the net shall be held at the surface of the water and the other down vertically. Then you cut two holes in the ice about forty feet apart (for that is a common length for Eskimo nets) and each a foot or eighteen inches in diameter. Between these two holes you cut a series of smaller holes just big enough to stick your arm into the water, and perhaps six to eight feet apart. Next you take a stick of dry, buoyant wood that is eight or ten feet long. You shove it down through one of the end holes until it is all in the water, when it floats up and rises against the ice. You have a string tied to the stick and this stick you fasten to one end of the net. Then you lay the string so that, while one end is still visible at your hole, the other end is visible below the next hole six or eight feet away. You now go to the second hole, put your hand into the water and slide the stick along under the ice until you can see it through the third hole. The stick, of course, pulls the string in after it and by the time you have worked the stick along to the furthest hole your net is set. You now take a rope that is about ten feet longer than the net and tie each end of the rope to one end of the net so as to make an "endless chain," the net being under the water and the rope on top of the ice.

During the night the holes all freeze over. You allow the small holes to remain frozen permanently but each time you go out to tend the net you open the two end holes and pull the net out of one of them. As you pull the net out the rope part of your endless chain is pulled into the water. When you have picked all the fish out of the net, you pull on your rope and thus drag the net back into the water.

—VILHJALMUR STEFANSSON, *Hunters of the Great North*

As we have said, a complex operation can be described with the purpose of putting the reader into a position to perform it himself. That is the implication in Stefansson's account, as his repeated *you* suggests. (It is also, we may remind *you*, the implication in *The Macmillan Handbook of English*.)

Often, however, and especially in cases involving modern pieces of machinery, a description is written not for the user, but for the layman, to give him at least some sense of how a complicated mechanism operates. In the following description of a space suit by an astronaut, notice how the language is addressed not to fellow astronauts, but to you and me.

Normally, unless the cabin pressure fails and we are threatened with a case of the bends—which would almost certainly be fatal—the suit serves mainly to keep us ventilated and provides us with a constantly refreshed supply of oxygen to breathe. It is a beautifully contrived mechanical environment. A steady stream of pure oxygen—which emanates from one of the two volleyball-size flasks we have mentioned earlier—enters the suit through the inlet valve near the waist. We plug this valve in as soon as we enter the capsule. The

49

oxygen then circulates through the entire suit and reaches all of our extremities to cool them off. A series of waffle-weave patches on our long-john underwear helps to keep the oxygen moving. The oxygen finally makes its exit through an outlet located near our right ear near the helmet. As it flows out, the oxygen takes with it whatever body odors, perspiration, carbon dioxide, water and other waste matter—like nasal discharge or bits of hair—it has picked up on its tour. The water and CO_2, of course, are normal by-products of the pilot's metabolism. The system dumps all of this into a marvelous bit of plumbing which traps out the waste and uses an electric fan to push the tired gas over a bed of activated charcoal. This filters out the odors and then the gas goes on through two tanks of lithium hydroxide to remove the deadly carbon dioxide. When it has been thoroughly cleaned, the oxygen then goes into a cooling device which removes the excess heat which it has picked up from our bodies. The hot gas is cooled by conduction in a heat exchanger. Here water takes up much of the heat, which is then discharged out of the capsule in the form of a puff of steam. One of the many things we have to worry about on a flight, incidentally, is making sure that this steam duct does not freeze up because of excess water flowing through the system. If that happened, the water would not get converted readily into steam, the steam duct would clog up and cease functioning, and so would the delicate systems which keep the Astronaut and his cabin cool. A device which Rube Goldberg himself would be proud of takes care of droplets of water which collect in the suit circuit at this point. The drops are soaked up by a little sponge which is struck by a small piston every thirty minutes to squeeze the water out and dump it into a storage tank. This, incidentally, is our emergency supply of drinking water. As soon as the oxygen has been purged of water, waste, odors, and carbon dioxide, it flows back into the suit and starts the same tour all over again. While all this is going on, a much simpler process is taking place in the separate atmosphere of the cabin. Here, a fan and a heat exchanger keep the cabin ventilated and cool. If the oxygen should start leaking from the cabin system, it can be replenished from the oxygen in the suit—after the Astronaut has had a chance to breathe it first.

—WALTER M. SCHIRRA, JR., *We Seven*

Local Color. The literature of travel, describing places unknown to the reader, has a long and distinguished history. Related to it is the growth of local-color writing, in nineteenth-century America, when people came to realize that their own communities were exotic and interesting in their own right.

Now every section of America has its literature of praise and interpretation. But works of travel and local color have had to change their emphasis in our own time, when increased mobility, general education, movies, and television have brought vividly to our senses the scenes of places formerly unknown. As a result, much writing about local color must now assume a considerable factual knowledge on the part of the reader, and the author nowadays may try instead to give his reader some special sense of the *feel* of the place. What impression of Chicago do you get from the following description?

Chicago is the great American city. New York is one of the capitals of the world and Los Angeles is a constellation of plastic, San Francisco is a lady, Boston has become Urban Renewal, Philadelphia and Baltimore and Washington wink like dull diamonds in the smog of Eastern Megalopolis, and New Orleans is unremarkable past the French Quarter. Detroit is a one-trade town, Pittsburgh has lost its golden triangle, St. Louis has become the golden arch of the corporation, and nights in Kansas City close early. The oil depletion allowance makes Houston and Dallas naught but checkerboards for this sort of game. But Chicago is a great American city. Perhaps it is the last of the great American cities.

The reporter was sentimental about the town. Since he had grown up in Brooklyn, it took him no time to recognize, whenever he was in Chicago again, that the urbanites here were like the good people of Brooklyn—they were simple, strong, warm-spirited, sly, rough, compassionate, jostling, tricky and extraordinarily good-natured because they had sex in their pockets, muscles on their back, hot eats around the corner, neighborhoods which dripped with the sauce of local legend, and real city architecture, brownstones with different windows on every floor, vistas for miles of red-brick and two-family wood-frame houses with balconies and porches, runty stunted trees rich as farmland in their promise of tenderness the first city evenings of spring, streets where kids played stick-ball and roller-hockey, lots of smoke and iron twilight. The clangor of the late nineteenth century, the very hope of greed, was in these streets. London one hundred years ago could not have looked much better.

—Norman Mailer, *Miami and the Siege of Chicago*

"Local color," let it be understood, is not necessarily a euphemism for squalor and the "realism" that depends on drunks

51

lying in the gutter, washed-out mothers hanging washed-out clothes, and a good, overall plastering of earthy expressions. All these may be present, but if your community does not possess an aged eccentric with a fine down-home dialect, don't feel you need to create one. The *reality*, as opposed to the fictitious realism, of a home town is a subject with infinite possibilities.

You could investigate the history of your community and write a paper on some phase of it, such as the pioneer days, the coming of the railroad, the Great Depression days. You could investigate local science—geology, botany, and so on—and write an article on the geologic structure of the region, the birds of the region, or the characteristic vegetation. Or, as in the passage you have just read, you could assume much of this information on the part of your reader and try for something more literary.

Here are some further suggestions for the writing of compositions about one's community:

1. Cultural resources
2. The teen-agers
3. What people do for a living
4. Contact with the past
5. Politics and government
6. The school system
7. Recreation: parks, etc.
8. Industrial domination
9. Commuters
10. Relation to other urban centers

The Personal Essay. A good deal of the reading and writing we have to do in this world, as every student knows, seems to be terribly serious, solemn, and pretentious. Every textbook (including this one) conveys the depressing order, "Now this is important—you must *get* it!" But it might be wholesome to conclude this collection of various types of writing by offering another kind of tone altogether. Here is a light personal essay, which, if it is out to prove anything at all, is doing so with considerable ease and good humor. The process of composing such a piece, though, is just as difficult and disciplined an activity as any other composing. You must have two essential tools: (1) a secure knowledge of the subject matter; and (2) a sure grip on the tone, which should not descend into exaggerated joking. Note how much Phyllis McGinley communicates about her view of the battle of the sexes through irony and implication. Notice too how skillfully she manipulates clichés about sex roles in catching your attention.

L A D I E S   O N   T H E   H I G H W A Y

That men are wonderful is a proposition I will defend to the death. Honest, brave, talented, strong and handsome, they are my favorite gender. Consider the things men can do better than women—mend the plumbing, cook, invent atom bombs, design the Empire waistline and run the four-minute mile. They can throw a ball overhand. They can grow a beard. In fact, I can think of only two accomplishments at which women excel. Having babies is one.

The other is driving an automobile.

Don't misunderstand me. Some of my best friends are male drivers. And they seldom go to sleep at the wheel or drive 90 on a 45-an-hour road or commit any other of the sins of which statistics accuse them. But insurance companies have been busy as bees proving that I don't get around among the right people.

New York State—where I live—has even made it expensive to have sons. Car insurance costs much more if there are men in the family under 25 driving than if there are only women. Obviously the females of the species make the best chauffeurs.

They ought to. They get the most practice. Aside from truck- and taxi-drivers, it is women who really handle the cars of the nation. For five days of the week they are in command—slipping cleverly through traffic on their thousand errands, parking neatly in front of the chain stores, ferrying their husbands to and from commuting trains, driving the young to schools and dentists and dancing classes and Scout meetings. It is only on Saturdays and Sundays that men get their innings, not to speak of their outings, and it is over week ends when most of the catastrophes occur.

Not that men are responsible for *all* the accidents. Some are caused by women—by the little blonde on the sidewalk at whom the driver feels impelled to whistle. Or by the pretty girl sitting in the front seat for whom he wants to show off his skill, his eagle eye, and the way he can pull ahead of the fellow in the red sports car.

But it isn't caution and practice alone which make the difference between the sexes. It's chiefly an attitude of mind. Women—in my opinion—are the practical people. To them a car is a means of transportation, a gadget more useful, perhaps, than a dishwasher or a can opener, but no more romantic. It is something in which we carry the

53

sheets to the laundry, pick up Johnnie at kindergarten and lug home those rose bushes.

Men, the dear, sentimental creatures, feel otherwise. Automobiles are more than property. They are their shining chariots, the objects of their affections. A man loves his car the way the Lone Ranger loves his horse, and he feels for its honor on the road. No one must out-weave or out-race him. No one must get off to a better jack-rabbit start. And no one, but no one, must tell him anything while he's driving. My own husband, ordinarily the most good-tempered of men, becomes a tyrant behind the wheel.

"Shouldn't we bear south here?" I inquire meekly on our Saturday trips to the country. Or, "Honey, there's a gray convertible trying to pass."

"Who's driving!" he snarls like Simon Legree, veering stubbornly north or avoiding, by a hair, being run into.

Women drivers, on the other hand, *take* advice. They are used to taking it, having had it pressed on them all their lives by their mothers, teachers, beaus, husbands, and eventually their children. And when they don't know their routes exactly, they inquire at service stations, from passers-by, from traffic officers. But men hate to ask and, when they are forced to do so, seldom listen.

Have you ever overheard a woman taking down directions on the phone? "Yes," she says affably. "I understand. I drive up that pretty road to the Danbury turn-off. Then I bear left at the little antique shoppe that used to be a barn—yellow with blue shutters. Then right at a meadow with two beech trees in it, and a couple of black cows. Up a little lane, just a tiny way beyond a cornfield, and that's your place. Yes. With a Tiffany-glass carriage lamp in front. Fine. I won't have any trouble." Nor does she.

A man has too much pride to take such precautions. "O.K." he says impatiently. "Two point seven miles off the Post Road. A left, a rotary, another left. Six point three to—oh, never mind. I'll look it up on the map."

When they don't insist on traveling by ear, men travel by chart. I've nothing against road maps, really, except the way they clutter up the glove compartment where I like to keep tissues and sun glasses. But men have a furtive passion for them.

When my husband and I are planning a trip, he doesn't rush out like me to buy luggage and a new wardrobe. He shops for maps. For days ahead of time he studies them dotingly; then *I* am forced to study them en route. Many a bitter journey have I taken past the finest scenery in America with my eyes glued to a collection of black and red squiggles on a road map, instead of on the forest and canyons we had come all the way across the country to behold.

"Look!" I cry to him as we rush up some burning autumn lane. "Aren't the trees glorious!"

"What does the map say?" he mutters. "I've marked a covered bridge about a quarter of a mile along here. That's where we turn."

If we should ever approach the Pearly Gates together, I know exactly how the conversation will run. "See all the pretty stars," I'll be murmuring happily. "And, oh, do look over there! Isn't that the City of Gold?"

"Never mind your golden cities," he'll warn me sternly, as he nearly collides with a meteor. "Just keep your eye on the map."

—PHYLLIS McGINLEY

PROBLEMS OF WRITING AND REVISING

Nature of the Plan or Outline

Every paper written needs a plan, although some plans spend their life cycles in the heads of the writers without ever emerging on paper in the form of outlines. Some plans take the form of a series of notes on the back of an old envelope. The experienced writer may plan almost subconsciously; some writers say that they do all their outlining mentally, whereas others say that they write out elaborate outlines on paper. But the inexperienced writer has everything to gain by using paper and pencil to record and clarify the planning that goes on in his head. Even when inspiration is powerful enough and spontaneous enough to leap onto a page without intermediate steps, *an outline of the finished work is an excellent check of organization and logic. If there are flaws in the product of inspiration, an outline may reveal them.*

The Informal Outline. A short paper should have a short outline. A few notes on a piece of scrap paper may suffice. Suppose the urge comes to write a thoughtful little essay on childhood memories. Seize your scrap paper at that moment and begin a list of things you recall from early childhood. Some recollections will be vivid, some won't. Perhaps the difficulty of remembering them at all strikes you. Jot that thought down too. Now sit back and consider what you have, a list of things that must once have impressed you and the thought that they are a good deal less impressive today. Think how the two might fit together. One solution is to begin with the result, the difficulty of remembering. Start your actual paper with a short paragraph developing that subject, lead in your list of memories, and then pause. What you need is a conclusion, although you may have already glimpsed one from reviewing your notes. A speculative paragraph on why these particular recollections should surface while a million other experiences lie undisturbed in the cerebral mud is one acceptable choice for rounding off the topic, but there are others. An appealing short essay can be written in this way and perhaps should always be. Its spontaneity would more than likely be dampened by the imposed order of a full-blown formal outline.

The Process of Synthesis. Making an outline is often spoken of as a process of dividing a subject. It is assumed that the thought mass exists in its entirety in the writer's mind, and in preparing it for the market he methodically slices it up into pieces called topics and subtopics. That may be true for some. For most of us outlining is a process of synthesis, not division. We usually begin with a problem and the necessity of doing something about it. Our first suggestion may be an ill-favored and disreputable little idea. We pull it out and look it over. It seems promising—possibly. But then we look about again—by thinking, by reading, by observing—and pull out other ideas to add to it. We jot down these ideas on paper. Some writers use file cards, which they can later organize in coherent order. Pretty soon, if we are fortunate, we have enough, or perhaps more than enough for our purpose. Then and only then can we begin to select and arrange and divide.

Let us remind ourselves here that in this process of writing a paper or a speech many things go on at the same time. We do not select a subject first, limit the subject second, plan next, outline next, and so on. We may think of a good illustration— and write it down quickly before it fades away; we are conscious of the persons who will read what we say; we have a sudden inspiration of a clever opening paragraph; we think of another important idea that just has to have a place somewhere; we add another thought brick to the structure. And so our essay grows. But the process cannot be prescribed; it is after all too chaotic.

Order of Presentation. The order in which you present your material to your reader will depend partly on what you have to say and partly on the sort of reader you are addressing. The following paragraphs will suggest five among many possible ways of constructing order.

The Chronological Order. If you are telling how something is made, how a game is played, how a system grew or developed in the course of time, you will naturally use the order of happening, called the chronological order. In topics such as the following the chronological order is inherent in the material: how to clean a rifle, how to organize and manage a formal dance, how to prepare for a final examination, how to operate a bulldozer, the history of tennis, the development of consumers' cooperatives, learning how to play the guitar. When a subject does not naturally call for chronological order, you can often achieve a clearer presentation by changing your approach so that you can use the order of time. The description of an airline terminal, for instance, can be made more attractive by first outlining its morning, afternoon, and evening features.

The Inductive Order (Order of Easy Acceptance). Occasionally you may gently lead your reader toward an unpalatable idea by starting with a presentation of numerous facts, instances, or observations that support your main idea. This technique may be used where it is necessary to prepare a reader's mind for a new idea, but inasmuch as most articles are read quickly, the device of surprise has limited uses. It can be tried, however, and can work. For instance, if you are advocating the adoption of an honor system in your school, you may get a more favorable response from your readers if you convince them first that a system of strict, paternalistic supervision has resulted in widespread dishonesty. If you are urging the establishment of teenage night clubs, you can begin by picturing the existing undesirable conditions: students on the streets, involved in drag races, etc.

The Deductive Order ("from the general to the particular"). It is often possible to win over your reader with a well-worded generalization or premise, the truth of which you substantiate in the body of your essay by citing specific examples. In logic the *syllogism* is a form of argument based on deduction. It consists of a *major premise*—"All men love peace"—a *minor premise*—"John Kennedy was a man"—and a *conclusion*—"John Kennedy loved peace." As you can see this method of argument has certain advantages. If you accept the major premise, the other two propositions must also be accepted; the force of logic helps drive the point home. Many readers also equate eloquent generalizations like "All men love peace" with the truth, even though such assertions may not hold up under scrutiny. In order to use this method successfully the writer must be sure that the generalization or major premise is workable and defensible. This means that the process of deduction should be tested before writing the essay; you cannot depend solely on the authority of your voice to carry you through. A useful rule is to make sure your generalization ("All men love peace") has been carefully qualified ("*Most* men love peace") so that the reader will not be able to point out obvious exceptions before you have had a chance to persuade him. (See the following section on logic for examples of fallacies that result from faulty deduction.)

Order of Enumeration. If you can divide your subject into several parts of equal importance, you may indicate the division in your opening paragraph and then discuss the parts one by one. We shall call this an order of enumeration. "Communism differs from socialism in four important aspects," you begin. "Before the Diesel engine could be used in light motor cars, automotive engineers had to solve the following three problems." You can see from such examples how a considerable number of subjects will adapt themselves to this sort of treatment. You must remember, however, that a formal enumeration of parts implies a serious and formal treatment of the subject.

Order of Easy Comprehension. If your subject is an organization, or a complicated piece of machinery, or an elusive abstract quality, such as *existentialism,* you may start with the simple elements of the subject and gradually work toward those more difficult to understand. This could be called an order from easy to hard, or from known to unknown.

Logic

Most of us are put off by the word *logic*. It connotes a cold, unfeeling, even devastating approach to life. Yet in writing for an audience that you are trying to sway, impress, cajole, or move in some way, logic can be a useful guide. It may even serve as the machete that you can wield to cut your way through a jungle of ideas or impressions in your own mind. One thing is sure: if you make too many errors in logic, your reader will soon begin to suspect the authority of your statements. Once lost, that reader is difficult to win back to your point of view with emotional appeals alone.

Below are a few of the more common errors in logic or reasoning. Try out your understanding of them by testing them against the arguments that appear in the editorial sections of newspapers or magazines.

False Analogy. *Analogy* is a means of arguing by comparing something to something else. Recently we have heard of a "war on poverty" conducted by the Federal government; and the argument in support of urgent funding for poverty programs has depended on the analogy. We are made to feel that we must *conquer* poverty and hunger before they conquer us.

False analogies result when the comparison does not rest on any basic similarities or when the analogy is substituted for a proof in an argument. To justify certain actions in governmental organizations by comparing the organization to a "team" that is out "to win" is an example of substituting an analogy for a proof. Government is not a game.

False Cause. *False cause* has several variations, but the most common one confuses cause with effect. Because American society is so impressed with statistics, we are often susceptible to false cause arguments that employ them. For instance, an irate speaker recently used the following statistics to "prove" that rock music is evil: "Of 1,000 girls who became pregnant out of wedlock, 994 committed fornication while rock music was being played." One wonders what the other six were doing!

The *post hoc, ergo propter hoc* fallacy is another example of false cause argument. Translated the phrase means "after this, therefore because of this," and it describes a statement asserting that two events are related because the first predicted the second. Those who claim there is a *direct* relationship between Herbert Hoover's election as president in 1928 and the stock market crash of 1929 are using the *post hoc* argument. By asserting that we came out of the Depression because we elected a *Democratic* president, an analyst of government is only compounding the error.

Begging the Question. Any argument that assumes the truth of the very point to be proved *begs the question.* One of the symptoms of this fallacy is circular reasoning, in which the conclusion of the argument simply restates the assumption. Those who claim that the country's moral fiber has been weakened by too much television watching and that we will grow strong again if we destroy television sets have assumed too much. They must first *prove* that the nation's morality has indeed become corrupted in the period since the invention of television.

Argumentum ad Hominem. An "argument against the person" might simply be called *avoiding the question,* since it draws attention to the character of the individual and not his or her assertion. We immediately think of *abuse* or *invective* as examples of *ad hominem* arguments: "He has never done an honest day's labor in his life, so how can he dare to introduce a bill improving the rights of the average worker?" But a speaker who uses emotional generalities to win our approval is also ignoring the question: "Many long years of loyal service to and love for this company qualify me to speak about what is best for its employees."

Non Sequitur ("it does not follow"). When the premises of an argument do not establish a firm basis for the conclusion, then the conclusion is called a *non sequitur.* Often the cause is a failure to provide a step in the argument: "I bought one of those cars and it turned out to be a lemon. The company later went out of business." More often the conclusion is based on irrelevant evidence: "Joe Namath uses those pantyhose, so they must be good." Notice how many companies attempt to "prove" the quality or popularity of their products by getting endorsements from famous people.

No doubt the most obvious error in argumentation is *overgeneralization.* It is not specifically an error in logic, though many people might claim that a failure to qualify any statements about events or people violates their sense of the real world. More important, hasty generalizations give the reader the impression that you have not taken the time to look closely at the evidence. They are the basis as well for *prejudice* and *bias:* "*All* Italians belong to the Mafia"; "The Irish are fighting with each other *all the time.*" We are especially susceptible to overgeneralization when our emotions are aroused. It was not until some time after World War II that many Americans chose to recognize that the Japanese had planned to inform us about the attack on Pearl Harbor *before* it took place, but their Washington ambassador was delayed because of problems in decoding the message from Tokyo.

When you find yourself using such words as *always, never, all, only,* and *every,* it is time to examine your statement in detail. Don't claim that *only* truck drivers sit in front of their television sets, beer cans in hand and watching football, until you have checked around. If you claim that *most* women want a home and husband, make sure that at least two-thirds in fact do or you will not only be open to a charge of overgeneralization but also to a charge of sexism. To avoid such serious predicaments, and to improve your writing, take advantage of the numerous qualifying terms available to you. Select the ones that accurately describe the facts in your argument: "*Some* men feel pressured by the company's affirmative action policy in hiring"; "She *often* wants me to do the shopping so that she can have more free time." Remember that the reader will heed statements based on a realistic assessment of the facts more readily than loose generalizations of the kind he or she hears frequently in informal and uninformed conversation.

Beginnings and Endings

Every writer faced with the task of setting his ideas down on paper is conscious of the overwhelming importance of an effective beginning. It seems as important as first impressions in the first interview with your employer, or the introduction to your future parents-in-law. There is something terrifying about it because it must be got over first and because its success, or lack thereof, is thought to color everything that follows. In writing, students spend entirely too much time getting started.

"The best way to begin is to begin. Do not write introductions. Just plunge in." All this is sound advice, but not very helpful to the beginner. One might as well tell him to learn to dance by plunging in—some persons do dance that way, after all. One needs to know what to do after plunging in. Another piece of advice, possibly more helpful, goes this way: "Just write down anything about your subject. Keep going until you get well into your first main topic. Then, in revision, cross out the first two paragraphs." This advice rings true, but it may result in lopping off a good idea or two. A cleansing and healing of the afflicted part may prove as effective as amputation and will certainly hurt less. Learn to diagnose ailments before prescribing surgery.

There are, however, a number of specific devices that a writer may use to introduce his subject appropriately and interestingly, just as there are similar devices for the easier task of appropriately ending his paper. Anyone glancing over a recent file of a serious magazine in which various kinds of articles appear—*Harper's,* for instance—is sure to find repeated examples of particular techniques for beginning as well as for ending. As the following selections will show, there is usually a close logical and rhetorical relation between the two. The moral for the student is clear: he who ends his paper without some kind of reference to his beginning is likely to give his reader a scattered or diffuse impression of his argument. To connect your beginning and ending is one obvious way to give your paper *organization.*

Eight possible ways to begin (among many) are illustrated below. In each case the author's ending is also quoted. Their relation is worth study. As always, your choice of any particular technique depends not only on personal taste but on the kind of article you are writing and the kind of reader you are addressing. In studying these illustrations, note how the various beginnings and endings are in part responses to the particular subject and tone that the author has chosen.

The Dramatized Example or Incident. A familiar opening is a dramatized example or incident from which a larger generalization is to emerge. Here is such an introduction in the first few sentences of an essay on jogging.

Just as I'm putting on my sneakers and adjusting my headband, my stomach begins revolting. You'd think after nearly two years of running I'd be used to it now. I never quite get my breath until I'm a full mile into the run. Then, I guess, my body consents because there's no turning back.
Most people like to jog. Not me.

The author proceeds to argue that she does not jog but instead runs, some six miles a day. In the course of the essay we discover that she is not simply describing her experiences in the course of a typical jogging session; she is extolling a particular approach to life. This point is dramatically restated in her concluding paragraph.

As I zip by the mirror-image houses, I see duplicity everywhere, in the lines on the people's faces, in the Eliotesque coffee cups. When I reach home, there's always some lunatic standing on my front lawn ready to chat, saying something or other about a neighbor's dog. And above it all, I feel my mind shaking hands with my body.

—Patricia Breen-Bond, "Running in the Rain"

The Anecdote. A related technique is to begin with an anecdote, true or fictitious, but told in the manner of the storyteller. Note how the author of the following passage transforms a true anecdote into something of a fable by means of the storyteller style.

When the Inquisitors summoned Galileo before them, they told him he must not find that the earth revolves around the sun. Galileo had been observing the heavens through a telescope: he had become convinced that the evidence warranted his conclusion. But the Inquisitors did not look through the telescope. They knew all about astronomy from reading the Bible. So against Galileo's telescope the Inquisitors employed another instrument: the rack. And by the rack, which could inflict pain on the astronomer's body, they undertook to cure the astronomer of his scientific error. Thus they prohibited the exploration of the heavens by the exercise of their physical power.

The essay then develops the thesis that the forces which move mankind forward, represented by Galileo's desire to explore the heavens, are like birds trying to free themselves from cages devised by forces symbolized by the Inquisitors' rack. The author concludes by recalling the image of oppression and the impulse for freedom.

It is a hope engendered in the human heart during the long ages in which the slowly emerging impulses of civilization, beset by barbarism, have struggled to be free.

—WALTER LIPPMAN, "The Will to Be Free"

The Autobiographical Incident. A similar opening technique is the illustrative incident taken from a moment in the writer's own life. Here the writer mixes autobiographical fact and humor to launch an essay on the effects of war.

I was born on the first day of the second month of the last year of the First World War, a Friday. Testimony abounds that during the first day of my life I never smiled. I was known as the baby whom nothing and no one could make smile. Everyone who knew me then has told me so. They tried very hard, singing and bouncing me up and down, jumping around, pulling faces. Many times I was told this later by my family and their friends, but, anyway, I knew it at the time.

The essay closes with a reference to the remarks of a famous British statesman on the end of World War I. Thus the writer provides a framework for her assertions about her early sophistication—she smiled only when she was bemused.

Since that time I have grown to smile quite naturally, like any other healthy and house-trained person, but when I really mean a smile, deeply felt from the core, then to all intents and purposes it comes in response to the words uttered in the House of Commons after the First World War by the distinguished, the immaculately dressed, and the late Mr. Asquith.

—MURIEL SPARK, "The First Year of My Life," *The New Yorker*

The Stereotype Refuted. A common device for opening an essay is to summarize stereotyped beliefs about a given subject, then proceed to refute them. Effectively done this opening can impress your audience with your learning and audacity. Here is a typical example.

The past few years in America have seen the gradual disintegration of the illusion that we are not a violent people. Americans have always admitted being lawless relative to Europeans, but this was explained as a consequence of our youth as a nation—our closeness to frontier days. High crime rates prior to World War II were regarded in much the same manner as the escapades of an active ten-year-old ("America is all boy!"), and a secret contempt suffused our respect for the law-abiding English. Today the chuckle is gone, the respect more genuine, for the casual violence of American life has become less casual, and its victims threaten to include those other than the disadvantaged.

The author then sets about to explain American violence as a reaction to sudden social change. He concludes by restating the opening reference to our general unwillingness to admit that we are threatened by "radical" plans to do something about our social dilemma.

The predominant feeling is that there is more change than anybody can tolerate already, so how can anyone even *consider* a radical reevaluation of the whole system. Or, to paraphrase a cartoon by Mell Lazarus: "I know I need to see a psychiatrist, but the idea scares me too much now—I'll go when I'm less anxious." Apparently, the idea not only scares us—it makes us mad enough to kill somebody.

—PHILIP SLATER, *The Pursuit of Loneliness*

The Shock Opening (Serious). A variation on the use of the stereotype is to begin an essay with a surprising or even shocking statement, one that is distinctly *not* a stereotype. Sometimes such a beginning may take the form of open hostility toward authority, as in this case.

Humanists for thousands of years have attempted to construct a naturalistic, psychological value system that could be derived from man's own nature, without the necessity of recourse to authority outside the human being himself. Many such theories have been offered throughout history. They have all failed for mass practical purposes exactly as all other theories have failed. We have about as many

65

scoundrels in the world today as we have ever had, and *many more* neurotics, probably, than we have ever had.

Then, having lured us into his argument with this shocker, the author must document his charges, and he concludes by re- minding us of the important distinction between theory and practice, culture and the individual.

A teacher or a culture doesn't create a human being. It doesn't implant within him the ability to love, or to be curious, or to philoso- phize, or to symbolize, or to be creative. Rather it permits, or fosters, or encourages or helps what exists in embryo to become real and actual. The same mother or the same culture, treating a kitten or a puppy in exactly the same way, cannot make it into a human being. The culture is sun and food and water: it is not the seed.

—Abraham Maslow, "Psychological Data and Human Values"

The Shock Opening (Humorous). Another kind of shock opening, far less aggressive in tone, can be achieved by putting forward an argument that is absurd on the face of it. Can the writer *mean* it? we ask. The writer in the following example gives us a ludicrous but somehow apt definition of bachelorhood.

The confirmed bachelor can be defined as the man who has the courage of his lack of convictions. Once he hasn't made his mind up, he really sticks to it. Swinging more and more wildly from his loosen- ing trapeze, he is another reeling acrobat in the disorganized circus of American love and marriage.

By turning to a more somber tone at the close of his essay, Herbert Gold makes us realize that although the bachelor in pursuit of the ideal woman is a romantic idealist, there is an- other side of his personality that is lonely and poignant.

Usually he does not find the girl of his dreams. That ladder to the stars lies folded in a closet somewhere. Another evening has been spilled away with a swell kid whose name he will soon forget.

We do not see him during those moments when he is alone in his apartment, wondering why. *Alone.* Back home alone to his cold bed, his vacant hopes, and his Dacron shirt drying in his bathroom.

—Herbert Gold, "The Bachelor's Dilemma"

66

Questions to Be Answered. We spoke previously of the rhetorical question, the question with only one possible answer, as an ending technique. It is also familiar as a beginning. But even more familiar, and clearly appropriate for many kinds of serious analytical essays, is to begin by asking questions that do not have easy answers. The effort to provide answers, then, becomes the central concern of the essay. Here is an example in which a poet questions the very act of writing poetry in the modern age.

Why is it that nowadays, when poetry brings in little prestige and less money, people are still found who devote their lives to the apparently unrewarding occupation of making poems? Is the poet a quaint anachronism in the modern world—a pathetic shadow of the primitive bard who, unable for some reason to take active part in the life of his tribe, won himself an honorable place in the community by singing of the exploits of hunters and warriors?

While part of the appeal of this essay is that the author cannot find adequate answers to these questions, he concludes by pointing out that the poet, like the rest of us, requires some of the same qualities we need in our own less glamorous work.

Each new poem I begin is an attempt at making and exploring. Each finished one is, in effect, a way of praising life, a sacrifice in life's honor. I need devotion, discipline, sincerity, skill, and above all, patience, if the poem is to come to anything; but I also need something I cannot cultivate—call it luck.

—C. DAY LEWIS, "The Making of a Poem"

The Appeal of Importance. In all the beginnings we have discussed, the author has been responsible for convincing his or her reader that the article will be worth the reading, that it is important or significant or amusing. Sometimes, instead of asking questions or telling stories to arouse interest, an author may simply *tell* the reader of the subject's urgency.

There is only too much reason to fear that Western civilization, if not the whole world, is likely in the near future to go through a period of immense sorrow and suffering and pain—a period during which, if we are not careful to remember them, the things that we are attempting to preserve may be forgotten in bitterness and poverty and disorder. Courage, hope, and unshakable conviction will be necessary if we are to emerge from the dark time spiritually undamaged.

After describing the political and social pressures that menace the spirit of Western civilization, the author concludes by emphasizing the need to learn lessons from adversity, if only to preserve the value of wisdom for future generations.

It is to the possible achievements of man that our ultimate loyalty is due, and in that thought the brief troubles of our unquiet epoch become endurable. Much wisdom needs to be learned, and if it is only to be learned through adversity, we must endeavour to endure adversity with what fortitude we can command. But if we can acquire wisdom soon enough, adversity may not be necessary and the future of man may be happier than any part of his past.

—BERTRAND RUSSELL, "If We Are to Survive This Dark Time—"

Writing the Paper

After you have thought your subject through, worked it over in your mind, laid out your general plan, and supplied as many details as you can, you must begin writing. How you write is a matter for you to decide. Write rapidly without pausing too often to struggle for the perfect sentence or the exact word if writing that way keeps composition from bogging itself to the axles and coming to a lame halt. The first draft devised in an act of creative passion, however, requires scrupulous revision, and initial speed is not necessarily an ultimate saver of time. If a slow, thoughtful progress suits you better, write slowly and thoughtfully, but do not neglect, even then, to revise critically.

Among professional writers no two work alike. Some write fast and revise slowly, changing words and phrases, crossing out and rewriting, copying the revised manuscript and then rewriting again, sometimes as many as fifteen times. Some chisel out every word in creative agony in their first draft—and never revise, but they are possessed of a rare confidence.

Although no two writers use an outline alike, the beginning writer can profit, here as elsewhere, by observing the practice of the skilled writer. A short outline for a short paper is probably so well fixed in the writer's mind by the time he has finished it that he can give it a quick survey, lay it aside, and proceed to write his paper from memory. In the composition of a long paper with a complex outline, especially when the writing is done from notes, it is best to study the notes and the section of the outline dealing with a small unit, lay both aside for the time, and write from memory. The writer does go back—and should, too—for a recheck of his material before revising his first draft. He gives himself freedom to add illustrations, examples, and typical cases that do not show in the outline. He also has the freedom to cut if that seems best in the writing.

Proportion. The amount of space that you give to each of the topics in your paper will depend on what you have to say and on your purpose in writing.

In general, certain things are unimportant. Long, rambling beginnings, formal conclusions (which often begin with "In conclusion . . ."), and digressions from the central idea should be severely cut or eliminated.

As for the rest, the principle is simple. Keeping in mind the old rule of "an interesting beginning and a strong ending," you will give relatively more space to the important topic that you have saved for the end of your paper. That topic is the fact or idea that you want to stress, both by placing it at the end and by saying more about it. You may, of course, introduce your last topic by some such phrase as, "And, finally, the most important . . . ," but telling your reader that an idea is most important is not the same as making him think and feel that it is. (We have suggested this difference in the eighth example under "Beginnings and Endings.") You need concrete details. You need evidence. And you also need to allow a certain amount of time for the idea to sink into your reader's mind.

Substance: Use of Details. To reach the mind of your reader, then, to make him understand and to persuade him to accept, you must in ninety-nine cases out of a hundred be specific and concrete. Generalities seldom convince. A vague essay on the need for international understanding and cooperation may earn a reader's passive mental agreement, but a concrete picture in terms of someone's actual experience will win him more directly. A lecture on man's inhumanity to man is one thing; a newsreel showing the inside of a concentration camp is something different. Your outline and much of your note-taking are often a series of generalities. They are the skeleton of your paper, with all the emotional appeal, the personality, and the warmth of a skeleton. You must cover the skeleton with living flesh. Explanations, specific details, instances, illustrations, concrete examples—out of these you build your finished essay. Think of yourself at this stage as a reporter gathering factual details about a news event: details supplying answers to *Who* was (were) involved; *What* was (were) involved; *Why, When, Where,* and *How* involved.

One way of placing yourself in a better position to put substance into your writing is to keep substance in mind from the beginning, during your preliminary note-taking and outlining. Be specific from the start. Actually few ideas come into your mind as abstractions unless you are merely pushing other people's words around like so many billiard balls. Abstractions usually start with an actual event of some sort. An abstraction such as the need for international understanding is likely to mean, if it means anything at all to you, something that *happened* in your experience. Perhaps it was a conversation with a South American; perhaps it was something you read in a foreign book; perhaps you saw a French movie. Whatever it was, your notion of a need for international understanding was a logical connection you made between all the pious and abstract talk you have heard on this subject and something definite that was part of your own life. When you begin your note-taking and outlining, do not forget this connection. We all know the sort of note or outline heading that means almost nothing and that gives the writer almost no help for proceeding. "Need for international understanding vital." What can you do about that except repeat it in other and even duller words? But suppose your notes read something like this: "Conversation with Juan, acquaintances from Cuba. Passionate defense of Castro's policies. 'You don't understand Cuba,' he says. Does he understand America? And what do we mean by 'understand'?" This is only a beginning, but it is promising. Obviously, abstract terms and headings are always necessary to hold an argument together and give it direction. But when your abstractions are divorced from the drama and experience of the daily events that gave them birth, you are on your way to writing mush.

Preparing the Final Draft: Revising, Proofreading. Many students, perhaps most students, do not know how to revise. Of all writing performances, revising is probably the least teachable, the most difficult to master. Too many young writers revise by simply copying over the choppy, rambling, or illogical sentences they have already perpetrated. Try to complete a draft of a paper at least a day or two before it is due. This means giving up the bad habit of composing *and* typing the essay the night before handing it in. Then take from the remaining time an hour or two when you are at your most alert, when you are feeling efficient and sensitive. Pick up your manuscript and begin to read. As you do so, try to *pretend it was written by somebody else.* In your role as just another reader of this composition, make quick notes in the margin of everything that makes you hesitate, for any reason. Ask yourself, How can I tell that this essay was written by an amateur, not a professional? Here are some of the kinds of evidence you may notice: weak transitions between sentences and paragraphs, loose logical connections between ideas, inexact use of certain words, a vague pronoun or two (*it* and *this* are regular offenders), a nonstop sentence, a series of very short sentences, a failure to organize the whole essay around a single theme.

After you have made notes of this sort, take steps to correct all these weaknesses, using your dictionary, thesaurus, and this *Handbook* as you need them. Then try reading your paper again, but this time read it *aloud,* and listen to yourself. A tape recorder can be very handy for this purpose, and for the general task of remembering certain details about your subject. If you do not have a recorder, ask your roommate, or your mother, to act as an audience for your pronouncements. Sometimes the person you choose will question points of your argument or style you have failed to notice. In the process you should be able to recognize more revisable items: harsh sound effects, awkward repetition of words, clauses and phrases that seem to have no connection with the main thoughts of sentences. When this analysis is completed, you are ready to begin shaping your final draft.

Attempts to make substantial changes while typing or writing this final copy are inadvisable, although you may notice one or two additional details for improvement. If you have carried out your rereading and revising process thoroughly, drastic changes during the copying will do more harm than good. But your final act of *proofreading* is absolutely essential. Now you are on the lookout, not for the logic and phrasing of your argument, but for those mechanical errors that so irritate and distract a reader. This is the time to make final corrections of punctuation and spelling. To many students such things seem trivial, and in a way they are, but, unfortunately, to ignore them is suicidal. The plain fact is that no matter how clever your words may be, if you spell them badly your reader (who is, after all, your instructor) will assume that you are ignorant and illiterate. He may be wrong but he cannot help himself. You would assume the same thing, about someone else's sloppy manuscript.

Finally, it is a fine thing to be proud of what you do. To hand in a clean, solid composition should be no less satisfying than to score a clean, solid block on the football field or to execute successfully a difficult piano recital. A performance is a performance. Admit that it is and never be content with less than the best you can do.

The Whole Essay

The following are selected questions about the essay as a whole. They are worth raising *before* you hand in the finished work, as they are certain to occur to an experienced reader like your instructor. As with the questions raised about grammar and mechanics these possible problem areas must be attended to carefully if the impact of your writing is to be strong and persuasive.

1. If you follow the *deductive approach* (see pp. 57–58), have you included your thesis statement in the opening paragraph? Is the rest of the essay organized and documented most effectively to prove the thesis?

2. If you follow the *inductive approach* (see p. 57), have you at least hinted at your thesis in the introduction? How long must the reader wait until he knows where you stand? (Another reader besides you should be asked about this matter.)

3. Does the concluding paragraph merely repeat the introductory one? (See "Beginnings and Endings," pp. 61–62.) Have you given your reader a sense that the argument has moved toward a conclusion? Does the essay just stop, or does it have an ending?

4. Are your paragraphs arranged so that the reader has the impression of moving from *least* to *most* important points? At any stage does a paragraph seem to digress unnecessarily from the mainstream of your argument? (See "Order of Presentation," pp. 57–58.)

5. Have you achieved smooth *transition* from paragraph to paragraph? Ask yourself, or your objective reader, whether or not the essay seems disjointed or choppy because the reader is forced to leap from topic to topic in successive paragraphs. (See § 39b in Section III, "A Handbook of Writing and Revision.")

6. If you argue by means of *comparison* and *contrast* (see pp. 60–61), are the similarities and differences discussed adequately explained? If the whole essay is a comparison and contrast of the American and Russian forms of government, for example, have you presented a *balanced* picture and reached some definite conclusion? To conclude by stating that both forms of government feature advantages and disadvantages is to leave the reader hanging.

7. Is the *tone* of your essay consistent? If you intend a lighthearted examination of laws against drug use, don't suddenly turn preachy or crusading at the close of your paper. Be sure you understand how *you* feel about the subject before presenting an opinion to the reader. (See §40b for a definition of *tone*.)

8. Have you used *active verbs* throughout? Check the number of *passive constructions* and if they represent more than a third of the verbs and verb phrases in your paper, revise the affected sentences. (See § 30c in the "Handbook.")

9. Does your essay stand as a *reasoned process* or does it consist of a series of unsupported assertions or opinions? Watch for clues in the openings of your sentences. "I believe . . . ," "I think . . ." are signs that the statements cannot stand alone and need your presence to convince the reader. (See pp. 59–61.)

10. Have you sufficiently defined and narrowed the topic? If

73

in looking over the paper you find it studded with overgeneralizations, you have probably taken on a topic that is too big. *Be sure to consult your instructor before beginning to be sure the subject can be covered adequately in the time and space allotted.* (See "Problems of Subjects and Focus," pp. 32–55.)

CONVENTIONS OF THE FORMAL OUTLINE

There are a number of conventions governing the formal outline:

1. The parts of the outline, heads and subheads, should be labeled by alternating figures and letters as follows: I, II, III, and so on; A, B, C, and so on; 1, 2, 3, and so on; a, b, c, and so on. Periods, not dashes, should be placed after these figures and letters.

2. No punctuation is needed after the topics in a topic outline. In a sentence outline, each sentence should be punctuated in the conventional manner.

3. The heads in any series should be of equal importance. That is, the heads numbered I, II, III, IV, and so on, should actually be divisions of the whole paper; heads numbered with capital letters should be coordinate divisions of heads numbered with Roman numerals; and so on.

4. Coordinate heads should be expressed in parallel form— that is, in a given series, nouns should be made parallel with nouns, adjectives with adjectives, and so on. But although parallel structure is desirable and logical, clearness and directness should never be sacrificed to gain strict parallelism. There are times when nouns and gerunds can live side by side in a formal outline.

5. In a topic outline, all heads and subheads must be topics. In a sentence outline, all heads and subheads must be sentences. Sentences should not run over from one head to another.

6. Each head and subhead should be as specific as it is possible to make it in an outline. Vague topics and sentences are bad because they tend to hide flaws in the logic or organization of the outline.

7. Using such headings as "I. Introduction," "II. Body," "III. Conclusion" is unnecessary and undesirable. Such divisions do not indicate correctly the structure of most essays or articles. Many papers written by students are too short for a formal introduction or conclusion. In most long papers the conclusion is simply the main topic which the writer wants the reader to hear about last—for reasons explained elsewhere. Separate introductions are used more often than separate conclusions in essays of six thousand words or more, but in the outline it is better to use a topic that tells what is said in the introduction than to use the vague "Introduction" itself.

8. Since an outline represents a grouping of parallel parts, it is illogical to have a single subhead under any head. A single subhead can usually be combined with its head with benefit to the logic and organization of the outline.

Here are two kinds of conventional outline examining a subject for a paper that might emerge out of our treatment of occupations, in the first part of this chapter.

TOPIC OUTLINE

Choices—In College and After

Thesis: The decisions I have to make in choosing college courses depend on larger questions I am beginning to ask about myself and my life work.

I. Two decisions described
    A. Art history or chemistry?
        1. Professional considerations
        2. Personal considerations
    B. A second year of French?
        1. Practical advantages of knowing a foreign language
        2. Intellectual advantages
        3. The issue of necessity
II. Definition of the problem
    A. Decisions about occupation
    B. Decisions about a kind of life to lead
III. Temporary resolution of the problem
    A. To hold open a professional possibility: chemistry
    B. To take advantage of cultural gains already made: French

A sentence outline is similar in organization to a topic outline. It differs from a topic outline in that every topic and subtopic is translated into a complete sentence, stating the central idea of the particular topic. The sentence outline has two advantages over the topic outline: (1) It forces the writer to study his material carefully so that he has something specific to say for each head and subhead; and (2), much more effectively than the topic outline, it conveys information in logical sequence to the reader. The topic outline merely states a series of subjects, rather like titles, which the writer intends to say something about. The sentence outline actually summarizes what he has to say.

Here is an example of a sentence outline, based on the topic outline we have just examined:

SENTENCE OUTLINE

Choices—In College and After

Thesis: The decisions I have to make in choosing college courses depend on larger questions I am beginning to ask about myself and my life work.

I. I have two decisions to make with respect to choosing college courses in the immediate future.
   A. One is whether to elect a course in art history or in chemistry.
      1. Since at one time I planned to be a chemical engineer and still have this career much in mind, professional considerations would indicate the choice of chemistry.
      2. On the other hand I enjoy art and plan to travel to see more of it; I need training in art history if I am going to be more than just another ignorant museum-goer.
   B. The second decision is whether to continue for a second year of French, beyond the basic college requirement.
      1. French might be practically useful to me, both in business (including engineering) and in the travel I hope to undertake.
      2. Furthermore I am eager to put to actual use, in the reading of good books, the elementary French I have already mastered.

3. But how necessary are these considerations in the light of other courses I might take instead?

II. My problem can be put in the form of a dilemma involving larger questions about my whole future.

A. On the one hand I want to hold a highly trained position in a lucrative profession.

B. On the other hand I want to lead a certain kind of life, with capacities for values not connected with the making of money.

III. I will have to make a decision balancing the conflicting needs I have described.

A. I will hold open the professional possibilities by electing chemistry.

B. I will improve and solidify what cultural proficiency in another language I have already gained, by electing French.

EXERCISES

EXERCISE 1, TOPIC OUTLINES. *Select a subject from each of the three lists on page 35 and prepare a topic outline to show how a composition might be written on this subject.*

EXERCISE 2, AN AUTOBIOGRAPHICAL ESSAY. *Reread the section called "Autobiographical Materials." Take preliminary notes on three incidents in your life that could be interpreted as expressing a dominant trait in your character. Write a five-hundred-word essay based on one of these. Try writing the essay in thirty minutes, without regard to style, punctuation, or word choice. Read over what you have written at the end of that time to discover how your mind works in selecting and rejecting details.*

EXERCISE 3, VIEWPOINT. *Describe an incident in which you met a friend at an airport or railroad station. Tell it from the point of view of yourself. Then rewrite the incident, telling it from the imagined point of view of the other person.*

EXERCISE 4, DESCRIPTION. *Describe a scene that has changed dramatically since you first knew it—a neighborhood, a building, a room. Use contrast in the manner of the "old soldier" on page 41.*

EXERCISE 5, THE BOOK OR MOVIE REVIEW. *Try in a single page to give a fair description of the last book you read or movie you saw.*

With what kinds of book or movie is this particularly difficult? With what kinds is it relatively easy?

EXERCISE 6, DIRECTIONS. *Make a list of some operations you believe you can perform better than someone else. (Examples: repairing a stereo, tuning an engine, hanging wallpaper.) Give directions for one of these, so clearly that even your instructor might be able to perform it adequately.*

EXERCISE 7, STYLE. *Find a short, serious essay written in formal style. Try rewriting it in the breezy manner of Miss McGinley (page 53). Is the essay still serious? And just what do you mean by "serious" here? Then try rewriting the original essay by parodying its formal style. Compare this version with your breezy treatment. What differences do you notice?*

EXERCISE 8, BEGINNINGS. *Select a subject that you want to use for an essay. Write four beginnings for it. With the help of your instructor pick out the most promising one and use it in writing your paper.*
1. Begin by using an imagined incident which illustrates the point of your paper or out of which a discussion may seem to arise.
2. Begin with evidence of the importance or the timeliness of your subject.
3. Begin with a shock opening.
4. Begin with a question or a series of questions.

EXERCISE 9, PROOFREADING. *Make a list of the errors you catch in your proofreading. Compare it with a similar list of corrections made by your instructor on your paper. Does this comparison suggest some hints for future proofreading? Are you missing something?*

EXERCISE 10, ANALYSIS. *Here are two uncorrected student essays that may be analyzed in the same way your instructor reads and corrects your work. Consider some of the following questions in a written critique of the papers: Are the subjects adequately focused and limited? What order of presentation does each writer choose? Does the writer follow the principles of that order? Is the essay coherent? What types of beginnings and endings are used? Does the writer use more active verbs than passive ones? Is there anything in particular that the writer might do to improve the essay?*

Uncorrected Student Essay 1[3]

Skewed Language

"Skewed language" is defined as biased or planted language. Many examples of skewed language can be found in English, especially with reference to women. The English language was formed to keep women in their inferior or secondary role.

Common examples of occupational names—postman, policeman, garbageman, fireman—give the impression that women can't hold these jobs. If a woman does hold a job, once thought to be only a man's job, she is labeled with lady or woman followed by the occupational name as in woman doctor, woman congressman, or lady engineer.

Our male-dominant standard of English is well illustrated in the words playboy and don juan. The feminine equivalents—loose woman or slut—have completely different connotations. While playboy is not degrading to the males, loose woman is certainly degrading to the females. Another example is the single male, the glamorous bachelor, as opposed to the single female, the old maid or spinster.

The English language also has many words that reduce women to animals. Chick, bunny, and mouse are common examples. Although some expressions for men also refer to animals, they are the big, strong animals like tiger, cat and fox, which show the dominance of male over female.

Throughout the entire English language, there are many derogatory and degrading words aimed at women but very few, if any, aimed at men.

Uncorrected Student Essay 2[4]

Law and Disorder

To my thinking the movie <u>Law</u> <u>and</u> <u>Disorder</u> was written for today's times and people. Most people are becoming more and more concerned with the amount of violence and crimes that occur and the increase of crime each year. There are many ideas as to what can be done to combat crime and protect the citizen and one idea is to form a group and patrol your own neighborhood. This is the idea the movie used and tried to show what could happen.

The crimes they used were possibly extreme or exaggerated, yet they do happen: a car is parked on a street and in five minutes is completely stripped; a man lowers himself by rope from the roof of an apartment building, climbs in an open window, takes the TV, ties it on the other end of the rope and he goes down to the next floor, while the TV goes to the

---

[3] Reprinted by permission of the author, Cheryl Boes.
[4] Reprinted by permission of the author, Virginia Stoker.

roof. All this happens while the occupant is in the kitchen fixing a sandwich.

The people living in this neighborhood were getting more furious each time the police were unable to protect them, so they decided to form a group to help the police and patrol their own neighborhood.

I thought the movie was quite good in pointing out some of the things that could happen. What began as trying to help the police turned into the group trying to be or thinking they <u>were</u> the police. Instead of wearing their own clothes they needed uniforms that looked like police uniforms, then they needed to act like policemen so they must drill. It was like watching a group of children so excited about their new game and one of the children has an idea to go one step further and another step until it is not at all what the game originally was. Not being satisfied with walking the streets they purchased an old police car with a siren that they put on top. Now they could ride around like policemen and with the radio go on police calls outside their neighborhood. They answered a police call and in trying to be regular policemen one of their group was shot and killed. Their police car had been shot at and they were a group of very confused frightened men.

The ending was not at all what they had thought it would be: I think they had hoped to be heroes and instead one person was dead, and I don't think they realized what they had done that caused his death.

To me the show was effective and I don't think it could have ended any other way. It gave the problem, the increase in crime and what we can do about it. It took one of many answers and showed what could happen.

3 *The Research Paper*

IMPORTANCE OF THE RESEARCH PAPER

The research paper is an important and extended exercise in writing. It is best understood as an essay or report derived from the collection of data by research. *Research* is grand search. It means looking for a particular kind of information on a particular kind of subject in a particular kind of medium, and sorting the relevant findings according to some plan. Although the preparation of a research paper may depend on concentrated study of books, articles, and reports in the library—the study, in short, of someone else's research—it may be written after almost any kind of information-gathering exercise. Careful observation of your family's patterns of behavior on rainy days is, in this sense, a form of research.

There are many values and skills to be acquired from writing a research paper:

1. Practice in preparing the term papers that will be required in many of your college courses.
2. Acquisition of interesting and perhaps useful information about a special subject.
3. An increase in the ability to distinguish between facts and opinions.
4. An improved ability to *judge* material as well as to find it, to evaluate its worth, to organize it, and to present it in attractive form.

These skills are useful whether you compose a report for your speech class, a speech for the AMA or Young Democrats, or an article for the school newspaper.

THE USE OF THE LIBRARY

Although we must always take into account differences in size and organization of different libraries, a study of the resources of a library can still be taken up under three main headings: (1) the card catalog, (2) the general reference library, and (3) the guides and indexes to periodicals and bulletins.

The Card Catalog: Basic Guide to the Library

The starting point for exploration of the library is, logically, the *card catalog,* a collection of cards listing every book (including reference books), bulletin, pamphlet, and periodical the library owns.

The cards are arranged alphabetically according to authors, titles, and subjects. In other words, a large and complete library will have every book listed on at least three separate cards. You can therefore locate a book if you know the author's name, or the title, or the subject with which it deals. A listing in the card catalog, however, is no more than a record that the library believes it owns the work in question. A book on the shelves is worth two in the catalog, so remember that books should be checked out of the library by due process, not carried out surreptitiously under a coat.

Magazines and bulletins are usually listed by title—that is, the card catalog will tell you whether or not the library owns a certain magazine or series of bulletins. The card for a given magazine or bulletin will tell you which volumes are bound and shelved (and usually the call number to be used in asking for them), and which are stacked unbound in a storeroom. In most libraries there will be a duplicate list of periodicals for use in the reference library room. For detailed information about the contents of periodicals, bulletins, and newspapers you will have to consult the periodical indexes. These are listed and explained on pages 91–93.

Here is a typical library card.

```
ML3551   Rosen, David M
.R68
              Protest songs in America, by David Rosen.
         Foreword by David Manning White. [Westlake Vil-
         lage, Calif.] Aware Press [1972]

             154 p.    20 cm.    $3.75
             Bibliography: p. 151–154

             1. Protest songs—History and criticism.
         2. Songs, American—History and criticism.
         3. American ballads and songs. I. Title.
```

1. ML3551.R68 is the call number, according to the Library of Congress system. (See pages 85–86.)

2. "Rosen, David M" is the author's name, last name given first. The date of the author's birth (and death) may or may not appear on a card.

3. "Protest songs in America . . . [1972]" gives the title of the book, the author, the writer of the foreword, the place of publication, the publisher, and the copyright date.

4. The next line explains that the book contains 154 pages, that the shelf size (height on the shelf) of the book is 20 centimeters, and that its price is $3.75. Pages 151–154 contain a bibliography of related works.

5. The titles at the bottom of the card tell under what subjects the book may be found in the catalog. You can find this work by looking under Protest songs—History and criticism; Songs, American—History and criticism; American ballads and songs; and under the book title.

The card just examined is an *author card*. A *title card* is just like an author card, except that the title is typewritten at the top.

A *subject card* is an author card with the subject typed, usually in red, above the author's name at the top.

```
American ballads and songs

PS3515      Huston, John, 1906—
.U83              Frankie and Johnny. Illustrated by Covarru-
            bias. New York, B. Blom, 1968.

                 160 p. illus.    18 cm.
            Reprint of the 1930 ed.

                 1. American ballads and songs. I. Covarru-
            bias, Miguel, 1904–1957, illus. II. Title.

            PS3515.U83FS 1968 812.54                    68–57190
            Library of Congress                             MARC
```

On the card just illustrated are two or three items not found in the specimen author card.

1. Both the Library of Congress and the Dewey Decimal call numbers are listed: PS3515.U83FS and 812.54. (Both numbering systems are described in the section that follows.)

2. "Library of Congress" indicates that the Library of Congress has a copy of the book.

3. The numbers and letters at the lower right are for the use of librarians in ordering copies of this card. They are of no interest to the general user of the card catalog.

To find information about a certain periodical consult your library's Serial Record. This collection of cards will tell you where to find the periodical in the library and how many and which volumes are available.

Call Numbers. A call number is a symbol or group of symbols used by a library to designate a particular book. It consists frequently of two parts: the first, or upper, is the classification number, the second, or lower, the author and book number. The call number is typed on the upper left-hand corner of the card-catalog card, on the spine or binding of the book, and often inside the book's front or back cover. In most libraries, before you may take out a book, you must fill out a *call slip*. On this slip should appear the call number, the name of the author, and the title of the work. Your signature and whatever supplementary information the library requires complete the call slip.

For the undergraduate, a knowledge of the systems used in devising call numbers is relatively unimportant. To satisfy a natural curiosity on the part of many students, however, the following brief explanation is given.

Two classification systems are used by libraries in this country: the Library of Congress system and the Dewey Decimal system.

The Library of Congress System. The Library of Congress system, found more frequently in college than in public libraries, uses the letters of the alphabet, followed by additional letters and Arabic numerals, as the basis of its classification.

A	General works	M	Music
B	Philosophy—Religion	N	Fine arts
C	History—Auxiliary sciences	P	Language and literature
		Q	Science
D	History and topography	R	Medicine
E and F	American history	S	Agriculture
G	Geography—Anthropology	T	Technology
		U	Military science
H	Social sciences	V	Naval science
J	Political science	Z	Bibliography and library science
K	Law		
L	Education		

The following table shows the larger subdivisions under one of these main classes:

G Geography—Anthropology

G	Geography (General)
GA	Mathematical and astronomical geography
GB	Physical geography
GC	Oceanology and oceanography
GF	Anthropogeography

GN Anthropology—Somatology—Ethnology
    Ethnogeography (General)
    51–161   Anthropometry—Skeleton—Craniometry
    400–499   Customs and institutions (Primitive)
    537–686   Special races
    700–875   Prehistoric archeology
GR Folklore
GT Manners and customs (General)
GV Sports and amusements—Games
    201–547   Physical training
    1580–1799 Dancing

The Dewey Decimal System. The Dewey Decimal system, devised by Melvil Dewey, uses a decimal classification for all books. The entire field of knowledge is divided into nine groups, with an additional group for general reference books. Each main class and subclass is shown by a number composed of three digits.

000	General works	500	Natural science
100	Philosophy	600	Useful arts
200	Religion	700	Fine arts
300	Sociology	800	Literature
400	Philology	900	History

The following table shows the first subdivision under the literature class and the beginning of the intricate system of further subdividing under the 820 group.

800 Literature
   810   American
   820   English
      821   English poetry
      822   English drama
         822.3   Elizabethan drama
            822.33   Shakespeare
   830   German
   840   French
   850   Italian
   860   Spanish
   870   Latin
   880   Greek
   890   Minor literatures

The Reference Library

The reference library consists of all the general reference works, such as encyclopedias and dictionaries, and collections of pamphlets, bibliographies, guides, maps, and pictures that are to be consulted for some specific information rather than to be read in their entirety. Reference books ordinarily may not be taken from the library. The following list of reference books should be a starting point for your exploration of possible subjects. It is wise to know what they are, where these books are shelved, and how they can be used to the best advantage. The date given is usually the date of the latest revision. In this rapidly changing world, the date of publication may be very important in a reference book.

General Encyclopedias. A student using the *Britannica* and the *Americana* should consult the annual supplements, the *Britannica Book of the Year* and the *Americana Annual,* for additional information.

Encyclopedia Britannica. 30 vols., 1975. Chicago: Encyclopedia Britannica, Inc. Since 1940 the *Britannica* has been kept up to date by continuous revisions. The 15th ed. is divided into a macropedia (19 vols.), consisting of long, fully detailed articles, and a micropedia (10 vols.) of dictionarylike format. Both are arranged alphabetically. A single-volume propedia, or index, is arranged according to topic. The micropedia and propedia may be used as indexes to macropedia articles.

Encyclopedia Americana. 30 vols. New York: Americana Corporation. Like the *Britannica,* the *Americana* is now kept up to date by continuous revision. Hence the date is necessary with any reference to it.

Collier's Encyclopedia. 24 vols., 1973. New York: Crowell Collier, and Macmillan Publishing Co., Inc. Continuously revised. Although written in a popular style designed for the general rather than scholarly reader, it is objective and authoritative.

Special Encyclopedias. A special or limited encyclopedia is available for almost any subject of importance that one can think of. You may find a long list by looking under "encyclopedias" in the most recent annual volume of the *Cumulative Book Index.* Many of these special encyclopedias, once useful and authoritative, have not been revised recently. The information

87

they contain is now dated. Others are valuable as historical records. Here are a few examples of this type of reference book:

The Catholic Encyclopedia. 15 vols. New York: McGraw-Hill Book Company, 1967. Although this work deals primarily with the accomplishments of Roman Catholics, its scope is very general. It is useful for subjects dealing with medieval literature, history, art, and philosophy.

The Jewish Encyclopedia. 12 vols. New York: Funk & Wagnalls, 1925.

McGraw-Hill Encyclopedia of Science and Technology. 15 vols. incl. yearbooks. New York: McGraw-Hill Book Company, 1960, 1966, 1971.

Encyclopedia of World Literature in the Twentieth Century. 3 vols. New York: Frederick Ungar Publishing Co., 1971.

Yearbooks. In addition to the general yearbooks listed here, there are yearbooks for many specialized fields. See the *Cumulative Book Index* or *Books in Print* for titles.

Britannica Book of the Year. Chicago: Encyclopaedia Britannica, Inc., 1938 to date.

Americana Annual. New York: Americana Corporation, 1923 to date.

Chambers' Encyclopedia Yearbook. London: International Learning Systems Corporation Limited, 1970 to date.

World Almanac and Book of Facts. New York: The New York World-Telegram and Sun, 1868–1967; Newspaper Enterprise Association Incorporated, 1967 to date.

Information Please Almanac. New York: Macmillan Publishing Co., Inc., 1947–1959; McGraw-Hill Book Company, 1960; Simon & Schuster, Inc., 1961 to date.

Economic Almanac. New York: National Industrial Conference Board, 1940 to date.

Statesman's Year-Book. London: Macmillan & Co., Ltd.; New York: St. Martin's Press, Inc., 1864 to date.

The Official Associated Press Almanac. New York: Almanac Publishing Company Incorporated, 1970 to date. (First published as *The New York Times Encyclopedia Almanac.*)

Guides to Reference Books. The following are the principal bibliographies of reference texts.

BARTON, MARY NEILL, and MARION V. BELL. *Reference Books: A Brief Guide.* 7th ed. 1970.

The Bibliographic Index. 1937 to date.

GATES, JEAN KAY. *Guide to the Use of Books and Libraries.* 2nd ed. 1969.

SHORES, LOUIS. *Basic Reference Sources: An Introduction to Materials and Methods.* 1954.

WINCHELL, CONSTANCE M. *Guide to Reference Books.* 8th ed. 1967.

A World Bibliography of Bibliographies. 4th ed., 5 vols. 1965–1966.

The Harper Encyclopedia of Science. Rev. ed. 1967.

Constance Winchell's *Guide* offers the best source of reference books in your field of interest. More specialized bibliographies and indexes can also be found in this volume.

Biographical Information. Biographical information can also be secured with the help of various periodical indexes (such as the *Readers' Guide to Periodical Literature*) and in very compressed form in your own desk dictionary.

Dictionary of American Biography. 20 vols., plus 3 supp. vols. New York: Charles Scribner's Sons, 1928–1973.

Dictionary of National Biography. 22 vols., plus 7 supp. vols. London: Oxford University Press, 1885–1971. The word *national* is sometimes confusing to students; it refers to the "nationals" of the British Empire, more recently known as the British Commonwealth of Nations.

Current Biography: Who's News and Why. New York: H. W. Wilson Company, 1940 to date. Published monthly, with six-month and annual cumulations.

Webster's Biographical Dictionary. Springfield, Mass.: G. & C. Merriam Company, 1971. A one-volume pronouncing biographical dictionary of over 40,000 names. It includes living persons.

Who's Who in America. Chicago: A. N. Marquis Company, 1899 and biennially to date.

Who's Who. London: A. & C. Black, Ltd.; New York: Macmillan Publishing Co., Inc., 1849 to date.

Biography Index. New York: H. W. Wilson Company, 1947 to date. This is a guide to biographical information in books and magazines.

Dictionaries and Books of Synonyms. The following books are useful for study of the changing meanings of words and for the discovery of synonyms.

New Standard Dictionary. New York: Funk & Wagnalls, 1935 to date.
New Century Dictionary. 3 vols. New York: The Century Company, 1927–1933. Based on the original *Century Dictionary,* 12 vols., 1911.
Oxford English Dictionary. New York: Oxford University Press, 1933. A corrected reissue of *A New English Dictionary on Historical Principles,* 1888–1933. The purpose of this work is to give the history of every word in the English language for the past 800 years. It contains many quotations illustrating meanings of words in various periods and full discussions of derivations and changes in meanings and spellings.
Dictionary of American English on Historical Principles. 4 vols. Chicago: University of Chicago Press, 1936–1944. This is especially useful to the student who wishes to learn the historical changes in the use and meaning of words in American English.
Webster's New Dictionary of Synonyms. Springfield, Mass.: G. & C. Merriam Company, 1968. A dictionary of discriminated synonyms with antonyms, analogues, and contrasted words.
HAYAKAWA, S. I. *Modern Guide to Synonyms and Related Words.* New York: Funk & Wagnalls, 1968.
KLEIN, ERNST. *A Comprehensive Etymological Dictionary of the English Language.* 2 vols. Amsterdam, New York: Elsevier Publishing Co., Inc., 1966–1967.
PARTRIDGE, ERIC. *A Dictionary of Slang and Unconventional English.* 2 vols. New York: Macmillan Publishing Co., Inc., 1967.
Roget's Thesaurus of the English Language in Dictionary Form. Rev., greatly enl. ed. New York: G. P. Putnam's Sons, 1965.

Gazetteers and Atlases. In a world of rapidly changing national boundaries and of former colonies emerging as independent nations, gazetteers and atlases are out of date almost as soon as they are printed. Most of the following works, however, are kept up to date by reasonably frequent revisions. Check the date on the book you are using.

The Columbia Lippincott Gazetteer of the World. A revision of *Lippincott's Gazetteer* of 1905. New York: Columbia University Press, 1962.
Rand McNally Commercial Atlas and Marketing Guide. Chicago: Rand McNally Company.
Encyclopaedia Britannica World Atlas. Chicago: Encyclopaedia Britannica Company, 1959. Rev. annually.
National Geographic Atlas of the World. 3rd ed. 1970.
The Times Atlas of the World. Rev. ed. 1968.

Books of Quotations. When you are in doubt about the source or wording of a passage that you can only vaguely recall, search out the complete passage in a book of quotations. These volumes are thoroughly indexed by key words.

BARTLETT, JOHN, and E. M. BECK. *Familiar Quotations.* 14th ed. Boston: Little, Brown and Company, 1968.
STEVENSON, BURTON. *The Macmillan Book of Proverbs, Maxims, and Famous Phrases.* New York: Macmillan Publishing Co., Inc., 1941.
————. *The Home Book of Quotations.* 10th ed. New York: Dodd, Mead and Company, 1967.

Guides and Indexes to Periodicals and Bulletins

Magazines and Bulletins. Indexes to magazines, bulletins, and newspapers are usually shelved in the reference room of the library.

When searching for something published in a magazine, you need to know two things: (1) Does the library subscribe to that periodical? (2) In what issue was the article published? The answer to the first question is on a card, found in either the general catalog or an additional special card file in the reference room. For an answer to the second question, look into a periodical index. (Your reference librarian can help you to locate these resources.)

Bulletins are listed in most indexes. In compiling your bibliography remember that a bulletin is treated as a periodical if it is published at regular intervals (that is, as a series), and as a book if it is a separate, single publication.

There is a special index for material published in newspapers. See page 93.

Poole's Index to Periodical Literature, 1802–1881, and supplements from 1882 to 1906. A subject index only. Materials such as poems and stories are entered under the first word of the title. Only volume and page numbers are given; dates are excluded.
Readers' Guide to Periodical Literature, 1900 to date. Entries are under author, title, and subject. Besides volume, paging, and date, it indicates illustrations, portraits, maps, and other materials. Since for

the student seeking a general topic this is the most important of the indexes, a sample of its entries follows:[1]

```
ALEXANDER, Donald Crichton
    Top tax official on rebates, refunds, audits;
    interview. il por U.S. News 78:19-20 Ap 14
    '75
                    about
    IRS's $287 billion man. il por Time 105:60-1
    Ap 7 '75 •
ALEXANDER, John
    George Washington shopped here. il Sat Eve
    Post 247:22-3 Mr '75
ALEXANDER, Tom
    Battered pillars of the American system: sci-
    ence. il Fortune 91:146-7+ Ap '75
    Plate tectonics has a lot to tell us about
    the present and future earth. il Smith-
    sonian 5:38-47 F '75
ALEXANDER and Baldwin, inc
    Hawaiian company invests its sugar profits.
    por Bus W p80-2 Ap 14 '75
ALEXANDER Botts, detective; story. See Up-
    son, W. H.
ALEXANDER Sprunt Jr sanctuary. See Bird
    sanctuaries—South Carolina
ALEXEYEV, Vasili. See Alekseev, V.
ALEXIAN brothers. See Brothers (in religious
    orders, congregations, etc)
ALFORD, Albert L.
    Education amendments of 1974. il Am Educ
    11:6-11 Ja '75
ALFRED the Great, king of England
    Golden dragon, by A. J. Mapp, Jr. Review
        Harper 250:104-5 Ap '75. J. Gardner
        Smithsonian 5:108+ Mr '75. B. Farwell •
ALGAE
    Polarizing fucoid eggs drive a calcium current
    through themselves. K. R. Robinson and
    L. F. Jaffe. bibl il Science 187:70-2 Ja 10
    '75
    Toxicology and pharmacological action of
    anabaena flos-aquae toxin. W. W. Car-
    michael and others. bibl il Science 187:
    542-4 F 14 '75
        See also
    Plankton
    Seaweed
```

Specialized Periodical Indexes. These include the following:

International Index to Periodicals, 1907 to date. This is the best index to periodical journals. It also indexes some foreign-language journals, especially those in German and French.
Agricultural Index, 1916 to date.
Art Index, 1929 to date.

[1] Reproduced by Courtesy of H. W. Wilson Company.

Biography Index, 1947 to date.
Book Review Digest, 1905 to date.
Education Index, 1929 to date.
Index to Legal Periodicals, 1908 to date.
Music Index, 1949 to date.
Public Affairs Information Service, 1915 to date. Indexes, periodicals, books, documents, and pamphlets relating to political science, sociology, and economics.
Quarterly Cumulative Index Medicus, 1927 to date. *Index Medicus,* 1879–1926. An author and subject index to periodicals, books, and pamphlets in the field of medicine.

Index to Newspapers. *The New York Times Index* can be used as an index to any daily newspaper in the United States, since the same stories will probably be found in all daily papers on the same day they appear in the *Times.* The London *Times Index* is a good source for articles of all kinds.

New York Times Index, 1913 to date.
Index to The Times [London], 1906 to date.

THE RESEARCH PAPER

The research paper, variously known as the *investigative theme,* the *term paper, library paper,* or the *research article,* is an exposition, based on research in a library, presenting the results of careful and thorough investigation of some chosen or assigned subject. You will no doubt also have occasions to write term papers based not on library research but on laboratory experiments, questionnaires, or your own critical reactions to something you have read; papers of that sort are organized and written like any other expository paper. Some English departments require a long analytical discussion based on material collected and printed in what is often known as a *source book* or *casebook.* This type of paper, which is sometimes called the *controlled-research* or *controlled-sources* paper, solves certain problems inherent in the research assignment, such as the need to plumb the library or assemble original data. Where the controlled-sources method is used, the instructor's directions should be followed exactly. The information that follows applies primarily to papers based on library investigation.

Summarized here are the values or purposes of the research paper:

1. It will teach you how to use the library efficiently.

2. It will acquaint you with the methods of scholarly documentation—that is, the use of bibliography and footnotes.

3. It will increase your ability to take usable notes.

4. It will teach you how to organize and combine material from a number of different sources.

5. It will give you practice in presenting material in a way that will appeal to your readers.

The research paper can be a project full of frustrations, however, unless you follow orderly procedures. Below is a commentary on the various steps that constitute an orderly, efficient approach to the job.

Decide on a General Subject or Field of Investigation

As soon as the research paper is assigned, many students will ask themselves: "Now what subject do I know something about?" A major in English may want to investigate some author or literary movement. A student in forestry may be especially eager to investigate the new uses of forest products. A student of home economics may wish to write on nutrition or consumer redress. In some ways this attitude is commendable; it approaches in method the theory of the "honors course" now so popular in colleges—the independent investigation in depth of some special field related to a student's major interest. But in other ways this attitude is a mistake. A student should indeed be interested in the subject of his investigation, but his interest may as well involve the thrill of exploring an unfamiliar field.

Of course, if the subjects are assigned the problem of choice does not exist, but if the student has a choice, either unrestricted or limited, the choice should be based on a knowledge of both what is desirable and what must be avoided. The following kinds of subjects are *not* workable; they lead only to frustration:

1. Subjects that are too broad. Broad or general subjects are

starting points. They must be limited or narrowed to usable dimensions.

2. Subjects on which little has been published anywhere.
3. Subjects on which the local library has little material.
4. Subjects that are so technical that the writer cannot understand his material, much less present it intelligibly to others.
5. Subjects that are too narrow or too trivial for a paper of the suggested length.
6. Subjects indistinguishable from those selected by your classmates.

It is impossible to list all the general interests that will appeal in every instance. The lists given here are merely suggestive:

1. Something related to the course you are taking or expect to take in college, such as literature, history, medicine, or political science.
2. Something coming out of your experience, such as your work during summer vacations, your military service, your travel or stay in a foreign country, the occupations of your parents. But remember that these are only the starting point for your library work.
3. Something related to your hobbies, your special talents, or your reading interests, such as photography, archeology, exploration, sports, aviation.

The advice of your instructor may be the last word on your choice of subject. If you have freedom of choice, however, or if you are urged to present several choices for your instructor's approval, the following list of general fields may help:

1. Archeology	12. Music
2. Art	13. Mythology
3. Aviation	14. Nature
4. Biography	15. Photography
5. Crime	16. Psychology
6. Drama	17. Sciences
7. Education	18. Sports
8. History	19. The theater
9. Language and literature	20. Utopias
10. Medicine	21. Warfare
11. Movies	22. Welfare

Make a Preliminary Check of the Library and Do Some General Reading

Before making a final decision on the general subject, it is best to spend an hour or two browsing in the library to see whether the subject will be satisfactory and to get an idea of how it can be limited. First look in the card catalog. Then check through some of the periodical indexes to ascertain the extent of the available published material in the selected field. Notice in what types of periodicals the information is to be found, and make a preliminary check, either through the general card catalog or through a special list of periodicals, to see which of the sources are available in the library. Look in the *Britannica* to see what it has on the topic. If there is only a limited amount of information on hand and several persons want access to it simultaneously, efforts at research will run into frustrating delays.

Limit the Subject

After selecting a general field of interest, you will, with the help of your instructor, select some part or aspect of it that can be effectively presented in the given space and time. If you are interested in American literature, you may decide to write about Robert Frost or Sylvia Plath. You may find it convenient to limit your subject still further and to investigate the early poems of Frost or the suicidal tendencies expressed in the works of Plath. These are merely suggested topics. The variety of possible topics is vast. How you limit a broad subject depends partly on the time or the space allowed, partly on the thesis of the paper, partly on the extent of available material. A scholarly probing of a very minor area is one thing; a more general presentation of facts, such as might be read before a club or a seminar, is another. In choosing a subject, always remember that it is impossible to narrow or limit a subject by excluding details. A research article should be interesting. Interest comes from the concrete details, the examples, and the imaginative touches in the writing. Note how this balance is achieved in articles on science or medicine in *Time* magazine.

Now let us take two or three of these general fields and suggest in each of them several topics narrowed down to what can be presented adequately in the time and space prescribed.

GENERAL SUBJECT: MOVIES

1. Hollywood stars
2. Famous directors
3. Horror movies—their history
4. The Western hero
5. Novels into films
6. The art movie
7. The history of film technology
8. The gangster film
9. Movies and 30s society
10. Silent comedies

GENERAL SUBJECT: WARFARE

1. Caesar's battles
2. Famous ancient sea fights
3. The strategy of siege
4. Air battles of World War I
5. World War II generals
6. War in literature
7. American antiwar movements
8. Modern weapons of war
9. The American draft system
10. Nuclear arms limitation

Prepare a Working Bibliography

A bibliography is a list of books, articles, bulletins, or documents relating to a given subject or author.

When you begin working on a research paper, arm yourself with a supply of 3 × 5 cards or slips of paper. On these cards make a list of references—one and *only one* to each card—that you hope will be useful. Collect the references from the card catalog, the encyclopedias, and the periodical indexes. Since there is always a great deal of wastage and frustration in defining a specific area of research, take out insurance by getting more references than you expect to use. As you proceed with your reading, refine the bibliography by adding new references and by discarding those you find useless.

Bibliographic Forms. It is unfortunate that bibliographic forms have not been standardized as completely as have the parts of an automobile. Recently, however, the Modern Language Association has moved toward standardization in the general field of literature, language, and the social sciences. The result of the move has been the publication of *The MLA Style*

Sheet. Although this pamphlet concerns itself primarily with the preparation of *learned articles* in humanistic fields, it may be used by undergraduates and graduates in the preparation of term papers and theses. The forms of bibliographies and footnotes used here are based on *The MLA Style Sheet,* insofar as the recommendations of the MLA are applicable to undergraduate work.[2]

(There are other forms used for bibliographies and footnotes, however, and your instructor may well recommend modifications of the MLA style. Use the form requested.)

Every bibliographic reference consists of the three parts necessary for a complete identification of the printed work used, and these parts are generally arranged in this order:

1. *The author's name.* (Write the last name first only where lists are to be alphabetized. If an article or pamphlet is unsigned, begin with the title.)
2. *The title.* (If it is a book, underline the title. If it is an article, essay, poem, short story, or any subdivision of a larger work, enclose it in quotation marks.)
3. *The facts of publication.*
   a. For a book, give the place of publication (with the abbreviated state, if needed for clarity, as *Garden City, N.Y.*), the name of the publisher in full, and the date.
   b. For a magazine article, give the name of the magazine, the volume number, the date, and the pages.
   c. For a newspaper article, give the name of the newspaper, the date, the section if the sections are paged separately, and the page.

Sample Bibliography Cards

The sample bibliography cards that follow illustrate the arrangement of items and the punctuation in various types of references.

---

[2] *The MLA Style Sheet,* 2nd ed. (New York: Modern Language Assn., 1970).

ARTICLE IN AN ENCYCLOPEDIA

Initials of the author identified in vol. I. Date of copyright from back of volume. Title of article in quotes. Underline title of reference book.

```
Atkinson, Richard J. C.

"Stonehenge." Encyclopaedia Britannica, 1958, XXI, 440-
441.
```

BOOK BY A SINGLE AUTHOR

Copy call number. Underline title of book.

```
PN1993.5  Bergman, Andrew
.U6
B38       We're in the Money:

          Depression America and Its Films.

          New York: New York University Press, 1971.
```

BOOK BY TWO OR MORE AUTHORS

All names after the first are in normal order.

```
PN45   Wellek, René, and Austin Warren.

.W36
1962   Theory of Literature.

       New York: Harcourt, Brace, 1949.
```

BOOK EDITED BY MORE THAN THREE PERSONS

et alii ("and others") abbreviated *et al.* (Do not underline.)

Ref.   Spiller, R. E., et al., eds.,
PS88   2 vols.
 .L522
1974   <u>Literary</u> <u>History</u> <u>of</u> <u>the</u> <u>United</u> <u>States</u>. 4th ed.
       rev.

       New York: Macmillan Publishing Co., Inc., 1974

BOOK EDITED

 811   Millay, Edna St. Vincent.
.M611x
       <u>Collected</u> <u>Poems</u>. Ed. by Norma Millay

       New York: Harper & Brothers, 1956.

SIGNED MAGAZINE ARTICLE
VIOLENCE

Assassinations and the bicentennial. P. P. Moulton. il [il-
lustrated] Chr. Cent. 90: 1120–2 N 14 '73

Moulton, P. P.

"Assassinations and the Bicentennial."

<u>Christian</u> <u>Century</u>, Nov. 14, 1973, pp. 1120–22.

UNSIGNED ARTICLE
WATERGATE case

After surrendering tapes, new pressures on Nixon. il por
[portrait] US News 75: 19–21 N 5 '73

"After surrendering tapes, new pressures on Nixon."

<u>U.S.</u> <u>News</u> <u>and</u> <u>World</u> <u>Report</u>, Nov. 5, 1973, pp. 19–21.

100

NEWSPAPER ARTICLE

James, John: The New Directors; illus. J 27, 1973, F Ed., p 7

> James, John.
>
> "The New Directors."
>
> Detroit News, Jan. 27, 1973, Final Ed., p. 7.

Bulletins are treated like books if they are published occasionally, and like magazine articles if they are issued periodically (at regular intervals).

OCCASIONAL BULLETIN

Parker, William Riley. The MLA Style Sheet. 2nd ed. New York: MLA, 1970.

PERIODICAL BULLETIN

"New Trends in Testing," Educational Research, HEW, Nov. 1974, 27–28.

Reading and Taking Notes

It is a good idea, before you begin to read and take notes, to collect a few fairly promising bibliography cards. Take your cards with you to the library. Look up several of your references. You might start with the encyclopedia articles, or with books that give an overview of your subject. The aim in this reading is to develop a preliminary understanding of the subject you are interested in exploring. Read for general information. While exploring, note those topics that seem to be most closely related to your particular subject. If your subject is the impact of a certain type of movie from the Thirties on social attitudes, be sure to record information about the backgrounds of screenwriters, directors, and the actors themselves. These topics, properly arranged, will become your first rough outline. They will be the headings to use on your note cards when you begin taking notes.

Reading and Skimming. The tortures of research, the dead ends, the crucial articles that turn out to be irrelevant, the books that cannot be located, plague everyone. But there will be fewer frustrations and less wasted time if you remember that what you have learned about writing must apply also to your reading. Good writing produces work organized so that its contents are evident quickly, easily, without confusion, without wasted effort. Those who write books, chapters, essays, or articles in magazines follow the same principles of writing that you have learned—so that *you* may get the information you want, easily, quickly, without confusion, without wasted effort. Here are some aids to quick reading and comprehension:

1. In a book examine first the table of contents, Preface, Foreword, or Introduction, the index (if it has one), the chapter headings, and the topics of the lesser divisions.

2. In an essay or article look for a formal statement of plan or purpose at the beginning. If it is a rather long essay or article—one of those five-part essays used by magazines for serious discussions, for example—look at the beginning of each part for a hint of the contents.

3. Glance through the essay, reading a topic sentence here, another one there, until you come to what you want. The process is called *skimming*.

Evaluating Your Sources. To expect a college freshman writing his or her first research paper to have the experience necessary to evaluate all sources is not exactly fair or reasonable. But any college student can learn a few hints or signs that will help distinguish the totally unreliable from the probably reliable. *The student should first realize that not all that gets into print is true.* Some—perhaps most—of it is as true and as reliable as honest and informed men and women can make it. Some of it is mistaken or biased opinion. The following suggestions will help in the evaluation of sources:

1. The first aid is the date of publication of the book or article. In some fields, such as chemistry, physics, and medicine, information even a few months old may be outdated. *Try to get the most recent facts possible.*

2. To a certain extent, judge the information by the authority of the publication in which it appears. The *Britannica,* for

instance, selects its authors with more care than does a newspaper.

3. A long, thorough treatment of a subject is probably more accurate than a short treatment of it, or a condensation.

4. Finally, if it is possible, find out something about the reputation of the author. Obviously a careful checking of authorities is a necessity in a scholarly thesis written for publication, and a desirable but often unattainable ideal in a freshman term paper. In practice, however, a college library can usually be trusted to winnow out most of the chaff before it buys. When in doubt ask your librarian for help.

The Topic Outline. Once the dimensions of a subject area have been established by preliminary exploration, it is time to organize the subject according to a *topic outline.* A topic outline, however, should consist of more than a simple record of information; it should also begin to sift the information in terms of what an intelligent, mature person approaching the matter with an open mind will most appreciate being told. A writer must always keep his reader in mind. What information is actually available is, of course, the primary restriction on any topic outline. From that point the topic outline is the result of selecting material appropriate to the writer's objective and the reader's interest. "Selecting" is the key word. A tabulation of everything ever thought about a subject is no more a topic outline than is a list embracing every conceivable perspective some imaginary reader might like to see explored. The writer must pick and choose, add to and discard from the working outline, until the paper is set in its final form. But if the first topic outline is bound to undergo change, it is nonetheless important as a necessary guide for note-taking. It is therefore better that its preliminary form include too much than too little.

Use of Note Cards. When you go to the library you should have with you a generous supply of note cards. These may be either the 3×5 cards that you use for your bibliography or some slightly larger, such as the 4×6 size. If you cannot obtain cards, cut notebook paper into quarters to make slips approximately 4×5 inches in size. Just as carry-on baggage should not be stowed in an aircraft's baggage rack, notes should not be written in a notebook. One loose piece of paper to each note is the only format permitting easy and frequent rearrangement.

Methods of Identifying Notes. Notes must be identified if you are to avoid confusion later on. Two simple methods of identifying notes are presented here:

1. As you take notes, write at the top of a card the topic under which the information falls. At the bottom of the card write an abbreviated reference to the source of your information. This reference may consist of the author's last name, an abbreviated title, and the exact page reference.

2. The second method is to number all the bibliography cards. Any number system will do as long as the numbers are not duplicated. Then instead of the reference at the bottom of the note card, write the number of your bibliography card and the page number. Of course, whichever method is used each note card must relate to a topic in the working topic outline.

Be sure to use the method that is recommended by your instructor.

The Form of Notes. A sample note card is given below, but before you study it, consider the following suggestions for note-taking:

1. Most notes will be in the form of a summary. Get what is essential and get it accurately, but do not waste words. In order to avoid any chance of inadvertent plagiarism, try to paraphrase what you read—that is, try to *use your own words, not the words of your source.* But dates, figures, and such matters must obviously be quoted accurately.

2. If you wish to quote the exact words of an author, copy your material in the form of direct quotations. Ordinarily you should not use direct quotations from your sources if a summary will serve. But if you wish to preserve the words of your source because of unusually apt or precise language, or for some other adequate reason, quote your source exactly. If you leave out a part of a quoted sentence, indicate the omission by means of spaced periods (. . .) called *ellipsis periods* or *suspension points.* Use three spaced periods, leaving a space between the word and the first period, if you omit words in the sentence, and four spaced periods (which include the period ending the sentence) if your omission follows a complete sentence. If you omit a

paragraph or more, use three spaced periods centered on the card and in a line of their own, with space above and below the ellipsis.

3. Let your first unbreakable rule be: "One topic to a card." Do not include in your notes on the same card material relating to two or more topics. You may have as many cards as you wish covering the same topic, but take care to label each card and cite the exact source of your notes on each card.

4. Make your notes accurate and complete enough to make sense to you when they become cold.

5. Use headings or topics that represent actual divisions of your outline. Too many topics will merely result in confusion. Let the working outline be your guide.

6. Finally, remember that every note card must have three pieces of information: (1) the heading or topic, which shows you where the information belongs; (2) the information itself (in quotation marks if you use the words of your source); (3) the exact source of the material (including page reference).

Plagiarism. In writing a paper based on research, it is very easy for a student to fall into unintentional plagiarism. Therefore, he or she should understand exactly what *plagiarism* is, and how it can be avoided. The procedure outlined in this chapter shoud help you to steer away from *borrowing without giving proper credit* through careful note-taking. In taking notes be sure to rephrase the author's material in your own words; do not merely alter a word here and there. The danger is that if you do alter only a few words, the language of your source will carry over into the final paper. To prevent this transference, rephrase and summarize in your notes. You will naturally do more rephrasing when you write your first draft and the final draft, thus reducing the possibility of copying. Since plagiarism can be a serious offense (in some cases students have been expelled for committing it), ask your instructor to explain his or her definition of the word, and to give you assistance in any doubtful instances.

Sample Note Card. If you follow the instructions on pages 101–105, you will have little trouble in taking usable notes. This sample is a summary. No sample cards are necessary for anything as obvious as a direct quotation.

I, A. 'Making rounds of folk music clubs - Reaction

Clubs such as the Commons, the Gaslight, the Wha? and Gerde's Folk City were ideal places for Dylan to try out new ideas. Critics and so fellow artists praised him as a musician and as a talker.

Scaduto, *Dylan: an Intimate Biography* p.274

Prepare the Final Outline

For most of you, the final outline is not the one you will write the paper from. In other words, the outline is usually in a state of flux until the paper itself is finished. It is subject to change until the last moment. If something that looked good at first later seems to be out of place, throw it out and improve the outline. The outline is a working blueprint, a simplified diagram of your paper, but it is no help to anyone if it forces you to construct something that at the last moment you feel is wrong. Change it if it needs changing.

For the conventions of the formal outline, turn back to Chapter 2 in this section. Then examine the outline preceding the sample research paper in this chapter.

Write a First Draft of the Paper

In the process of writing a paper based on research in the library, most writers—whether students or professionals—work up the outline slowly and gradually as they collect notes. The whole process is one of synthesis, of gradual putting together, of sifting and rearranging, which of course includes throwing away unusable material as well as filling in unexpected gaps. It is time to begin writing when the working outline adequately defines the limits of the paper's content and when an approach to the subject, and possibly to the reader, is clear. It may be that you even have thought of an interesting beginning. So, take your note cards and outline at this point, and, on the table in front of you, spread out your note cards for your first section. Read them over to freshen in your mind the sequence or flow of thought—and then you are on your own.

As you write, whenever you come to borrowed material, either quoted or paraphrased, include the reference in parentheses in the right place in the text or between horizontal bars running from margin to margin, the first immediately below the material. Later copy your footnotes, in the approved form, at the bottom of each page as you prepare the final draft of your paper.

When you quote verse, you may run two lines together in your quotation if you indicate the end of a line by a slash (/), but if you quote more than two lines you should center the quotation on the page. If you quote prose of some length, you should separate the quotation from your text by indention. *No quotation marks are used when quotations are marked by indentions.* Ask your instructor if single or double spacing is required for indented quotations. Study the sample research paper at the end of this chapter for examples of these conventions.

Write a Final Draft with Footnotes

The Final Draft. Go over your first draft carefully before adding the footnotes and copy it for final submission. Keep the following principles in mind: (1) unity and direction of the paper as a whole; (2) interest, supplied by fact and example; (3) organization of the paper as a whole and of the separate paragraphs; (4) correctness of sentence structure; and (5) correctness of punctuation and spelling.

Footnotes: Where Needed. Whether in a college term paper or in a scholarly research article, footnotes are required:

1. *To acknowledge and identify every direct quotation.* Quoted material, as we have indicated earlier, should always be quoted exactly, word for word, except where deletions are indicated and either enclosed in quotation marks or indented. Footnotes are not used with familiar sayings or proverbs; everyone knows that these are quoted. (Expressions such as "all the world's a stage" or "all that glitters is not gold" are examples. But be careful to avoid these clichés; the library paper, like any other essay, requires aptness and freshness of language.)

2. *To acknowledge and identify all information that has been used in the paper or thesis in paraphrased, reworded, or summarized form.* Of course, facts of general knowledge need not be credited to any one source.

3. *To define terms used in the text, to give additional information that does not fit into the text, and to explain in detail what has been merely referred to in the text.*

4. *To translate unusual foreign phrases.*

Numbering and Spacing Footnotes. To indicate to the reader that a footnote is being used, place an Arabic numeral immediately *after* the material referred to and a little above the line. Do not put a space before the number or a period after it, either in the text or in the footnote. Place the same number *before* and a little above the line of the note at the bottom of the page. Each note should be single-spaced, and there should be one line of space between notes.

Footnotes should be numbered consecutively, starting from *1*, in a paper intended for publication; in a typed or handwritten paper, however, it is often required that they be numbered beginning with *1* on each page. Some instructors and editors prefer that footnotes appear on a separate sheet(s) at the end of the essay. Use the style your instructor recommends.

The Form of Footnotes. The first time you use a footnote to refer to any source, give the same information that is given in the bibliographic entry, and the exact page from which your information is taken: the author's name (but in the natural order, *not* with the last name first), the title of the work, the facts

108

of publication, and the exact page reference. The punctuation in the footnote is changed in one important respect—instead of periods, as in the bibliography, commas and parentheses are used to separate the three parts of the reference. Later references to the same source are abbreviated. If only one work by an author is used in your paper, the author's name with the page reference is enough. If more than one work by the same author is used, the author's name and a shortened form of the title (with exact page reference, of course) will suffice. Book publishers' names are given in the shortest intelligible form—*Macmillan,* not *Macmillan Publishing Co., Inc.,*—when they are included.

The forms illustrated here are those recommended by *The MLA Style Sheet,* 2nd ed., with the addition of the publishers' names. For scientific papers the forms are slightly different, and the student who writes papers for publication in scientific journals should follow the rules set up by those journals.

Models for Footnotes—Books

BOOKS BY ONE AUTHOR

[1] Andrew Bergman, *We're in the Money: Depression America and Its Films* (New York: New York University Press, 1971), p. 18.
[2] Philip Roth, *The Great American Novel* (New York: Holt, Rinehart and Winston, 1973), p. 200.

LATER REFERENCES

[3] Bergman, p. 21. (The MLA recommends use of *p.* or *pp.* [*pp.* is the plural abbreviation] only with works of a single volume.)
[4] Roth, *Novel,* p. 218. (Latin reference tags, such as *ibid., loc. cit.,* and *op. cit.,* are now considered redundant. See pp. 112–113.

TWO OR MORE AUTHORS

[5] René Wellek and Austin Warren, *Theory of Literature* (New York: Harcourt, Brace, 1949), p. 45.

EDITED BOOK

[6] Christopher R. Reaske, ed., *Seven Essayists: Varieties of Excellence in English Prose* (Glenview, Ill.: Scott, Foresman, 1969), p. 75.

109

BOOK EDITED BY MORE THAN THREE EDITORS

⁷ M. H. Abrams et al., eds., *The Norton Anthology of English Literature,* (New York: Norton, 1968), I, 33.

REPRINTED BOOK

⁸ L. C. Knights, *Drama and Society in the Age of Jonson* (1937; rpt. New York: Norton, 1968), pp. 146–149.

BOOK REVIEW

⁹ Cyrus Colter, rev. of *The Unfinished Quest of Richard Wright,* by Michel Fabre, *New Letters,* 40 (Spring, 1974), 108–114.

DISSERTATION

¹⁰ Hugh J. Ingrasci, "The American Picaresque Novel Between the World Wars," Diss. Michigan 1972, p. 10.

TRANSLATED WORK OF TWO OR MORE VOLUMES

¹¹ H. A. Taine, *History of English Literature,* trans. H. Van Laun (New York: 1889), IV, 296.

Models for Footnotes—Articles

ARTICLE IN A JOURNAL

¹²Jay Halio, "Three Filmed *Hamlets,*" *LFQ,* 1 (1973), 316–320. (Note that the journal's name, *Literature/Film Quarterly,* is abbreviated, and *p.* or *pp.* is not used for page numbers.)

ARTICLE IN AN ENCYCLOPEDIA

¹³ Richard J. C. Atkinson, "Stonehenge," *Encyclopaedia Britannica* (1958), XXI, 440.

ARTICLE FROM A MONTHLY MAGAZINE

¹⁴ H. Keppler, "New Look in Eclipses," *Modern Photography,* Nov. 1963, 93.

ARTICLE IN A WEEKLY MAGAZINE

¹⁵ Muriel Spark, "The First Year of My Life," *The New Yorker,* 2 June 1975, pp. 37–39. (When the volume number is not given, the page number is identified by *p.* or *pp.*)

UNSIGNED MAGAZINE ARTICLE

¹⁶ "An End to Kindness," *Time,* 2 June 1975, p. 43.

SIGNED NEWSPAPER ARTICLE

[17] John James, "The New Directors," Detroit *News,* 27 Jan. 1973, Final Ed., p. 7, cols. 1–4. (The edition and column numbers are not essential, but they are helpful pieces of information. The city where the paper is published is not generally underlined.)

ARTICLE IN AN EDITED COLLECTION

[18] Mary Lascelles, "Shakespeare's Pastoral Comedy," in *Pastoral and Romance: Modern Essays in Criticism,* ed. Eleanor Lincoln Terry (Englewood Cliffs, N.J.: Prentice-Hall, 1969), p. 119.

Miscellaneous

INTERVIEW

[19] Tom Jones, personal interview on popular music, Kansas City, Mo., 6 Jan., 1972.

QUOTATION CITED IN A SECONDARY SOURCE

[20] Gourmet Fields, "The Most Delectable Food I Ever Tasted," as quoted in *W. C. Fields by Himself,* ed. Ronald J. Fields (Englewood Cliffs, N.J.: Prentice-Hall, 1973), pp. 4–5.

ARTICLE REPRINTED IN A COLLECTION

[21] Robert B. Heilman, "Wit and Witchcraft: An Approach to *Othello,*" *The Sewanee Review,* 64 (Winter 1956), rpt. in *Shakespeare: Modern Essays in Criticism,* ed. Leonard F. Dean (New York: Oxford University Press, 1961), pp. 294–310.

FILM

[22] *The Taming of the Shrew* (1966), dir. Franco Zeffirelli; s. Elizabeth Taylor, Richard Burton. USA/Italy: Royal Films International F.A.I. Prod. (There is as yet no standardized form for footnoting films. The above citation includes as much information as is available, though the main elements are the title, date of release, director, country, and production company.)

RECORDING

[23] Bob Dylan, "Desolation Row," *Highway 61 Revisited* (Columbia Records, 1965).

Roman Numerals. Because Roman numerals have a restricted use, students are sometimes unfamiliar with them. The following brief explanation may be helpful:

The key symbols are few in number: 1 = I, 5 = V, 10 = X, 50 = L, 100 = C, 500 = D, 1,000 = M.

Other numbers are formed by adding or subtracting. The three main principles involved are as follows: (1) A letter following one of equal or greater value is added value. (2) A letter preceding one of greater value is subtracted value. (3) When a letter stands between two of greater value, it is subtracted from the last of the three and the remainder is added to the first. Try this explanation with the following examples:

R U L E 1

2 = II	20 = XX	200 = CC
3 = III	30 = XXX	300 = CCC
6 = VI	60 = LX	600 = DC
7 = VII	70 = LXX	700 = DCC

R U L E 2

4 = IV	40 = XL	400 = CD
9 = IX	90 = XC	900 = CM

R U L E 3

19 = XIX	59 = LIX	1,900 = MCM

Abbreviations in Footnotes. Although the number of abbreviations used in research papers at the graduate-school level is large—and often confusing to the lay reader—only a few are of immediate concern here.

anon. Anonymous.
c., ca. *Circa,* "about." (Used with approximate dates.)
cf. *Confer,* "compare." (should not be used when *see* is meant.)
ch., chap. Chapter.
chs., chaps. Chapters.
col., cols. Column, columns.
ed. Edited, edition, editor.

e.g. *Exempli gratia* [ĕg·zĕm′plī grā′shĭ·à], "for example."

et al. *Et alii* [ĕt ā′lĭ·ī], "and others."

f., ff. And the following page (f.) or pages (ff.).

ibid. *Ibidem* [ĭ·bī′dĕm], "in the same place." (*Ibid.* refers to the note immediately preceding. *The MLA Style Sheet* recommends substituting either the author's name or an abbreviated title; either is unambiguous and almost as brief as *ibid.*)

i.e. *Id est,* "that is." Do not use for "e.g."

l., ll. Line, lines.

loc. cit. *Loco citato* [lō′kō sī·tă′tō], "in the place cited." (*Loc. cit.* refers to the same passage cited in a recent note. It is used with the author's name but is not followed by a page number.)

op. cit. *Opere citato* [ŏp′ĕ·rē sī·tā′tō], "in the work cited." (*The MLA Style Sheet* calls this "the most abused of scholarly abbreviations," and recommends instead the use of the author's name alone or with an abbreviated title.)

The Fair Copy. After you have finished your final draft, you should prepare a clean copy for submission. Chapter 2, in Section III of this book, gives some general rules that you should follow unless your instructor has some other preference. The sample research paper at the end of this chapter will also assist you.

Prepare a Final Bibliography

Your final bibliography should include all the articles and books cited by your paper in the footnotes, plus whatever additional source information your instructor specifies. A bibliography can be prepared quickly and simply by gathering the bibliography cards for the footnotes in the final draft and arranging the citations taken from them in alphabetical (index, not dictionary) order by author, or by title when no author is given.

To alphabetize titles in index order, remember that (1) initial articles (*a, an, the*) are disregarded and (2) alphabetization is by word, with short forms of the same word coming first no matter what letter the second word starts with. For instance, *New York* always precedes *New Yorkers:*

> *New York: Dylan's Early Days*
> *New York: The Folksong Clubs*
> *New York Audiences*
> *New York Critics*

To alphabetize names in index order, you will also need to bear in mind a few variations from dictionary order. *Mc-* and *M'-* are alphabetized as if spelled *Mac-*. When two authors have identical last names, alphabetize by first names first, second names next: *Norman, Marie B.* precedes *Norman, Mary A.* An initial takes precedence over a spelled name that begins with the same letter, and a last name followed by a single initial takes precedence over a last name followed by two initials: *Norman, M.* precedes *Norman, M. B.,* and both precede *Norman, Mary A.* Use the titles (or dates, if titles are identical) to alphabetize a number of works by the same author writing alone. When there are collaborators, use the following order: (1) single author; (2) author and collaborator; (3) author "et al."; (4) title; (5) date, with the earliest first:

JONES, A. B. *My Life and Times.* New York: Jones Publishing Company, 1975.
———and TOM SMITH. *Friendly Enemies.* New York: Jones Publishing Company, 1973.
———et al. *Relatives.* New York: Jones Publishing Company, 1973.
———et al. *Topical Essays.* New York: Jones Publishing Company, 1971.
———et al. *Topical Essays.* New York: Jones Publishing Company, 1974.

The form of the individual entries has already been treated on pages 98–101. See also the bibliography accompanying the sample paper that follows.

Sample Outline and Library Paper

The following sample outline and library paper are reproduced here, not as perfect models to imitate, but as examples of conscientious and competent work.[3] (The student has used a *sentence* outline here; for a sample of the *topic* outline, turn back to pp. 74–75.)

[3] Reprinted by permission of the author, Harry Lee Wheeler, Jr.

Obviously a Generation of Believers

<u>Thesis</u> <u>Sentence</u>: Bob Dylan's music, marked by its variety of
moods, has had a powerful influence on the social and political conscience of an entire generation of young people.

   I. Dylan's earliest performances (in 1961) gave no promise
     of his later greatness.
     A. He made the rounds of folk music clubs in New York.
     B. His style, though attractively unpredictable, was
       still mainly imitative.
  II. With the release of "Blowin' in the Wind" (1962), Dylan
     became "troubadour of the Movement."
     A. His music carried a message of protest.
     B. He achieved an image of success without selling out.
     C. His music spoke directly to an increasingly restless
       audience: American college students.
 III. The release of <u>Another</u> <u>Side</u> <u>of</u> <u>Bob</u> <u>Dylan</u> (1964) marked a
     move to fuse elements of folk and rock music.
     A. Dylan tried to put his music on a level with his lyr-
       ics.
     B. As had happened with other popular singers, he soon
       found himself increasingly imitated.
  IV. Between 1965 and 1967, Dylan found yet another voice:
     one of cynicism and doubt.
     A. This mood fit that of the student anti-war protest-
       ers.
     B. Answers to questions about their identities were
       sought in Dylan's songs by many people.
     C. In the three brooding albums from this period,
       Dylan's words achieved a poetic quality they had not
       held before.
   V. After a near-fatal motorcycle accident in 1966, Dylan's
     music became softer, "the poetry of faith and salva-
     tion."
     A. "John Wesley Harding," though less controversial and
       more folk-like than his most recent music, reached
       out to the working class of the future.
     B. <u>Nashville</u> <u>Skyline</u> caught on as Dylan's audience began
       to move away from psychedelic to folk music.
  VI. Today Dylan tours the country to sold out audiences who
     still listen to his words and look for their meaning.

Obviously a Generation of Believers

By Harry Wheeler
Freshman English 120
29 March 1974

117

Obviously a Generation of Believers

In the late summer of 1969, 200,000 young people from both sides of the Atlantic gathered on the Isle of Wight in the English Channel to pay tribute to a man they had long followed. The crowd waited in poor facilities through two days of preliminary concerts and adverse weather conditions, making clear their commitment to the performer they had come to see. Though the performance lasted less than an hour and was three hours late, the huge audience was wild with enthusiasm, caught willingly in the magic of the words and sounds of this prophet they had oftened turned to.[1]

Bob Dylan has been called a prophet, a poet, a genius, and a Christ at various times in his career. He has been seen as an angry young rebel, a bitter, lashing oracle of the impending doomsday, a self-satisfied artist expounding the joys of salvation, and finally a true messiah leading us into the new consciousness.[2] In short, Bob Dylan has been a powerful force on the social and political conscience of an entire generation.

Few people could have noticed as a skinny, nineteen-year-old arrived in New York City on a cold winter morning in January 1961. Fewer would have predicted that years later, through a journey spanning nearly a decade, they would be following down roads he had so painfully and controversially paved. For these people could not have foreseen that the words of Bob Dylan would become the voice of his emerging generation, and that this man would become the most influential artist of the turbulent period that lay before them.

-2-

Once established in New York, Bob Dylan began the usual routine of folk musicians in coffee houses and cabarets. He performed at such establishments as the Commons, the Gaslight, the Wha?, and Gerde's Folk City. Although performing at the usual places and playing traditional folk music, Dylan soon demonstrated to established folk artists and critics that he was unique. Victoria Spivey said of him in 1961: "Dylan's a born genius of a musician."[3] Len Kunstadt commented in the same year on his erratic, unpredictable genius.[4] Israel Young, member of the board of Sing Out!, a respected folk music journal of the 1960s, stated in 1961: "I'm very excited by Bob Dylan. . . . Purely from the way he talks he seems to have greatness in him. . . ."[5]

1961 also brought what every young performer anxiously awaits—a review in the New York Times. Robert Shelton, music critic for the Times, wrote of Bob Dylan's performance at Gerde's Folk City:

> . . . Although only twenty years old, Bob Dylan is one of the most distinctive stylists to play in a Manhattan cabaret. . . . There is no doubt he is bursting at the seams with talent. . . . Mr. Dylan is vague about his antecedents and his birthplace, but it matters less where he has been than where he is going, and that would seem to be straight up.[6]

Soon after Shelton's review was published, Columbia Records sent John Hammond out to sign Dylan to a five-year contract. Dylan was the first of the younger male folk singers to be signed by a major record label.[7] Impressed with Dylan's musicianship, Columbia pushed for an early release of his first album. Released in March 1962 and entitled simply Bob Dylan, the album was a moderate success; but the material on

it was obsolete before it reached the public. Dylan had already moved into an area different from his traditional folk
album represented. As Dave Van Ronk, an established folk artist saw it, Dylan had emerged into the twentieth century.[8]

"Blowin' in the Wind" was written in April 1962 and
quickly became the anthem of the radical civil rights activists. It made Dylan the acknowledged leader of the protest
movement. At the same time, all the forces which had been af-
fecting Dylan began to take the form of a series of bitter
songs with social themes. His villains were the people whom
he calls the "Masters of War," those who profit from the manufacture of weapons, the hypocrites who claim that "With God
on Our Side" they can justify any evil act they wish to commit:

> When the Second World War
> Came to an end
> We forgave the Germans
> And we were friends
> Though they murdered six million
> In the ovens they fried
> The Germans now too have God
> On their side.[9]

Dylan's success was mounting rapidly, when in 1962 Gil
Turner wrote in Sing Out! that Dylan had become the most pro-
lific and important song writer in America.[10] At one point
Turner refers to him as "the Elvis Presley of folk music,"[11]
a reference which indicates Dylan's mastery of popular style.
In a prophetic closing remark, Turner states: "I believe his
most significant and lasting contribution will be in the
songs he writes."[12]

-4-

Dylan's career was now on a phenomenal upward swing, gaining new followers as his reputation increased. This rise was evidenced by the audience's reaction at the Newport Folk Festival of 1963, which was, as Anthony Scaduto describes it, Dylan's first major concert:

> . . . When the three days of traditional and folk–protest music . . . were over, Dylan was being hailed as the "crown prince" of folk music by the mass media. Newport was also the scene of the transformation of Bob Dylan—hobo minstrel, into Bob Dylan—the eclectic poet–visionary hero who was single–handedly orchestrating a youth revolution. . . . And they loved him. For the many who had never heard Dylan or his songs before, the effect was electric. They had come to take part in a movement, and they had discovered a prophet.[13]

For the next year, Bob Dylan was at the head of the radical movement growing up among the young. For them, the Dylan image had been formed: he was truly an idolized artist; he was making it big, but he wasn't selling out. His music was real because it struck out against injustice and bigotry in an amazingly human way. Perhaps *Life* magazine expressed it best in a portrait of Dylan dedicated to finding the real person in the cloud of praise and criticism that had hung over him up to this time. The article calls Dylan the most important songwriter in the past twenty years, and treats his unconventional style and appearance objectively. It emphasizes that Dylan alone is giving young audiences what they want—protest directed at their enemies and spoken in their voice. "In his songs Dylan talks most compellingly to young people. They are drawn by his style, his voice, and the stories he tells. But there is something more that attracts them, a feeling that Bob Dylan is on their side."[14] Indeed it ap-

–5–

121

peared that Dylan possessed charisma that writers until now had attached only to political leaders. He was a hero: "a poet of the people—especially the young, the disoriented, the idealists, the activists who believed they could build a new world."[15] He had also won critical acclaim, his work was being hailed as the most progressive and influential music in years, and he was becoming a huge commercial success. But Dylan had never been locked into one step for very long, and his restless nature was clearly at work within him as he moved beyond his former position once again.

With the release of <u>Another</u> <u>Side</u> <u>of</u> <u>Bob</u> <u>Dylan</u> in 1964, the folk musician and political figure was dead forever. His friends and supporters were shocked by this change, and many began to call out for the old Dylan in public forums. <u>Sing</u> <u>Out</u>! editor Irwin Silber published a long, impassioned plea in the form of an open letter for Dylan to return to social protest. The letter contained evidence of a deep concern and high praise, calling Dylan's songs "inspired contributions which have already had a significant impact on American consciousness and style."[16] Silber's plea and those of others were well meant but too late, because Dylan had already abandoned folk music and the mood of protest with which it had become identified.

The spring of 1965 brought a surprising fusion of the two apparently opposite styles of folk lyric and rock music, the fusion of the two styles pioneered and made popular by Bob Dylan. Paul Nelson saw the move as the logical extension of the quest for truth; his statement that "Time if nothing

-6-

else will vindicate Bob Dylan's 'New Music'" proved indisput-
ably sound.[17] Several months later, Robert Shelton observed
that "if imitation is the sincerest form of flattery, then
Bob Dylan should be the most self-satisfied performer in
America, as he [is]* certainly the most imitated."[18] Dylan
himself claimed that the move was designed to put his music
on a level with his lyrics.[19] But the cause of the fusion was
microscopic in importance compared to its effect. Dylan
achieved with this new music a height of public attention af-
forded very few artists. The shift to popular music gave his
poetry new emphasis, and he was beginning to reach unprece-
dented numbers of young people. Other artists were recording
his music at this time: the Byrds' recording of "Mr. Tambourine Man" had become a bestseller in at least seven countries. Carl Oglesby, former president of the Students for a
Democratic Society, felt that Dylan was exactly in step with
the mood of the nation's young. They had grown increasingly
frustrated with involvement in causes and, with the help of
Dylan's music, were beginning to explore seriously their own
minds.[20]

From this point (1965) until much later in the decade,
Bob Dylan was the performer youth turned to for answers to
their questions about identity and reality. Newsweek predicted the longevity of this trend when it hailed popular
music as the wave of the future and placed Dylan at its
head.[21]

---

*When you insert a word or phrase in a quotation to provide smoother transition,
or to achieve agreement in tense, etc., use brackets to avoid confusion.

-7-

123

In the three record albums he produced between 1965 and 1967, Dylan created visions of a dark and sinister under- world, where lies are accepted as beauty and truth, and al- ienation and falseness become the absurd reality.[22] The gen- eration Dylan was reaching identified with this message; they felt the same pressures and responded with the same horror to the picture Dylan's songs painted. A poll of major colleges listed Dylan as the "most important contemporary poet in America" because of what he had done to awaken the minds of a generation.[23] A Princeton student expressed it this way: "It's the words. Either you understand him or you don't. I can't explain why he's so great, but he knows what it's about!"[24] Novelist John Clellon Holmes expressed much the same enthusiasm in his answer to a question about Dylan's im- portance in modern society: "I think it's safe to say that no one years hence will be able to understand just what it was like to live in this time without attending to what this astonishingly gifted young man has already achieved."[25]

That achievement was almost cut short by a near-fatal motorcycle accident in 1966, an accident that had a major ef- fect on Dylan's personal outlook and his career. During the recuperation period he lived at his home in Woodstock, New York, where he switched roles from participant to observer of the American scene. The result of Dylan's observations emerged with him seventeen months later in the form of the album, John Wesley Harding. Gone in this album are the dark images and deep bitterness which had characterized Dylan's music in the mid-sixties. These are replaced by the poetry of faith and salvation, by songs which look optimistically to the future. Dylan's new direction was exactly in step with what Carl Oglesby refers to as the Movement. According to him, Dylan was reaching out for a different constituency, the white working class of the future.[26] Whatever his motives, Dylan's move into relative simplicity and lyricism was reem—phasized in his next album, Nashville Skyline.

Nashville Skyline appeared just at the time when young people were moving away from psychedlic music. As Scaduto sees it Skyline was like a clear country stream, lacking the irony and ambiguity of words and sounds that had marked so many acid rock songs.[27] This album shows a happy, content Bob Dylan so in love with life that all his songs have a romantic theme, without the old skepticism that once cut so deep. Al—though many Dylan followers no doubt felt, like the folk art—ists of the early sixties, that they had been betrayed, and that Dylan was no longer in touch with their troubled times and minds, it eventually became clear that Bob Dylan was still one step ahead of musical trends and still held the po—sition of leader of millions of young people.

But it was not until January 1974 that the leader re—turned to the place where he could be seen and heard: the performing stage. In that month his long—awaited cross coun—try tour became a reality. As David DeVoss acknowledged in Time:

> . . . For thousands of young Americans, Bob Dylan is one of the very few personalities to emerge intact from the '60's whirlwind. A vindicated Cassandra who, in crystallizing once vague discontents, transformed dissent from an intellectual

—9—

125

hobby to a public cause, Dylan sang about the turmoil of a generation. The generation listened. Now it remembers.[28]

Never in the history of American popular music has a tour aroused so much public interest. Within a few hours after tickets went on sale, post offices along the route received letters containing ticket requests in excess of five million. "One trade paper calculated that 7.5% of the population of the U.S. had requested tickets to see Dylan," wrote David DeVoss.[29] Judging from the uproar for encores and the inevitable standing ovations, Dylan's tour was a striking success. More important, however, it signalled his reentry into the performing circuit at a time when new fans were ready to experience the sounds that had moved their older brothers and sisters. The tour demonstrated that thousands of young people are still "listening to his words and looking for their meaning."[30]

Two writers who have participated in the listening and looking over the past decade provide fitting comment on the lasting quality of Bob Dylan's music and poetry. Anthony Scaduto, Dylan's biographer, summarizes the impact of selected songs on society:

As much as any man, Bob Dylan has given shape and substance to our time. With such songs as "Blowin' in the Wind" and "The Times They Are A-Changin'" he awakened in young America a social conscience that had lain dormant throughout the Fifties. "Tambourine Man," "Chimes of Freedom," "Visions of Johanna," inspired unknown thousands (perhaps millions) to embrace a new lifestyle, to drop out of society and seek salvation in communes or drugs or oriental religion.[31]

Looking back, Paul Nelson paid perhaps the ultimate compli-

126

ment to this most important and controversial artist:

It is hard to claim too much for a man who in every way revolutionized modern poetry, American folk music, popular music, and the whole of modern—day thought; even the strongest praise seems finally inadequate. Not many contemporary artists have the power to actually change our lives, but surely Dylan does——and has.[32]

And will.

Footnotes

[1] "Pop Music Festival Rocks English Channel Island," New York *Times*, 31 August 1969, p. 46, cols. 5-8.

[2] Anthony Scaduto, *Bob* *Dylan:* *An* *Intimate* *Biography* (New York: Grosset and Dunlap, 1971), p. 274.

[3] Quoted by Scaduto, p. 96.

[4] Quoted by Scaduto, p. 96.

[5] Quoted by Scaduto, p. 99.

[6] "Bob Dylan: A Distinctive Folk Song Stylist," New York *Times*, 28 September 1961, p. 16, cols. 1-4.

[7] Scaduto, p. 98.

[8] Bob Dylan, personal interview by KUDL-FM, 18 March, 1974.

[9] "With God on Our Side," by Bob Dylan. © 1963 Warner Bros. Inc. All Rights Reserved. Used by permission.

[10] "Bob Dylan--A New Voice Singing New Songs," *Sing* *Out!*, March 1962, rpt. in *Bob* *Dylan:* *A* *Retrospective*, ed. Craig McGregor (New York: Wm. Morrow and Co., 1972), p. 22.

[11] Turner, p. 23.

[12] Turner, p. 27.

[13] Scaduto, p. 148.

[14] "Angry Young Folk Singer," *Life*, 10 April 1964, p. 114.

[15] Scaduto, p. 146.

[16] "An Open Letter to Bob Dylan," *Sing* *Out!*, April 1964, rpt. in *Bob* *Dylan:* *A* *Retrospective*, pp. 66-8.

[17] "Bob Dylan: Another View," *Sing* *Out!*, May 1966, rpt. in *Bob* *Dylan:* *A* *Retrospective*, p. 107.

[18] "Pop Singers and Songwriters Racing Down Bob Dylan's Road," New York *Times*, 27 August 1965, p. 17, cols. 3-4.

[19] Quoted in Steven Castin, "Folk-Rock's Tambourine Man," *Look*, 8 March 1966, p. 76.

[20] Scaduto, p. 177.

[21] "Folk and the Rock," *Newsweek*, 20 September 1965, p. 88.

-12-

128

Footnotes (cont.)

22 Scaduto, p. 221.

23 Jules Siegel, "Well, What Have We Here?," <u>Saturday Evening Post</u>, 30 July 1966, pp. 32-36.

24 Quoted in John Clellon Holmes et al., "Is Bob Dylan the Greatest Poet in the United States Today?," New York <u>Times</u>, 6 June 1965, rpt. in <u>Bob Dylan: A Retrospective</u>, p. 167.

25 Holmes, p. 167.

26 Scaduto, p. 249.

27 Scaduto, p. 259.

28 "Dylan: Once Again, It's Alright Ma," <u>Time</u>, 21 January 1974, p. 54.

29 "Once Again," p. 54.

30 "Once Again," p. 57.

31 Scaduto, p. i.

32 Quoted in Bob Dylan, <u>Blonde on Blonde Songbook</u> (New York: Warner Bros., 1966), p. ii.

-13-

Bibliography

"Angry Young Folk Singer." Life, 10 April 1964, pp. 109–14.

"Bob Dylan: A Man and His Music." Interview by Dave Van Ronk
on KUDL–FM, 18 March, 1974.

Bob Dylan: A Retrospective. Ed. Craig McGregor. New York:
William Morrow and Co., 1972.

Castin, Steven. "Folk–Rock's Tambourine Man." Look, 8 March
1966, p. 76.

DeVoss, David. "Dylan: Once Again, It's Alright Ma." Time, 21
January 1974, pp. 54–57.

Dylan, Bob. Blonde on Blonde Songbook. New York: Warner Bros.
Publications, 1966.

————. "With God on Our Side." New York: M. Whitmark and
Sons, 1963.

"Folk and the Rock." Newsweek, 20 September 1965, p. 88.

"Pop Music Festival Rocks English Channel Island." New York
Times, 31 August 1969, p. 46, cols. 5–8.

Scaduto, Anthony. Bob Dylan: An Intimate Biography. New York:
Grosset and Dunlap, 1971.

Shelton, Robert. "Bob Dylan: A Distinctive Folk Song Stylist." New York Times, 28 September 1961, p. 16, cols. 1–4.

————. "Pop Singers and Songwriters Racing Down Bob Dylan's
Road." New York Times, 27 August 1965, p. 17, cols. 3–4.

Siegel, Jules. "Well, What Have We Here?" Saturday Evening
Post, 30 July 1966, pp. 32–36.

4 *The Letter*

THE FORMAL LETTER AND ITS PARTS

Every letter is a composition. Each is in some degree governed by the considerations that govern other kinds of writing. But when you dash off a note to the deliveryman, you need not worry very much about your grammar and punctuation. Your first draft is probably adequate. On the other hand, a letter to a prospective employer may be the most important document you ever write, one in which every detail may count. The variety of letters is enormous. In every letter you write, however, even the one to the deliveryman, you are explicitly expressing yourself to one other individual. *A letter is not an essay intended for general interest; it is, usually, a private communication between you and another person.* In no other writing, therefore, is the emphasis so heavily on the character of your reader, what you know and expect of that person.

Your letter to the deliveryman probably needs no improvement; the test of it is whether you get the package left next door. Furthermore no one, not even an English teacher, should presume to tell you how to write your most personal correspondence. You know best what ought to go into it. (The history of literature, however, provides many a love letter composed with grace and style, even if true love never did run smooth.)

What a teacher *can* help you to write, and what this chapter is concerned with, are all those relatively formal letters, letters addressed to individuals you don't know intimately or otherwise composed under circumstances inappropriate to a casual style. These include not only letters of application and business letters, but all those letters you have to write to people, especially older people, with whom you are not on easy terms.

Formal letters, then, are governed by considerations similar to those you must have in mind for all compositions. You should be clear, well organized, coherent. You should be careful about spelling, grammar, and punctuation. But in addition to these familiar injunctions, there are certain other laws, or conventions, of usage that the letter writer cannot ignore.

These are the parts of a letter:

1. The heading.
2. The inside address.
3. The salutation or greeting.
4. The body of the letter.
5. The complimentary close.
6. The signature.

For each of these parts usage has prescribed certain set forms. These forms should not be ignored or altered, especially in business letters. Conformity, not originality, is a virtue here.

The Heading

The parts of a heading, written in the following order, are *the street address, the name of city or town, the name of the state, the date.* A printed letterhead takes the place of a typed address. On paper with letterheads, the writer types the date either directly under the letterhead or flush with the right-hand margin of the letter.

[Letterhead]

September 23, 1975 [or] September 23, 1975

A growing number of letter writers, influenced possibly by European practice, or by the military services, are writing dates with the number of the day first, the month next, then the year—all without punctuation—for example, 23 September 1975. There is a logic and simplicity to this form that may in time win universal acceptance.

On paper that does not have a letterhead, the writer types the heading at the right according to one of the following forms:

Block form with open punctuation—that is, end punctuation is omitted. This form is rapidly becoming almost universal.

132

```
                              327 East Walnut Street
                              Springdale, Wisconsin  54875
                              September 23, 1975
```

Indented form, with closed punctuation. Final punctuation is usually omitted.

```
                              76 Belmont Street,
                                Canton, Iowa  52542
                                September 23, 1975
```

Whichever form he uses, the writer should be consistent throughout the letter—in the heading, in the inside address, and in the address on the envelope.

The Inside Address

In a business letter *the inside address is the address of the person written to.* The envelope of a business letter is often discarded before the letter reaches the intended recipient. Repeating the address ensures that the addressee's identity is not accidentally lost and that it remains on any copy of the letter kept in the sender's files.

In a personal letter the inside address is usually omitted, though it may be added at the bottom of a fairly formal personal letter, in the lower left-hand corner. The first line of the inside address should be flush with the left-hand margin of the letter. Either the block form or the indented form may be used.

```
Mr. H. G. Warren
Warren & Stacey, Builders
132 First Avenue
Ogden, Maine  03907

Dear Mr. Warren:
```

or

```
Parr Oil Company,
  20 Main Street,
    Helena, Illinois  61537

Gentlemen:
```

The block form, illustrated first, is preferred by a majority of letter writers for business purposes.

133

The name of the person addressed in a business letter should be accompanied by a personal title. The use of a personal title is correct even when a business title follows the name. Common personal titles are *Mr., Mrs., Miss* (or *Ms.*), *Dr., Professor, Messrs.* A business title designating the office or function of an individual should not precede the person's name but should either follow the name immediately if the title is short or, if it is long, appear on the line below.

```
Mr. T. C. Howard, Secretary      Mr. William R. Jones
Pueblo Rose Society              Personnel Manager

Dr. James L. Pendleton           Ms. Laura Jackson
Director of Admissions           Treasurer, City Action Club
```

The inclusion of a business title usually implies that the writer is addressing the reader in his or her capacity as holder of a particular office or authority. In such cases, answers may properly be made by an assistant who speaks for his or her superior, or by a successor, should the original addressee have left office for some reason.

The Salutation or Greeting

The following forms are correct for business and professional letters:

```
Gentlemen:                       Ladies:
Dear Sir:/Dear Sirs:             Dear Madam:
Dear Mr. Jackson:                Dear Miss (or Ms.) White:
```

In personal letters the range of greetings is unlimited, but somewhere between the inappropriately formal *Sirs* or *Madam* at one extreme, and an inappropriately affable *Hi Swinger* at the other, we may mention the following as usually appropriate:

```
Dear Jack,      Dear Mr. Howard,      Dear Miss (or Ms.) Brown,
```

We also ought to be aware that a great deal of modern business is transacted on a first-name basis, even when the relations between the parties are entirely professional.

134

Correct usage in addressing government officials and other dignitaries will be found in a good desk dictionary such as *Webster's New World Dictionary,* the *American College Dictionary,* or *Webster's Eighth New Collegiate Dictionary.* Local newspapers will also provide titles and addresses of government officials.

A colon is used after the salutation in a business letter; either a colon or a comma may be used in a personal letter. A comma is considered less formal. A dash—appropriate enough for a letter to an intimate friend—should be avoided in formal letters.

The Body of the Letter

The composition of business letters is a subject much too complex to be discussed here except in a very introductory way. A good letter, again, obeys the principles of any good writing. It should be clear, direct, coherent, and courteous. A student who can write a good class paper ought to be able to write a good business letter. But there are whole college courses devoted to the subject, and the interested student should either enroll in such a course or consult one of the numerous special guidebooks available.

At its best, the efficient and graceful composition of a business letter is a genuine art. Much more flexibility is required than is generally understood. There are times when a letter must speak very formally, as if in the abstract voice of its letterhead, a large and impersonal corporation. There are other times when warmth and genial good fellowship are appropriate. The executive who can say no without hurting a reader's feelings is a valuable person to the company. But these skills, however interesting and important, are beyond the range of this handbook.

The Complimentary Close

Correct forms for the complimentary close of business letters are as follows:

Yours truly,	Faithfully yours,
Yours very truly,	Sincerely yours,
Very truly yours,	Yours sincerely,
Respectfully yours,	Cordially yours,

135

It is now considered bad taste to use a participial phrase in closing a letter, such as *Hoping you are well.* A comma is the usual punctuation after the complimentary close; only the first letter is capitalized. In ordinary formal business letters, *Yours truly* or *Yours very truly* is the accepted form. In business letters between persons who know each other well, *Yours sincerely* and *Cordially yours* are used, or even, more informally, *Sincerely* and simply *Yours.*

The Signature

For the ordinary person it is correct to sign a business letter as he or she would sign a check. If possible, you should write your name legibly. But just to make sure, it is desirable to type the name under the signature.

Some of the conventions that govern the form of a signature are the following:

1. Neither professional titles, such as *Professor, Dr., Rev.,* nor academic degrees, such as *Ph.D., LL.D., M.A.,* should be used with a signature.

2. An unmarried woman should not sign herself as Miss Laura Blank, but she may place *Miss* (or *Ms.*) in parentheses before her name if she feels that it is necessary for proper identification.

3. A married woman or a widow who elects to adopt her husband's last name signs her own name, not her married name. For example, *Diana Holoday Brown* is her own name; *Mrs. George Brown* is her married name. She may place *Mrs.* in parentheses before her signature, or her married name in parentheses under it.

4. When a secretary signs her employer's name to a letter, she may add her own initials below the signature.

The following is an example of a business letter, of the type that might be written to a business organization from a private individual:

37 North Cove Road
Los Gatos, California   95030
June 18, 1975

Acme Camera Shop
876 Fifth Street
Palo Alto, California   94302

Gentlemen:

I am returning to you a lens which you sent me, on my order, on June 16. The lens is a 35—mm F 2.5 (wide angle) P. Angenieux Retrofocus, with a bayonet mount to fit the Exacta camera. The number of the lens is 463513.

You will notice by holding the lens against a bright light that there is a distinct scratch on the front element. As the lens is guaranteed to be free from imperfections, I am returning it to you for a replacement.

Will you kindly send me a new lens as soon as you can? I must have it by June 25, as I am leaving then on a camera trip to Utah.

You have my check for $120, dated June 12, in payment.

Yours very truly,

Martin H. Hanson

Martin H. Hanson

LETTERS OF APPLICATION

One of the most difficult and probably most important letters that you will have to write is the letter of application for a job. Of course it is impossible to say what will appeal to every employer, but there are certain general guides. In applying for work you usually have to fill out a printed application form. So will five hundred others applying for the same job. The letter you write will help you stand apart from the crowd.

A letter of application should be direct, sincere, and informative. It must not be vague; it must not grovel in undue modesty or boastfully promise what cannot be delivered. It should not include irrelevant personal information. Something is to be gained, as it often is in other types of writing, by putting yourself in the place of the person you are addressing. Suppose *you* were a busy personnel manager, shuffling through dozens of

137

letters of application. What would attract you favorably? Obviously, long-windedness would not.

An effective letter of application contains the following components:

1. An introductory statement in which the writer indicates that he or she has heard of a possible vacancy.
2. Personal data.
3. Record of education.
4. Personal experience in the job area.
5. References.
6. Request for an interview.

Probably the most important section is the one in which you outline how your experience or education has a vital bearing on the job for which you are applying. This is difficult to write, but it can also be decisive.

```
                              37 Twenty-third Street
                              Corvallis, Oregon  97330
                              April 10, 1975

Mr. F. C. McVey
Personnel Officer
Department of Parks and Recreation
City of Portland, Oregon
Portland, Oregon  97208

Dear Mr. McVey:

    Ms. Jane Ryan, one of the counsellors on your staff, has
informed me that you will need several guides for your resi-
dence camps this summer. I wish to apply for a job as a camp
guide.

    I am twenty years old and in excellent health.

    Two years ago, when I was eighteen, I graduated from
Central High School, where I took the college preparatory
course with emphasis on botany and geology. With this back-
ground, I am trained to point out many interesting natural
phenomena to the children.

    When I was in high school, I spent my weekends and vaca-
tions working for Bert's Camping Equipment, where I learned a
great deal about the operation and maintenance of various
types of outdoor equipment. Mr. Bert Jenkins will write you
about my work there.

    Since then I have worked at various jobs to earn money
for my college education. I am now finishing my first year in
the division of arts and sciences at Oregon State College.
```

After graduation from high school I spent a year working for the Ochoco Ranch, near Knappa, Oregon, where I taught hiking and horseback riding to beginners. Then last summer I entered the Yosemite Mountainclimbing Club, an experience that taught me a good deal about organizing outings of various kinds. Here I also learned to conduct nature trips. I believe that my experience should qualify me for this job.

The following employers have given me permission to use their names as references:

> Mr. H. D. Winslow
> Ochoco Ranch
> Knappa, Oregon 97601

> Mr. Karl Swensen
> Yosemite Mountainclimbing Club
> Yosemite National Park, California 95389

I would appreciate the opportunity to call at your office for an interview at any time that you designate. My telephone number is 753-5948.

> Yours very truly,
>
> *Jane Williamson*
>
> Jane Williamson

Sometimes a shorter letter of application, though for a more permanent position, may be used as a supplement to other records—college grades, statements of recommendation—that are forwarded to an employer by a placement service. Here is an example of such a letter, in which it is wise not to repeat much of the information that the employer already possesses in the official dossier.

> 1401 Ridge Avenue
> Columbus, Ohio 43215
> May 10, 1975

Dr. Leroy Faust
Superintendent of Schools
Shaker Heights, Ohio 44120

Dear Dr. Faust:

I understand from our local placement office that a position as third grade teacher is open for next fall in your school system. I believe I am qualified for that position. My record of training at the University School of Ohio State University is being forwarded to you, and as you will see, I maintained a "B" average at the University and completed all

139

necessary requirements in teacher training. I hold a temporary teacher's certificate for the state of Ohio. This letter
is meant to convey, in addition, my great enthusiasm for
teaching and my personal interest in becoming a part of your
system.

Though I have done no classroom teaching beyond that
provided by my university courses, I believe my devotion to
young people may in part compensate for inexperience. My enthusiasm for teaching those younger than I began early in my
life, and was increased by my years as a leader in Boy Scout
work. Summer jobs as a camp counselor, involving instruction
in outdoor activities for young children, improved my confidence in handling the eight-to-ten age group. Considerable
testimony from parents and from the children themselves convinced me that I have been successful in reaching these young
people.

Naturally I am eager to become a part of a school system
so well thought of as yours at Shaker Heights. I am available
on short notice for interview, at your convenience.

Sincerely yours,

James A. Clark

James A. Clark

SOME FAMILIAR FAULTS TO AVOID

Do not omit pronouns, prepositions, and articles where they
are grammatically necessary. If your letter should begin with *I*
or *we*, begin with *I* or *we*.

QUAINT
Received your letter yesterday.
Am writing to you in reply . . .
Have not heard from you . . .

BETTER
I received your letter yesterday.
I am writing to you . . .
I have not heard from you . . .

Do not close a letter with a sentence or a phrase introduced
by a participle.

140

INDIRECT

Hoping to hear from you soon . . .

Hoping for an early answer . . .

Thanking you again for your past favors . . .

Trusting to hear from you by return mail . . .

Do not write *yours, your favor,* or *your esteemed favor* for *letter.*

AFFECTED

In reply to yours of the 20th . . .

Your esteemed favor at hand, and in reply . . .

And avoid certain other trite and stilted expressions frequently used in business letters.

In reply would say . . .

Yours of the 10th inst. received . . .

And contents thereof noted . . .

Your valued favor . . .

And oblige, Yours truly . . .

Enclosed please find . . .

PUBLIC LETTERS

We have spoken of letters as, usually, private communications from one individual to another. The exception is the public letter in which the writer, while ostensibly addressing a single person, is in fact addressing a larger audience. An obvious example is the letter to the editor, in which the greeting *Dear Sir* might more accurately read *Dear Everybody* or *Dear World.* Many business letters, without being directed to the world, are intended for more than one reader—a committee, a sales force, a staff of officers. Modern duplicating methods are so cheap and efficient that any member of an organization may expect to find his semipublic report to a superior photocopied and spread all over the office. When this happens, of course, his errors of expression, his misspellings, and his vague logic are photocopied too.

The composition of a public, or semipublic, letter requires a special kind of skill. When addressing a group of individuals—a committee, for example—one must often be aware of the likes and dislikes of particular individuals among one's readers. Sometimes these likes and dislikes conflict. How can one persuade some of one's readers without offending others? What modified expression of one's own view might win a majority approval, or at least acquiescence? Astute corporate and bureaucratic officials often report that every word they write is chosen for its suitability to a variety of possible responses from readers whose prejudices may be, or are known to be, in conflict. If there is any excuse for the astounding circumlocutions of *officialese* (see §25g in the "Handbook"), it is the need to perform verbal high-wire acts to the detriment of precise, vigorous prose.

EXERCISES

EXERCISE 1, A LETTER OFFERING SUGGESTIONS. *Write a letter to the principal of your high school in which you suggest two or three specific ways students might be better prepared for your particular college.*

EXERCISE 2, A LETTER OF CORRECTION. *Write a letter to your college newspaper in which you correct a wrong impression produced by a news story that has just appeared in the paper. Make your letter courteous, dignified, and logical.*

EXERCISE 3, A LETTER REQUESTING A SPECIAL PRIVILEGE. *Write a letter to your dean or instructor in which you request permission to take your final examinations several days before the scheduled period. Give your reason clearly and convincingly.*

EXERCISE 4, A LETTER URGING ACTION. *As secretary of a student organization, write a letter to the members urging them to pay their dues.*

EXERCISE 5, A LETTER OF PROTEST. *As a member of the same organization, write a letter to its secretary protesting his undue anxiety about the members' dues.*

EXERCISE 6, A LETTER OF APPLICATION. *You plan to work at one of the national parks during the summer. Write a letter of application. Apply for some position that you could fill. Give adequate information about yourself and your qualifications.*

EXERCISE 7, A LETTER TO A CONGRESSMAN. *Write to your congressman requesting an interview with him when you visit Washington in a month's time.*

EXERCISE 8, A LETTER REQUESTING PAYMENT. *A man for whom you worked last summer owes you thirty dollars. Write him a letter that will induce him to pay you what he owes you.*

EXERCISE 9, A LETTER TO THE EDITOR. *Write to your local newspaper complaining about the ear-splitting noise made by motorcycles zooming past your house late at night. Use humor to address the problem and in such a way as to make even motorcyclists want to support you.*

THE ELEMENTS

OF STRUCTURE:

SENTENCES AND

PARAGRAPHS

1 *The Sentence:*

Grammatical Patterns

WHAT IS GRAMMAR?

Grammar is the systematic description of language as it is, or was, spoken. Definitions of grammar, however, need not be so succinct. The editors of *Webster's Third New International Dictionary,* who try to phrase their definitions for the layman as well as for the scientist, define grammar as "a branch of linguistic study that deals with the classes of words, their inflections or other means of indicating relation to each other, and their functions and relations in the sentence as employed according to established usage and that is sometimes extended to include related matter such as phonology, prosody, language history, orthography, orthoepy, etymology, or semantics."[1]

The subject of this book is the grammar of contemporary American English, and a genuinely scientific or linguistic approach to it would develop a *descriptive grammar,* a grammar in which there were no rules handed down but, instead, generalizations derived by observing at large how all persons speak and write American English.

Distinction Between Grammar and Usage

Unfortunately, a strictly descriptive approach to our language poses a problem. The scientific grammarian recognizes no such thing as good grammar or bad grammar, for the way each individual speaks and writes is *a* valid grammar, following

---

[1] *Webster's Third New International Dictionary,* p. 986.

patterns acquired or established during a lifetime. To acknowledge only that everyone has a grammar, however, is to ignore the practical consideration that a grammar must be reasonably understandable to at least two people if language is to serve its function, which is to let Ferdinand tell Isabella that he is unexpectedly called to a business meeting in Las Vegas, that he has lost the car keys, or that the laundromat won't take Canadian quarters. If we concede that grammar is not only a unique and variable phenomenon but a potential and desirable common medium, we open the door to the *prescriptive grammarian*, the grammarian ready to say, "The grammar I choose shall be the common one." Oppressive as that declaration sounds, two facts support it: it has a practical foundation and a well-established reputation. Many people do think there is a right and a wrong way to put words together. As long as that belief survives, and it shows little sign of going away, there is reason for learning what people think is correct. The problem is that the term *grammar* can cover both the scientific analysis of language as it comes spontaneously off a multitude of speakers' tongues and the concept of a proper and an improper speech. Only the second meaning involves the speaker's judgment, the conscious selection of one phrasing over another in response to some external measure of propriety, such as occasion, subject, audience, argument, or simply the opinion of society. The linguist dealing with issues of grammatical judgment uses the term *usage* to avoid confusing the imposed conventions of language with the grammar of unpremeditated utterance. For our purposes, however, the distinction is unnecessary. Correct usage, like any other form of functioning language, has its grammar too. A handbook having as its objective the improvement of its readers' use of language must make judgments, make comparisons, and point out appropriate and effective language patterns in terms of the standards of its day. When we speak of grammar in this book, we mean the descriptive grammar of usage as defined by the speech and, especially, by the writings of men and women whose sensitivity to the precise, effective use of language has earned them faithful audiences and enduring respect. They at once follow and lead the conventions of correct usage.

148

It is important to remember that correct usage can be led. No grammar known has proved unchangeable like the law of gravity, and good grammar is constantly in the process of modification. That is why we map even its cultivated landscape descriptively, in terms of what is actually happening.

Is a Knowledge of Grammar Helpful?

Many students, at some time or other, question the value of a knowledge of grammar as an aid to better writing. What part of grammar is useful? What part is useless? The answer must be different for every different person. Many people write well and speak well without knowing much about grammar, but for those who by reading this book admit their capacity for self-improvement, grammar is both a convenient chest of tools and a practical code of communication. Like a chest of tools it enables the student to build effective sentences and to repair faulty ones. It is a code or a technical vocabulary, understood by both teacher and learner, necessary in learning and teaching.

How, for instance, can a student correct the eccentricities of such a sentence as, "This is strictly between he and I," if he knows nothing about pronouns, about prepositions, or about the conventional uses of the objective case? How can a teacher explain the punctuation of phrases and clauses in a series if the student does not know what phrases and clauses are? When a person says, "I done pretty good in the test today," he expresses his thought with absolute clearness—but clearness is not enough. How can this speaker learn to make the statement in a more generally acceptable form, and how can a teacher help him learn it, if he does not have some understanding of verb forms in current usage? Or the accepted use of adjectives and adverbs? A knowledge of grammatical terms will at least provide a common ground of explanation between student and instructor, and a mutual understanding of the technical vocabulary involved is the first requisite in the explanation of any procedure.

THE PARTS OF SPEECH
OR WORD CLASSES

Words are classified according to their *function* or *use in the sentence* into what are called parts of speech. Notice that in this system of classification it is the *use in the sentence* that always determines the part of speech of a word in a given situation. Many words, especially those that have been in the language for a long time, have acquired several uses, just as they have acquired many meanings. In your desk dictionary, look up a few simple, everyday words that occur to you as you glance about the room: *glass, floor, wall.* You immediately think of such uses as *the glass in the window, you live in a glass house, we glassed in our porch,* and you see the word *glass* used as a noun, as an adjective, and as a verb. Now make the same test for *floor* and *wall.*

The parts of speech are *nouns, pronouns, verbs, adverbs, adjectives, prepositions, conjunctions,* and *interjections.*

The Noun

A *noun,* also called a *substantive,* is a word that names something. It may name a person, a thing, a place, an animal, a plant, an idea, a quality, a substance, a state, an action. Use each of the following properly in sentences and try to determine under which classification each noun falls: *man, lion, city, oak, book, liquids, beauty, affection, flight, stupor, relativity.* When a noun names a person, a place, an object, it is called a *concrete noun;* when it names a quality, an idea, a mental concept, it is called an *abstract noun* Concrete nouns name physical, visible, tangible objects; abstract nouns name things that do not have a physical substance. For the practical value of this information, see § § 21, 24, 26. A proper noun is the official name of some individual person, place, or object; a common noun names any one of a class or kind. In English, proper nouns are capitalized; common nouns are not. See §8.

NOUNS

When the *inverter* was fixed, the *gantry* moved away, the *cherrypicker* maneuvered its *cab* back outside the *capsule,* and the *count* went along

150

smoothly for 21 *minutes* before it suddenly stopped again. This time the *technicians* wanted to double-check a *computer* which would help predict the *trajectory* of the *capsule* and its impact *point* in the *recovery area.*

—ALAN B. SHEPARD, JR., *We Seven*

The *knowledge* he has acquired with *age* is not the *knowledge* of *formulas,* or *forms* of *words,* but of *people, places, actions*—a *knowledge* not gained by *words* but by *touch, sight, sound, victories, failures, sleeplessness, devotion, love*—the human *experiences* and *emotions* of this *earth* and of oneself and other *men;* and perhaps, too, a little *faith,* and a little *reverence* for the *things* you cannot see.

—ADLAI STEVENSON, speech at Princeton

The Verb

A *verb* is a word (or group of words) that expresses action, occurrence, being, or mode of being. See §3 and §6.

VERBS

The high grey-flannel fog of winter *closed off* the Salinas Valley from the sky and from all the rest of the world. On every side it *sat* like a lid on the mountains and *made* of the great valley a closed pot. On the broad, level land floor the gang plows *bit* deep and *left* the black earth shining like metal where the shares *had cut.* On the foothill ranches across the Salinas River, the yellow stubble fields *seemed to be bathed* in pale cold sunshine, but there *was* no sunshine in the valley now in December. The thick willow scrub along the river *flamed* with sharp and positive yellow leaves.

It *was* a time of quiet and of waiting. The air *was* cold and tender. A light wind *blew up* from the southwest so that the farmers *were* mildly hopeful of a good rain before long; but fog and rain *do not go together.*

—JOHN STEINBECK, "The Chrysanthemums"

The Pronoun

A *pronoun* is usually defined as a word that takes the place of a noun. And, like a noun, can be called a *substantive.* This brief definition, useful enough as a practical shortcut, must be modified by pointing out that certain pronouns, such as *none, nobody, anything,* and the impersonal *it,* do not take the place of any noun but are words more or less arbitrarily classified by grammarians and lexicographers as pronouns. Pronouns are further classified as personal, demonstrative, relative, interrogative, and indefinite. See §4. The following table indicates how certain words usually function in these classes. It must be understood, however, that some of these words may also be used as other parts of speech.

PERSONAL
I, you, he, she, it, they, we, them, thee, thou

DEMONSTRATIVE
this, that, these, those

RELATIVE
who, which, what, that, whoever, whatever, whichever

INTERROGATIVE
who, which, what

INDEFINITE
one, none, some, any, anyone, anybody, someone, each, somebody, nobody, everyone, everybody, either, neither, both

The Adjective

An *adjective* is a word that modifies (describes or limits) a noun or pronoun. It may denote quality, quantity, number, or extent. The articles *a, an, the,* and the possessive forms of nouns and pronouns, when used to modify nouns, are here considered in the classification of adjectives. Pronouns have two forms of the possessive: the first form (*my, our, your, her, his, its, their*) when placed before a noun functions as an adjective; the second form (*mine, ours, yours, his, hers, theirs*) functions as a pronoun.

ADJECTIVES
It was *an eloquent, sharp, ugly, earthly* countenance. *His* hands were *small* and *prehensile,* with fingers knotted like *a* cord; and they were continually flickering in front of him in *violent* and *expressive* pantomime.

—R. L. STEVENSON

The place through which he made *his* way at leisure was one of *those* receptacles for *old* and *curious* things which seem to crouch in *odd* corners of *this* town, and to hide *their musty* treasures from *the public* eye in jealousy and distress.

—Charles Dickens

One of *our* men saw *your* horse throw you and break through *the* fence. They left *their* work, at *my* suggestion, and ran to see if you needed help.

PRONOUNS
That horse of *mine* is a problem. May I borrow one of *yours* to get me back to the ranch?

The Adverb

An *adverb* is a word that modifies a verb, an adjective, or another adverb. Less commonly an adverb modifies a preposition, a phrase, a clause, or a whole sentence. Adverbs express the following relations in a sentence: time, place, manner, degree, frequency, affirmation or negation. See also §5.

TIME
It will rain *tomorrow*. The guests will *soon* be here. They are *now* arriving.

PLACE
Come *in*. Leave your umbrellas *outside*. Place them *here,* please.

MANNER
She expresses herself *crudely*. Her sister sings *beautifully*. She learns *quickly*.

DEGREE
You are *very* kind. This is *too* good. It is *entirely too* expensive.

FREQUENCY
She is *always* pleasant. She called *twice*. It rains *often*. It *never* snows.

AFFIRMATION OR NEGATION
Do *not* go there. *Certainly,* he will return. *Yes,* he was there. *No,* you must *not* see him. *Perhaps* he will call you. *Undoubtedly* he is busy.

153

The Preposition

A *preposition* is a word used to show the relation between a substantive (noun or pronoun), called the object of the preposition, and some other word in the sentence. A preposition thus introduces a group of words called a phrase, which may be used as an adjective, as an adverb, or, less frequently, as a noun. Many prepositions are single, short words:

at the game, *by* the house, *in* the room, *for* payment, *from* home, *off* duty, *on* land, *above* the clouds, *after* the ball, *around* her neck, *before* dawn, *behind* his back, *between* dances, *below* the covering, *over* the top, *through* the skin, *until* daybreak

There are also a number of so-called group prepositions, the use of which you can readily see:

by means of, in front of, on account of, in place of, with respect to, according to, because of, in addition to, in spite of.

The Conjunction

A *conjunction* is a word that connects words, phrases, or clauses. Conjunctions are either coordinating or subordinating. Adverbs used as connectives, either coordinating or subordinating, are called *conjunctive adverbs.*

The words commonly used as coordinating conjunctions are *and, but, for, or, nor, yet, both—and, not only—but also, either—or, neither—nor.* In contemporary usage, *so* is used as a coordinating conjunction in loose, informal writing and in speech, but its use should be avoided in most serious writing except in direct quotations.

Some of the words used as subordinating conjunctions are *if, although, though, that, because, since, so that, in order that, as, unless, before, than, where, when.*

Correlative conjunctions (conjunctions used in pairs) are *both—and, not only—but also, either—or, neither—nor.*

Some words commonly functioning as adverbs may be used as conjunctions: *how, why, where, before, after.* Such connectives as *however, therefore, nevertheless, hence,* and *accordingly* are often classified as conjunctive adverbs. In modern prose they are commonly used as transitional expressions. There is no profit in worrying over the question of whether they are transitions or conjunctive adverbs; the only important fact here is that in modern writing these expressions, with the exception of *hence, thus,* and *still,* are usually not placed at the beginnings of clauses in compound sentences. They function more accurately when they are set within the clauses. See §14 for a discussion of the punctuation that should be used with these transitional expressions.

The Interjection

An *interjection* is a word or group of words used as an exclamation expressing sudden or strong feeling. Note that an exclamation point is not the inevitable punctuation of an interjection. For most interjections, especially the mild ones, a comma or a period is sufficient. Examples are *Ah, Alas, Oh.*

THE VERBALS

The *verbals*—gerunds, participles, and infinitives—are mutations. They are derived from verbs and have some of the forms and functions of verbs, but they serve primarily as other parts of speech. Verbals may have tense forms, they may take complements, and they may be modified by adverbs. In these contexts they are like verbs. Their primary function, however, is as nouns, adjectives, and adverbs.

The Gerund

A *gerund* is a verbal used as a noun.

The man began *shouting* incoherently. [Note that *shouting* is the object of the verb *began.* It is modified by the adverb *incoherently.*]

Writing a poem is not easy. [*Writing* is the subject of the verb *is,* and has *poem* as its object.]

His eligibility for office was established by his *having been* so successful as governor. [Note the form of the gerund. Note also that it takes the adjective *successful* as its complement.]

The Participle

A *participle* is a verbal used as an adjective. It is, of course, also used as a part of a verb phrase, as in "He *was reading* a book." It may appear in a few uses with an adverbial sense, as in "They came *bringing* gifts" or "The boys ran off, *shouting* protests." Our main concern, however, is with the adjective use of the participle: "*driving* rhythm; *framed* picture." Note also such sentences as "He *was asking* you a question" and "Teasing him was *asking* for trouble," in which *asking* is a part of the verb phrase in the first combination and a gerund in the second.

The *tired* men again faced the *howling* wind. *Gripping* the rope, they slowly pulled the *mired* truck past the *waiting* soldiers. They noted a staff car *turning* in their direction. *Having saved* the truck, they relaxed for a moment. [Note here the tense forms and the positions of the participles.]

The Infinitive

An *infinitive* is a verbal that may be used as a noun, an adjective, or an adverb. The infinitive may be recognized by its sign *to*. Occasionally the sign is omitted.

Mary did not want *to drive* her car. [Used as a noun object of the verb *did want*. Note that it takes an object.]

Mary hoped *to be taken* home. [Note the passive form.]

We did not dare *refuse* her request. [Note the omission of the sign *to*.]

She had no car *to drive*. [Used as an adjective to modify *car*]

She was happy *to come* with us. [In adverbial sense, modifies *happy*]

To watch her happiness was a pleasure. [In noun sense, as subject of verb *was*]

156

EXERCISES

In such use the infinitive can replace or be replaced by its participle, as, "*Watching* her happiness was a pleasure." Note, however, that the meaning changes slightly.

EXERCISES

EXERCISE 1, PARTS OF SPEECH AND VERBALS. *Identify the parts of speech and the verbals in the following selections:*

I have but one lamp by which my feet are guided, and that is the lamp of experience. I know of no way of judging of the future but by the past. And judging by the past, I wish to know what there has been in the conduct of the British ministry for the last ten years to justify those hopes with which gentlemen have been pleased to solace themselves and the house.

—PATRICK HENRY

We hold these truths to be self-evident, that all men are created equal, that they are endowed by their Creator with certain unalienable rights, that among these are life, liberty, and the pursuit of happiness. That, to secure these rights, governments are instituted among men, deriving their just powers from the consent of the governed.

—*The Declaration of Independence*

EXERCISE 2, VERBALS. *Identify the verbals in the following sentences. The verbals are gerunds, participles, and infinitives.*

1. Attending a church wedding is fun; I usually like to go.
2. Being a devoted clubwoman, Mother has social obligations to consider.
3. Father, a tired and harried executive, tries to avoid being involved in her affairs.
4. Coming home, still absorbed in his office problems, he tries to be courteous to a roomful of women without revealing that he is unable to recall a single name.
5. Having finished his social chores, Father retreats to his study.
6. One day Mother took my protesting father to church to watch two strangers being married.

7. The day being hot and muggy, Father sat there sweltering in his tight formal suit.
8. Wishing to avoid an argument, Father pretended to be enjoying himself.
9. Sitting in the next pew were two old and respected friends of the family.
10. Having bowed politely, he began to study the expressions on the faces of the assembled guests.

THE ELEMENTS OF THE SIMPLE SENTENCE

Defined in terms of form or pattern, a *sentence* is a basic unit of language, a communication in words, having as its core at least one independent finite verb with its subject. In addition to being a basic unit, the sentence is a natural one. It nearly always contains two pieces of information the listener as a user of language is conditioned to expect from it: who or what is involved, and what does he, she, or it do or feel. When it leaves out one or the other component, the sentence, if it is still a sentence, is responsible for justifying the sense of insufficiency it creates. Because examples without both parts are uncommon, we speak of sentences in general as complete units, capable of standing alone without the support of supplementary comment.

On the basis of the types of clauses, coordinate and subordinate, that enter into their structure, sentences are classified as simple, complex, and compound.

The following sentence diagrams are included to help you identify the main parts of a sentence. In a *simple sentence* the parts are referred to as *subject* and *verb,* and the diagram divides them in the following way:

$$S \mid V$$

A sentence containing a *direct object* looks like this in diagram form:

Addition of an *indirect object* is signified in the following way:

Subjective and *objective complements* are identified by slanted lines:

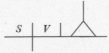

Articles, adjectives, prepositions, and other *modifiers* are indicated by slanted lines below the main line:

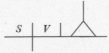

Whenever a *phrase* is *subject* or *object* in the sentence, it is represented by the following symbol:

Subject and Verb: The Independent Clause

The *simple sentence* contains a single independent clause. In it, the subject, the verb, or both may be made up of two or more things or actions. A multiple subject or verb is a *compound* one.

> The *independent clause* is a basic unit of grammar that will occur again, and what it is should be understood now to avoid confusion later. An independent clause, which may be a sentence in its own right, as the definition of a simple sentence implies, is a group of words containing a subject and a verb, and perhaps a modifier, that relies on no external information for meaning. The independent clause is complete, just as the average sentence is complete, which is why the independent clause constitutes the basic form of sentence. The examples below are both sentences *and* independent clauses.

S   V
Men are working.

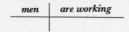

S   S   V
Boys and girls play.

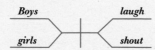

S   S   V   V
Boys and girls laugh and shout.

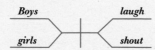

Complements

Some verbs express a general action, and the sentences they
help to form have a sense of completeness. Other verbs, however, require a third element—in addition to subject and
verb—to form a complete expression. That element is called a
complement (related to *completion*). There are three main types of
complements: *direct objects, indirect objects,* and *subjective complements.* Less common are the *objective complement* and the *retained
object.*

The Direct Object. The *direct object* of a verb denotes that
which is immediately acted upon or receives the direct action of
the verb.

S   V   O
Mary bought a hat.

Mary	bought	hat

V   O
Read this book.

(You)	read	book

160

V   S   V   O
Did you hear him?

The Indirect Object. The *indirect object* names, without the use of a preposition, the one to whom or for whom the action involving a direct object is done.

Mother told *me* a story.

He taught *us* a lesson.
I gave the *dog* a bath.

Note that when *to* or *for* is expressed, the substantive following becomes the object of a preposition, as in "Mother told a story to me," "Dr. Jones taught mathematics to us," "She gave a dollar to the man."

The Subjective Complement. The *subjective complement* refers to the subject and describes or limits it. It is often called a *predicate substantive* if it is a noun or pronoun, and a *predicate adjective* if it is an adjective. See also §5.

Tom is a *major* now. [Predicate substantive]

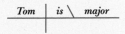

It looks *good* to me. [Predicate adjective]

$$\text{It} \mid \text{looks} \diagdown \text{good}$$

A common error committed by beginning writers is the misuse of adverbs for subjective complements. In the sentence above, "It looks *well* to me" would be incorrect—and sound pretentious as well. Verbs such as *seem, become, go, remain,* and *prove* often invite the misuse of an adverb complement. Verbs of the senses—*feel, look, smell, sound, taste*—also require adjective subjective complements.

161

He felt *bad* about it. [not *badly*]

It tastes *sour* to me. [not *sourly*]

The air smells *foul* tonight. [not *foully*]

The Objective Complement. The *objective complement,* used with verbs such as *elect, choose, make, call, appoint,* and the like, refers to the direct object.

They made her their *chairperson.*

They	made / chairperson	her

They called him *crazy.*

The Retained Object. The *retained object* is used with a verb in the passive voice.

They were given *food.*

They	were given	food

He was taught a good *lesson.*

A simple sentence may have adjectives, adverbs, and phrases as modifiers. Do not be confused by the number of these modifiers. Diagramming the sentence will help you to show it is still a simple sentence.

The little boy gave his mother a red rose.

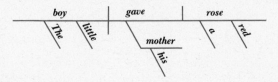

Phrases

In its general, loose sense, a *phrase* is any group of words. Thus we say that a man "phrases his thoughts" when he puts them into words, or that a woman expresses her ideas in "well-balanced phrases" when her sentences are well built and rhythmical. The word *phrase* in its general sense has its legitimate place in the language. In the study of grammar, however, the word refers to one of three kinds: the verb phrase, the prepositional phrase, or the verbal phrase.

The verb phrase, which is not discussed in this chapter, is actually a verb consisting of more than one word, such as *have been persuaded, has loved, will be honored.*

The Prepositional Phrase. A *prepositional phrase* consists of a preposition, its object, and modifiers of the phrase or any of its parts.

A prepositional phrase may be used as an adjective.

A graduate *with a knowledge of mathematics* and a desire *for advancement* should find a job *in one of the new industries.* [Note that the first phrase modifies *graduate,* the second modifies *knowledge,* the third modifies *desire,* the fourth modifies *job,* and the fifth *one.* Note also that the second phrase is a part of the first and the fifth is a part of the fourth.]

He must have studied several subjects *of no particular value.* [The phrase, a modifier of *subjects,* has within it two modifiers. *Must have studied* is an example of a verb phrase.]

The father *of the child* [adjective] watched *from the window* [adverb].

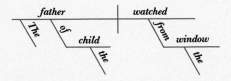

A prepositional phrase may be used as an adverb.

Slowly he walked *toward the door.* [The phrase functions as an adverb of place or direction, modifying the verb *walked.*]

She sat *on a stool* and selected a cherry *from the basket.*

If you are angry *at your best friend,* you must be careful *with your speech.* [Here the phrases function as adverbs modifying adjectives.]

163

Under the bridge two tramps had built a fire.

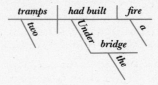

A prepositional phrase may be used as a noun. This use is quite rare.

The best time for study is *in the morning. On the mantel* would be a good place for it. [The first phrase is used as a noun subjective complement; the second is used as the subject of the verb *would be.*] *For me to criticize his work* would be presumptuous. [With *for*]

The best time *for study* is *in the morning.* [As adjective and as noun]

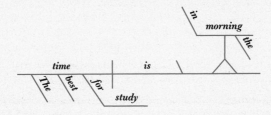

The Verbal Phrase. A *verbal phrase* consists of a participle, a gerund, or an infinitive and its complements and modifiers.

The Participial Phrase. A participial phrase consists of a participle, its complement, if it has one, and any modifiers of the phrase or any of its parts. It is generally used as an adjective. A thorough understanding of the uses of participial phrases is of practical value to any writer because their misuse results in a stylistic fault known as the *dangling modifier.* For a discussion of dangling modifiers, see § 29.

The car *now turning the corner* belongs to my father. [The phrase modifies *car.* The participle is modified by the adverb *now,* and it has for its object the noun *corner.*]

The letter, *stamped and sealed,* lay on the table. *Distracted by the sudden noise,* the speaker hesitated and then stopped in his oration. [Note the possible positions of·the participle in relation to the word it modifies.]

164

Having given him the required amount, I left the store. [Notice that within the participial phrase there is another participle, *required,* modifying *amount.*]

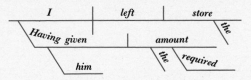

The Absolute Phrase. The absolute phrase is made up of a noun or pronoun (a substantive) followed by a participle. The substantive has no grammatical relation to any word in the sentence outside the phrase; it stands as an independent element. An absolute phrase cannot become a dangler. Note the following examples carefully.

Our assignment having been finished, we asked for our pay. [*Having been finished* modifies *assignment.*]

If the same thought is expressed as a participial phrase, *"Having finished our assignment,* we asked for our pay," it is no longer grammatically independent of the rest of the sentence. In that case the assignment has to have been finished *by* somebody or something that the remainder of the sentence is required to furnish, whereas in the absolute phrase it is simply given as finished by a person or persons unknown.

The class having been dismissed, the teacher wearily picked up his books.
We hunted toward the north, *each taking one side of the ridge.* [The substantive is *each.*]

The Gerund Phrase. A gerund phrase consists of a gerund, its complement, if it has one, and any modifiers of the phrase or any of its parts. A gerund phrase is always used as a noun; it may therefore function as the subject of a verb, as a complement, or as the object of a preposition.

Arguing with him does little good. *Piloting a speed boat* requires great skill. [In both sentences the gerund phrase is used as a subject. By this time you should be able to identify the modifiers and the complements.]

165

Willard enjoyed *watching television.* [Direct object].

You can get the address by *stopping at our house.* [Object of preposition]

I should call that *violating the spirit of our agreement.* [The phrase is used as an objective complement referring to *that.*]

Hearing that song brings back sad memories to me. [Subject of verb]

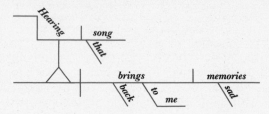

Mary objected to *my telling the story.* [Object of preposition]

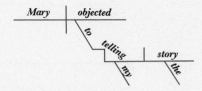

The Infinitive Phrase. An infinitive phrase, like other verbal phrases, may have a complement and modifiers. In addition it may have what is called the *assumed subject* of the infinitive. The assumed subject of an infinitive is in the objective case. An infinitive phrase may be used as an adverb, an adjective, or a noun.

We stood up *to see better.* [Modifies the verb]

We are happy *to have you back with us.* [Modifies an adjective]

Whether to believe him or to call mother was a real problem for me. [A noun, used as the subject of the sentence]

We knew him *to be the worst troublemaker in school.* [Notice that the infinitive *to be* has *him* as its assumed subject. "We knew him; he was the worst troublemaker in school" puts an actual subject in place of the assumed one, and, incidentally, takes the sentence out of the *simple* class.]

My orders were *to deliver the guns.* [Noun used as subjective complement]

166

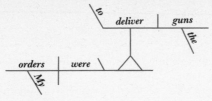

I am happy *to see you again.*

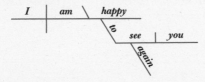

She wanted me *to drive the car.*

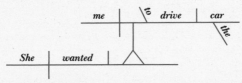

EXERCISES

EXERCISE 1, PARTICIPLES. *Pick out the participles in the following sentences and tell what word each participle modifies.*

1. The astronauts' spacecraft is a complicated machine.
2. Compressed to a minimum, it is the size of a telephone booth.
3. In spite of its reduced area, it contains thousands of instruments.
4. In it are over seven miles of wire winding back and forth.
5. Only a genius could design this amazing machine.
6. The engineers were faced with several puzzling limitations.
7. Every bit of needed equipment had to be miniaturized.
8. Having succeeded in solving one problem, they faced another.
9. The completed system had to have duplicates for safety.
10. In addition, this seemingly snarled and confused mechanism had to be made to function automatically.

167

EXERCISE 2, PARTICIPLES AND GERUNDS. *Pick out each gerund and participle in the following sentences and tell how each is used.*

1. Most students entering college enjoy being welcomed to a new experience.
2. Having been duly warned and advised, they return to their normal routines.
3. Some students, impressed and perhaps disturbed by the advice, resolve to become devoted scholars.
4. Urged on by curiosity, some begin exploring their new and exciting surroundings.
5. Finding old friends and making new contacts are in themselves rewarding experiences.
6. There are always a few lost, unhappy souls who, unable to make new friends, amuse themselves sadly by browsing in the library.
7. Some even think of writing home to surprised and pleased parents, thereby revealing their homesickness without actually admitting it.
8. The happiest are the extroverts, adjusted to life anywhere, taking life day by day as it comes and not worrying much about it.
9. Classes soon start, and then loneliness is forgotten in the excitement of meeting new professors, buying books, and getting a routine of studying established.
10. College life becomes a challenging adventure, demanding much from each student and giving much in return.

EXERCISE 3, PHRASES. *In the following sentences pick out each phrase and tell whether it is prepositional, participial, gerund, or infinitive.*

1. My brother urged me not to miss the concert.
2. I telephoned Margie early in the afternoon.
3. Thanking me warmly, Margie agreed to accompany me.
4. Getting two tickets was the problem of the moment.
5. Knowing the condition of my bank account, I decided to get help from my friends.
6. A friend in need seems to be the only kind of friend that I have.
7. I found everyone in great need of financial help.
8. In despair I decided to test my brother's fraternal loyalty.

9. He had a long sermon to give me, but in the end he agreed to help me.
10. Looking very pretty, Margie added beauty to an evening of exciting music.

THE ELEMENTS OF THE COMPOUND SENTENCE

A *compound sentence,* as the name indicates, is made by compounding or joining two or more simple sentences. The parts are of equal or *coordinate* grammatical weight. Each has its own subject and verb. Such joining may involve the use of conjunctions and proper punctuation. See §§13 and 14. The examples used here are shorter than the typical compound sentence.

She should not take risks; she has three small children.
I warned her, but she was persistent.

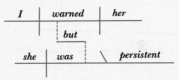

The walk was slippery, and she fell and hurt herself badly.

Note that the parts of a compound sentence must relate to each other. Do not make two independent sentences into a compound one. Similarly, writing is smoother if two related thoughts are compounded rather than given as two separate sentences.

THE ELEMENTS OF THE COMPLEX SENTENCE

We have seen that simple sentences are units structurally and grammatically complete, and that compound sentences can be broken up into such complete and independent units. A

169

thought expressed in a simple sentence is thereby given primary rank or importance. Ideas expressed in the coordinate units of a compound sentence have equal weight. It is of course quite possible for communication to function, as it were, on a single plane without degrees of structural emphasis. Modern English, however, has developed a system whereby many differences in the relationship of one idea to another, or of one fact to another, can be expressed by differences in grammatical structure. It has developed and perfected the dependent clause and the complex sentence.

Clauses

In the many possible variations of the useful complex sentence, the notion that main clauses are for big ideas and subordinate clauses are for lesser ideas is often completely lost. Perhaps it is better to think of a complex sentence only in grammatical terms—main or coordinate clauses are at the top level structurally; dependent clauses are dependent structurally. In the following examples pick out what you think is the important idea in each sentence and then decide whether it is in the grammatically independent clause.

He had a feeling that his number was up, that he would die on the beach.

It seems that the entire invasion fleet was heading for the wrong beach.

It should be added that a sudden and unexpected last-minute order from Hitler kept the Germans from moving up their panzer divisions.

A *complex sentence* has at least one main clause, grammatically independent and able to stand alone, and one or more dependent clauses.

Like the independent clause, the *dependent clause* will appear in numerous grammatical and mechanical situations, and knowing one when it appears is important to forming and punctuating sentences correctly. A dependent clause must hang on to an independent clause to have meaning. The clause *the cheaper of the two dishwashers ranked higher in the performance ratings* leaves no one in doubt as to what is involved or what it did. By themselves, the words *which we did not buy* don't even make a splash in the imagination as they fall. A combination works: *The cheaper of the two dishwashers, which we did not buy, ranked higher in the performance ratings.* Because *which we did not buy* only adds to a thought instead of constituting one, its position in the expression of the thought is *subordinate,* of lesser importance; the thought it is added to is a *main* clause. The subordinate or dependent clause may function as a noun, an adjective (as in the example), or an adverb.

A dependent clause is often joined to the main clause by a relative pronoun, *who, which, that,* or by one of the numerous subordinating conjunctions, such as *after, although, as, because, before, if, since, unless, when, where, why,* but sometimes the sign of dependence or subordination is omitted, as in the following examples:

The progress [*that*] *they made in college* depended on the friends [*whom*] *they had found.*

I realized [*that*] *he had not understood the error* [*that*] *I had pointed out to him.*

The boy [*whom*] *he referred to* was the one who had begged, "Say [*that*] *it isn't so, Mister!*"

The Noun Clause. A dependent clause may be used as a noun.

AS SUBJECT OF A VERB
What he says means little to me.

AS OBJECT OF A VERB
She thought *that she would go to Paris.*

AS SUBJECTIVE COMPLEMENT
Her explanation was *that she was bored with life.*

171

AS OBJECT OF A VERBAL

Be sure to accept *whatever she offers you.*

AS OBJECT OF A PREPOSITION

It depends upon *how many can play Saturday.*

AS AN APPOSITIVE

His first argument, *that women are inferior to men,* was easily proved false.

EXAMPLES

What he told the officers was never revealed. [Noun clause used as subject]

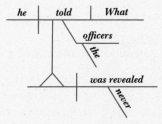

The teacher said *that the answer was correct.* [Noun clause used as object]

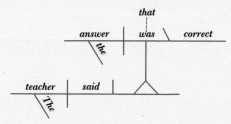

Give it to *whoever calls for it.* [Noun clause used as object of a preposition]

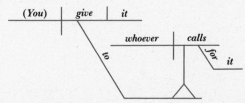

The Adjective Clause. A dependent clause may be used as an adjective. Adjective clauses are either restrictive or nonrestrictive. An important thing to remember in this connection is that restrictive clauses are *not* set off by commas. See §13.

R E S T R I C T I V E

We needed a car *that was rugged and light.*

Do you know anyone *who has two tickets to sell?*

A teacher *who speaks poor English* is badly handicapped.

Try to remember the exact time *when you saw the accident.*

Isn't this the shop *where you found your bargains?*

N O N R E S T R I C T I V E

I have been reading *Jaws, which was written by Peter Benchley.*

We camped that night near Maupin, *where we found some moss agates.*

My father, *who is a lapidary,* was delighted with the find.

I am rooming with John Cooper, *who is now a sophomore.*

A restrictive clause helps to identify the word it modifies. It points it out. It says, "That particular person or thing and no other." In the second group of sentences, no identification is added. The person or thing is already identified, sometimes by name, sometimes by other means.

Note that if you are looking for structural signals to recognize clauses, the words *where, when,* and *why* may introduce adjective clauses. Think of them in terms of "place where," "time when," and "reason why," and you will not be confused. These three words, however, have other uses too. See the examples given below.

A D J E C T I V E   C L A U S E S

We found no reason *why he should be held.*

He was seen near the place *where the crime had been committed.*

It was the hour *when graves and tired students yawn.*

This is the boy *who brought the papers.* [Adjective clause modifying *boy*]

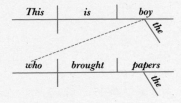

In the examples below the words introduce clauses that are not adjectival.

ADVERBIAL CLAUSES

You will begin writing *when I give the signal.* [Modifies the verb]

Put it back *where you found it.* [Modifies the verb]

NOUN CLAUSES

We never did know *where he found it.* [Object of *did know*]

Why he went home is a mystery to me. [Subject of verb *is*]

The Adverbial Clause. A dependent clause may be used as an adverb to show time, place, cause, condition, concession, comparison, manner, purpose, or result.

TIME

You must sit still *while the orchestra plays.*

Parents may come in *before the main doors are opened.*

He played professional football *until he was drafted.*

After you finish your test, hand in your papers to me.

PLACE

I will go *where they send me.*

He hid *where no one thought to look.*

CAUSE

He grows roses *because he loves flowers.*

Since no one volunteered, James finished the work himself.

I can't go with you, *as that would be breaking my promise.*

CONDITION

If I were he I should invest in tax-exempt bonds.

Children will not be admitted *unless they are accompanied by their parents.*

In case you have no parents, any adult will do.

CONCESSION

I agreed to go with him *although I was very tired.*

No matter what he says, I shall not be angry.

174

COMPARISON

He is as honest *as the day is long.*

Jack is older *than I am.*

MANNER

Marion looks *as if she were ready for bed.*

He speaks *as a tactful man should speak.*

PURPOSE

They came to America *in order that they might find religious freedom.*

RESULT

The night was so stormy *that we could not see the highway.*

ADDITIONAL EXAMPLES

Carol is prettier *than I am.* [An adverbial clause of comparison]

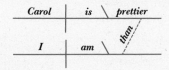

The whistle blew *before the ball was fumbled.* [An adverbial clause of time, modifying the verb *blew*]

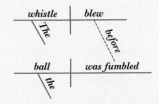

We found no reason why he should be held *until he is arraigned.* [An adverbial clause modifying an adjective clause]

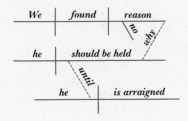

175

EXERCISES

EXERCISE 1, NOUN CLAUSES. *In the following sentences pick out each noun clause and tell whether it is used as the subject of a verb, as the complement of a verb or verbal, or as the object of a preposition.*

1. At noon they told me that I was selected to be the first to jump.
2. Why they handled the selection in such a way puzzled me at the time.
3. I forgot to tell them what my target was.
4. My assistant and I joked about what we had planned to do that night.
5. Then I remembered that my wife must be informed.
6. The starter wanted to show me what I should do with the timing watch.
7. Of course I realized that he was joking.
8. I had expected severe anxiety after the final count and the start.
9. That there was little nausea came as a pleasant surprise.
10. I announced that everything was going according to schedule.

EXERCISE 2, ADJECTIVE CLAUSES. *Pick out the adjective clauses in the following sentences and tell what word each clause modifies. Be able to tell which clauses are restrictive and which are nonrestrictive.*

1. I have been reading books that tell about human rights.
2. One writer asserts there is no such thing as a natural right.
3. His contention, which I agree with, is that all rights are made by man.
4. I asked him where we got the rights that are mentioned in the Declaration of Independence.
5. The author I speak of is a man whom my father knew at Harvard.
6. He rubbed his chin with a gesture that indicated he was thinking deeply.
7. I understood the reason why he was careful about his choice of words.
8. "The rights you mention," he said, "are rights that men had to fight for."

9. We talked about the reasons why Jefferson called them unalienable.
10. It is a pleasure to know people with whom you can discuss ideas.

EXERCISE 3, ADVERBIAL CLAUSES. *Pick out the adverbial clauses in the following sentences.*

1. The rain that had been threatening us all day came before we had finished our work.
2. We were working where the rocks had to be blasted out.
3. Because the traffic was heavy, we kept one lane of the road open.
4. Before each blast was set off, two girls waved the traffic to a halt.
5. Ashley, who was more experienced than I, told me what to do.
6. Although we had never had an accident, we worked under constant tension.
7. When the highway was clear, I pressed the handle down, and a long strip of roadway shuddered as if it were writhing in agony.
8. While the traffic waited, the bulldozers quickly shoved loose rocks off the open lane so that the cars and trucks could proceed again.
9. I think that some of the drivers were as relieved as we were.
10. While we were clearing off the rocks, the downpour came; soon the cut was so muddy that we had to stop work for the day.

2 *The Sentence:*

Rhetorical Patterns

THE PROBLEM OF EFFECTIVENESS

Effective use of language is not always a correct use of language. "I git thar fustest with the mostest men" is a famous formula for winning battles from the lips of Confederate General Nathan Bedford Forrest. It is not correct according to the standards set by the educated speaker, the experienced, careful worker with words, but it is more effective, in the right place, than "I arrive on the scene first with the greater number of troops." Indeed, one might suspect the leader who used the alternative of being a desk-bound campaigner.

Is effectiveness, then, independent of correctness? Absolutely not. Those few happy accidents in which ignorance has stumbled upon a successful phrasing are too rare to count on as a principle to follow. Correctness comes first. When it is well in hand, experiments within its bounds can be made for that desirable state of correctness, effectiveness. Only when correctness is understood beyond the possibility of error can it be abused and misused for the sake of incorrect effectiveness, and even then it will always risk looking just sloppy.

Correctness is important because it is universally functional. A misspelled word in a business letter or a misused verb in an interview can brand an otherwise able teacher or professional person as careless and perhaps unreliable in his or her own field. Bad spelling and bad grammar show; educated people notice them immediately. Crudity in vocabulary or usage makes many persons wince. In your college courses, many an otherwise excellent answer, test paper, or report may get a lower grade because of slips in spelling or grammar. Outside college, in industry, in business, in the professions, these mistakes can be even more damaging. It is no mystery, then, why we stress correctness in our language studies.

To be realistic about effectiveness, as distinguished from correctness, let us admit freely, before we go into this matter of improving something that is adequate, that for most routine occasions "correct" writing is good enough. We are here concerned with the student who is not satisfied with merely "correct" writing, the student who is disturbed that although he writes correctly and honestly, he is yet ineffective. Some of the qualities of effective communication are stressed elsewhere in this book. It is well to review them here briefly before we continue discussing sentence patterns. Diction is important. The words a writer uses should be exact, fresh, alive. Picture-making words are better than vague, general words. A fresh perspective can flavor a style. Humor can lighten and liven it. Even such devices as spacing on the page and use of properly opaque paper are important.

In this chapter we are dealing primarily with the grouping or arrangement of words in sentences—not exclusively, of course, because no skillful juggling of poorly chosen words can make effective sentences. First, let us examine sentence unity.

SENTENCE UNITY

The problem of unity in a sentence is primarily one of "not enough" or "too much."

Not Enough in the Sentence

The completeness or unity of a sentence is based, in one sense, on its structure. As we shall see later, it is also based on its thought or content. The sentence, however, is not a formula or an unchangeable pattern. On the contrary, it is a unit of such variety and flexibility that no rule, only the good sense of the writer, can decide when "not enough" becomes "complete," and when "complete" becomes "too much."

Obviously, a sentence is "not enough" when it is not grammatically complete; that is, when it does not have an expressed or implied subject and verb or a required object. For a discussion of sentence fragments see §1 of "A Handbook of Writing and Revision."

Too Much in the Sentence

A sentence may have "too much" in several ways. First, two unrelated ideas of the same weight and importance may be thrown together to make a compound sentence. The proper cure for this sort of fault is subordination. Second, a sentence may appear bulging and baggy from having too many related minor details thrown into it. Finally, a sentence may lack unity because the writer tossed into it some unrelated minor detail that popped into his mind while he was writing.

UNRELATED DETAILS

The library, old and dusty and well lit with bright new fixtures, was a melancholy place to work. ["Melancholy" seems related to "old and dusty" but not clearly to the new lighting.]

UNIFIED

The library, though well lit with new fixtures, was old and dusty and a melancholy place to work.

UNRELATED DETAILS

After the Communists took control in Vietnam, freedom of the press, which is guaranteed by a Constitutional amendment in the United States, was suppressed by the new regime. [If the sentence is about Vietnam, the reference to the United States is merely thrown in. If it is part of a contrast between the two governments, it might be acceptable.]

UNIFIED

After the Communists took control in Vietnam, freedom of the press was suppressed by the new regime.

UNRELATED DETAILS

The good sense of the chairman, who is a corpulent individual, is respected by all who know him. [His good sense has nothing to do with his shape.]

180

UNIFIED

The good sense of the chairman is respected by all who know him.

Overloading a sentence with details can obscure its unity and destroy its clearness and order. If the details are important, they should be told in separate sentences where they can be given proper value. If they are unimportant, they may be omitted.

CONFUSED

Military training teaches a person to stand up straight and walk with his head up; this helps in future life because it becomes a habit and so many people have the bad habit of walking stooped and this leads to poor health and poor appearance.

Military science teaches also common courtesies, not only to your superior officers but to everyone to whom courtesy is due; for instance when you enter offices, or the courtesies you should use when you are using firearms while hunting or shooting in the presence of another person.

The remedy for sentences like these is a return to the first principles of thought communication: say one thing at a time; say it as simply and clearly as possible; say it so that it cannot be misunderstood.

What does the reconstruction suggest the writer meant to say in these sentences?

REVISED

Military training teaches a person to stand erect and to walk with his head up. [That is enough for one sentence.] Good posture [Is that what the writer meant by "this" and "it"?] becomes habitual. It leads directly to better health and better appearance.

Military science also teaches common courtesy, not only to officers superior in rank but to everyone. [Are there some persons to whom "courtesy is not due"?] For instance, it teaches one how to enter an office, or how to handle firearms with safety to others. [These two examples are so badly chosen that no sentence can make them apt or congruous.]

181

USES OF SUBORDINATION

A child normally expresses his thoughts and impressions in simple sentences. He will say, for instance, "My trike was lost. I found my trike. It was back of the garage. I lost it last night. It was wet. It rained on it." The child's baby-sitter, several years older than he, probably would report the situation like this: "Bobby found his tricycle behind the garage. He left it there last night when it began to rain." An older person might have said, "Bobby found his tricycle behind the garage, where he had left it last night when it began to rain." As a child's mind matures and he begins to perceive that not all circumstances and thoughts are of the same importance, he learns to give certain details of his communication a primary and others a secondary position in a sentence. In other words, he learns to use *subordination*. He learns to place minor or contributing facts and ideas in dependent constructions in his sentences.

Let us first look at parallel versions of the same paragraph, the first written largely on the same plane, a little like the style of a sales promotion brochure, the second as a modern author wrote it. Compare the two carefully.

VERSION A

No regular reader of these pages should be surprised by the claim that violence on television leads to real violence. We have pointed out on numerous occasions that the link between the two is obvious. And we have argued for a reduction of and change in scheduling of violent programs. Now the National Commission on the Causes and Prevention of Violence has connected TV and violent behavior, especially in children. As a result of these findings, the major networks should now stop finding excuses and begin changing their programming.

VERSION B

That violence on television begets violence, particularly among the poor and disorganized, should come as no surprise to anyone with a smattering of psychology, sociology, or for that matter, common-sense logic. Nor should it astonish any reader of these pages where, for the past decade, we have pounded away almost every month at the obvious link between TV violence and violent behavior patterns with some but by no means enough success in a crusade to reduce the proportion and timing of violence on the home screen. At any rate, the case is now official: findings of the National Commission on the Causes and Prevention of Violence conclusively connect TV with violent behavior, especially in children. And it may be wise for the titans of broadcasting to stop throwing their hands in the air and declaring that they can do nothing at all about the dangerous drivel they show by the hour because that is what the American people want and the three chains would go out of business overnight if mayhem, killings, tortures, and outright brutality were reduced by, say, 30 per cent.

—RICHARD L. TOBIN, "When Violence Begets Violence"

Accuracy and Variety: The Dependent Clause

By this time you should be familiar with the various types of dependent clauses and with the structural signals that show their dependence. In the following examples, does the revision improve the accuracy of expression, give unity to sentences, or relieve the monotony of too many clauses on the same level?

A. I well remember a strange conversation I had with a man once. This man was a friend of mine. He and I had served together in the Marines.
B. I well remember a strange conversation I once had with a friend of mine, with whom I had served in the Marines.
A. Do not be in too much of a hurry to join an organization. Study its membership before you join.
B. Before you join an organization, investigate its membership.
A. Space suits are personalized garments. You must make many alterations on one of them. Otherwise it will not fit properly. In this respect it is like a bridal gown.
B. Because space suits are personalized garments, you need to make more alterations on one of them to make it fit properly than you do on a bridal gown.

—WALTER M. SCHIRRA, JR., *We Seven*

The Useful Participial Phrase

The substance of a coordinate clause may be better expressed in a *participial phrase*.

183

COORDINATE

My decision to enter college came suddenly, and I encountered several obstacles.

PARTICIPIAL

Having made a sudden decision to enter college, I encountered several obstacles.

But the participial phrase, useful as it is, contains several built-in dangers: it can become a dangler (see §29); its overuse can produce a stiff, awkward style; and, if the wrong detail is subordinated, it can distort rather than clarify meaning. And, finally, it can distort rather than clarify the writer's thought if he has subordinated the wrong detail. With these cautions in mind, study and analyze the following examples:

A. A law school or a medical school can be an essential part of a great university. Each school must be properly staffed and directed.
B. A law school or a medical school, if properly staffed and directed, can be an essential part of a great university. [Past participles]
A. I could not overcome my difficulty. I could not understand it.
B. Unable to understand my difficulty, I could not overcome it. ["Being" is understood in the sentence.]
A. There was one problem not solved by the Commission. This was how to widen the highway without moving the historic church.
B. The problem left unsolved by the Commission was how to widen the highway without moving the historic church.

Gerund and Infinitive Phrases

Gerund and infinitive phrases may be used on occasion to gain economy and compactness in writing.

A. For three days he punished me. He refused to eat my desserts.
B. For three days he punished me by refusing to eat my desserts.
A. Their working hours were shortened. This resulted in more spare time for recreation and enjoyment.
B. Shortening their hours of work resulted in more time available for recreation and enjoyment. [Note how the vague *this* has been avoided.]

184

A. The housewife has children whom she must clothe. She must take care of them and worry about them. The married professional woman has all these duties and, in addition, must face the sometimes harsh demands of her job.

B. The housewife has children to clothe, to care for, to worry about; the married professional woman has all these duties and, in addition, must face the sometimes harsh demands of her job.

Conciseness: The Prepositional Phrase

A prepositional phrase may be used to express a detail more accurately and more concisely than a clause or a sentence.

A. We wrote our exams at separate tables. There was a proctor in front of us. Another one stood behind us.

B. We wrote our exams at separate tables, with one proctor in front of us and another behind us.

A. The professor repeated his instructions. It was to help those who came late.

B. For the benefit of the latecomers, the professor repeated his instructions.

A. The examination was over. Then the students got together and compared their answers.

B. After the examination the students got together to compare answers.

A. I turned in my exam. I did not stop to go over my answers.

B. I turned in my exam without a second glance at my answers.

Notice that in the first examples above traits of informal conversation—shortened sentences, unsubordinated thoughts—stand out.

Compactness and Economy: The Single Word

A minor detail worth only a single word instead of a whole sentence or a clause is better expressed in a single word.

A. There were two new girls, and they both wore green double-knit dresses that had short sleeves.

B. The two new girls both wore short-sleeved dresses of green double-knit.

185

A. The house was old. The lawn around it was enclosed by yew hedges. These hedges were neatly clipped.
B. The lawn around the old house was shut in by neatly clipped yew hedges.

Uses of the Appositive

Like clauses, phrases, and verbals, the appositive (i.e., a word or phrase in apposition restating another word or phrase in terms that expand or define it) may be used to express details the writer wishes to subordinate. Consider this piece of autobiographical writing:

A. I was born in Middleville, Ohio. It's a small town. Most of the people in it are farmers. They raise cows for milk and a lot of apples. Still, it's the county seat of Whiteside County.

Obviously this is a wordy passage, marred by many faults in addition to a lack of subordination. It can be improved by the use of appositives:

B. I was born in Middleville, Ohio, a small dairy and apple-farming community and the seat of Whiteside County.

The following groups of sentences will further illustrate the resources of the appositive:

A. Lutetium was discovered in 1905. It is a chemical element. It is one of the rare-earth elements. The name comes from *Lutetia*. In ancient days Paris was called that.
B. Lutetium, a chemical element, member of the rare-earth group, was discovered in 1905; its name was derived from *Lutetia*, the ancient name of Paris.
A. The custom of kissing under the mistletoe was once an old Druid religious ceremony. It is now a pleasant part of our Christmas.
B. The custom of kissing under the mistletoe, once an old Druid religious ceremony, is now a pleasant part of our Christmas.
A. Tony is a congenial sort of person, and he hasn't made an enemy in his life.
B. Tony, a congenial sort of person, has not made an enemy in his life.

186

USES OF SUBORDINATION

To sum up the subject of subordination, two parallel versions of one more paragraph are given below. The sentences in the second version use dependent clauses or phrases to give a more effective allocation of meaning and emphasis. As a result, the writing in the second paragraph should seem more mature, more sophisticated, more accurate in conveying different shades of meaning, and more pleasing in style.

VERSION A

A great deal of traditional cultural education was foolish. That must be admitted. Boys spent many years acquiring Latin or Greek. At the end they could not read a Greek or Latin author. Neither did they want to. Of course this was not true in a small percentage of cases. Modern languages and history are preferable to Latin and Greek. This is in every way true. They are more useful, and they give much more culture, and it all takes less time. An Italian of the fifteenth century had to learn Latin and Greek. Everything worth reading was in those languages or in his own. These languages were indispensable keys to culture. Since that time great literatures have grown up in various modern languages. Development of civilization has been very rapid. A knowledge of antiquity has become less useful. A knowledge of modern nations and their comparatively recent history has become more useful in understanding our problems. The traditional schoolmaster's point of view was admirable at the time of the Revival of Learning. Now it is unduly narrow. It ignores what has been done since the fifteenth century. History and modern languages are not the only things contributing to culture. Science contributes too. But science must be properly taught. Education should have other aims than direct utility. It is possible to maintain this viewpoint. It is not necessary to defend the traditional curriculum. Utility and culture are not incompatible. They only seem to be. But they must be understood broadly.

VERSION B

It must be admitted that a great deal of the traditional education was foolish. Boys spent many years acquiring Latin and Greek grammar, without being, at the end, either capable or desirous (except in a small percentage of cases) of reading a Greek or Latin author. Modern languages and history are preferable, from every point of view, to Latin and Greek. They are not only more useful, but they give much more culture in much less time. For an Italian of the fifteenth century, since practically everything worth reading, if not in his own language,

187

was in Greek or Latin, these languages were the indispensable keys to culture. But since that time great literatures have grown up in various modern languages, and the development of civilization has been so rapid that the knowledge of antiquity has become much less useful in understanding our problems than knowledge of modern nations and their comparatively recent history. The traditional schoolmaster's point of view, which was admirable at the time of the Revival of Learning, became gradually unduly narrow, since it ignored what the world has done since the fifteenth century. And not only history and modern languages, but science also, when properly taught, contributes to culture. It is therefore possible to maintain that education should have other aims than direct utility, without defending the traditional curriculum. Utility and culture, when both are conceived broadly, are found to be less incompatible than they appear to the fanatical advocates of either.

—BERTRAND RUSSELL, *In Praise of Idleness and Other Essays*

LONG AND SHORT SENTENCES

Has the length of sentences much to do with effectiveness, as it has with style? Turn back to the last two selections, which you have just studied for subordination. Version A contains twenty-eight short sentences; version B has only ten sentences, most of them fairly long. Both selections say essentially the same thing—but the first seems aimless, undeveloped, and at times misplaced in emphasis.

Before we arrive at any hasty decision that a paragraph of long, complex sentences is more effective than a paragraph of short, simple ones, we should compare the ways in which two men, both good writers, chose to report similar moods of contentedness. The first man wrote his piece in very short sentences.

Across the open mouth of the tent Nick fixed cheese cloth to keep out mosquitoes. He crawled inside under the mosquito bar with various things from the pack to put at the head of the bed under the slant of the canvas. Inside the tent the light came through the brown canvas. It smelled pleasantly of canvas. Already there was something mysterious and homelike. Nick was happy as he crawled inside the tent. He had not been unhappy all day. This was different though. Now things were done. There had been this to do. Now it was done. It had been a hard trip. He was very tired. That was done. He had made his camp. He was settled. Nothing could touch him. It was a good place to camp. He was there, in the good place. He was in his home where he had made it. Now he was hungry.

He came out, crawling under the cheese cloth. It was quite dark outside. It was lighter in the tent.

Nick went over to the pack and found, with his fingers, a long nail in a paper sack of nails, in the bottom of the pack. He drove it into the pine tree, holding it close and hitting it gently with the flat of the ax. He hung the pack up on the nail. All his supplies were in the pack. They were off the ground and sheltered now.

Nick was hungry. He did not believe he had ever been hungrier. He opened and emptied a can of pork and beans and a can of spaghetti into the frying pan.

"I've got a right to eat this kind of stuff, if I'm willing to carry it," Nick said. His voice sounded strange in the darkening woods. He did not speak again.

—Ernest Hemingway, *In Our Time*

And now notice how differently another man says almost the same thing, "This is the place I had searched for, where for the moment I was happy and at peace."

Beyond Blake Avenue was the pool parlor outside which we waited all through the tense September afternoons of the World's Series to hear the latest scores called off the ticker tape—and where as we waited, banging a ball against the bottom of the wall and drinking water out of empty coke bottles, I breathed the chalk off the cues and listened to the clocks ringing in the fire station across the street. There was an old warehouse next to the pool parlor; the oil on the barrels and the iron staves had the same rusty smell. A block away was the park, thick with the dusty gravel I liked to hear my shoes crunch in as I ran round and round the track; then a great open pavilion, the inside mysteriously dark, chill even in summer; there I would wait in the sweaty coolness before pushing on to the wading ring where they put up a shower on the hottest days.

Beyond the park the "fields" began, all those still unused lots where we could still play hard ball in perfect peace—first shooing away the goats and then tearing away goldenrod before laying our bases. The smell and touch of those "fields," with their wild compost under the billboards of weeds, goldenrod, bricks, goat droppings, rusty cans, empty beer bottles, fresh new lumber, and damp cement, lives in my

189

mind as Brownsville's great open door, the wastes that took us through the west. I used to go round them in summer with my cousins selling near-beer to the carpenters, but always in a daze, would stare so long at the fibrous stalks of the goldenrod as I felt their harshness in my hand that I would forget to make a sale, and usually go off sick on the beer I drank up myself. Beyond! Beyond! Only to see something new, to get away from each day's narrow battleground between the grocery and the back wall of the drugstore! Even the other end of our block, when you got to Mrs. Rosenwasser's house and the monuments works, was dear to me for the contrast. On summer nights, when we played Indian trail, running away from each other on prearranged signals, the greatest moment came when I could plunge into the darkness down the block for myself and hide behind the slabs in the monuments works. I remember the air whistling around me as I ran, the panicky thud of my bones in my sneakers, and then the slabs rising in the light from the street lamps as I sped past the little candy store and crept under the fence.

—ALFRED KAZIN, "The Block and Beyond"

We may notice that out of the thirty-five sentences in the Hemingway selection, twenty-seven are fewer than ten words long. Hemingway was obviously striving to give the effect of random thoughts and impressions going through the mind of his character, who at the end of a long day of tramping was relaxed and happy and not disposed toward much thinking. In the Kazin selection, which is taken from a personal reminiscence and not a novel, all of the sentences are twenty words long or longer. Only the exclamations "Beyond! Beyond!" break this pattern—and do so with dramatic effect. There is a complex mood here, as the image of children playing in a wading ring contrasts with the symbolically foreboding image of a single child hiding behind a grave marker. Both writers, however, are trying to convey a feeling of homelike pleasure and mystery about the scenes they describe.

VARIATIONS IN ORDER

Sentences should fit the thoughts they contain, or, as in the Hemingway selection just analyzed, the mood they are creating. Most sentences, without any conscious effort on the writer's

part, fall into an instinctive pattern, subject—verb—complement. This natural pattern is not sacred; it can be changed to
make a statement more exact or more attractive by inverting
the elements or shifting the modifiers, but it should be left alone
unless there is something to be gained by tampering. The following pairs of sentences illustrate changes of emphasis created
by varying the word order.

A. They elected him their president. [Now change the basic S–V–C
   order.]
B. Him they elected their president. [What word is emphasized here?]
A. All six hundred rode into the valley of death. [Normal order]
B. All into the valley of death rode the six hundred. [Note the change
   of emphasis because of the inversion.]

—ALFRED, LORD TENNYSON

It is relatively easy to throw modifiers around (*the cry was
loud—loud was the cry*) or to shift from the active to passive voice
(*Susan hit me—I was hit by Susan*), but an alternative order should
not hinder the linking of one sentence to another. The following
parallel versions suggest a few possibilities, and indicate a few
difficulties, in shifting sentence parts for the sake of variety.

VERSION A

If you want to see and hear what happens and to be so close to the
bull that you will have the bullfighter's point of view, the best seat is
the barrera. The action is so near and so detailed from the barrera that
a bullfight that would be soporific from the boxes or the balcony is
always interesting. You see danger and learn to appreciate it from the
barrera. An uninterrupted view of the ring is also available from it.
The sobrepuertas are the only other seats, besides the first row in the
gallery and the first row in the boxes, where you do not see people
between you and the ring. You see these seats as you enter the various
sections of the ring as they are built over the doorways through which
you enter. You get a good view of the ring and a good perspective from
them, as they are about half-way up the sides of the bowl, yet you are
not as distant as in the boxes or gallery. They are good seats, yet they
cost about half as much as the barreras or the first row of gallery or
boxes.

VERSION B

The barrera is the best seat if you want to see and hear what happens and to be so close to the bull that you will have the bullfighter's point of view. From the barrera the action is so near and so detailed that a bullfight that would be soporific from the boxes or the balcony is always interesting. It is from the barrera that you see danger and learn to appreciate it. There too you have an uninterrupted view of the ring. The only other seats, besides the first row in the gallery and the first row in the boxes, where you do not see people between you and the ring, are the sobrepuertas. These are the seats that are built over the doorways through which you enter the various sections of the ring. They are about half-way up to the sides of the bowl and from them you get a good view of the ring and a good perspective, yet you are not as distant as in the boxes or gallery. They cost about half as much as the barreras or the first row of gallery or boxes and they are very good seats.

—ERNEST HEMINGWAY, *Death in the Afternoon*

It is worth noting that Hemingway has used relatively long sentences for descriptive purposes. Compare them with the shorter ones in the preceding fragment of his writing. Sentence variety based on function is important.

LOOSE AND PERIODIC SENTENCES

A *periodic sentence* is a complex sentence in which the main clause comes at the end, as "Just as the technicians were locking the hatch in place, one of the bolts broke." A *loose sentence* is a complex sentence in which the main clause comes first, followed by dependent clauses and other modifying elements, as "I realized that I had discussed the wrong topic only after I had handed in my paper." Short sentences are often periodic; long sentences tend to be loose. Since the mind grasps the thought of a short sentence, or even of a moderately long one, quickly, it is only in long sentences that periodic structure has any noticeable psychological effect.

192

The periodic sentence builds suspense. It tends to hold up the meaning until the end, to force the reader to consider first the various details on which the main thought is based. It makes him or her wait. Overused periodic structure is a little like an aged drunk holding your lapel and breathing into your face to tell his life story.

Notice in the following paragraph how a skillful writer combines the two types of complex sentences. In writing, the occasional conscious change from a loose to a periodic sentence, like tightening the belt, helps keep things from dragging.

For the kind of courage which does not consist in repression, a number of factors must be combined. [Periodic] To begin with the humblest: health and vitality are very helpful, though not indispensable. [Loose] Practice and skill in dangerous situations are very desirable. [Simple: periodic effect] But when we come to consider, not courage in this and that respect, but universal courage, something more fundamental is wanted. [Periodic] What is wanted is a combination of self-respect with an impersonal outlook on life. [Periodic] To begin with self-respect, some men live from within, while others are mere mirrors of what is felt and said by their neighbors. [Loose] The latter can never have true courage; they must have admiration and are haunted by the fear of losing it. [Loose] The teaching of "humility" which used to be thought desirable was the means of producing a perverted form of this same vice. [Periodic] "Humility" suppressed self-respect but not the desire for the respect of others; it merely made nominal self-abasement the means of acquiring credit. [Loose] Thus it produced hypocrisy and falsification of instinct. [Simple: periodic effect] Children were taught unreasoning submission and proceeded to exact it when they grew up; it was said that only those who have learned how to obey know how to command. [Loose] What I suggest is that no one should learn to obey and no one should attempt to command. [Loose] I do not mean, of course, that there should be no leaders in cooperative enterprises; but their authority should be like that of a captain of a football team, which is suffered voluntarily in order to achieve a common purpose. [Loose] Our purposes should be our own, not the result of external authority; and our purposes should never be forcibly imposed upon others. [Loose] This is what I mean when I say no one should command and no one should obey. [Loose]

—BERTRAND RUSSELL, *Education and the Good Life*

193

PARALLEL STRUCTURE AND BALANCE

One of the rhetorical devices available to writers is known as the *balanced* or *parallel* construction. At its elementary level, the device is a thoroughly practical means of improving an awkward sentence by making a noun parallel with another noun, a gerund with another gerund, a phrase with another phrase, a clause with another clause.

SCATTERED

Choose a house that is spacious, with a good exposure to the sun and that people like to look at. [An adjective, a phrase, a clause]

PARALLEL

Choose a house that is spacious, sunny, and attractive. [Three adjectives]

SCATTERED

I was glad to be there for the lecture and to see how the models work. [A noun and a clause]

PARALLEL

I was glad to be there for the lecture and the demonstration of models. [Two nouns]

SCATTERED

I have only one suggestion to make: cultivate friends who you think are loyal, have a cheerful disposition, and who are ambitious. [An adjective, a verb, and an adjective]

PARALLEL

I have only one suggestion to make: cultivate friends who you think are loyal, cheerful, and ambitious. [Three adjectives]

For a discussion of the "false parallel," see §32.

Forced into service when it is not required to give wandering sentences focus, parallel structure becomes a conspicuous art. Carried too far it becomes a mannerism. Used judiciously, however, to fit thought and occasion, it will seldom reach the

point of affectation. In his essay on studies, Francis Bacon deftly
balances phrase with phrase without excess.

```
Reading maketh a full man;
conference a ready man;                  and
writing an exact man.                    And therefore
      if a man write little       |—|    he had need to have
                                            great memory;
      if he confer little         |—|    he had need to have a
                                            present wit; and
      if he read little           |—|    he had need to have
                                            much cunning,
to seem to know what he doth not.
```

As Bacon's contemporaries not only tolerated but admired
rhetorical mannerisms, we should, perhaps, marvel at Bacon's
restraint rather than at his elaboration. You can find other examples of skillful parallelism in the work of present-day writers,
as in many of the selections quoted in Section I, Chapter 1:
Winston Churchill, page 16, Judge Oliver Wendell Holmes,
page 18, and J. R. Oppenheimer, pages 19–20.

Antithesis

Antithesis is another effective way of achieving balance in
sentences. The device is a favorite of political speakers like
Churchill and, more recently, President John F. Kennedy:
"Ask not what your country can do for you; ask what you can do
for your country"; "Those who make peaceful revolution impossible will make violent revolution inevitable." The second
example vividly illustrates how balance is achieved by opposing
"peaceful" to "violent," and "impossible" to "inevitable." As
with parallel structure, antithesis can be carried too far by the
beginning writer striving to sound like a great orator. Remember that both devices tend to be more appropriate to speech-
making than to the essays you are likely to write.

In the following selection, notice the varied and pleasing
rhythm of loose and periodic sentences throughout, the frequent use of balance, and here and there the effective development of climax. Notice too how the argument, like the style in
which it is presented, is both compelling and balanced.

195

As I see it, the United States is the first nation—though so complex and unclassifiable an entity almost resists definition as a single unit—to suffer/enjoy the death throes of the Renaissance. How could it be otherwise, since our nation is sensitive, energetic, swarming with life, and, beyond any other developed nation in the world, the most obsessed with its own history and its own destiny? Approaching a kind of manic stage, in which suppressed voices are at last being heard, in which *no extreme viewpoint is any longer "extreme,"* the United States is preparing itself for a transformation of "being" similar to that experienced by individuals as they approach the end of one segment of their lives and must rapidly, and perhaps desperately, sum up everything that has gone before.

It is easy to misread the immediate crises, to be frightened by the spontaneous eruptions into consciousness of disparate groups (blacks, women, youth, "the backlash of the middle class"); it is possible to overlook how the collective voices of many of our best poets and writers serve to dramatize and exorcize current American nightmares. Though some of our most brilliant creative artists are obsessed with disintegration and with the isolated ego, it is clear by now that they are all, with varying degrees of terror, saying the same thing—that we are helpless, unconnected with any social or cultural unit, unable to direct the flow of history, that we cannot effectively communicate. The effect is almost that of a single voice, as if a communal psychoanalytic process were taking place. But there does come a time in an individual writer's experience when he realizes, perhaps against his will, that his voice is one of many, his fiction one of many fictions, and that all serious fictions are half-conscious dramatizations of what is going on in the world.

Here is a simple test to indicate whether you are ready for the new vision of man or whether you will fear and resist it: Imagine you are high in the air, looking down on a crowded street scene from a height so great that you cannot make out individual faces but can see only shapes, scurrying figures rather like insects. Your imagination projects you suddenly down into that mass. You respond with what emotion—dread or joy?

In many of us the Renaissance ideal is still powerful, its voice tyrannical. It declares: *I* will, *I* want, *I* demand, *I* think, *I* am. This voice tells us that we are not quite omnipotent but must act as if we were, pushing out into a world of other people or of nature that will necessarily resist us, that will try to destroy us, and that we must conquer. *I will exist* has meant only *I will impose my will on others.* To that end man has developed his intellect and has extended his physical strength by

196

any means possible because, indeed, at one time the world did have to be conquered. The Renaissance leapt ahead into its own necessary future, into the development and near perfection of machines. Machines are not evil, or even "unnatural," but simply extensions of the human brain. The designs of our machines are no less the product of our creative imaginations than are works of art, though it might be difficult for most people—especially artists—to acknowledge this. But a great deal that is difficult, even outrageous, will have to be acknowledged.

If technology appears to have dehumanized civilization, this is a temporary failing or error—for the purpose of technology is the furthering of the "human," the bringing to perfection of all the staggering potentialities in each individual, which are nearly always lost, layered over with biological or social or cultural crusts. Anyone who imagines that a glorious pastoral world has been lost, through machines, identifies himself as a child of the city, perhaps a second- or third-generation child of the city. An individual who has lived close to nature, on a farm, for instance, knows that "natural" man was never *in* nature; he had to fight nature, at the cost of his own spontaneity and, indeed, his humanity. It is only through the conscious control of the "machine" (i.e., through man's brain) that man can transcend the miserable struggle with nature, whether in the form of sudden devastating hailstorms that annihilate an entire crop, or minute deadly bacteria in the bloodstream, or simply the commonplace (but potentially tragic) condition of poor eyesight. It is only through the machine that man can become more human, more spiritual. Understandably, only a handful of Americans have realized this obvious fact, since technology seems at present to be villainous. Had our earliest ancestors been gifted with a box of matches, their first actions would probably have been destructive—or self-destructive. But we know how beneficial fire has been to civilization.

—Joyce Carol Oates, "New Heaven and Earth"

REPETITION, SOUND, AND RHYTHM

Balance, parallel structure, and apposition are, in a sense, forms of repetition—repetitions primarily of phrasing or structure rather than of words, although within balanced phrases words may be repeated. Note this repetition in the quotation from Bacon on page 195:

a full man	write little	he had need to have great memory
a ready man	confer little	he had need to have a present wit
an exact man	read little	he had need to have much cunning

Then in the selection just quoted note the repetition of structure:

its own history	its own destiny
his voice is one of many	his fiction one of many fictions
it is easy to misread	it is possible to overlook
more human	more spiritual

that will necessarily resist/ that will try to destroy/ that we must conquer.

Single words may be repeated for emphasis or for a smoother rhythmic flow of sounds, quite apart from a balance of structural units, as you will notice in the following:

as you *love* your *country,* I *love* my *country.* . . .

—Adlai Stevenson

Before *parents* can be *parents* they must have lived a good part of their lives.

—Carl Van Doren

we shall fight in France, *we shall fight* on the seas and oceans, *we shall fight* with *growing* confidence and *growing* strength in the air . . . *we shall fight* on the landing grounds. . . .

—Winston Churchill

Euphony

Good prose should be easy to read aloud. Pleasing audible effects depend partly on an avoidance of harsh sounds or combinations of letters difficult to pronounce and partly on combinations of sounds, stresses, and variations in pitch that appeal to our sense of hearing. *Cacophony* is the name for jarring and harsh sounds. Many tongue twisters are familiar examples of cacophony.

She sells sea shells. . . .
The Leith police dismisseth us.

Euphony is the word that describes pleasing sounds. Some of the pleasure we get from good prose comes from various patterns of stresses called *rhythm*. Occasionally—and largely by accident—prose rhythms approach the regular metric forms of verse, but any conscious effort to arrange prose accents in poetic forms is usually out of place. The rhythms of prose are irregular—and yet one feels that in rhythmic prose there is an appropriate music. Read the following passage aloud, always remembering that the syllables stressed may be stressed in many different degrees:

Thus from the grim gray of their skies they had alchemied gold, and from their hunger, glorious food, and from the raw bleakness of their lives and weathers they had drawn magic. And what was good among them had been won sternly, sparely, bitterly, from all that was ugly, dull, and painful in their lives, and, when it came, was more rare and beautiful than anything on earth.

—THOMAS WOLFE, *Of Time and the River*

The final selection in this chapter was written many years ago, but it has lost none of its freshness and power. The prose rhythms in it cannot be felt through silent reading. It should be read aloud.

A man may read a sermon, the best and most passionate that ever man preached, if he shall but enter into the sepulchres of kings. In the same Escorial where the Spanish princes live in greatness and power, and decree war or peace, they have wisely placed a cemetery, where their ashes and their glory shall sleep till time shall be no more; and where our kings have been crowned, their ancestors lie interred, and they must walk over their grandsire's head to take his crown. There is an acre sown with royal seed, the copy of the greatest change, from rich to naked, from ceiled roofs to arched coffins, from living like gods to dying like men. There is enough to cool the flames of lust, to abate the heights of pride, to appease the itch of covetous desires, to sully and

199

dash out the dissembling colors of a lustful, artificial, and imaginary beauty. There the warlike and the peaceful, the fortunate and the miserable, the beloved and the despised princes mingle their dust, and pay down their symbol of mortality, and tell all the world that when we die our ashes shall be equal to kings', and our accounts easier, and our pains and our crowns shall be less.

—JEREMY TAYLOR (1613–1667)

3 *The Paragraph*

WHAT IS A PARAGRAPH?

One beauty of our native tongue is that English can always borrow from another language when it is at a loss for words. *Paragraph*, for example, is derived from two Greek words, *para*, "beside," and *graphein*, "to write." It was at one time a mark, usually ¶, written in the margin of a manuscript beside the place where a unit or subdivision of the text was to begin. The conventional signal now used to indicate a new paragraph is of course indention—that is, beginning a line a little to the right of the margin. (In some situations paragraphing is indicated instead by a skipped line and a new sentence beginning at the left-hand margin.) However it is marked, paragraphing can be considered a form of punctuation. It suggests that the reader is to make a major pause in his progress—as much as several seconds if he is reading aloud—and that he is to prepare himself for a new unit of discourse following, in some reasonable order, the one he has just finished.

The function of this punctuated, or paragraphed, unit varies with different kinds of prose. In dialogue, the paragraph often marks off a single speech of a character. In description it may divide the details of a scene or object being presented. Paragraphs may be organized in a simple sequence of time, as when one writes instructions on the operation of a machine. They may mark off units into which a subject has been divided, a familiar textbook formula (three causes of a war, four classes of a society). In discussions of facts and ideas—usually spoken of as exposition—a common paragraph unit comprises a step in a logical argument. Since it is exposition that most concerns students, we give our attention primarily to such paragraphs. If we speak of a paragraph of exposition, for the moment at least, as a related group of sentences calculated to advance an argument, with or without a summarizing or topic sentence, we probably come close to describing the actual practice of writers.

Almost anyone who begins a sentence with a dependent clause—for instance, "When I saw him on the street yesterday . . ."—has a pretty good idea as he does so what his main clause is going to say. "When I saw him on the street yesterday, he looked perfectly well." Similarly, an experienced writer, composing an introductory sentence in a paragraph, has a fair idea of how that sentence is going to relate to the major point of his paragraph—a point he may be preparing to state in what is called a *topic sentence* later on. In terms of larger structures yet, a practiced writer is aware of what a particular paragraph is going to contribute to the whole point of a developing article, or even a book. A writer should be ready constantly to change schemes, for he learns as he composes. But enormous quantities of waste motion are saved if he maintains a maximum awareness of the various relationships between a particular unit being written and all the other units of which it is to become a working part.

For the beginning writer, simultaneous coordination of all these relationships comes hard, and planning paragraphs by outline as one plans whole essays is advisable, at least in the early attempts. The topic sentence of a paragraph is that sentence that states the subject of the paragraph, suggests the attitude taken toward the subject in the paragraph, and, usually, anticipates the paragraph's conclusion. Experimental drafting of a few topic sentences can be helpful, even when the writer knows that the topic sentence may have to be rewritten and that it need not be the opening sentence. (The topic sentence of this paragraph is the last one.) Any procedure, in fact, that helps the student recognize a number of possible relations between the component sentences of the paragraph is useful.

The most familiar diagnosis of poor paragraphs in exposition is that they lack organization. By this one means:

1. *Lack of coherence*—that is, unrelated statements are made; relations between statements are not clearly shown.
2. *Lack of unity*—that is, digressions from the main thought or the topical idea are made; irrelevant details are included.

See § § 38 and 39.

202

As we have already hinted, it is fruitless to consider paragraphs in isolation from the larger units of which they are a part. Perhaps the fairest way to approach the paragraph as a single piece is to concentrate on introductions, the first paragraphs in expository essays. One can study an introductory paragraph without the sense that one has missed what went before it, for there is nothing before it except the title. What we shall do here, therefore, in the next few sections of this chapter, is to consider in some detail several introductory paragraphs of the sort found in essay collections. In each case, the writer is *introducing* his reader to the exposition that is to follow. This work on the paragraph can be related to the section "Beginnings and Endings" in Section I, Chapter 2, where larger problems of organization are considered.

KINDS OF INTRODUCTORY PARAGRAPHS

Coherence in Paragraphs

We have said that the writer in his first paragraph is introducing his reader to his exposition, but introducing can be done in so many different ways that the statement is not very helpful without some elaboration. There are at least three common and useful ways a paragraph can introduce a piece of expository prose.

First, the paragraph can contain a statement of a thesis to be argued. This is an obvious and sensible mode of beginning, as if to say, "Here is what I am going to show you." Often such a paragraph will include a reference to general opinion on the subject and how the writer's treatment will differ.

Second, the paragraph may tell a story, or begin to tell one, even though it will be clear that the whole essay is not fiction at all. The story will then be used as an example or a piece of evidence to support a thesis being argued.

Third, the paragraph may concentrate on a single key term to be defined, as a way of launching the demonstration to come.

203

In addition to setting the stage for what is to follow, an introductory paragraph introduces something of immense importance to the whole: the writer. Or, perhaps we should specify, that particular self he or she wishes to put forward for the particular circumstances and purposes of the writing. The way sentences in a paragraph relate to each other to introduce an argument, then, must be appreciated not only as a strategy in logic but as the image of a personality that assumes a definite relation (or *tone*) toward us. While writers are exposing *arguments,* they are dramatizing through language a *person* speaking formally, informally, intimately, or distantly, as the case may be. The composition of a well-organized paragraph requires paying as much attention to tone as to the logical arrangement of ideas. In the good writer, the argument and the voice presenting it are fused.

The Paragraph as a Statement of a Thesis to Be Argued

In expository writing it is of course common practice to state at the outset the thesis or argument that the writer proposes to advance in his essay. For one thing, this is simple politeness to the reader. Often the statement is preceded or immediately followed by a reference to general prevailing opinion on the subject, or to past treatments of it by other writers. The reader is to assume that such opinion and such past treatments are to be qualified, or perhaps demolished utterly, by the new treatment the author is putting forward. This approach can, however, come dangerously close to a formula: "Contrary to the view generally held on the subject, which naively assumes thus-and-so, I shall soon convince you that this-and-that is really the case." The student using this approach, therefore, should take note of the various ways in which professional writers modify the formula.

Let us begin with an uncomplicated piece of prose from a popular American magazine, *The Atlantic Monthly,* and watch the formula at work.

[1] Anyone who has casually turned on his television set since the beginning of the 1963–64 season might gain the impression that television is in the same old rut, only deeper. [2] A closer examination of the landscape, however, discloses that the world of television is in quite an upheaval. [3] Strange new forms of television are starting to emerge, some of them never anticipated, even by most insiders. [4] New hybrids and seemingly implausible alliances are taking shape. [5] As a consequence, decisive changes appear to be in prospect, with a wider diversity of programming from which to choose and, hopefully, an improvement in what is available to the discerning viewer.

—VANCE PACKARD, "New Kinds of Television"

[1] The first sentence expresses the general opinion from which the writer will differ; he is going to do more than "casually" turn on a television set. Note his informal air with his reader, as in that final colloquial phrase, *same old rut*.

[2] Here is the topic sentence, linked with the preceding one by the transitional adverb *however* and by the repetition of *television*.

[3] This sentence spells out the "upheaval" by presenting evidence, or at least by restating the theme of change in other terms.

[4] These phrases are variations on *strange new forms;* note the biological metaphor.

[5] The opening phrase here is another clear transitional expression, apparently referring not only to the preceding sentence but to the entire paragraph, as the author gives us another restatement of *upheaval*. He ends with language in dramatic opposition to his beginning, where television was assumed to be "in a rut."

As you see, the writer has taken pains to connect his sentences to one another by the use of transitional phrases and by seeing to it that succeeding sentences enlarge upon or define references in previous sentences. A clear case is the fourth sentence, as it plays variations on *strange new forms.* Throughout, his tone, as we have suggested in our analysis of his first sentence, is informal and easy with the reader, and perhaps his inside jokes based on clichés from botany, geology, and evolution (*strange new forms, world in upheaval, new hybrids, implausible alliances*) help to maintain this pose of comfortable knowledge held in common with the reader. But we cannot believe that the writer is thoroughly serious in suggesting an analogy between the great theory of evolution, on the one hand, and the current situation in television, on the other.

Some readers might find this tone offensively chummy; some would single out the word *hopefully* in the last sentence to sub-

205

stantiate a charge of diffidence and indecisiveness. However you may respond to the writer's tone or thesis, it is easy enough to see that he is playing a variation on the formula we have suggested, which, in this case, would read in the raw: "Contrary to general opinion that television is in the same old rut, it is in fact in a state of rapid change that may produce better programs for discriminating viewers (of which select set the reader and writer are indubitably parts)." The next passage, from the same magazine, begins with a paragraph using the same formula, but with a different tone. Read it the first time quickly to get a sense of the person speaking here.

[1] The conflict of the generations is neither a new nor a particularly American story, but it is perhaps exacerbated by the self-consciousness and the partial segregation of teenage culture, to such an extent that both old and young are exceptionally vulnerable to their mutual criticisms. [2] I do not care to add to the complacency of my agemates who, from their clubs, pulpits, and other rostrums, attack the alleged "softness" of the young, whom they have themselves brought up, while failing to see the difficulties young people face today precisely because the manifest hardships with which earlier Americans coped have been, for millions, attenuated. [3] These hardships cannot be artificially restored, at least for people over twelve; however, I believe that college students are now beginning to find new ways to become active politically, and hence responsible humanly.

[1] The first sentence connects what is to follow with an ageless problem—the conflict of the generations—and suggests a modern climate of opinion in which the assumptions the author is about to attack can flourish.

[2] Here the author, aware of the climate of opinion he described in his first sentence, explicitly separates himself from those holding the prevailing view of teen-age "softness." He does so because he recognized (first sentence) how vulnerable the young are to such attacks. Note the subtle but clear relation between the two sentences.

[3] *These hardships* repeats an important word from the preceding sentence. Then the key clause of the whole article follows, introduced by the connective *however.* In spite of their loss of traditional hardships, young people are learning to act responsibly.

—DAVID RIESMAN, "Where Is the College Generation Headed?"

The difference in tone between the two paragraphs, which should be obvious on a first quick reading, may be explained by a number of differences in their rhetorics, at least some of which we can mention here. For one thing, note the length of the sentences: whereas Vance Packard, in a paragraph of just over one hundred words, writes five sentences, David Riesman, in a considerably longer paragraph, writes only three. Riesman's vocabulary is also sophisticated; some of his words (*exacerbated, attenuated*) may have sent you to the dictionary. Riesman expects a good deal of his reader. He addresses him formally, he does not avoid complex ways of talking, and he does not make things any easier by introducing colloquial language or an intimate tone, as Packard does. The relations between Riesman's sentences are not immediately obvious. There are no in-jokes, about evolution or anything else, and indeed we may feel some alienation in this speaker's crack about his agemates in their pulpits and rostrums. How can we account for such difference in rhetoric and tone? We cannot assume that the two writers are addressing different audiences, for both these articles appeared in different issues of the same magazine. Nor is the difference primarily that they are dealing with different subjects, although this no doubt has something to do with it. Rather, the answer is to be found in the individual decision of each writer to project a different speaking personality. His precise motives for making such a decision are mysterious, and would probably be as difficult to discover entirely as the motives for most human behavior.

Let us now examine one more introductory paragraph built on the same formula, contrary-to-general-opinion-I-shall-demonstrate-thus-and-so. This one is from a famous essay about language itself.

[1] Most people who bother about the matter at all would admit that the English language is in a bad way, but it is generally considered that we cannot by conscious action do anything about it. [2] Our civilization is decadent, and our language—so the argument runs—must inevitably share in the general collapse. [3] It follows that any struggle against the abuse of lan-

[1] Informal, abrupt, colloquial (*in a bad way*). Realistic, almost tough, in the admission that not many do bother about language. *It is generally considered* introduces the prevailing view which the writer will oppose.
[2] The words between the dashes relate to *it is generally considered* and make it clear the writer does not agree.
[3] *It follows that* relates to the *argument* preceding and is ironic insofar

guage is a sentimental archaism, like preferring candles to electric light or hansom cabs to aeroplanes. [4] Underneath this lies the half-conscious belief that language is a natural growth and not an instrument which we shape for our own purposes.

—GEORGE ORWELL, *Shooting an Elephant and Other Essays*

as the writer is opposed to the logic he is reproducing.

[4] *Underneath this* provides the transition, continuing the bogus argument. Language is not a natural growth at all, it is an instrument which we shape.

In this clear expression of a point of view about language, note the signals by which the writer keeps reminding us that we are not to agree with general opinion. What we *are* to do is to "struggle against the abuse of language"—and note the favorably loaded implications of a word like *struggle*. This is a vigorous, serious voice addressing us, even though it speaks to us at some points informally and even colloquially.

We have now seen three examples of expository paragraphs, all employing variations of a familiar formula: "Contrary to a generally held view, I propose the following thesis." Each paragraph is constructed of sentences knit together with transitional devices, some more obvious than others, but all at least competently handled. The tone of the three writers is quite different, from Packard's easy informality, to Riesman's academic distance, to Orwell's mixture of tough-colloquial intimacy with a very serious purpose. Note that the writer's choice about his tone is not necessarily a function of his subject: Orwell's subject is at least as important as Riesman's, yet his tone is considerably less formal.

The Paragraph of Anecdote as Evidence for a Thesis

We begin this section with an article, written about the same time as Orwell's and on the same subject, that takes a similar stand on the abuses of language. But see how differently the argument is begun by Jacques Barzun.

[1] Like five million other people I spend part of each day in a New York bus, and some of that time my eyes

[1] A disarming opener: note how the author specifically makes himself no better than anyone else.

rest on the sign:

PLEASE REFRAIN FROM
CONVERSATION WITH OPERATOR
WHILE BUS IS IN MOTION

We are to sense the humor of this pretentious sign even before he labels it with *this foreign-language text.*

[2] After some years of dumb staring, it has come over me that this foreign-language text means, "Please do not talk to the driver between stops." [3] But this knowledge does not make me sure that I shall ever understand that other sign, found in every shop, which reads: "Illumination is required to be extinguished before these premises are closed to business." [4] Before it, I find I have only one thought: "WHOM is speaking?"

—JACQUES BARZUN, "How to Suffocate the English Language"

[2] Three linked phrases: *part of each day, some of that time, after some years.*

[3] *This knowledge* refers to *it has come over me.*

That other sign, yet similar, of course, in its stuffiness.

[4] *Before it:* note the transitional phrase, with its reference to the *other sign.*
The author's joke on grammar at the end implies that his reader shares his immediate recognition of absurdly ungrammatical forms.

The next sentence of this article, beginning its second paragraph, opens with the phrase "These public displays of literary ineptitude . . . ." The anecdote of seeing the sign on the bus, it is clear, is to be taken as one piece of evidence for a larger fact. The sign about illumination is another piece of evidence. This technique is a form of what is called the *inductive approach,* starting with a specific occasion or instance and moving to a generalization. One advantage to using a personal anecdote as evidence is that the reader momentarily enjoys the comfortable feeling of being told a story. It provides a pleasant avenue into what may turn out to be a tough neighborhood before the trip is over, and it distracts the reader from questioning the truth of the evidence. If a generalization begins the discussion there is every likelihood the reader will stop to say "I can think of exceptions." And if the writer immediately provokes the reader's antagonism, the rest of his argument will have an uphill fight. In a story narration, however, the speaker's relation to his

209

reader is easy and good-humored; he is having fun with his subject.

In another example of personal anecdote as an introductory device, we confront a speaker who is puzzled by a common belief about the qualifications of job applicants. What begins as a somewhat humorous curiosity in the writer's mind quickly becomes a fact of business life which leads him to some careful self-examination. Notice how dramatically the tone shifts, in the second paragraph, from lighthearted bafflement to sober exposition of fact.

[1] I used to think it curious, if not a bit sad, as I began to notice that the only men who stated their height on résumés I'd receive were those six feet or taller. Why, I puzzled, would these résumé writers think anyone could possibly care how tall an editor is—unless the dejected fellows were scraping the barrel of their assets for something to say about themselves.

[2] One day I realized they weren't as off-base as I had thought. I chanced upon a sociological study, which found that when the starting salaries of graduates of the same business college were compared, the taller men's salaries were significantly higher. In addition, another social psychology experiment had 140 recruiters make a hypothetical choice between two equally qualified applicants, one man six feet, one inch, and the other five feet, nine inches. Only one percent chose the short man.

— LEONARD H. GROSS, "Short, Dark, and Almost Handsome"

[1] Note the off-handed way in which the fact of the applicants' size was communicated to the author. Colloquialisms like *a bit sad* and *scraping the barrel* also convey the author's mood of bemused condescension about the matter. Though not a specific incident, this generalized anecdote accomplishes the task of involving the reader in the writer's puzzlement.

[2] With *One day* we shift to a serious discussion while retaining something of the colloquial flavor with *off-base,* a baseball metaphor that nicely characterizes the gamesmanship of the applicants. By citing the two sociological studies, the author has appealed to authority and has impressed us with "scientific" findings. The final, short sentence, with its revealing fact, gives a dramatic close to the paragraph.

The third paragraph of this essay begins "These revelations stirred up some suppressed anxieties . . . ," thereby applying the anecdote to the feelings of the author himself on the subject of height. We read on: "Being somewhat undersized all through childhood, I worried if I'd reach that critical five feet eight that enabled you to be a cop or a fireman (these occupations being symbols for the worrisome question—'Will I be a Real Man?')." Note the reference to general opinion, so familiar in our earlier examples, an opinion from which the writer will explicitly diverge: "Height can only be a factor insofar as it represents 'Authority' and transmits a strong and dependable image, . . ." Now we know that we are to take the anecdote as a piece of evidence for a much more serious concept, namely the role of height in determining success for men in our society. But the writer does not entirely lose his good-natured storytelling manner, as his humorous but sensible observation at the close of the third paragraph proves: ". . . a hose will smother more flames than the foot of a fireman even as big as Wilt Chamberlain ever could."

The use of stylistic techniques borrowed from fiction has been increasing in expository writing, especially in some journalism. The two samples of anecdote we have been looking at both originated, presumably, from the writers' own experience, something they saw or directly heard about. When a reporter takes the larger step of assuming he is a kind of novelist, describing scenes he has never seen and thoughts of people he could not have known about, then the dangers are obvious. Newswriting that attempts to be especially lively, such as you will find in *Time,* runs this risk of dishonesty. But the novelist's manner is tempting to aspiring writers, especially to historians who wish to paint the actions of the past with color and vividness. Here is a serious professional historian beginning a piece of writing on early America.

[1] Out to the limitless distance ran the ocean. [2] From its near edge, the generations of Europeans had watched the turbulent waters recede into the unknown space, within which imagination crowded all the fantastic beings of fable. [3] Here began the end of the world; the mariners hugged the margins of the continent, fearful

[1] Note the suspense created here: "What ocean?" we ask.

[2] *Its:* a simple, clear transition by means of a pronoun.
See how the historian takes the liberty of assuming how their imaginations worked.

[3] *Here:* transition.

as in Odysseus' day of losing sight of the familiar universe of rising cliffs and jutting promontories that was their home.

More subtle links provided by *limitless distance, turbulent waters, unknown space, fantastic beings, fearful . . . of losing sight of . . . home.*

—Oscar Handlin, "Shaped in the Wilderness: The Americas"

We may have to read on a bit, beyond this theatrical opening, before we know what Handlin is talking about (the European coastline, it turns out, about 1600). The mystery and suspense created here, as we have said, are traditionally characteristic of the novelist, not the writer of exposition. The student essayist should imitate this kind of paragraph with caution.

The Paragraph as a Definition of a Term

The point of a piece of exposition often depends on one or two significant words. Many of the significant words have been so mauled by excessive handling that they are invoked less for their meaning than for their easy capacity to adapt to a variety of meanings without retaining the shape of any. *Liberal, idea, tolerance* are three of them. Anyone writing an essay making important use of such terms must anticipate a reader's very proper question: What do you mean by that? In the following three opening paragraphs, definition of one of these terms is the central problem the paragraph must solve, or at least face. Within this definition of common function, however, the paragraphs again differ markedly in tone.

[1] Any education that matters is *liberal.* [2] All the saving truths and healing graces that distinguish a good education from a bad one or a full education from a half-empty one are contained in that word. [3] Whatever ups and downs the term "liberal" suffers in the political vocabulary, it soars above all controversy in the educational world. [4] In the blackest pit of pedagogy the squirming victim has

[1] Strong, terse statement, italicizing the crucial term.
[2] Links: repetition of *education* and the final phrase, *that word,* which refers to the italicized term.

[4] *Pedagogy* is a linking echo of *education.*

212

only to ask, "What's liberal about this?" to shame his persecutors. [5] In times past a liberal education set off a free man from a slave or a gentleman from laborers and artisans. [6] It now distinguishes whatever nourishes the mind and spirit from the training which is merely practical or professional or from the trivialities which are no training at all. [7] Such an education involves a combination of knowledge, skills, and standards.

—ALAN SIMPSON, "The Marks of an Educated Man"

Note again the repetitions of *liberal,* the key word.
[5] The phrase *liberal education* combines the two.
[5, 6] Sentences 5 and 6 are linked and balanced by the references to time in each: *in times past* and *now.*
This is the crucial sentence of the definition.

[7] *Such an education*—i.e., a liberal one—again reinforces the links between the sentences.

The writer is now ready to proceed with his discussion of "knowledge, skills, and standards." He has set up a working definition of *liberal,* however general it may be, and he has set it apart from its political connotations. The tone is serious, and the reader, although he is expected to share the values of education here referred to, is certainly not left with the impression that the speaker knows him intimately. This is formal discourse.

We now look at another problem with a word, the word *idea.* Here is a distinguished composer beginning an essay on the creative process in the writing of music.

[1] The word "idea" is a very vague term for what we really mean when we talk of the composer's creative imagination. [2] The German word *Einfall* is the perfect expression needed in our situation. [3] *Einfall,* from the verb *einfallen,* to drop in, describes beautifully the strange spontaneity that we associate with artistic ideas in general and with musical creation in particular. [4] Something—you know not what—drops into your mind— you know not whence—and there it grows—you know not how—into some form—you know not why.

[1] The speaker concedes immediately that he has a problem of definition.

[2] *Word* is repeated; *in our situation* refers also, more generally, to the first sentence.
[3] *Einfall* repeated; *describes beautifully* refers to *is the perfect expression* in the sentence preceding.

[4] This unorthodox punctuation is Hindemith's attempt to express in words *the strange spontaneity* he mentioned in the previous sentence.

213

[5] This seems to be the general opinion, and we cannot blame the layman
if he is unable to find rational explanations for so strange an occurrence.

[5] *This* refers, perhaps a little
vaguely, to the thought processes
just described.

—PAUL HINDEMITH, "How Music Happens"

Hindemith's tone is a good deal lighter and friendlier than
that in the previous passage, partly because of his clever mim-
icking of popular responses to the word *idea* in musical creation.
(All those dashes!) Notice that the writer expresses some charity
for those who know less than he does—"we cannot blame the
layman." He is a little more human, a little less formidable,
than the preceding writer.

You will recognize the reference to "general opinion" in the
final sentence, an opinion with which Hindemith is about to
disagree in the rest of his article, at least to the extent of describing a composer's process of creating music in something
like rational terms. The paragraph of definition, in this case,
not only deals with a term, but in doing so also uses the first
technique described in this chapter, the argument in contrast to
prevailing opinion. Methods, it is important to make clear, are
often successfully combined, as in the example just given. Our
process of critical analysis is based on a completed process, and
in practice the writer does not ask beforehand, "Now which of
three, or six, or fifteen techniques should I use in this paragraph?" The practical question is much harder: "How can I so
organize this paragraph that the reader will respond exactly as I
want?" Knowing the categories of critical analysis will not,
alone, solve all paragraphing problems—reading will discover
plenty of excellent introductory paragraphs that seem to fit
none of the categories—but it will help the inexperienced
writer, who must sometimes choose an opening self-consciously
and deliberately, as when answering an examination question.

Of the three elusive words mentioned, *tolerance* gives off the
deepest sound and seems to defy all but the most piously respectable approach. Must the appropriate tone for defining it
be impersonal or strictly formal? Not necessarily. We must not
press too hard our notions of appropriateness, for, as already
noted, subject matter and tone are not the same thing. It does

214

not follow that because a topic is supposed to be serious, we must necessarily speak of it seriously. *Consistency* in the way we speak of it is another matter; "the departed" at the beginning should not turn up as "the stiff" near the end, unless the best we can afford is cheap humor. The quality of tone is the writer's own decision, and in the case of some great writers, as the following passage should show, the decision can be surprising.

[1] Can you define tolerance? [2] I can't, any more than I could define love or faith, or fate, or any other abstraction. [3] My mind slips about, tries a definition, finds it won't quite work, drops it, tries another, and so on. [4] And people whose minds are better than my own seem to be in the same plight here. [5] They propound definitions, they defend them stoutly and philosophically, but sooner or later the definition crumbles under the onslaught of some other philosopher, and the world is left where it was. [6] Well, not quite where it was. [7] Despite the failure, two valuable things have occurred. [8] Firstly, the human mind has been exercising itself, and my goodness, how desirable that is! [9] It has been trying to discover something, and it has become stronger and more agile in consequence, even though nothing has been discovered. [10] And, secondly, the abstract subjects on which it has exercised itself have gained in prestige. [11] Tolerance is important, no one can deny that, and if it is talked about so that people dispute what it is, or isn't, its importance should be maintained or increased.

—E. M. FORSTER, "Toward a Definition of Tolerance"

[1] Definition problem immediately stated, and the reader directly involved (*you*).

[2] The speaker, with his informal contractions (*can't*), cheerfully admits his own limitations.
Links: *define,* sentence 1; *define,* 2; *definition,* 3; *definitions,* 5.

[4] *And* connects the writer's mind with everyone else's.

[5] This sentence echoes, in more elegant language, the way in which the speaker described his own train of thought in sentence 3.

[6] *Well:* highly informal. *Where it was:* another linkage by repetition.

[7] The *failure* summarizes what has been described so far.

[8, 9, 10] Familiar logical organization: *firstly, secondly.* (*First* and *second* are now the preferred adverbial forms.) The speaker is jocular, of course, about minds exercising themselves, implying it does not happen very often!

[10] *Gained in prestige* links with *important* and *importance* in the final sentence.

[11] *Tolerance* returns us neatly to the first sentence.

215

These introductions suggest the conclusion that success in creating such paragraphs in exposition is a matter of at least two interrelated processes. First, it is necessary to have logical internal *organization:* to provide links between sentences so that the reader has a sense of rational sequence in the paragraph. Second, it is necessary to maintain a consistent personality, or *tone* (attitude toward material and audience), throughout the paragraph.

PROBLEMS OF INTERNAL ORGANIZATION

What we have already noted about internal structure in opening paragraphs applies to a considerable extent to paragraphs within the body of an essay. Most paragraphs, wherever they may appear, are built around a *central theme* or *idea,* which is often expressed in a single *topic sentence*. And most paragraphs are made up of sentences connected by transitional devices that can be identified. We will now take a look at some additional techniques for organizing, or unifying, or holding together expository paragraphs.

In the following paragraph, notice how all the details have been chosen to relate to the initial topic sentence and its key phrase, "old dark house." This is a simple approach that consists of seeing to it that all the items of a list belong in that list, but it is not as easy as it looks.

The Haunting is set in that pleasantly familiar "old dark house" that is itself an evil presence, and is usually inhabited by ghosts or evil people. In our childhood imaginings, the unknowable things that have happened in old houses, and the whispers that someone may have died in them, make them mysterious, "dirty"; only the new house that has known no life or death is safe and clean. But so many stories have used the sinister dark house from-which-no-one-can-escape and its murky gardens for our ritual entertainment that we learn to experience the terrors as pleasurable excitations and reassuring reminders of how frightened we used to be before we learned our way around. In film, as in story, the ambience is fear; the film specialty is gathering a group who are trapped and helpless. (Although the women are more easily frightened, the men are also powerless. Their superior strength doesn't count for much against unseen menaces: this may explain why the genre was often used for a male comedian—like Bob Hope in *The Ghost Breakers*. Russ Tamblyn serves a similar but feeble cowardly-comic function in *The Haunting*.) The action is confined to the house and grounds (the maze); the town is usually far away, just far enough away so that "nobody will hear you if you scream."

—Pauline Kael, "Zeitgeist and Poltergeist; or, Are Movies Going to Pieces?"

Still another technique of unifying a paragraph is to build all or most of the sentences around a comparison or a contrast. Comparison requires finding similarities in two things. Usually the more familiar thing or idea is used to explain the less familiar one: to explain the game of squash show how it is similar to tennis, the more familiar game. In what ways is piloting a plane like driving a car? How are Canadians like their continental neighbors in the United States? Contrast, on the other hand, is telling what a thing is not like. How does college life as you see it now differ from college life as you thought it would be? How does the Western way of living differ from the Oriental way? How does capitalism differ from communism? How does propaganda differ from news? These are typical subjects that invite treatment by contrast, not in paragraphs alone but also in entire essays or articles.

A white-collar employee of an American corporation visiting a Soviet institution of comparable rank will be in for some surprises. [Topic sentence] For one thing the offices of the establishment will be secondary to the plant, instead of vice versa which is usually the case in the United States. Also the visitor will note that a considerable number of executive officers in a Russian industrial organization, even engineers, are women. On a superficial level other points can be mentioned. First, there is little of the personal byplay and banter that accompany much American business endeavor and office routine; no coffee break, for example. Bosses are aloof. Second, lunch takes place in a cafeteria on the premises, maintained by the establishment; no corner drugstore, bar, or hotdog stand. Third, nobody has to catch the 5:25; commuting, if any, is by bus. Another point is that jobs are different in function. No Soviet plant has a public relations department or advertising

217

department, office for employer-employee relationships, or even a sales manager and staff. Salesmanship, the first of all occupations in America, does not exist in our sense at all.

—JOHN GUNTHER, *Inside Russia Today*

The following, with its touches of grim humor that so few people associate with the author, may inspire you to compare and contrast your chosen occupation with others:

The great liability of the engineer compared to men of other professions is that his works are out in the open where all can see them. [Topic sentence] His acts, step by step, are in hard substance. He cannot bury his mistakes in a grave like the doctors. He cannot argue them into thin air or blame the judge like the lawyers. He cannot, like the architects, cover his failures with trees and vines. He cannot, like the politicians, screen his shortcomings by blaming his opponents and hope that the people will forget. [Note how the use of phrases, "like the architects" and "like the politicians," breaks the monotony of each repetition.] The engineer simply cannot deny that he did it. If his works do not work, he is damned. That is the phantasmagoria that haunts his nights and dogs his days. He comes from the job at the end of the day resolved to calculate it again. He wakes in the night in a cold sweat and puts something on paper that looks silly in the morning. All day he shivers at the thought of the bugs which will inevitably appear to jolt its smooth consummation.

On the other hand, unlike the doctor his is not a life among the weak. Unlike the soldier, destruction is not his purpose. Unlike the lawyer, quarrels are not his daily bread. To the engineer falls the job of clothing the bare bones of science with life, comfort, and hope. No doubt as years go by people forget which engineer did it, even if they ever knew. Or some politician puts his name on it. Or they credit it to some promoter who used other people's money with which to finance it. But the engineer himself looks back at the unending stream of goodness which flows from his successes with satisfactions that few professions may know. And the verdict of his fellow professionals is all the accolade he wants.

—HERBERT HOOVER, *The Memoirs of Herbert Hoover: Years of Adventure*

Specific transitional words and phrases in the preceding paragraphs help relate the component sentences to each other. We have been using such terms as *echo, refer,* and *link* to signify these relations. We can now summarize these connecting expressions as follows:

1. *Conjunctions and transitional adverbs,* which include words and phrases such as *and, but, yet, however, therefore, consequently, moreover, accordingly, at the same time, as a result, for example, on the other hand, finally.*
2. *Pronouns,* such as *this, that, these, those, his, her,* and *its,* which refer to an antecedent in a previous sentence. It is extremely important that the young writer make sure references of pronouns are clear. See §27 in the "Handbook."
3. *Repetition of key words,* of which examples, particularly clear in paragraphs of definition, appear in earlier pages of this chapter.
4. *Parallel structure,* through which the reader is led back to sentences phrased in similar forms.

For a close study of connectives, transitions, and internal organization, follow the themes and variations, almost like musical motifs, in the following passage:

[1] The first sentences of this book were written nearly two years ago. [2] *Outside my window* on *that* spring *morning,* as on *this,* a *bird sang.* [3] *Outside a million windows,* a million *birds* had *sung* as *morning* swept around the globe. [4] Few men and few women were so glad that a new day had dawned as *these birds* seem to be.

[5] Because my *window* looks out on a southern landscape, my *bird* is a cardinal, with feathers as bright as his half-whistled song. [6] Farther *north* in the United States he would be a *robin,* more likely than not—less colorful and somewhat less melodious but seemingly no less pleased with the world and his place in it. [7] Like *us,* *robins* have *their* problems but *they* seem better able to take *them* in *their* stride. [8] *We* are likely to awake with an "Oh, dear!" on our lips; *they*

[2] Introduces key words. Pronouns *that* and *this.*

[3] Repeats *Outside . . . window, bird,* and *morning; sung* echoes *sang.*

[4] Pronoun *these.* Repeats *birds.*

[5] Again repeats *window.* Repeats *bird.*

[6] Contrasts *north* with *southern* in sentence 5. Introduces key word.

[7] Repeats *robin. Their* contrasts with *us.* Pronouns.

[8] *We* ties in with *us.*

219

with "What fun!" in their beaks.
[9] Mr. Sandburg's peddler was re-
markable because he seemed so *terribly
glad* to be selling fish. [10] Most robins
seem *terribly glad* to be eating worms.

[9, 10] Repeated phrase, *terribly
glad.*

[11] For some time I have been
thinking that I wanted to write a book
about the *characteristics* and *activities* of
living things. [12] During the week or
two just before, I had been wondering
with what activity or characteristic I
should begin. [13] Reproduction,
growing up, and getting a living are
all, so I said to *myself,* fundamental
activities. [14] Combativeness in the
face of rivals, solicitude for the young,
courage when danger must be met,
patience when hardships must be endured, are all typical *characteristics.*
[15] But *my cardinal* proposed a different solution. [16] Is any *characteristic*
more striking than the joy of life instead?

[11] Introduces two key words—
characteristics and *activities.*

[12] Repeats key words.

[13] Pronoun refers to *I.* Repeats key
word.

[14] Repeats key word.

[15] *My cardinal* refers to *cardinal* in
sentence 5.
[16] Repeats key word.

—JOSEPH WOOD KRUTCH, *The Great Chain
of Life*

ORGANIZING PARAGRAPHS
IN SEQUENCES

To understand how paragraphs are related to one another is
to begin to see how a whole essay is organized. A paragraph that
reflects a list of items to be considered is one obvious illustration. But note that in the following piece of historical writing,
the authors have subtly given their third "factor" an added
importance by granting it a paragraph to itself.

As late as 1808, when the slave trade was abolished, numerous
Southerners thought that slavery would prove but a temporary evil.
[Summary of preceding paragraph]
*But during the next generation the South was converted into a section which for
the most part was grimly united behind slavery.* [Topic sentence of the

paragraph] How did this come about? Why did the abolitionist spirit in the South almost disappear? [Questions to be answered by what follows] For one reason, the spirit of philosophical liberalism which flamed high in Revolutionary days gradually became weaker. [One possible answer] For another reason, a general antagonism between puritanical New England and the slaveholding South became evident; they differed on the War of 1812, the tariff, and other great issues; and the South felt less and less liking for the so-called Northern idea of emancipation. [A second possible answer] But above all, certain new economic factors made slavery more profitable than it had been before 1790. [This third possible answer provides a topic sentence for the whole section to follow, comprising the following two paragraphs.]

One element in the economic change is familiar—the rise of a great cotton-growing industry in the South. [First example of an "economic factor" topic sentence of the first half of the paragraph] This was based in part on the introduction of improved types of cotton, with better fibers [one explanation of the rise of the cotton industry], but in much larger part on Eli Whitney's epochal invention in 1793 of the "gin" for cleaning cotton [second explanation]. Cotton culture rapidly moved westward from the Carolinas and Georgia, spreading over much of the lower South to the Mississippi River and, eventually, on into Texas. *Another factor which placed slavery on a new basis was sugar growing.* [This second "economic factor" provides a topic sentence for the second half of the paragraph.] The rich, hot delta lands of southeastern Louisiana are ideal for sugar cane; and in 1794–1795 an enterprising New Orleans Creole, Étienne Boré, proved that the crop could be highly profitable. He set up machinery and vats, and the crowds which had come from New Orleans to watch the boiling-off broke into cheers when the first sugar crystals showed in the cooling liquid. The cry, "It granulates!" opened a new era in Louisiana. A great boom resulted, so that by 1830 the state was supplying the nation with about half its whole sugar supply. This required slaves, who were brought in, in thousands, from the Eastern seaboard.

Finally, tobacco culture also spread westward and took slavery with it. [Third "economic factor" and topic sentence of this paragraph] Constant cropping had worn out the soil of lowland Virginia, once the greatest tobacco region of the world, and the growers were glad to move into Kentucky and Tennessee, taking their Negroes with them. Thereafter the fast-multiplying slaves of the upper South were largely drained off to the lower South and West. This diffusion of slavery relieved many observers, because it lessened the risk of such a slave insurrection as

221

Nat Turner's Rebellion, a revolt of sixty or seventy Virginia slaves in 1831—which, incidentally, did much to increase Southern fear of emancipationist doctrines.

—ALLAN NEVINS AND HENRY STEELE COMMAGER,
The Pocket History of the United States

Here is a similar technique of dividing one's subject into parts and permitting the paragraph divisions to punctuate these parts.

The Soviet Union's cosmic rocket added a new member, if a miniscule one, to the system of planets revolving around the sun since eons past. Its success is a dramatic step toward sending rockets to seek out secrets of the solar system—and perhaps to explore some of the measureless space beyond. And it has stimulated men further to look up at the "stars that sweep, and turn, and fly," and ponder the nature of the universe. [This statement introduces the next idea, which is the heart of the piece.]

Space, from earthman's point of view, has three main divisions. [Main topic sentence] *The first and smallest is the solar system.* [Topic sentence of first subdivision] The sun, with a diameter of 864,000 miles and its mighty force of gravitation, holds the nine known planets in their elliptical orbits. In addition, the solar system includes thirty-one satellites of the planets (not counting the earth's artificial satellites); thousands of asteroids, which are rather like tiny planets; comets and meteors. As astronomical distances go, the size of the solar system is not astronomical: it is only about 7,350,000,000 miles across. [Particulars and details to clarify the topic sentence]

The next division of space is "our" galaxy: an aggregation of about 100 billion stars. [Topic sentence of second subdivision] Our sun is an average star in this "Milky Way." The nearest star to us after our sun is so distant that it takes light four and one-half years to travel to us. The galaxy itself is so vast that it takes light 100,000 years to travel from one edge of it to the other. Yet ours is a medium-sized galaxy. [Particulars and details]

Beyond our "Milky Way" is the third division of space—all the rest of the universe. [Topic sentence of third subdivision] In the unimaginable reaches of this really outer space are countless numbers of aggregations of suns. All these galaxies rotate and move in space. The most powerful telescopes can find no end to them. [Again, particulars and details]

—*The New York Times Magazine,* "To the Planets and Beyond"

The next example is from an essay in which the writer describes and illustrates creativity in many kinds of activity. Her major device for linking paragraphs is the repetition of the word *imagination.* See what other ways of making transitions you can identify.

Imagination is a kind of blind spot in the average, nonwriting member of society. Because, of course, everybody has imagination. If you have the thought, "Everyone hates me"; or if you consider it a good idea to see what is the matter with the light fuse by poking your finger into the socket; or if you suppose that you can sail a boat because you have seen other people do it; or if you conclude that a friend has turned against you, when in fact her brusqueness was the result of not thinking about you at all; those are all examples of an undisciplined imagination. It is obvious how dangerous such imaginings can be.

Malicious gossip—which takes the place of creation in noncreative lives—of course draws heavily on the imagination. Fear and superstition have their roots in imagination. The fact is that imagination is antisocial in that it is not in any relation at all to everyday reality. Then what is imagination in relation to?

Probably because of such destructive phantasies as those I listed, imagination hasn't a terribly good reputation in our society. Of course, to say that so-and-so is lacking in imagination is understood as not a compliment. But if I call someone a dreamer; or remark that someone has a head full of fancies; or say to someone, "That's all your imagination"—those are not compliments either. It might be objected that such disparagements only apply to those who might be called the amateur dreamers; that a novelist, for instance, is expected to have a highly active imagination. Yet to say "She certainly has a *lively* imagination" isn't praise either. That old phrase "Nothing but imagination," is one of the commonest, one of the most damning, in use today. I would point out, however, that even the greatest novels are "nothing but" paper, ink, a certain amount of miscellaneous information, and imagination.

The space age opening before our eyes is "nothing but" the end result, scientifically supported, worked out with infinite toil, of man's first mad, unreasonable image of himself flying. When it was first entertained, a good while before Daedalus, that image was about as adapted to reality as if I were to feel the urge to lie, like Ariel, in a cowslip's bell. Yet today we do fly. Science fiction once prophesied, in its apparently wild flights of fancy, many of the aerial feats that have come to pass. Are these the only phantasies which are allowed to come to pass? May not what science fiction calls teleportation also come to pass, along with the contents of that bottle in *Alice in Wonderland* marked DRINK ME, and may it not be possible for some woman in the future to become tiny and find herself curled inside that golden cup?

—NANCY HALE, "The Two-Way Imagination"

In reading the essays of professionals, as well as those written by classmates, it is helpful to develop a sensitivity to various techniques of transition from paragraph to paragraph. "How has the writer connected these parts?" can be your repeated question—and sometimes you will find that both professional and amateur have not connected them as well as they might. Similarly, when writing your own compositions, you can develop a critical awareness of paragraph sequence by giving regular attention to the endings and beginnings of paragraphs. Fairly early in the development of reading skill, and eventually in the development of proficiency in writing, this awareness of how paragraphs can be linked together becomes almost automatic—and an impressive feature of a mature style.

EXERCISES

EXERCISE 1, SENTENCE ORDER. *The following paragraphs are composed with a scrambled order of sentences. In each case, reorder the sentences so as to make a paragraph with the best possible internal organization. Do not rewrite any sentence. You will probably find the paragraphs increasing in complexity as you proceed.*

1. A realistic attitude toward the Panama Canal and the zone is not a retreat. An accommodation can be worked out with American patience and understanding. It is, instead, acceptance of a situation that could become intolerable in the face of American intransigence. Various of these points can be negotiated. A dubious treaty formulated two generations ago cannot be expected to stand today. But in the end, Panamanian sovereignty in Panama is not likely to be negotiable.

2. The furrier told her they were killed humanely, but all skins are sold at auction and he has no way of knowing how they were killed. The great majority are trapped. Take the First Family, for example. President Ford accepted a wolfskin coat, though the wolf is threatened with extinction. They are all professed animal lovers, yet look at the record. Susan Ford chose a fox-trimmed muskrat coat for graduation.

3. Making these parents live up to their obligations would prevent a drain on taxpayer's dollars and perhaps provide a higher level of support for the families. In about one-half of these cases fathers do not live at home and do not contribute to the support of the family. Federal officials estimate that about one-half of the absent fathers are financially capable of paying toward the living expenses of their families. A recent count showed there are about 3.4 million families in the Aid to Dependent Children program in the United States.

4. Rock music stars are often maligned in the press because of their appearance. Mick Jagger and Alice Cooper have been labeled in a similar way because of their make-up and costumes. The Beatles were called "effeminate"—and worse—when they first appeared in their unique haircuts. Without the easy access to name-calling these pundits would probably have to resort to the hard task of learning something about contemporary music. Until they are forced to do their homework, we can expect to see an unabated flow of sardonic but ephemeral adjectives in the reviews of rock concerts by "mainstream" music critics. This habit of labeling and packaging what is new or threatening is typical of American critics writing for major newsmagazines.

5. It is not hard to understand why assembly-line courts have become the rule and not the exception. Hundreds of people get divorced every day. When they realize how the system operates they find it easy to lose respect not only for the courts, but also for the law in general. Society also suffers under this system. Our courts are already bogged down in litigation. And the divorce laws encourage suits, countersuits, petitions, cross-petitions, depositions, claims, counterclaims, and long, bitter battles over property settlements. This atti-

225

tude will inevitably spread; it has already done great harm to the reputation of the judiciary, the legal profession, and, consequently, our very system of government. People must wait weeks or even months for court dates.

EXERCISE 2, INTRODUCTORY PARAGRAPHS. *Look through an anthology of modern essays, noting the introductory paragraphs. Find a paragraph stating a thesis to be argued, one telling an anecdote, and one offering a definition. Find one using a combination of these methods. Find one that fits none of these categories. Can you invent a useful fourth category to contain it?*

EXERCISE 3, WRITING INTRODUCTORY PARAGRAPHS. *Write three possible opening paragraphs for an essay, "The Roles of the Sexes in America Today." Use each of the three approaches outlined in the first part of this chapter.*

EXERCISE 4, TONE. *Rewrite your three paragraphs, drastically changing the tone (e.g., from serious to humorous, distant to familiar) in each case.*

EXERCISE 5, PARAGRAPH VARIETY. *Locate examples of the following:*

1. A paragraph with a topic sentence at the end.
2. A paragraph used as a transition between two topics of an essay.
3. A paragraph with a light tone on a heavy subject.
4. A paragraph within which the tone shifts.
5. A paragraph summarizing a section of an essay or chapter.

EXERCISE 6, REVISING A PARAGRAPH. *In the following passage, revise and combine the sentences, inserting transitions where necessary, in order to produce a logical and readable paragraph:*

Students of the English language have divided its historical growth into three main periods; the Old English Period, from 450 to 1100, was the first one. The Middle English Period lasted from 1100 until 1500. The Modern English Period began in 1500 and lasted up to the present time. The people of England

226

EXERCISES

did not stop speaking one kind of language and begin speaking another in any one year. The change was gradual. There were definite historical events occurring at the times mentioned which caused a more rapid change in the language of the people of England. The Angles, Saxons, and Jutes invaded England in 449. The Norman Conquest occurred in 1066. The English Renaissance began about 1500.

227

A HANDBOOK OF

WRITING AND

REVISION

1 *Grammar and Usage* 1

§ 1. SENTENCE FRAGMENTS

Fragmentary sentences should be avoided in expository writing.

A grammatically complete sentence is a pattern of communication in words that is based on a verb with its subject. The essential core of a complete sentence is at least one verb with its subject or subjects. Structurally the sentence must be an independent unit, capable of standing alone. Dependent units, such as phrases, clauses, appositives, and similar groups of words, are not sentences, and should not be written as sentences. When any one of these dependent units is written and punctuated as a sentence, it is called a *sentence fragment*

Of course there are also nonconforming patterns in writing and speech—especially in informal speech or written dialogue—which we may call legitimate fragments, or non-sentences, or unconventional sentences. They exist in our language, and their special uses must be understood. In expository writing, however, even legitimate fragments are usually objectionable. These patterns are discussed below.

Legitimate Sentence Fragments

Fragments of various kinds, verbless and subjectless sentences, with or without understood additions that would make them complete grammatically, are commonly used in speech. In narrative writing they are necessary to reproduce dialogue naturally. By some writers they are also used for special stylistic effects, especially in novels and short stories. In some of the fragments either the subject or the verb is understood; in others,

1

no amount of ingenious interpretation will supply a subject or a predicate. We must accept them for what they are—language patterns correctly punctuated as sentences. Here are examples:

THE COMMAND

Drive your car to the last platform. Please drive carefully. Then stop your motor. Open the trunk and let me look into your suitcases. [The typical pattern of the *imperative* sentence omits the subject.]

THE QUESTION

Why the delay, officer? A wreck ahead? How bad? Anyone hurt? Two elderly women? Oh, not seriously.

THE EXCLAMATION

Another fumble! Oh, what luck, what awful luck! Three fumbles already and no recoveries.

BITS OF DIALOGUE

"Tough luck," he said. "No stuff today, eh?"
"Yeah," I answered, "trying for corners."
"Keep it low. Curve 'em. Dr. Larkin's sure-fire cure for pitchers."

SPECIAL EFFECTS — THE ''POINTING-OUT'' METHOD OF DESCRIPTION

Sam Clark's Hardware Store. An air of frankly metallic enterprise. Guns and churns and barrels of nails and beautiful shiny butcher knives.

Chester Dashaway's House Furnishing Emporium. A vista of heavy oak rockers with leather seats, asleep in a dismal row.

Billy's Lunch. Thick handleless cups on the wet oilcloth-covered counter. An odor of onions and the smoke of hot lard. In the doorway a young man audibly sucking a toothpick.

The warehouse of the buyer of cream and potatoes. The sour smell of a dairy.

—SINCLAIR LEWIS, *Main Street*

Ineffective Sentence Fragments

An *ineffective sentence fragment* may be revised by (1) attaching the fragment to the sentence with which it logically belongs, (2) completing its form by adding the necessary words, (3) rewriting the passage.

232

1. SENTENCE FRAGMENTS

The four main types of ineffective sentence fragments are listed below and their corrections indicated by examples:

1a. A dependent clause should not be written as a complete sentence.

If you remember that a dependent clause usually begins with a connective that relates it to the main clause, you can guard against some types of fragments. For adjective clauses look for the relative pronouns *who, which,* and *that,* and the relative adverbs *when, where,* and *why.* For adverb clauses look for the subordinating conjunctions *after, although, as if, because, before, if, since, though, unless, when, where,* and *while.* Noun clauses are almost never miswritten as fragments. Another helpful fact to remember is that the fragment usually *follows* the main clause, to which it may be joined in correction.

FRAGMENT

He spent his life preaching social justice. *Which was a startling concept in his day.*

REVISION

He spent his life preaching social justice, which was a startling concept in his day. [Add fragment to main clause.]

FRAGMENT

The animosity that his ideas excited is incredible. *Although a few brave men praised him.*

REVISION

The animosity that his ideas excited is incredible, although a few brave men praised him. [Add clause to sentence.]

FRAGMENT

The officer came to the alley where the man was last seen. *And where the stolen gems were probably hidden.*

REVISION

The officer came to the alley where the man was last seen, and where the stolen gems were probably hidden. [The second *where*-clause also modifies *alley.*]

233

1

1b. A verbal or a prepositional phrase should not be written as a complete sentence.

F R A G M E N T

The two boys took the first faint trail to their left. *Hoping it would take them to a river.*

R E V I S I O N S

The two boys took the first faint trail to their left, hoping it would lead them to a river. [Join phrase to main sentence.]

The two boys took the first faint trail to their left. They hoped it would lead them to a river. [Supply subject and verb to make the fragment a sentence.]

F R A G M E N T S

They plodded along the trail all day. *Without a rest. Without stopping to eat what food was left.*

R E V I S I O N

Without a stop to rest or to eat what food they had, they plodded along the trail all day. [You may also revise by putting the prepositional phrases after the main clause.]

F R A G M E N T

The railroad made Virginia City a lumber center. *Its population leaping from three hundred to five thousand in three years.* [This is a participial phrase of the special type called the absolute phrase. See page 165.]

R E V I S I O N

The railroad made Virginia City a lumber center. Its population leaped from three hundred to five thousand in three years. [Change the participle to a verb to make a complete sentence. You may also join the phrase to the main clause.]

1c. An appositive phrase should not be written as a complete sentence.

Guard against this fault especially when the phrase is introduced by such words as *namely, for example, such as,* and the like.

F R A G M E N T

Some games are called contact sports. *Namely, football, basketball, and ice hockey.*

234

1. SENTENCE FRAGMENTS

REVISION

Some games, namely football, basketball, and ice hockey, are called contact sports.

FRAGMENT

New problems face the woman entering college. *Such as budgeting her money and her time for study.* [*Budgeting* is in apposition with *problems.*]

REVISION

New problems, such as budgeting her money and her time for study, face the woman entering college. [Place the appositive near *problems*, not at the end of the sentence.]

FRAGMENT

We found the case transferred to Juvenile Court. *A development that completely puzzled us.* [*Development* is in apposition with the whole idea expressed in the main clause.]

REVISION

We found the case transferred to Juvenile Court, a development that completely puzzled us. [Add the appositive to the main clause.]

1d. Any verbless chip or fragment of a sentence, whether you can classify it or not, should not be allowed to stand as a sentence.

Some fragments are written because the writer was in too much of a hurry to think; others are written because the writer has carried over into writing the exclamatory nature of very informal speech. The following examples will make the points clear:

FRAGMENTS

Just a lazy weekend vacation. No work. No worries. That's what he promised me.

REVISIONS

Just a lazy weekend vacation with no work or worries—that's what he promised me. [The dash indicates a sharp break in the construction.]

What he promised me was a pleasant weekend vacation, with no work and no worries.

235

1

FRAGMENT

Unexpectedly I dropped in on her daughter. *Just a friendly call, no party.*
[The writer of this was making notes, not sentences.]

REVISION

Unexpectedly I dropped in on her daughter. I intended this to be just
a friendly, informal call. [Make a sentence out of the fragment.]

EXERCISES

EXERCISE 1, RECOGNIZING SENTENCE FRAGMENTS. *Copy
the following sentences. Some of them are complete. Some are fragments. If
a sentence is complete, underline its subject once and its verb twice. If the
group of words is a clause, encircle the subordinating connective. If it is a
verbal phrase, encircle the verbal.*

1. *Main Street* being Sinclair Lewis's first really important
   novel.
2. Although he had already published two or three full-length
   stories.
3. A native of Sauk Center, Minnesota, he wrote about the
   people he knew best.
4. At first, the natives of Sauk Center were very indignant.
5. Resenting his slurs against them and their way of life.
6. They insisted that his novel was not a true picture of their
   town.
7. That his characters were caricatures and his town a mon-
   strosity.
8. Finding that his fame brought them notice and recognition.
9. Gradually capitalizing on their notoriety in profitable ways.
10. Merchants adopted "Gopher Prairie" as a sort of brand
    name for several of their commercial enterprises.

EXERCISE 2, ELIMINATING SENTENCE FRAGMENTS. *In
some of the following word groups you will find sentence fragments. Eliminate each fragment either by joining it to the main clause or by rewriting it
as a complete sentence. Be able to tell whether rule 1a, 1b, or 1c applies.*

1. Last summer, while on our way from New York to Denver,
   we stopped at University Park, Pennsylvania, to visit a
   friend of ours. Whom we had not seen since our college days.

2. The college is now a state university, and the town, once called State College, is now known as University Park. Names of towns being subject to quick changes.
3. The town is not exactly inaccessible, as some say. Neither is it close to a modern turnpike or expressway.
4. The drive to the city took us across several ranges of hills. The road at times narrow and curving but never difficult to take at reasonable speeds.
5. I was amazed at the extent and attractiveness of the campus. Situated as it was in the beautiful Nittany Mountains.
6. We found our friend in the college infirmary, where he had his office. And where he has worked with the students for many years.
7. His face showed at once that he had aged and gained weight. And his hair, or what was left of it, having turned gray.
8. He said he could leave his office early, drive us about the campus, and then take us out to dinner. Which was an offer that we accepted with many thanks.
9. Talking with an old friend usually revives old memories. Such as college pranks, football games, and wartime experiences.
10. Leaving him the next morning, we felt that he had led a happy, useful, and rewarding life. A fact that we spoke of at odd moments most of that day.

2

§ 2. RUN–TOGETHER SENTENCES

When two or more complete sentences are combined in a single sentence, they must be properly separated from one another.

A sentence made up of two or more independent, coordinate clauses, properly joined and punctuated, is called a *compound sentence*. (See page 169.) The usual means of joining these independent clauses are (1) a semicolon, (2) a conjunction, (3) a comma and a conjunction, (4) a semicolon and a conjunction. (See also § § 13 and 14.)

237

2a. The comma splice may be corrected in several ways.

The use of a comma to join independent, coordinate clauses (except in certain infrequent situations that will be discussed later) is called a *comma splice* or a *comma fault.* It should be avoided in college writing. A comma splice may be corrected in one of the following ways. The student should choose the method of revision that produces the most effective sentence.

1. The comma splice may be corrected by *subordinating one of the two independent sentences.* (If the student puts both statements in the same sentence, he must believe that one is closely related to the other. A subordinate clause can express this relation specifically.)

SPLICE
We all went home after the picnic, it had started to rain.

BETTER
We all went home after the picnic because it had started to rain.

SPLICE
The food was fine except for the cake, I didn't like it.

BETTER
The food was fine except for the cake, which I didn't like.

2. The comma splice may be corrected by *inserting a coordinating conjunction after the comma.* (These conjunctions are *and, but, for, or, nor, yet.*)

SPLICE
We were looking for a shady spot, we couldn't find one.

BETTER
We were looking for a shady spot, but we couldn't find one.

3. The comma splice may be corrected by *using a semicolon instead of a comma if the sentences are close enough in meaning to be combined into a compound sentence.*

238

2. *RUN-TOGETHER SENTENCES*

SPLICE

We finally found a satisfactory place, it was breezy but quiet.

BETTER

We finally found a satisfactory place; it was breezy but quiet.

If you wished instead to subordinate, then the sentence would look like this:

We finally found a satisfactory place, which was breezy but quiet.

4. The comma splice may be corrected by *using a period to separate the two coordinate clauses.* In simple examples, such as the ones we are discussing here, the danger of this alternative is a series of very short sentences that look choppy.

CORRECT BUT CHOPPY

We finally found a satisfactory place. It was breezy but quiet.

Note that the choice of a solution for the run-together sentence, like all choices in writing, can affect the tone of the statement. In the last revision above, the choice of two very short sentences makes the speaker sound matter-of-fact and distanced, almost like a police officer reporting details of an investigation. The decisions you make about grammar relate directly to the way your words affect the reader.

LEGITIMATE COMMA JUNCTIONS

The use of a comma to join coordinate clauses is more common in novels, stories, and some types of journalistic writing than in expository prose. In any case the clauses so joined are likely to be short and simple, and are most likely to occur in the following situations:

1. *When the clauses are arranged in the "a, b, and c" order.*

EXAMPLES

The shrubs were leafy and well-shaped, the walks had been carefully raked, and the fountain shone in the sunlight.

The dog growled, the cat spat, the mouse fled.

2. *When the series of statements takes the form of a climax.*

239

2

EXAMPLES

I came, I saw, I conquered.

The sun is growing warm, frogs are waking in the marshes, planting time will soon be here.

3. *When the statements form an antithesis, or are arranged in the "it was not merely this, it was also that" formula.* This is an effect particularly characteristic of traditional stylists.

EXAMPLES

It was more than an annoyance, it was a pang.

—WINSTON CHURCHILL

To allow the Mahdi to enter Khartoum would not merely mean the return of the whole of the Sudan to barbarism, it would be a menace to the safety of Egypt herself.

—LYTTON STRACHEY

Two familiar situations in writing invite the comma splice. One such danger point is immediately following tags such as *he said* in dialogue.

DIALOGUE

"That's right," said Paul. "I'd almost forgotten her name." [A period is the usual punctuation, although a semicolon is occasionally used.] "No one remembers the good things I have done," she complained; "no one ever does." [Semicolon used here.]

"Yes, I know, sir," said Jones. "I warned him to be careful." [Period used here.]

The other danger concerns conjunctive adverbs such as *however, moreover,* and so on.

ADVERBS

The prisoner told a long story of atrocities; however, his companion did not agree with his version of what had happened to them. [Use a semicolon before the conjunctive adverb. By using a semicolon and relocating the adverb within the second clause, you can achieve a smoother transition: ". . . atrocities; his companion did not agree, however, with his version . . ."]

240

When I registered for engineering, I had two high school subjects to make up; moreover, I had forgotten most of the algebra I ever knew. [Use a semicolon before the conjunctive adverb.]

2b. The fused sentence may be corrected by the same methods as the comma splice.

The fused sentence is one in which two sentences are run together with no punctuation at all between them. It is an extreme example of the same carelessness that produces the sentence fragment and the comma splice.

In the following pairs of sentences, the first is a fused sentence followed by a unified one.

At first I wondered if I should speak to her she seemed to be so wrapped up in her thoughts.

She seemed so wrapped up in her thoughts that at first I wondered if I should speak to her. [Subordination]

I almost decided to walk by and pretend I did not see her she might think I was intruding.

Fearing that she might think I was intruding, I almost decided to walk by and pretend not to see her. [Subordination]

I was lonesome I decided to speak and I said hello in a weak voice.

As I was lonesome, I decided to speak to her, and I said hello in a weak voice. [Subordination]

EXERCISES

EXERCISE 1, SUBORDINATING CLAUSES. *Correct each of the following sentences by subordinating one or more of the run-together coordinate clauses.*

1. Some people like an ocean voyage in winter, they want to escape the frost and snow at home.
2. A few are likely to be bored on a ship it is such a closed-in community.
3. The weather may be fine for days, however, it may change abruptly, everyone gets seasick.

2

4. The food is usually rich and plentiful, it would be unfortunate not to enjoy it.
5. Deckchairs are the rule in sunny weather, in bad weather one stays below.
6. Who would not appreciate seeing the islands of the West Indies, we have heard so much about them?
7. The stewards on shipboard are uniformly pleasant and efficient, they have been so well trained, they know exactly what to do.
8. Vacations at sea are within the reach of many people today they were a luxury for a privileged class not so very long ago.
9. Air travel is much faster, of course, nevertheless a week on a ship can be far more restful.
10. Most people are glad to get home, however, you can tell by looking at their happy faces as they step ashore.

Exercise 2, Subordinating with Phrases and Appositives. *Revise each of the following sentences by using subordination of a rank below that of a subordinate clause (a phrase or an appositive).*

1. Success in life, they say, requires two principal qualities, they are perseverance and innate talent.
2. This is like most such generalizations it is hard to put to practical use.
3. A person has perseverance, or innate talent, how can you distinguish?
4. Many people apparently have perseverance and talent, they still do not conspicuously succeed.
5. Such statements are misleading they are so simple, they are falsely profound.

Exercise 3, Revising an Informal Paragraph. *Here is a paragraph composed in a style approximating informal speech. Rewrite it by revising its fragments and run-together sentences in any way you think appropriate.*

I'm disgusted with him. The liar. Telling me all the time how honest he was, too. He wanted to borrow my car, I knew he didn't even have a license, his roommate told me that. I should have said no to him, I know I should. Right to his face. I'm soft-hearted, you know how I am. In spite of all past disappointments. I wonder where my car is, it's been quite a long time now. That thief.

Notice again, as you do this exercise, how the tone changes with the changes in grammar. Is the speaker in your revision more angry than the original speaker, or less? Is he closer to his imaginary listener, or further away?

3

§ 3. SUBJECT–VERB AGREEMENT

A verb must agree in number with its subject.

Once it is understood that a singular verb matches a singular noun and a plural verb a plural noun, there is nothing very difficult in recognizing that "The *boys are* playing in the yard" is standard English, whereas "The *boys is* playing in the yard" is not. As long as subject and verb lie close together, and it is obvious whether the subject is singular or plural, there should be no problem in applying the principle of agreement in number. Confusion arises when the complexity of a sentence or the peculiarity of a subject obscures the immediate relation between subject and verb. Problems in agreement fall into three main categories:

1. When several other words intervene between the subject and verb, or when the word order is unusual, the writer or speaker may forget for the moment just what the subject is and so make an error.

2. When the subject seems to be simultaneously singular and plural—"everybody," "gymnastics," "the whole family," "either of us," "a group of people"—or when its number seems to be a matter of choice, the writer can easily become confused over the number to be reflected in the verb.

3. Because usage differs according to situation or occasion, the writer may not know which rule best suits a given occasion. The forms recommended in this book, however, are appropri-

3

ate and correct in all varieties of English—formal or informal, written or spoken. In very informal situations, other forms may *also* be current.

It is often helpful to make a quick diagram of the grammatical subject and verb of a sentence.

3a. **Plural words that intervene between a singular subject and its verb do not change the number of the subject.**

E X A M P L E S

The *racket* of all those engines *was* deafening. [*Racket was,* not *engines were.* "Of all those engines" is a phrase modifying *racket,* and this of course does not make *racket* plural.]

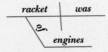

One of the many techniques he explained to us *was* that of flycasting. [*One* technique *was flycasting.*]

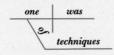

3b. **When words are added to a singular subject by *with, together with, as well as, in addition to, except,* and *no less than,* the number of the subject remains singular.**

E X A M P L E S

The *teacher,* as well as his principal, *was* exonerated. [*Teacher was*]
The *boy,* together with three companions, *was* discovered the next day. [*Boy was*]

These expressions may be logically considered as introducing modifiers of the subject. They do not have the force of *and,* which is the word that compounds a subject and makes it plural.

3c. **In sentence patterns that depart from the typical subject-verb-complement order, watch for the following situations in particular.**

244

3. SUBJECT-VERB AGREEMENT

1. The Subject Following the Verb. Mental transposition into normal order will clarify agreement of subject and verb.

3

EXAMPLES

Scattered over the floor *were* the *remains* of the evening's feast. [*Remains were scattered*]

Browsing peacefully in her vegetable garden *were* a large *elk* and three mule *deer*. [*Elk and deer were*]

2. Introductory *It*. Introductory *it*, as in "It is the people who matter," is always followed by a singular verb, no matter whether the noun that follows is singular or plural. *It* in such cases is an expletive, often called the *preparatory subject*, preparing the way for the real subject to come. Nevertheless it controls the verb. No one would say, "It are the people." (The preparatory subject is often used as a carry-over from spoken English. In the first example below note how much more direct the statement becomes after eliminating "It is . . . that" and rearranging word order: "We must consider her happiness." When you find yourself using the "It is" or "There are" constructions to excess, try rephrasing your sentences without them.)

EXAMPLES

It is her *happiness* that we must consider. [*It is happiness.* But try rephrasing: We must consider her happiness.]

It is the *colleges* that must take up the burden. [*It is colleges.* Rephrased: Colleges must take up the burden.]

3. Introductory *There*. In present-day English, usage seems to be divided in regard to the number of the verb when the preparatory *there* introduces a sentence.

In sentences in which the noun that follows the verb is *plural*, most writers and speakers will use a plural verb.

EXAMPLES

There *are*, if I counted right, exactly *thirteen* persons at this table. [*Persons are*]

There are, you must admit, several *degrees* of guilt. [*Degrees are*]

245

3

4. Introductory *What*. *What* as a preparatory subject may be either singular or plural according to what the writer means. If it serves in the sense of *the one thing that,* it is singular, and the only caution to observe is that all related verbs should respect its singular status—even when its subjective complement consists of more than one thing.

EXAMPLE

What is interesting about this model *is* the seven speed settings available. [*The one thing about this model is.* . . .]

It is usually clear when *what* must be plural.

EXAMPLE

For *what are* doubtless good reasons, responsibility for maintaining the reservoir has been transferred from the Sewage Authority.

Even with logic on your side, it is advisable to avoid constructions like the following:

Pterodactyls were not birds; *what* they were *was* reptiles. [Balance is preserved by saying simply, ". . . they were reptiles."]

When the subject following the verb consists of a number of nouns, the first of which is singular, there is a tendency to make the verb singular. Those who are conscious of the requirements of grammatical agreement, and who have time to plan their sentences, will use the plural verb in such cases.[1]

EXAMPLES

From Long Island to San Francisco, from Florida Bay to Vancouver's Island, there *is* one dominant race and civilization, one language, one type of law, one sense of nationality.

—FREDERIC HARRISON, *Memories and Thoughts*

At Valenciennes, where there *was* a review and a great dinner. . . .

—LYTTON STRACHEY, *Queen Victoria*

---

[1] Examples here used are quoted from David S. Berkeley's "An Agreement of Subject and Verb in Anticipatory *There* Clauses," *American Speech,* May, 1953. By kind permission.

3. SUBJECT-VERB AGREEMENT

There *is* much manganese and chrome, and enough uranium in the slag heaps of the Johannesburg gold mines to make its extraction worth while.

—*Harper's Magazine*

3d. The verb agrees with its subject, not with its subjective complement.

If the difference in number between subject and complement produces an awkward sentence, it is better to rewrite.

RIGHT
The one last *object* of her love *was* three Siamese cats. [Not *object were*]

REWRITTEN
She had nothing left to love except her three Siamese cats.

RIGHT
Our *worry was* the frequent storms that swept the lake. [Not *worry were*]

REWRITTEN
We worried because storms frequently swept the lake.

3e. A compound subject joined by *and* takes a plural verb.

Again, do not be distracted by unusual word order or by intervening phrases.

EXAMPLES
The *rest* of the manuscript and the *letter* from Whitney *seem* to have been destroyed in the fire. [Not *seems*]

A heavy *coat* or *windbreaker* and a fur *cap are* recommended as additional equipment. *Are* both an *overcoat* and a *parka* necessary? [Not *overcoat and parka is*]

When several singular subjects represent the same person or thing, however, or when they form one collective idea, a singular verb is used.

247

3

The *sum* and *substance* of the book *is* that all men are created equal.

The *tumult* and the *shouting dies.* . . .

—RUDYARD KIPLING, "Recessional"

Our *ally* and *neighbor* to the south, the Republic of Mexico, *maintains* a quiet border.

But notice the difference that an article (*a, an, the*) can make.

E X A M P L E S

The blue and gold sweater is very becoming.
The blue and the gold sweaters are very becoming.

A red and white rose is in bloom.
A red and a white rose are in bloom.

3f. **When subjects are joined by** *neither—nor, either—or, not only—but also,* **the verb agrees with the nearer subject.**

When both subjects are singular, the verb is singular; when both subjects are plural, the verb is also plural. But when one subject is plural and the other singular, formal usage prescribes that the nearer subject dictates the number of the verb. In informal usage there is a tendency to make the verb always plural. One way to avoid an awkward sentence—as well as an awkward decision—is to recast the sentence entirely.

F O R M A L

Neither the *students* nor their *teacher is* quite prepared.

Neither *you* nor *I am* going there now.

I N F O R M A L

Neither the *students* nor their *teacher are* quite prepared.

*You are*n't going there now and neither *am I.*

3g. **After** *each, every, each one, everyone, everybody, anybody, nobody, none, either,* **and** *neither* **the singular verb is used in formal English.**

3. *SUBJECT-VERB AGREEMENT*

EXAMPLES

Each of us *is* willing to pay *his* share of the expenses. [Note that *his,* referring to *each,* is also singular.]

Every American *knows his* (or *her*) duty.

Has anyone seen her?

I doubt that *anybody knows* who wrote the song.

The rule as stated here represents the practice of most writers. Exceptions can easily be found, in both formal and informal writing. In an attempt to interpret usage, it is said that the *intention* of the writer determines whether the singular or the plural is to be used. But that is a razor-edge distinction for a student to make. When you say "*Each* of the boys *tells* a different story," the choice is clear, but it is a less obvious matter of right between "*None* of the boys *is* telling the truth," and "*None* of the boys *are* telling the truth." You may justify the first as formal usage and the second as informal usage. The simplest solution is to say, "All the boys are lying."

3h. With a collective noun a singular verb is used when the group named by the noun is regarded as a unit; a plural verb is used when the noun is regarded as indicating the individuals of a group.

Common collective nouns that are troublesome are *class, band, number, family, group, public, committee.*

EXAMPLES

The *number* of failures *was* surprising. [*The number* is usually construed as a single unit.]

A *number* of students *are* failing this term. [*A number* refers to individual items or members of a group and is therefore plural.]

The whole *family is* here. [The modifier indicates that *family* is considered as a single unit.]

The *family are* all attending different churches. [Here the reference is to the individuals of the family.]

Since there is considerable range for individual choice in the use of collective nouns, *consistency* must be the student's guide.

3

Once you have spoken of a group as a single unit, you should not, without some explanation, refer to it as a plural.

EXAMPLES

The *platoon are* removing their knapsacks. *They are* getting ready for a mock charge.

The *class was* assembled promptly and proceeded with *its* assignment.

3i. When the subject is a title, the name of a book, a clause, a quotation, or some other group of words expressing a single idea, the verb is singular.

EXAMPLES

Bolts of Melody is a collection of Emily Dickinson's poems.

All men are created equal is a statement of dubious truth.

   This rule also applies to expressions signifying number, quantity, distance, time, amount, or extent. When the subject is expressed as a unit, the verb is singular.

EXAMPLES

Twenty years is an unusual time to wait for an editor to make up his mind.

Five hundred words is long enough for most daily themes.

Thirty miles is a tiring day's walk.

   But when the amount is meant to be made up of separate units, the plural verb is used.

EXAMPLES

The first *ten years* of every marriage *are* the hardest to endure.

There *are five hundred words* in his essay.

3j. Several words ending in -*s* are governed by special rules of usage.

   A number of nouns ending in *-ics* are considered singular when they refer to a branch of study or a body of knowledge (*linguistics, physics, mathematics, civics, economics*), but are usually

250

plural when they refer to physical activities, qualities, or phenomena (*acoustics, acrobatics, tactics, phonetics, athletics*).

Other words likely to cause trouble are listed below.

Usually singular: *news, measles, mumps, gallows.*

Usually plural: *scissors, tidings, riches, trousers, means, falls* [water].

Either singular or plural: *headquarters, politics, alms.*

3k. **A singular verb is used with a relative pronoun referring to a singular antecedent, and a plural verb is used with a pronoun referring to a plural antecedent.**

E X A M P L E S

It is good to associate with *students who are* courteous. [*Who* refers to *students,* a plural noun.]

He is the only *one* of the family *who intends* to enter college. [*Who* is singular because it refers to *one.*]

Now notice the difference between the last example above and the following construction: "She is one of those girls who are always getting into trouble." If you shift this about to read, "Of those girls who are always getting into trouble, she is one," you can see that *who* refers to *girls* and is therefore plural. But in practice the singular verb is very common, especially in speech: "She is one of those girls who is always getting into trouble."

E X E R C I S E S

EXERCISE 1, RECOGNIZING SUBJECTS AND VERBS. *Some of the difficulty with agreement, as we have seen, is simply a matter of making sure just what the subjects and verbs in sentences are. In the following sentences write* S *above each subject and* V *above each verb.*

1. As he said, there were a police officer and a crowd of people in front of our house.
2. The police officer, as well as most of the crowd, was looking up at the sky.
3. One of several things that I worried about was a fire.

3

4. Neither burglars nor a fire is ever far from a homeowner's thoughts.
5. Every one of my neighbors is worried about fires.
6. The sum and substance of it is that we have poor fire protection.
7. Smoke, as well as fire and water, causes much damage to a burning house.
8. Looking up toward the treetops in front of our house were three small boys.
9. The number of people inspecting our residence was growing steadily.
10. The news that finally reached us was reassuring; the excitement was about a kitten frantically trying to descend from its perch on a tall tree.

EXERCISE 2, CORRECTING ERRORS IN SUBJECT-VERB AGREEMENT. *Correct the errors in each of the following sentences. Tell what rule applies.*

1. The outcome of all those meetings and conferences were the appointment of a committee.
2. In colleges and in governments there is usually a type of person that love to serve on committees.
3. This committee, with the Dean of Administration, serve as a check on other committees.
4. There seems to be several explanations why this was called a standing committee.
5. If my mathematics is correct, this committee sat from two to six the first day.
6. Four hours are a long time for a standing committee to sit.
7. Each of the members have a different cause to champion.
8. Neither the dean nor the chairman admit saying, "A camel is a greyhound designed by a committee."
9. One man complained that the acoustics in the auditorium was poor.
10. The outcome of all their deliberations were that the questions under discussion should be referred to a new committee.

1. The teacher remarked that his use of salacious expressions were unfortunate.
2. Either you or I am going to tell him to watch his language.
3. Linguistics are not exactly his strong point; he is much better at athletics.
4. Athletics, whether you believe it or not, do require some skilled teaching.
5. The salary of a football coach, thirty thousand a year, is much more than the average professor earns.
6. There seems to be several reasons why this is so.
7. The public know that a good fullback is hard to find, and it is willing to pay the price required.
8. But many a good fullback were lost to the world because he could not pass his entrance examinations.
9. My uncle is one of those who do not believe that a knowledge of poetics is useful in a business office.
10. After his long career as a little-known author, one of his novels were made into a motion picture.

4

§ 4. PRONOUNS

Be careful to use the right form of the pronoun.

Nouns in modern English change their form for the plural and for the possessive. Plurals are discussed in § 19. The possessive forms are discussed in § 15. There are very few problems connected with the form changes of nouns.

Some pronouns, however, change their forms for person, number, and case, and thereby cause the student of the English language numerous difficulties. In English there are three cases: the *nominative* or *subjective,* the *possessive,* the *objective.* There are also three persons: the *first* person indicates the speaker; the

4

second person indicates the one spoken to; the *third* indicates the one spoken about.

The forms of the personal pronoun are shown in the table below:

SINGULAR NUMBER

	FIRST PERSON	SECOND PERSON	THIRD PERSON *Masc.*	*Fem.*	*Neuter*
Nominative:	I	you	he	she	it
Possessive:	my, mine	your, yours	his	her, hers	its
Objective:	me	you	him	her	it

PLURAL NUMBER

	FIRST PERSON	SECOND PERSON	THIRD PERSON
Nominative:	we	you	they
Possessive:	our, ours	your, yours	their, theirs
Objective:	us	you	them

The relative and interrogative pronoun *who* has only three forms:

Nominative:	who
Possessive:	whose
Objective:	whom

There are also a number of *indefinite* pronouns, such as *another, anybody, anyone, anything, both, each, either, everybody, everyone, everything, few, many, neither, nobody, none, one, somebody, someone.*

The intensive pronouns (used for emphasis) and the reflexive pronouns (used to point the action back toward the subject) are *myself, himself, herself, itself, yourself, yourselves, ourselves, themselves.* Be careful not to overuse these intensive pronouns.

INTENSIVE

The general *himself* gave the order. I *myself* will carry it out.

REFLEXIVE

"You can easily hurt *yourselves*," I said, but they picked *themselves* up.

4. *PRONOUNS*

MISUSED

Everyone, including *myself,* was surprised by the announcement. [The objective case, *me,* is appropriate.]

My wife and *myself* were invited to Harry's party. [My wife and *I*]

Nominative Case

4a. The nominative case is used when the pronoun is the subject of a verb.

The student should watch out for three trouble spots in connection with the use of the nominative case:

1. A parenthetical expression, such as *they think, they say, we believe,* etc., between *who* (*whoever*) and the verb may confuse the writer.

EXAMPLES

Jones is one senior who we think could teach this class. [Not *whom we think,* but *who could teach*]

A young man who we believe was the driver of the car is being held.

Who did you say brought us these cherries? [Not *whom did you say*]

We agreed to accept whoever they thought was the best foreman. [Not *whomever*]

S	V	O	S	V	C	S	V	C
who	*could teach*	*class*	*who*	*was*	*driver*	*whoever*	*was*	*foreman*

2. The fact that a *who* or *whoever* clause follows a preposition may confuse the writer into using the wrong case.

EXAMPLES

Send a card to *whoever* asks for one. [Not *to whomever. Whoever* may seem to be attracted into the objective case by its position after the preposition. But it is the subject of the verb *asks.* The whole clause is the object of the preposition.]

Settle the question with *whoever* wrote the report. [Not *with whomever,* but *whoever wrote*]

4

3. In clauses of comparison, with *than* and *as,* the nominative is used with the implied verb.

EXAMPLES
She can usually see more in a painting than *I* [can see]
No one knows that better than *she* [knows it]

Comparison between two clauses, the verb of one of which is implied, constitutes what is called an *elliptical* sentence.

4b. **In standard literary English, the nominative-case form is used when the pronoun is a subjective complement after the verb *be*.**

In conversation, "it's me" is generally accepted, and in most conversational situations "it's *I*" or "it is *I*" would sound affected and silly. As for "it's *us*" or "it's *them,*" probably the best advice —*in conversation*—is to follow your ear and your sense of propriety. You should do the same when writing dialogue. Outside quotation marks, however, standard written English requires the nominative in all such uses.

EXAMPLES
It is *we* who must bear the burden of the tax program, even though it was *they* who initiated it.
It was *he* (or *she*) who made the plans for the meeting.

Possessive Case

4c. **The apostrophe is not used with personal pronouns to form the possessive case; the apostrophe is used, however, with those indefinite pronouns that can be used in the possessive.**

The possessive forms of the personal pronouns are *my, mine, your, yours, his, her, hers, its, our, ours, their, theirs.*
The possessive forms of the indefinite pronouns are *anybody's, anyone's, everybody's, nobody's, no one's, one's, somebody's.*

256

WRONG

The furniture is *their's,* but the house is *our's.*

The bush is dying; *it's* leaves are covered with mildew.

RIGHT

The furniture is *theirs,* but the house is *ours.*

The bush is dying; *its* leaves are covered with mildew.

Note carefully the distinction between *it's,* which means *it is,* and *its,* which is the possessive form of *it.* Note also that when *else* follows the indefinite pronoun, such as *anybody, somebody, someone,* the apostrophe and *s* are added to *else,* not to the pronoun.

RIGHT

It's [contraction of *it is*] *anybody's* guess *whose* [possessive form of *who*] horse will win this race.

Would you like to ride in somebody *else's* car?

I wouldn't trust someone *else's* judgment.

4d. In standard English the general practice is to use the possessive form of the pronoun when it precedes a gerund.

Please note that here we do not use *general* in the sense of *universal.* We mean, "Most do; some don't." It is easy enough to find exceptions in the writing of reputable authors.

EXAMPLES

I cannot understand *his refusing* to do that for me.

Her driving off so abruptly was most unfortunate.

I told them about *your resigning* from office.

In these sentences the verbals *refusing, driving, resigning* are gerunds. They are used as object, as subject, and as object of a preposition, in that order. When the verbal is a participle, however, the objective case is correct.

EXAMPLES

We saw *them waving* a flag. [Them in the act of waving]

I found *him using* my typewriter. [Him in the act of using]

257

4

With nouns introducing or modifying gerunds, usage varies. There are situations in which the possessive is desirable; there are others in which it is difficult or clumsy, and therefore it gives way to the objective.

EXAMPLES

The family resisted the idea of *Mary's leaving* home.

The prospect of *nations fighting* one another again is almost unthinkable.

It was hard to imagine so many *buildings being constructed.*

4e. **Instead of the apostrophe-*s* form, the *of*-phrase may be used to show possession when the situation calls for it.**

1. Ordinarily, the *of*-phrase is used for inanimate objects: "the back of the building," "the top of the totem pole," "the hem of the dress" (*not* "the dress of my sister"). However, notice such forms as "in an hour's time" and "a week's pay." In some cases either form may be used; in other cases only one form is possible.

2. The *of*-phrase may also be used when the simple possessive form would separate a noun from its modifier.

EXAMPLE

The trustworthiness of a man who never thinks twice is highly questionable. [Not "The man's trustworthiness who never thinks . . ."]

The double possessive is a construction long established in standard English.

EXAMPLES

friends of Jane's   that old lover of mine   a colleague of his

Objective Case

4f. **The objective case of the pronoun is used when the pronoun is the direct or indirect object of a verb or verbal.**

DIRECT OBJECT

We liked *him*. Mother called *her*. Father tried to pay *him*. Punishing *him* did little good.

258

4. PRONOUNS

Mother served *them* their dinners. I agreed to read *him* a story.

The need for objective case in a pronoun object that immediately follows a verb or verbal is easy to recognize. A fault is obvious in sentences such as "I saw *she* at the game" and "Father bought *we* a new surfboard." Three kinds of construction, however, may pose some difficulty.

1. *Who* and *whom* may be confused when they appear out of their normal subject-verb-object pattern. In questions, *who* beginning the sentence is used in informal speech for both the subject and the object forms, but formal writing requires *whom* as object.

CONVERSATIONAL
Who did you want to see?
I'd like to know *who* they're going to elect.

FORMAL
Whom can we trust at such a moment in history? [We can trust *whom*.]
He was the one *whom* they finally selected. [They selected *whom*.]

2. When the pronoun is the second of two objects connected by *and*.

EXAMPLES
Mr. Case told John and *me* to make the decision. [Not *John and I*]
Everyone was astounded when the association chose for membership both *her* and *me*. [Not *her and I*]

3. When the pronoun is the object of an implied verb, after *than* and *as* in clauses of comparison.

EXAMPLES
He always gave Jack more than [he gave] *me*.
Mary told me more about it than [she told] *him*.

By reviewing paragraph 3, §4a, you can observe the difference when the nominative pronoun is used as the subject of the implied verb in similar constructions:

259

4

EXAMPLE

Mary told me more about it than *he* [told me].

4g. The objective case form is normally used when the pronoun is the object of a preposition.

Here again trouble arises not when the pronoun immediately follows a preposition, as in "I said to *her*" [not, of course, to *she*], but when the pronoun comes before its preposition or when it is the second of two objects.

EXAMPLES

It is difficult to predict *whom* the electorate will vote for. [For *whom*]

Whom could we turn to at a time like this? [To *whom*]

There was some controversy between *him* and *me*. [Not *him and I*]

Informal, conversational usage accepts *who* as the objective form, especially in questions, in which the pronoun may begin a sentence or a clause, such as "*Who* did you call for?" of "*Who* are you talking to?" But it is *not* acceptable, in either speech or writing, to use a nominative pronoun linked with a noun in the objective case, as in "of we citizens" or "between we men and women." Be wary, in fact, of using these constructions in formal writing, even with the proper objective pronoun. "A body of us citizens went to see the mayor" is not a very effective, serious sentence.

4h. The objective case is proper when the pronoun is the assumed subject or the complement of the infinitive *to be*.

EXAMPLES

Everyone wanted *him* to be the leader of the movement.

The woman whom I thought to be *her* turned out to be someone else.

4i. A pronoun should agree with its antecedent in number, gender, and person.

The antecedent of a pronoun is the word or words to which the pronoun refers. If the antecedent is singular, the pronoun should be singular; if it is plural, the pronoun should be plural.

4. *PRONOUNS*

First one woman cast *her* vote.

Then three men cast *their* votes.

An old man cast *his* vote.

The man and his wife had left *their* house early.

The responsibility will probably fall to *me, who am* the oldest one present. [The awkwardness that agreement seems to cause here can be avoided by a simple revision: ''I am the oldest one present.'']

We prefer to speak to *you, who are* the president.

Here as elsewhere, when questions of usage arise, we must distinguish between what is customary in formal usage and what is accepted in conversational, informal situations. We shall discuss the problems of agreement in terms of certain typical trouble spots that often require more than one kind of answer.

1. In situations that call for more or less formal English, it is customary to use a singular pronoun to refer to any of the following: *anybody, anyone, everyone, everybody, nobody, no one, somebody, someone, person.*

In informal English, especially in conversation, these words, although they take singular verbs, are quite generally felt to be collectives (plural in sense), and the pronouns referring to them are often plural. In addition, all sorts of special situations arise. For instance, *each, every, everybody, everyone* have a general meaning of "all, or a group, but taken individually." Apparently it is the "group" sense that is dominant in influencing the number of the pronoun referring to one of these words. In some cases, when the group consists of both males and females, the speaker uses the plural form because he feels that neither *his* nor *her* is quite accurate. Finally, in some situations, such as in this sentence, "Everybody started to laugh, but in a moment *they* realized that the speaker was not joking," the singular form just would not make sense.

FORMAL AGREEMENT

England expects every man to do *his* duty. [No question of gender here]

261

Everyone must do *his* part in this war.

Nobody has a right to think that *his* happiness is more important than the happiness of others.

OFTEN ACCEPTED IN CONVERSATION

Somebody must have left *their* coat here.

Everyone ought to feel that *their* vote really counts.

By "often accepted," however, we do not mean universally accepted, even in conversation, and in any case a stricter agreement is required in formal written English.

2. Either a singular or plural pronoun may be used to refer to a collective noun, depending on whether the noun designates the group as a whole or the members of the group. *Consistency is the governing principle.* The construction should be either singular or plural, but not both.

INCONSISTENT

The cast *is* giving *their* best performance tonight. [The verb is singular but the pronoun is plural.]

The team *is* now on the floor, taking *their* practice shots at the basket. [Again, verb and pronoun indicate a shift in number.]

CONSISTENT

The cast *is* giving *its* best performance tonight.

The team *are* on the floor now, taking *their* practice shots. [The team is thought of as being more than one person.]

3. Ordinarily one of the masculine pronouns, *he, his, him,* is used to refer to one of these "group taken individually" words. *He or she, his or her, him or her* are now generally accepted as substitutes.

EXAMPLES

Every *person* in the audience was requested to put *his* [or *his or her*] name to the petition.

4. *PRONOUNS*

It has also been common and correct to use one of the masculine pronouns when the antecedent of the pronoun gives no indication of gender but might refer to either a man or a woman.

EXAMPLES

Every *author* is responsible for proofreading *his* book.

The good *cook* does not wash *his* own dishes.

To follow this practice is still correct; however, it is also correct (and sometimes desirable) to acknowledge both genders in the pronoun.

EXAMPLES

The *writer* must make up *his or her* mind on the question.

What secretary would let the boss dictate to *him or her* during the lunch break?

The average homeowner hasn't a moment to call *his or her* own; *he or she* spends *his or her* free moments struggling to keep *his or her* private castle from decaying until it is offensive to *his or her* neighbors.

The last example shows the awkwardness of sustaining the doubled pronoun construction throughout frequent references. When the *he and she*'s begin to pile up and overwhelm everything else in a sentence or paragraph, the awkwardness can be overcome by using a plural construction. "Average homeowners haven't a moment to call *their* own; *they* spend their free moments . . . to keep *their* . . . to *their* . . . ." It may sometimes be best to recast the whole to avoid the need for pronouns altogether.

Note: The shorthand device *he/she* should never be used in any sort of formal exposition; it has no oral equivalent and labels its writer as someone who has no thought for the sound of words.

4. In modern usage, the relative pronoun *who* is used to refer to persons and occasionally to animals, but *whose* may refer to persons, animals, or things, especially when *of which* produces an awkward construction. The relative pronouns *that* and *which* may refer to persons, animals, places, things, and ideas.

263

4

My brother, *who* is an art critic, particularly admires modern painting. It is a taste *that* I cannot understand. He once gave me a painting, *which* I hung upside down in my room. It is a masterpiece *whose* meaning is obscure, at least to me. But my best friend, *whose* critical taste I admire, thinks it magnificent. The whole experience is one *that* I find most perplexing.

For at least a century many respected writers have used *that* and *which* interchangeably as relative pronouns, often making their choice on the assumption that *which* is somehow more refined than *that*. Between the two words, however, there is a distinction that very precise writers may wish to observe. *That* is a *restrictive* relative pronoun. It introduces a clause that particularizes or identifies the antecedent so that the antecedent may not be mistaken for anything else.

E X A M P L E

Bring me the umbrella *that* is drying in the hall. (There may be half a dozen umbrellas lying around, but I want only the one *that* is drying in the hall.)

In a *nonrestrictive* clause, one that adds information about an antecedent but does not single the antecedent out, *which* is the proper, formal relative pronoun.

E X A M P L E

Bring me my umbrella, *which* is drying in the hall. [*Drying in the hall* is only one of many details—color, size, style—the speaker might have offered. Note too that a nonrestrictive clause, unlike a restrictive one, is usually enclosed by commas.]

See "A Guide to Usage," page 467.

5. When *one* is the antecedent, American usage prefers *he* and *his* (or *he or she, his or her*) to the repetition of *one*, which is regarded as too formal.

T O O F O R M A L

One must not lose one's temper when one is being criticized for one's conduct. [Most people would regard this as affected. The formality,

264

however, does avoid the problem of identifying *one* in any particular gender.]

ACCEPTED FORMAL ENGLISH

A person must not lose his temper when he is being criticized for his conduct.

If one were to read between the lines, he would quickly detect the irony in Swift's calm proposal.

The informal equivalent of these expressions is the second person pronoun.

INFORMAL

You mustn't lose your temper when being criticized for your conduct.

6. Pronouns used in apposition are in the same case as their antecedents.

EXAMPLES

The reward was divided among us three, George, Tom, and *me*. [Not *I*]

They had told *us*—*him* and *me*—to report to headquarters immediately.

EXERCISES

EXERCISE 1, CASE OF PRONOUNS. *In the following sentences, tell whether each of the italicized pronouns is used as the subject of a verb, the complement of a verb or verbal, or the object of a preposition.*

1. *I* wonder whether *you* will walk downtown with Harris and *me*.
2. *We* must visit a lawyer *whom* *we* talked to last week.
3. *I* usually try to bring along *whoever* wants to come, if *he* asks *me*.
4. *Neither* of us is quite sure what the lawyer wants *us* to do.
5. *Who* else do *you* suppose would care to come with *us*?
6. A woman can often be of assistance to *us* men in such cases if *she* wishes.
7. *It* was *she* who helped *us* last time.

8. *Everyone* knows a lawyer can be difficult for those of *us* who are unsure of *themselves.*
9. If *he* says, "Try to remember *whom* you met that day," I am likely to forget *whoever* it may have been.
10. *You* are more quick-witted than *I,* so come along.

EXERCISE 2, CORRECTING PRONOUN ERRORS. *Correct every error in the use of pronouns in the following sentences. Assume that your corrected sentences are to appear in a college theme, not in informal conversation.*

1. Thompson, who is more energetic than me, is the man they must have for the job of chairman.
2. We voters, of course, are the only ones who's preference matters.
3. Of all we men whom I think should be available for office, Thompson is the first who comes to mind.
4. But the whole question, as I say, is up to we voters, who will cast our ballots on Friday.
5. When a person casts their ballots, they have to consider very carefully who they should vote for.
6. At any rate Thompson is the man whom I feel sure will be most adequate to serve us all, and everybody will be pleased with their new leader.
7. If I were him I would be overjoyed at their showing so much confidence in me.
8. Yesterday a man said to Thompson and I that they would probably give him or me their vote.
9. You probably know to who I am referring.
10. No one could be more pleased by such information than me, who is always eager to serve.

EXERCISE 3, FORMAL AND INFORMAL ENGLISH. *For each of the following sentences, provide two versions, one of which can be, but need not necessarily be, the form given here. One version should be appropriate to conversational speech, and one appropriate to graceful, formal, written English. In some cases (as in the first sentence), you should revise wording that may be formally correct but that is awkward or stuffy. In some cases you may feel that your two versions should be identical; after all, good written prose and good conversation may employ in very many instances exactly the*

4

same language. *Do not be afraid to remove pronouns altogether in the interests of realistic speech or graceful prose.*

1. It is I who am best prepared of all those whom you have available for the task which we have been discussing.
2. I wonder who he's talking to—me?
3. One should not exaggerate one's virtues in order to impress one's listener with one's superiority.
4. Who is it? It is I.
5. Some people whom I know intimately are likely to assert that which they know with altogether too much passion.
6. Everybody has their own opinion about that.
7. I wonder who he's going to call on next.
8. Somebody left their raincoat on this rack; he will have to come and get it.
9. Those to whom I have spoken on the subject which is before us have made the point that all is lost which is not pursued vigorously, and I am bound to agree with their opinion.
10. Whoever I need, I get.

§ 5. ADJECTIVES AND ADVERBS

Distinguish between adjectives and adverbs and use the correct forms of each.

Adjectives modify nouns. Adverbs modify verbs, adjectives, other adverbs, or groups of words, such as phrases and clauses, even when they are whole sentences. One superficial sign of distinction between the two is that most adverbs end in *-ly.* A few adjectives, such as *friendly and lovely,* also have the *-ly* ending, and a number of common adverbs, such as *fast, far, here, there, near, soon,* do not. Usually these are not hard to recognize.

ADJECTIVE

That's a *friendly* gesture.

He is a *violent* man.

She is a *lazy* person.

267

5

ADVERB

Butter it *only* on one side.

She learns *fast.*

I shook him *violently.*

He sat *lazily* in the sun.

Actually the difference between adjectives and adverbs depends not on a distinctive form or ending but on the way the words function in sentences. Thus a number of familiar words are used as either adjectives or adverbs, depending on function. In the list below, note that *when the word modifies a noun, it is used as an adjective; when it modifies a verb, an adjective, or another adverb, it is used as an adverb.*

EXAMPLES

	ADJECTIVES	ADVERBS
deep	We dug a *deep* well.	He dug down *deep.*
early	I am an *early* bird.	They sent us home *early.*
fast	He is a *fast* walker.	He walks much too *fast.*
little	It is a *little* book.	The book is *little* read.
right	I wish I had the *right* answer.	I wish I could do it *right.*

S	V	O
I	had	answer

right

S	V	O
I	could do	it

right

5a. The clumsy or awkward use of a noun form as an adjective should be avoided.

In our flexible language, as we have seen, words commonly used as nouns can also function as adjective modifiers, as in: a *bird* dog, a *house* cat, an *ivory* tower, an *iron* rod, a *silk* dress, a *flower* pot, the *city* streets, the *Chicago* fire. These are absolutely natural and legitimate uses. The objection is to awkward or ambiguous uses, as in the following examples:

AWKWARD

We heard a communism lecture.

It was really a heart attack sign.

5. *ADJECTIVES AND ADVERBS*

Then we heard the governor of New York's speech.

She's really a fun person to be with.

BETTER

We listened to a lecture explaining communism.

It was a symptom of a heart attack.

Then we heard the speech made by the governor of New York.

You'll have a lot of fun in her company.

5b. Use the adjective after certain linking verbs, such as *be,* *become, appear, seem, prove, remain, look, smell, taste, feel.*

A linking verb is completed by a subjective complement, either a noun or an adjective. The adjective complement describes the subject.

The girl was *quiet.* [The *quiet* girl]

$$\underline{\quad girl \quad | \quad was \backslash \quad quiet \quad}$$

The little boy appears *happy.* [The *happy* little boy]

Hyacinths smell *sweet.* [*Sweet* hyacinths]

$$\underline{\quad hyacinths \quad | \quad smell \backslash \quad sweet \quad}$$

This water tastes *bad.* [*Bad* water]

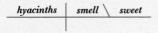

The report proved *true.* [*True* report]

With some of the verbs, when the word in the predicate refers to the manner of the action and not to the subject, it is, of course, an adverb, and the adverb form must be used.

EXAMPLES

The boy appeared *unexpectedly.*

The man felt *carefully* for the door.

She looked *quickly* at me.

We tasted the water *suspiciously.*

269

5

5c. Use the adverb form for a word that modifies a verb, an adjective, or another adverb.

ADVERB MODIFYING A VERB

He dresses *well* [not *good*], but his manners are poor.

During the summer I improved my tennis game *considerably*. [Not *considerable*]

Although he talks *cleverly* [not *clever*], his arguments are shallow.

ADVERB MODIFYING AN ADJECTIVE

My uncle was *really* [not *real*] happy to see us again.

It was *awfully* [not *awful*] generous of you to help us out.

ADVERB MODIFYING ANOTHER ADVERB

He slid down the hill *considerably* [not *considerable*] faster than he had crawled up.

He *almost* [not *most* or *mostly*] always takes a walk before breakfast.

Most of the difficulties center in a few words, of which the following are typical: *bad—badly, good—well, sure—surely, real—really, most—almost, awful—awfully, considerable—considerably*.

The words *most* and *almost* present a special problem. In formal usage, *almost* is the accepted modifier in such expressions as: almost all were saved; summer is almost here; we almost never see him; almost everyone respects him. But in informal conversation, *most* is widely used in those situations. In your writing it is best to follow formal usage.

5d. Certain colloquial uses of adjective and adverb should be avoided: *type, like, -wise*.

UNDESIRABLE

This *type* screw won't go into that *type* wood.

BETTER

This kind of screw will not go into that kind of wood.

UNDESIRABLE

I slid down the hill *like*, and then I saw this, like, glow in the sky.

270

5. *ADJECTIVES AND ADVERBS*

BETTER

I slid down the hill, and then I saw a glow in the sky.

UNDESIRABLE

Moneywise I was in favor of it, but *fraternitywise* I was against it.

BETTER

The proposal was good financially, but I disapproved of it in the interest of the fraternity.

5e. When an adverb has two forms (the short and the *-ly* forms), any difference in their use or meaning is determined by idiom.

The following adverbs—and a few others—have two forms:

bright—brightly	high—highly	near—nearly
cheap—cheaply	late—lately	right—rightly
close—closely	loose—loosely	tight—tightly
deep—deeply	loud—loudly	wrong—wrongly

The adverbs in these pairs are not always interchangeable. Nor is there any quick and easy way of learning how to distinguish them in meaning and function. Using them in sentences, as in the following, will help.

IDIOMATIC	INEFFECTIVE IDIOM
Lately the son has been staying out late.	Late the son has been staying out lately.
The dog crept close to me.	The dog crept closely to me.
Nobody was near.	Nobody was nearly.
He was highly respected.	He was high respected.
The girl slowly opened the door.	The girl slow opened the door.
Go slow. Drive slow.	
Go slowly. Drive slowly.	

5f. Observe the distinction between the comparative and the superlative.

271

5

The positive form of an adjective or adverb assigns a quality to the word it modifies, as in "a *big* bed," "he walked *rapidly*." The comparative degree is formed by adding -*er* to the positive or by using *more* or *less* with the positive, as in "a *bigger* bed," "he walked *more rapidly*."

The superlative degree is formed by adding -*est* to the positive form, or by using *most* or *least* with the positive. The superlative degree ranks the modified word highest or lowest in a class. It implies that there are at least three things in a class: "a *big* bed," "a *bigger* bed," "the *biggest* bed." [See also §33.]

The comparative degree, then, is used when referring to two persons or things; the superlative degree is used when three or more persons or things are involved.

COMPARATIVE

He was *taller* than his brother.

Of the two boys, John was the *more intelligent* and the *more cooperative*.

She learned faster than I.

SUPERLATIVE

He was the *tallest* boy on the basketball team. [More than two]

John was the *most intelligent* and the *most cooperative* boy in school. [Highest in a group consisting of more than two]

She learned fastest of us all.

Some words are compared irregularly:

many	more	most	much	more	most
bad	worse	worst	good	better	best
little	less *or* lesser	least	well	better	best
little	littler	littlest			

Adjectives of more than two syllables rarely take -*er* and -*est* to form comparatives and superlatives. Forms such as *famouser* or *magnificentest* are not modern English. In formal writing, there is some objection to comparative or superlative forms of adjectives that name qualities thought of as absolute, such as *more perfect, most perfect, most unique;* but these forms, and others such as *straightest, blacker, most complete,* are found in both formal and informal English.[1]

Those who object to modification or qualification of *unique, perfect, complete, black,* and other words that express absolute states or qualities may use *most nearly unique, more nearly* or *most nearly perfect, most nearly complete, most nearly black,* and so on. When the makers of our Constitution wrote, "We the people of the United States, in order to form a *more perfect* union . . . ," they may have had *more nearly perfect* in mind. Or they may have accepted usage without giving it much thought.

In modern English one does not combine two superlatives to form a kind of super-superlative. The same principle applies to comparatives.

WRONG

That is the *most unkindest* thing you could have said.

RIGHT

That is the *most unkind* thing you could have said.

WRONG

He finally reached the *more remoter* regions of the country.

RIGHT

He finally reached the *remoter* regions of the country.

EXERCISES

EXERCISE 1, RECOGNIZING ADJECTIVES AND ADVERBS.
Copy the following sentences. Underline each adjective once and each adverb twice.

1. Her spirits were high because the sun shone bright on her wedding day.
2. You may be right, but the little boy does not appear lazy.

---

[1] Bergen Evans and Cornelia Evans, *A Dictionary of Contemporary American Usage,* pp. 105–107.

5

3. The elderly teacher was considerably provoked because the bright boys protested loudly against the assignment.
4. When he awoke after a deep sleep, he noticed that the cold morning air smelled fresh and sweet.
5. All decisions regarding high policy must be highly respected, whether they are right or wrong.
6. Then, too, a lively conversation with the kindly old man was an awfully pleasant price for a delicious dinner.
7. The room smells stuffy, the milk tastes sour, the oilcloth feels gritty, the toast appears sooty, and the prospect for a happy day looks poor.
8. The housekeeper is coming early, I am sure, for everything looks wrong in my room.
9. Really, I feel well, although I did not sleep well last night.
10. Things look bad everywhere today.

EXERCISE 2, CORRECTING ADJECTIVE AND ADVERB ERRORS. *Correct the error in the form or use of the adjective or adverb in each of the following sentences.*

1. In the window she saw a mink coat that was richer and luxuriouser than anything she could imagine.
2. His manners were courtly and he spoke friendly to me, but I could not trust him.
3. All the players felt unhappily after losing the game, and I sure felt bad about it too.
4. You have been so good to me that I feel cheaply because I cannot repay you.
5. Lately he has taken to driving his sports car real fast.
6. I am most ready; my paper is near finished.
7. There is considerable merit in your paper ideawise, but structurewise it is badly arranged.
8. When I compare it with the one written by Anne, it is real hard to say which is worst.
9. He held the bat closely to his chest and then hit the ball highly in the air.
10. Sit tight; the doctor is near ready to see you.

EXERCISE 3, CHOOSING CORRECT ADJECTIVE AND ADVERB FORMS. *In each of the following sentences select the correct form of the adjective or adverb.*

1. I was (really carefully, real careful, really careful) about mounting the horse.
2. In spite of his education, he still does not read (well, good).
3. We drove (slow and careful, slowly and carefully) over the icy roads.
4. When we lost our way, Tracy (sure, surely) felt (bad, badly).
5. Like most careful persons, he takes his driving (real serious, really seriously).
6. Eugene is the (tallest, taller) of the two forwards on the team.
7. Tony did (good, well) on his English test.
8. Tony is (carefuller, more careful) than Eugene.
9. Eugene's history essay was (more perfect, more nearly perfect) than Tony's.
10. Harriet looked (curious, curiously), but actually she was only amused.

6

§ 6. VERB FORMS

The appropriate form of the verb should be used.

A student who is uncertain about the right form of a verb turns to the dictionary for help. We omit guides for pronunciation:

lay, *v.t.* [LAID, LAYING]
lead, *v.t.* [LED, LEADING]
lie, *v.i.* [LAY, LAIN, LYING]
look, *v.i.*

A dictionary gives what are known as the *principal parts* of a verb, or as many of them as are necessary. Verbs are *regular* or *irregular,* and this distinction controls the amount of information that the dictionary gives. The regular verbs form their past tense and their past participle by adding *-d, -t,* or *-ed* to the present: "I *looked,*" "I *have looked.*" Therefore only one part (*look*) is sufficient. But the irregular verbs change the present stem form to make the past tense and the past participle: "I *lie* on the floor," "I *lay* on the floor," "I *have lain* on the floor." The dic-

6

tionary gives as many principal parts as are necessary to indicate all the forms of the verb—or its *conjugation*. In the case of *lie,* the dictionary lists all the principal parts—namely, the past tense, the past participle, and the present participle. When the dictionary does not list the past participle of an irregular verb, it is assumed that it is the same as the past tense, as in "I *lead,*" "I *led,*" "I *have led.*"

An abridged conjugation of the verb *take* follows. For other forms and their uses, see §6a The principal parts of *take* are *take, took, taken, taking.*

INDICATIVE MOOD

ACTIVE VOICE — **PASSIVE VOICE**

Singular	*Plural*	*Singular*	*Plural*

PRESENT TENSE

I take	we take	I am taken	we are taken
you take	you take	you are taken	you are taken
he takes	they take	he is taken	they are taken

PAST TENSE

I took	we took	I was taken	we were taken
you took	you took	you were taken	you were taken
he took	they took	he was taken	they were taken

FUTURE TENSE

I shall (will) take	we shall (will) take	I shall (will) be taken	we shall (will) be taken
you will take	you will take	you will be taken	you will be taken
he will take	they will take	he will be taken	they will be taken

PRESENT PERFECT TENSE

I have taken	we have taken	I have been taken	we have been taken
you have taken	you have taken	you have been taken	you have been taken
he has taken	they have taken	he has been taken	they have been taken

PAST PERFECT TENSE

| I had taken | we had taken | I had been taken | we had been taken |

276

you had taken	you had taken	you had been taken	you had been taken
he had taken	they had taken	he had been taken	they had been taken

FUTURE PERFECT TENSE

I shall (will) have taken	we shall (will) have taken	I shall (will) have been taken	we shall (will) have been taken
you will have taken	you will have taken	you will have been taken	you will have been taken
he will have taken	they will have taken	he will have been taken	they will have been taken

IMPERATIVE FORMS: take, be taken

INFINITIVE FORMS: to take, to have taken, to be taken, to have been taken

GERUNDS: taking, having taken, being taken, having been taken

PARTICIPLES: taking, taken, having taken, being taken, having been taken

Tenses

6a. The correct tense forms of the verb should be used.

1. **The Present Time.** Present time may be expressed by three main verb forms. The *simple present* tense form usually expresses general or habitual action: "I *work*," "he *teaches*," "she *lives* in Albany," "they *drive* a Mazda." To express action as going on at the present time we use the *progressive* form of the present: "I *am working*," "he *is teaching*," "she *is living* in Albany," "they *are driving* a Mazda." There is also a present auxiliary form, "do," which is used for emphasis (I *do work*), for negations (she *does* not *teach*), and for questions (*does* she *live* in Albany?).

2. **The Past Time.** Past time is usually expressed by the *past tense,* as in "I *studied*," "she *played* the piano," "he *taught*," "I *worked*." Past time may also be indicated by the present tense form (called the *historical present*), as "The captain *looks* at me, and I *stare* back at him, and he *says* to me . . ." It is a device that

277

6

should be avoided in writing, except as part of dialogue, or in narrative writing that expresses vivid feelings and sense impressions.

3. **The Perfect Tenses.** The *present perfect* tense shows that an act has been completed prior to the present.

EXAMPLES

The men *have taken* all the tickets.
All the tickets *have been taken.*

The *past perfect* tense shows that an act was already completed before some specified or understood time in the past.

EXAMPLES

I *had heard* about the news before you told me.
He *had* already *paid* his respects to his hostess.

The *future perfect* tense, which is less common than the others, indicates a future act as having already taken place, in relation to some specified or understood time in the future.

EXAMPLES

He *will have counted* the money by the time you arrive to collect it.
By late this afternoon the money *will have been counted.*

4. **The Future Time.** Future time may be indicated in several ways. It may be indicated by the *present tense with an adverb or an adverbial phrase of time.*

EXAMPLES

We *arrive* in Chicago in *thirty minutes.*
Our wedding *takes* place *next June.*

The future may also be indicated by using *going to* or *about to* with the verb.

EXAMPLES

We *are going to stay* overnight in Chicago.
He *is about to declare* himself a candidate.

Shall—Will, Should—Would. Finally, and most obviously, the future may be indicated by using *shall* or *will* with the verb. Attitudes toward the use of *shall* and *will* have provoked controversy because the words are another illustration of the language in rapid change, and when usage changes quickly, controversy often arises. But the distinction between *shall* and *will,* once considered vital to educated English, now no longer seems so important. In modern informal speech, most people use *will* and *would* (or the contractions *I'll, he'll, he'd, you'd*) for all expressions of the future, and many do the same in writing. Others, at least in writing, use *shall* and *should* for the first person singular and plural, and *will* and *would* for the second and third persons. Once again, these seemingly trivial choices have their effect on tone: to maintain the *shall—will* distinction is to add a slight touch of traditional formality to the style.

Those who do maintain the distinction observe, in general, the following rules: for simple future, *shall* with the first person, *will* with the second and third persons; for the emphatic future, *will* for the first person, *shall* for the second and third persons.

EXAMPLES

I shall discuss the uses of verbs, and you will observe the appropriate forms.

You will have to study diligently if you are to put them to good use.

In asking questions, *shall* is ordinarily used with the first and third persons and *will* with the second person when a request for permission is implied: "*Shall* I wrap it up for you?" "*Shall* he take you home?" "*Will* you do it?" A note of formality may be imparted to a question if the speaker uses the form that he anticipates in the answer: "*Shall* you be at the meeting?" "I *shall.*"

To express habitual or customary action, *would* is generally used in all three persons; *should,* however, may be found in the first person.

EXAMPLES

She *would* read in the library instead of playing baseball with the gang.

She *would* sit in her rocker and knit all day long.

I *would* [*should*] be grateful for your advice.

279

Should is often used in the sense of *ought,* although in some sentences *ought* may imply a slightly stronger sense of obligation.

6

EXAMPLES

He really *should keep* his mouth shut. [He *ought to* . . .]

The policy *should have been defined* long before this. [The policy *ought to have been defined* . . .]

Sequence of Tenses. Use the tenses that show the correct relation of time between the main verb and the subordinate verb. When, for example, a verb indicates action that took place before the action of the main verb, and the main verb is in the past tense, then the subordinate verb must of course be past perfect.

EXAMPLE

After I *had talked* with him for a while, he *was* more agreeable.

Be careful to use the correct tense of infinitives and participles. Notice in the following examples that the time indicated by the verbal is always in relation to the time expressed by the main verb. That is, a present infinitive indicates the same time as the main verb, even when the main verb is past.

EXAMPLES

I was very pleased *to hear* from you. [Not *to have heard*]

She intended *to go* home, but she did not make it. [Not *to have gone*]

With participles, a past tense of the participle must be used to indicate a time previous to the main verb.

EXAMPLES

Having played tennis all day, we were tired. [Not *playing*]

Talking as we walked along, we soon arrived at the house. [Not *having talked*]

Careless Shifts in Tense. In telling a story or recounting an event, it is undesirable to shift from past to present or from present to past unless there is a real change in time of the action being described. For this reason the use of the historical present must be undertaken warily. (See also §§31 and 40.)

CARELESS SHIFT

I *went* out the door and *walked* slowly down the street, where the traffic *seemed* even more noisy than usual. Suddenly a man *approaches* me from an alleyway. "Look!" he *says,* and *thrusts* a piece of paper into my hand; but when I *looked* at it I *saw* nothing. I *continued* my walk.

THE SUBJUNCTIVE

6b. The subjunctive mood is used in a number of situations in formal writing.

The only uses of the subjunctive the student need be concerned about in speech and writing are the following:

1. In *if*-clauses expressing doubt or impossibility of the condition (usually referred to as "condition contrary to fact").

EXAMPLES

If she *were* here, you would not say that.

Were he with us today, he would be gratified at this scene. [This word order now has a somewhat old-fashioned ring.]

Note that when the condition is *not* contrary to fact, the subjunctive is not used.

EXAMPLE

Either he was here or he was not. If he was here, then he must know what happened.

2. In *that*-clauses expressing a wish, request, or command.

EXAMPLES

The president has ordered that all prisoners *be* treated equally.

I desire that he *come* here at once. [Again, note the relative formality of these sentences using the subjunctive. *Compare:* I want him to come here at once.]

3. In main clauses to express hope, wish, or prayer, usually in traditional and stereotyped patterns.

EXAMPLES

God *be* with you.

Long *live* the king!

"The rules *be* damned!" shouted the losing coach.

6

    With regard to the form of the verb, we can say that for most verbs the subjunctive form differs from the indicative in only the third person singular of the present tense.

INDICATIVE		SUBJUNCTIVE	
I take	we take	if I take	if we take
you take	you take	if you take	if you take
he takes	they take	if he take	if they take

[*Note: If* here is only an indicator of the subjunctive mood. *Should* is also sometimes used for the same purpose.]

EXAMPLE

We recommend that he *take* the entrance examination.

    The verb *to be* is a special problem. The problem may be simplified by saying that the subjunctive of *to be* uses:
1. *Be* in all forms of the present tense.
2. *Were* in all forms of the past tense.
3. *Have been* in all forms of the present perfect tense.

EXAMPLES

Be it ever so noisy, there is no place like home.

Were you as busy as I was at that moment, you would not have asked me to help you.

Having been asked to speak on flying, I will try my wings at it.

Voice

6c. The passive voice of the verb should not be overused.

    In most writing, and especially narrative and descriptive writing, the active voice is preferred as more direct, vivid, and emphatic than the passive voice. It is obviously simpler and

282

clearer to say "I hit the intruder on the nose" than "the intruder was hit on the nose by me." But the passive voice has its legitimate uses, as the first sentence in this paragraph should testify. It is indispensable when *the action of the verb is more important than the doer, when the doer of action may not be known,* or *when the writer may wish to place emphasis on the recipient of the action rather than on the doer.*

6

EXAMPLES

A sum of twenty thousand dollars was collected from a number of sources.

Another man was fired last night.

All the bridges were destroyed during the war.

It is not the passive voice in itself that is objectionable—it is the overuse or misuse of it. Constant repetition of passive verbs can create an effect of deadness in the action of the prose, as if nothing *did* anything but instead sat around waiting for something *to be done to it.*

The passive voice becomes the scapegoat if not the actual criminal when there is a shift in point of view in a group of sentences. Notice what happens in the following sentences:

CONFUSED

One girl may be writing a letter; a book absorbs the attention of another. As usual someone sat in her chair sound asleep. Constant whispers could have been heard by the lecturer. [The effect here is similar to that found in a carelessly edited film, where an actor exits screen left and reappears screen right without any visible reason for the flip. Continuity is lost.]

CONSISTENT

During the lecture, one girl is writing a letter; another is reading a book. As usual someone sits sound asleep. Several people are whispering constantly.

The passive voice, on the other hand, may be useful in enabling a writer to maintain his point of view through several sentences.

6

SHIFT IN POINT OF VIEW

She sat absorbed over her book. A frown could be seen on her face. Then a long whistle from outside interrupted her thoughts. She glanced in annoyance toward the window. Then she smiled as if what she saw there amused her.

CONSISTENT POINT OF VIEW

As she sat there frowning, absorbed over her book, her thoughts were interrupted by a long whistle from outside. Annoyed, she glanced through the open window. Then she smiled in amusement at what she saw there.

EXERCISES

EXERCISE 1, PRINCIPAL PARTS. *With the help of your dictionary, if necessary, find the principal parts of the following verbs. List the form given, the past tense, the past participle, and the present participle or gerund; for example,* begin, began, begun, beginning.

bear	dive	know	raise	spring
blow	drink	lay	ride	sting
break	drive	lead	ring	swim
bring	eat	lend	rise	take
burst	get	lie	set	throw
buy	go	lose	shake	wake
choose	grow	prove	sink	write

EXERCISE 2, TENSES. *Make necessary corrections of tenses in the following sentences.*

1. I was eager to have learned German since I planned to go to Europe.
2. I told everyone I bought my ticket two days before.
3. Learning the language in a few weeks, I was ready to go at last.
4. I should have purchased a round trip, but I failed to do so.
5. Will you be in Berlin at any time this summer?
6. The year before, I had traveled in England so that I could have spent some time with a friend of mine there.
7. Shall I try it once more?

8. By midnight we shall have reached our first destination.
9. I was pleased yesterday to have heard from you at last.
10. Knowing what a good correspondent you are, I look forward to hearing from you soon.

EXERCISE 3, THE SUBJUNCTIVE. *In the following sentences select the correct forms from those given in parentheses.*

1. I requested that an invitation (be, is, was) sent to them immediately.
2. We all wish we (are, were) with you at this time.
3. He demanded that their disruptive behavior (cease, ceased, ceases) at once.
4. We suggested that he (withdraw, withdraws) these demands.
5. He looks as if he (is, were) angry, but one cannot be sure.
6. I know he (is, were) angry because I heard him swear.
7. My suggestion is that he (bring, brings) you along with him.
8. Finally someone made the motion that the whole discussion (is, be, was) dropped.
9. If Jack (is, were) here at last, you (should, would) not treat me so.
10. Since Jack (is, were) here at last, you will not treat me so.

6

2 *Mechanics*

§ 7. MANUSCRIPT: FORM AND REVISION

7a. In the preparation of manuscript, follow standard procedures and any special instructions given you by your English instructor.

1. *Use standard typewriter paper or, for handwritten papers, the 8½ x 11 ruled theme paper.* Most English departments require composition students to use regulation typewriter paper, unruled if the themes are typewritten, ruled if the themes are handwritten. If you use narrow-ruled notebook paper for a theme, write on every other line.

2. *Write legibly.* If you write by hand, make your writing easy to read. Write with a good pen and use black or dark blue ink. Do not use red, violet, or green ink. Form all letters distinctly, especially those that might be confused with other letters. Dot your *i*'s and cross your *t*'s. Do not decorate your letters with unnecessary loops and flourishes. Indicate paragraphing clearly by indenting about an inch.

3. *Type legibly.* If you use a typewriter, see that the ribbon is fresh and the type clean. Adjust your margin properly. Always double-space your typing. Space five spaces for paragraph indentations, one space between words, and two spaces after the end punctuation of a sentence. If you must delete material in typing, type over it with a capital *M* or use one of the convenient correction tapes or liquids. *If you must cross out any considerable portion of your material, type your page over again.* Never begin a line with a punctuation mark, such as a comma, a period, a question mark, or an exclamation point, that belongs at the end of the preceding line.

4. *Label your themes correctly.* Use the method of labeling pa-

7

pers recommended by your instructor. Follow his or her instructions exactly. If the themes are to be handed in on flat, unfolded sheets of paper (the method preferred by all publishers), the correct place for the name, the page number, and the theme number is the upper right-hand corner of each page. Of course, you should never write on the back of the paper.

5. *Be careful about the correct placement and capitalization of the title.* Write the title on the first line of the first page only, or about two inches from the top of the sheet. Center the title on the page. Capitalize the first word and all important words in the title. The usual practice is to capitalize all nouns, pronouns, verbs, adverbs, and adjectives, and all prepositions that stand last or contain more than five letters. Do not underline the title or enclose it in quotation marks, unless the title is a quotation, and you wish to emphasize that it is quoted. Do not use a period after it, but you may use a question mark or an exclamation point if the sense of the title calls for either of these marks. Leave a space of about an inch between the title and the first line of your theme. Do not repeat the title on succeeding pages.

6. *Use proper margins.* Leave margins of an inch at the top and at the left of each page. Do not crowd your words at the right or at the bottom of the page. Some instructors like a wide margin at the right as well as at the left of the page so as to have room for comments and corrections. After the first page, begin writing on the first line.

If you are quoting verse, center your quotation on the page and follow the line arrangement of the poem from which you are quoting. No quotation marks are needed. If the quotation does not end a paragraph, begin the next line of your composition flush with the left margin.

7. *Make deletions and corrections clearly.* Parentheses and brackets are never used to delete or cross out a word. These marks have other uses.

To delete material, draw a horizontal line through it. In typing, material may be deleted by typing a capital *M* over it—if the section to be crossed out is not too extensive.

If you wish to insert a correction in your text, mark the point of insertion with a caret ($_\wedge$) and write the inserted material above the caret.

287

7b. Revise your manuscript carefully, both before you hand it in and after it has been returned to you for correction.

1. *Go over the first draft of your paper and copy it for final submission.* In revising your first draft, you should consider the following checklist:

   a. Has the paper an objective, a central idea, a direction?
   b. Is the content made interesting by facts and examples?
   c. Is the organization, in the whole paper and in the separate paragraphs, as logical as possible?
   d. Are there obvious errors in sentence structure to correct, such as the period fault, the comma splice, failure of verbs and subjects to agree?
   e. Are the punctuation and spelling correct?

2. *Revise your paper carefully after the instructor has returned it to you.* Make every correction indicated or suggested by your instructor. If he or she refers you to a handbook section, first study the section carefully to see how it applies to your error. Then, in pencil or a distinctive color of ink, draw a horizontal line through the word or words you wish to cancel, and in the space above, between the lines, write the revised version. If for any reason you do not have the time to revise the returned paper, at least make sure that you know what the faults indicated are and how you *would* revise them had you the time.

On pages 290–291, you will find the process of correction and revision illustrated.

On page 290 are two paragraphs of prose filled with elementary errors. The instructor has used section numbers from this "Handbook" to show the student where each kind of error is discussed and the correction explained. If the instructor had wished to be more explicit, he or she would have underlined the points of error.

On page 291, the same selection appears. This time the instructor has used correction symbols, according to the system indicated on the inside of the back cover of this book. The student has revised his sentences, in response to the instructor's corrections, by writing between the typewritten lines.

If your instructor indicates by a note or a comment in the margin that some part of your page is confused, undeveloped, or illogical, rewrite the section criticized. Whenever the revision is short, you may write between the lines. When you rewrite a number of sentences or paragraphs, however, you should first make your corrections on the face of your manuscript, and then recopy the entire page.

3. Once you have revised a page or an entire theme, it is a good idea to ask your instructor's opinion of the revision. Of course, the instructor may require you to hand in the revision, in which case it is an even better idea.

8

§ 8. CAPITALS

A *capital letter* is a kind of punctuation mark, designed to draw the reader's attention to itself for a particular reason. These reasons have been formalized in standard practice. There are reasons, then, for the appearance of every capital, and they should not be abused in overcapitalization.

8a. Capitalize the first word of every sentence, including frag-
    ments punctuated as sentences, and the first word of any
    group within a sentence that is understood as a sentence in
    its own right.

E X A M P L E S

What now? Who knows? Nobody.

He replied, "There is little hope left."

The main question is, When do we eat?

Do *not* capitalize the first word of (a) an indirect quotation, (b) a direct quotation that is not a complete sentence or that is made a structural part of the new sentence in which it is quoted, (c) the part of a direct quotation that follows dialogue tags such as *he said,* unless the part begins a new sentence.

E X A M P L E S

Everyone said that the statement was untrue. [Indirect quotation. *Compare:* Everyone said, "The statement is untrue."]

Why I Came

7

12   Why did I come to college. That is a hard question,
2 it cannot be answered in a few words. From one point of
19 view, it seems abserd that I should be here without
15/19 knowing why I am here. Its true my parents allways
wanted me to go to college. They probably never quite
analyzed their reasons for wanting me to go. They wanted
1 me to better myself. To learn a profession or a trade.
11 They felt that a well educated person would be able to
6/29 lead an easier life than they lived. Knowing the hard
6/13 life they lived their attitude seems reasonable to me.
13 From another point of view however, it seems logical to
me that I should come to college to find out why I came
to college. I am not sure that I can find all the answers. My college work may give me one answer to my
1 question. Or maybe several of the many possible answers.
41 While I do not expect to find all the answers, after
19 four years here I may know more definately what the
question means.

28   I have talked with other freshmen about their rea-
19/21 sons for comeing to college. They have many solutions.
1 Most of them talk about economic security. Which of
course is a legitimate objective. Others talk about a
25a life of service to others. If you talk long enough about
the subject, you will hear about cultivation of the mind
and the emotions. These are ideas I will try to discuss
here.

SAMPLE THEME MARKED BY THE INSTRUCTOR

7. MANUSCRIPT: FORM AND REVISION

Why I Came

Ques. Why did I come to college/?That is a hard question,
RS ~~it~~ *which* cannot be answered in a few words. From one point of
Sp view, it seems ~~absurd~~ *absurd* that I should be here without
Pn/ *Sp* knowing why I am here. It's true my parents ~~allways~~ *always*

wanted me to go to college. They probably never quite

analyzed their reasons for wanting me to go. They wanted
PF me to better myself/ ~~To learn~~ *by learning* a profession or a trade.

Pn They felt that a well-educated person would be able to
Tnse
Dng lead an easier life than they *have* lived. ~~Knowing~~ *Because I know* the hard
Tnse
C life they *have* lived, their attitude seems reasonable to me.

C From another point of view, however, it seems logical to

me that I should come to college to find out why I came

to college. I am not sure that I can find all the an-

swers. My college work may give me one answer to my
PF question/ ~~Or~~ *or* maybe several of the many possible answers.
Gr ~~While~~ *Although* I do not expect to find all the answers, after
Sp four years here I may know more ~~definately~~ *definitely* what the

question means.
Sub ~~I have talked~~ *As I talk* with other freshmen about their rea-
Sp/Ex sons for ~~comeing~~ *coming* to college/, ~~They have many solutions.~~ *I encounter many ideas.*
PF Most of them talk about economic security/, ~~Which~~ *which* of

course is a legitimate objective. Others talk about a
Wd
Rep life of service to ~~others.~~ *humanity* If you talk long enough about

the subject, you will hear about cultivation of the mind

and the emotions. These are ideas I will try to discuss

here.

SAMPLE THEME AS CORRECTED BY THE STUDENT

291

Most people feel, like the speaker in Wordsworth's sonnet, that "we lay waste our powers." [Direct quotation made a structural part of the new sentence]

"I wish I could tell you," he added, "what I really mean about that."

8

In quoting poetry or any other document, follow the original exactly in respect to capitalization. In writing out a title, capitalize the first word and all other words except conjunctions and prepositions of less than five letters. An exception is a short preposition ending the title, which should be capitalized. For further information on the special problems of titles, see §10a

8b. Proper nouns and adjectives are capitalized.

A *proper noun* names some particular person, place, or object; a *common noun* indicates one of a class of persons, places, or objects. In practice the distinction is usually not difficult.

Capitalize:

1. Names of persons, places, buildings, ships, and so on: John H. Farley, Wisconsin, the Washington Monument, the *Constitution,* Middletown Township, Chinatown, Israel.
2. Names of political and geographic divisions if they are part of a proper name: Union of South Africa, Northwest Territory, Dominion of Canada. [But *not:* a union of states, the territory toward the northwest]
3. Names of historic events or epochs: the Middle Ages, the Black Death, World War I, the Depression, the Sixties.
4. Names of nationalities, religious groups, and languages: English, Mormon, Slavic, Japanese. [Note that these can be used either as nouns or as adjectives.]
5. Adjectives derived from proper names: Byronic, Assyrian, Scottish. [A few such adjectives, used in special senses, such as *roman* or *italic* type, are often considered common rather than proper.]
6. Names of organizations: United States Steel, the Red Cross, Congress of Industrial Organizations, United Nations, Phi Beta Kappa.

7. Days of the week, names of the months and of particular holidays: Easter, Good Friday, Veterans Day, the second Monday in March.

As a rule, difficulties arise only when the same word is used both as a proper noun and as a common noun; some of these difficulties are discussed in § §8c and 8d below.

8

8c. Any title used preceding a name or as a substitute for the name is capitalized.

A *title* is always capitalized preceding a name; following a name, it is capitalized only to show particular respect or distinction.

EXAMPLES

Captain Townsend; Prince Philip; Pope Paul; Henry Kissinger, the Secretary of State; *but:* D. H. Jones, the chairman of the committee.

Notice that these words are *not* capitalized when they are not used as a title for a particular, named person. The article *a* is usually a signal that a common noun follows.

EXAMPLES

A queen's consort is usually a prince.

He was promoted to captain.

When will they elect a new pope?

Abbreviations after a name, such as Esq., Ph.D., M.D., F.R.S., are usually capitalized and not spaced. The following, however, are correct either with or without capitals: Jr., jr., Sr., sr. (*and note also* No., no.; A.M., a.m.; P.M., p.m.). Be consistent.

8d. Common nouns are capitalized only when they are used in the sense of proper names.

1. Capitalize *North, South, East, West, Northwest, Far East* only when these words refer to specific geographical divisions. Do not capitalize when they refer to directions.

EXAMPLES

The South is gaining industrially at the expense of the Northeast.

I turned south at the crossroads.

8

2. Capitalize the words for educational and other institutions only when they are a part of some name, not when they are used as common nouns.

EXAMPLES

The school was near Memorial Hospital, not far from the University of Maryland.

I attended high school there. It was called Beaverbrook High.

Many universities are looking for a good president.

I should like to work for the Smithsonian Institution or the Metropolitan Museum, but not all museum work interests me.

3. Capitalize the names of particular courses of study, such as *Mathematics 42, Physical Education 485b.* But do not capitalize such terms when they are used to refer to general areas of learning: *mathematics, physical education, history, law.* Remember, however, that names of nationalities and languages are always capitalized: *French history, English literature, Mexican art.*

4. Capitalize words denoting family relationships (*mother, father, uncle, grandfather*) only when these words stand for an individual who is called by that name. Again, be alert for the signal of a common noun, such as an article or possessive preceding the word.

EXAMPLES

A mother is often a twenty-four-hour laborer. My mother was such a person. One day I said to her, "Do you work as hard as Grandmother did, Mother?" She only replied that mothers have always worked hard.

The dictionary can often be useful in determining standard practice of capitalization. But in most doubtful cases, as our examples illustrate, it is necessary to recognize just how a word serves in a particular context.

294

EXERCISES

8

EXERCISE 1, SUPPLYING CAPITALS. Copy the following sentences, supplying capitals where necessary.

1. north central airlines serves many communities in the great lakes region.
2. there are a number of colleges and universities in the region, including minnesota and the university of wisconsin.
3. wisconsin is famous for its courses in journalism, but it also offers programs in all the liberal arts including english, anthropology, history, physics, and so on.
4. the badgers, as the football team is called, finds players from the fond du lac area and from many schools along lake michigan.
5. everyone knows that in the middle sixties wisconsin's football team contributed much to building the "big ten image."
6. the university's president has been an important figure in midwest history, especially through his efforts in bringing federal and state support to the school in madison.
7. I have tried to convince my brother to take north central when he flies west to visit us in wisconsin.
8. during world war II barracks were built on the campus to house united states soldiers, many of whom were of norwegian ancestry.
9. the state capitol is located in the center of town, and the legislators have adopted a romantic attitude about madison's beauty.
10. the governor and other public officials are still trying to overcome the bad publicity engendered during the days of mccarthyism.

EXERCISE 2, SUPPLYING CAPITALS. Here is a piece of administrative English, of the sort that might appear on a college bulletin board. Again, supply capitals where necessary, and only where necessary.

registration for the fall term will take place in walker hall from monday at 9 a.m. till wednesday at 4 p.m. all students will bring high school records and identification cards with them. the fol-

295

9

lowing courses will not be offered this year: economics 13, english 5, french 15, chemistry 37. students expecting to major in physical science should see professor adkins. those expecting to enter law school must elect political science 43. please interview without delay the professor who has been designated as your adviser.

§ 9. ABBREVIATIONS AND NUMBERS

9a. In ordinary writing, abbreviations are usually avoided (with a few standard exceptions).

The following are usually written out, although in footnotes, bibliographies, tabulations, and addresses they may be abbreviated to conserve space:

1. Names of countries and states: Canada [not *Can.*], West Virginia [not *W.Va.*], North Dakota [not *N.Dak.*].
2. Names of the months and days of the week: September [not *Sept.*], Monday [not *Mon.*], Friday [not *Fri.*].
3. Christian names: Charles [not *Chas.*], Robert [not *Robt.*], Edward [not *Edw.*].
4. Names of college courses, titles of professors, and other words frequently abbreviated in campus conversation: professor [not *prof.*], educational psychology [not *ed. psych.*], political science [not *poli. sci.*].
5. The titles *The Reverend* [not *Rev.*] and *The Honorable* [not *Hon.*], at least in formal situations. These titles are used with the person's full name, not with just the last name.
6. The following words: number, volume, chapter, page, and [not &], street, avenue, manufacturing, company, mountain, Christmas.

POOR

He was looking forward to Xmas vacation next Dec.

BETTER

He was looking forward to Christmas vacation next December.

296

9. *ABBREVIATIONS AND NUMBERS*

POOR

This class meets on Tue., Thurs., and Sat.

BETTER

This class meets on Tuesdays, Thursdays, and Saturdays.

POOR

He worked in N.Y. for the Macmillan Pblg. Co.

BETTER

He worked in New York for Macmillan Publishing Co., Inc. [It should be remembered that sometimes a company name is properly composed of abbreviations and ought to be written accordingly, e.g., Macmillan Publishing Co., Inc. As there may be a legal reason for the use of abbreviations in company names, try to find out what the company's letterhead says and use that.]

POOR

Some day she hopes to be a prof. of poli. sci.

BETTER

Some day she hopes to be a professor of political science.

POOR

Wm. and Chas. live on Jerome Ave., near Dilmore St.

BETTER

William and Charles live on Jerome Avenue, near Dilmore Street.

The following abbreviations are customary and appropriate:

1. Titles before proper names: Dr., Mr., Mrs., Ms., M., Messrs., Mme., Mlle. [*Ms.* is an "abbreviation" of no known word, and there has been some controversy over its right to a period (Ms.). A consensus appears to be forming that withholding the period is in some sense a denial of the legitimacy of the abbreviation, and we recommend, therefore, that it be written *Ms.* to preclude any suggestion of inferiority to *Mr.* or *Mrs.*]

2. Certain designations after names: Jr., jr., Sr., sr., D.D., M.D., Ph.D.

3. With dates only when necessary for clearness: A.D. and B.C.: Octavian lived from 63 B.C. to A.D. 14. [Note that B.C. fol-

9

lows the year, A.D. precedes it. It has been argued by some non-Christians that the abbreviations B.C. and A.D. misrepresent a true, universal reckoning of history. The alternatives proposed are B.C.E. (Before the Christian [or Common] Era) and C.E. (the Christian [or Common] Era).

4. Certain expressions usually abbreviated in informal and in technical writing, though written out when a more formal effect is desired: i.e., e.g., viz., etc. These actually stand for *id est, exempli gratia, videlicet, et cetera,* but they are written out as *that is, for example, namely, and so forth.*

5. Names of government agencies and certain other well-known organizations: TVA, CARE, NATO, CREEP. Note that the last three of these are pronounced as single words, rather than as series of letters. Abbreviations pronounced as words are known as *acronyms.* Note also the omission of periods. When in doubt about the punctuation, consult your dictionary.

Observe that it is not customary to space after periods within most abbreviations, except that initials representing names *are* spaced: A. L. Jones.

9b. In general writing (i.e., writing that is not statistical), most numbers are written out whenever they can be expressed in one or two words, or in a simple phrase.

EXAMPLES

She is about twenty-five years old.

She earned nearly eight thousand dollars last year.

She was able to buy three and a half acres of land.

For the use of the hyphen with compound numbers see §11

A *number* beginning a sentence is usually spelled out. If it cannot be easily written out, recast the sentence so that the number does not stand at the beginning. Be consistent and avoid referring to eight thousand dollars as $8,000 later in the same essay.

EXAMPLES

Thirty-five persons attended the ceremony. [Not *35 persons . . .*]

She paid a price of $4,550 for the property. [Not *$4,550 was paid . . .*]

298

9c. Figures (or numerals) are used for the following:

1. Dates: March 20, 1974; *not* March twentieth, nineteen hundred seventy-four. [Note that the day of the month is separated from the year by a comma.]
2. Street and room numbers: 415 State Street; *not* four hundred fifteen State Street; Union Hall 216, *not* Union Hall two hundred sixteen.
3. Page numbers: page 334; *not* page three hundred thirty-four.
4. Decimals, percentages, mathematical and technical statistics.
5. Several numbers occurring in the same paragraph or section, if the numbers refer to different quantities of the same thing and if one of the numbers would ordinarily be given in figures.

EXAMPLE

These systems are at distances ranging from 100,000 to 1,500,000 light years, their diameters range from 4,000 to 45,000 light years, and the total luminosities from 20 to 500 million times the luminosity of the sun.

Notice in the last example that commas are used to separate the figures into units—thousands, hundred thousands, millions—for clearness and convenience in reading. Commas are not used, however, in dates, serial numbers, telephone numbers, or social security numbers. In some of these it is customary to use hyphens to divide complex numbers into groups.

EXERCISES

EXERCISE 1, CORRECTING ABBREVIATION ERRORS. *Correct the errors in the use of abbreviations in the following sentences.*

1. Our route took us through Mich., Wis., and Minn.
2. The Stoic philosopher Seneca lived from 4 B.C. to 65 A.D.
3. This author was not born until after 1917 A.D.

9

4. English lit and math are my best courses.
5. We were in Vt. and Mass. for the rock festival.
6. Thos. Jones took me to the game with Hancock Hi.
7. I think that our chem labs are poorly designed.
8. One of the profs there said they were firetraps.
9. Professor L.B. White and Doctor A.G. Black are my chem lecturers.
10. Rev. Holmes was our convo speaker.

EXERCISE 2, IDENTIFYING ABBREVIATIONS. *Identify each of the following abbreviations. Consult your dictionary.*

1. ad lib
2. ASCAP
3. BMR
4. CIO
5. colloq.

6. ESP
7. f.o.b.
8. q.v.
9. TNT
10. S.J.

11. UNESCO
12. S.R.O.
13. USAFI
14. NCAA
15. op. cit.

EXERCISE 3, SPELLING OUT NUMBERS. *In the following sentences encircle the numbers that should have been written out in words.*

1. He will inherit the estate when he reaches the age of 21.
2. The estate consists of a ranch, some stocks, and $35,600 in bonds.
3. Brenda was given an expensive car on her 18th birthday.
4. Her sister Diana, who is 16, is in love with a boy 3 inches shorter than she.
5. Margaret's birthday parties are awkward, for she was born on December 26, 1950.
6. Although a member of the 4-H Club for 6 years, she does not know what the four *H*'s stand for.
7. Timmy, an 8th grader, told her his scholastic average for 2 years is 86.55.
8. He has just bought a 90mm lens for his Exakta, which is a 35mm single lens reflex camera.
9. In 1940 McMillan and Abelson produced element 93, named *neptunium* after the planet Neptune.
10. 36 boys can be housed in the dormitory at 218 South 36th Street.

§ 10. ITALICS

Italics are used to set words apart in a variety of situations.

The word *italics* refers to print. In handwriting or in typing, a word to be understood as in *italics* is underlined.

TYPEWRITTEN

In the June 2, 1975, issue of <u>Time</u> there is a review of Richard Condon's <u>Money Is Love.</u>

PRINT

In the June 2, 1975, issue of *Time* there is a review of Richard Condon's *Money Is Love.*

In business letters, instead of being underlined, the words are usually typed in capitals, as: TIME, MONEY IS LOVE.

Usage varies greatly in regard to the use of italics. The principles or statements of usage in this section refer to more or less formal usage. Newspapers, as a rule, do not use italic type. The *New York Times Book Review* follows British practice and uses quotation marks for titles of books. *Harper's Magazine* italicizes the titles of books, magazines, and newspapers, but uses quotation marks for titles of musical compositions. If you are writing for publication, the only sure guide is the style sheet of the magazine you are aiming at.

The following rules are usually observed in college papers of a formal nature.

10a. When referred to in formal writing, titles of books, plays, newspapers, magazines, musical compositions, and works of art as well as names of ships are usually underlined in manuscript and printed in italics.

EXAMPLES

Huckleberry Finn

Mozart's *The Marriage of Figaro*

Michelangelo's *Pietà*

Scientific American

the Portland *Oregonian*

the *Queen Elizabeth II*

301

Quotation marks are generally used for titles of chapters or subdivisions of books and for titles of short stories, magazine articles, newspaper articles, and short poems.

10

EXAMPLES

The stories in Maugham's *East and West,* such as "Rain" and "The Letter," could have appeared in a magazine, such as the *Atlantic,* before being published in book form. Later, as a play, *Rain* enjoyed a long run.

The definite article *the* and the name of the city before the title of a newspaper are usually not italicized: the St. Louis *Post-Dispatch.* Some periodicals, however, prefer the italicized article: *The New Yorker.* [Note that *The* in such use requires a capital.]

10b. Foreign words and phrases that are still not Anglicized are italicized (underlined) when used in writing.

A number of terms pronounced like foreign words are nevertheless considered so much a part of our language that italics are *not* used. Examples include: cliché, staccato, blitzkrieg. Some dictionaries will tell you if a word is still considered foreign and therefore must be italicized. Different dictionaries use different symbols for this purpose.

10c. In formal writing, words, letters, and figures, referred to as such, are usually italicized.

You have seen this procedure exemplified many times in this book, where italics have been used to mark off a word being discussed *as a word.* But in informal writing, quotation marks may be used for the same purpose. As always, be consistent in the form selected. In definitions, the word to be defined is commonly set in italics (underlined) and the definition is enclosed in quotation marks.

FORMAL STYLE

We realize the humorous intention when somebody invents from the noun *swashbuckler* a verb to *swashbuckle,* or to *buttle* and *cuttle* from *butler*

302

and *cutler,* but it is not so well known that the same process (probably with the same humorous intent behind it) gave us such sober words as *burgle, sidle, edit, grovel, beg,* and *greed.*

—Owen Barfield, *History in English Words*

Thus words like *sapolio, oleomargarine, brillo,* a name for steel wool used in polishing, *fermillac,* fermented milk, *sozodont,* the name of a tooth powder, and dozens of others like these betray at least a moderate degree of familiarity with the classical languages.

—George P. Krapp, *The Knowledge of English*

A nasturtium is a pretty flower, but the word *nasturtium* actually means "a nose twister." Few persons remember that *sabotage* means "throwing your wooden shoes into the machinery."

INFORMAL STYLE

Many people confuse "imply" and "infer."

The European "7" is written differently from ours.

10d. Italics may be used to give special emphasis to a word or phrase.

The use of italics or underlining for emphasis can be badly abused in formal writing, where it is likely to appear as a weak effort to give importance to words that ought to be important without such mechanical help. Furthermore, excessive underlining has associations with trivial dialogue, often of a juvenile flavor. ("My *dear,* you should have seen her *hair.* I mean you should have *seen* it. *Really!*") In a similar way, italics have been liberally used by some modern novelists, notably J. D. Salinger, to suggest the up-and-down stresses of emotional speech. "I was *born* here. I went to *school* here. I've been *run over* here—*twice,* and on the same damn *street.*"

But in formal exposition, it is conventional to use italics for emphasis far more sparingly, usually only when the sentence would not be immediately clear without them.

EXAMPLES

Emotions represented in literature are, neither for writer nor for reader, the same as emotions in "real life"; they are "recollected in tranquillity"; they are "expressed"—that is, released—by analysis; they are the *feelings* of emotions, the perceptions of emotions.

—RENÉ WELLEK AND AUSTIN WARREN, *Theory of Literature*

10

Every writer should be clear *who he is* for the purpose of writing— whether himself, or the representative of a point of view, or the spokesman of a particular group.

—ROBERT GRAVES AND ALAN HODGE, *The Reader over Your Shoulder*

EXERCISES

EXERCISE 1, ITALICS AND QUOTATION MARKS. *Copy the following paragraph, underlining for italics and adding quotation marks where necessary. Use the formal conventions.*

Webster's New World Dictionary, like other such works, includes helpful lists of synonyms for many familiar words. Listed under crowd, for example, you will find throng, multitude, swarm, mob, host, and horde, with precise differences indicated. An introductory article called Guide to the Use of the Dictionary is of further assistance to the reader searching for a mot juste. A subsection of this article, titled The Synonymies, treats antonyms as well, and concludes: "the antonym sad heads a synonymy that includes melancholy, dejected, depressed, and doleful, all antonymous to happy."

EXERCISE 2, ITALICS AND QUOTATION MARKS. *Copy the following paragraph in the same way, underlining for italics where necessary and adding quotation marks in the proper places.*

Eliot's The Love Song of J. Alfred Prufrock has long since supplanted Hiawatha and the Gettysburg Address as a set piece for young elocutionists. Prufrock has become the poem of a whole generation born long after it was written, and no doubt Eliot's Collected Poems owes at least some of its success to the popularity of this one poem. His religious poems, such as Ash Wednesday, and his plays, such as Murder in the Cathedral, are all very well, but apparently young people today prefer to think of themselves as junior Prufrocks.

304

§ 11. SYLLABICATION
AND HYPHENS

11a. The awkward division of a word at the end of a line
of handwritten or typewritten manuscript should be
avoided.

In printed matter, where a perfectly even right-hand margin
is mandatory, we have become accustomed to a number of
word divisions at the ends of lines. In handwritten or typewritten papers, however, it is usually unnecessary to divide
many words. For clearness and ease in reading, it is wise to
observe the following cautions about dividing words at the end
of a line:

1. Never divide words of one syllable, such as *eighth, rhythm,
signed, burned.* Note that the *-ed* ending in the past-tense form
must not be split off as a syllable when it is not pronounced as a
syllable.

2. Never divide a word so that a single letter is allowed to
stand by itself, either at the end of a line or the beginning of the
next line, as in *a-/mount, a-/round, e-/lope, greed-/y, read-/y.*

3. Try to avoid dividing proper names.

4. Try not to separate a name and the initials that go with it.

5. Try to avoid dividing the last word of a paragraph or a
page. In print such a division is often necessary, but in manuscript it can be easily avoided.

11b. If a division of a word is necessary, the division should be
made between syllables and a hyphen placed at the end
of the line.

Assume that your reader is pronouncing your sentence aloud
and divide words so that both parts are pronounceable. You
must divide correctly between syllables and your best resource
in doing so is your dictionary, where syllables are clearly indicated. The following cautions should be of additional help:

1. Divide compound words on the hyphen, and try to avoid a

11

second hyphen: self-/evident, *not* self-evi-/dent; college-/trained, *not* col-/lege-trained.

2. In words with prefixes, divide on the prefix: non-/sensical, pre-/caution, ante-/diluvian. Note that these words are ordinarily written solid; they are not hyphenated compounds.

3. In words with suffixes, divide on the suffix: boy-/ish, dog-/like, youth-/ful, fall-/ing, yell-/ing.

4. As a rule, when a word contains double consonants, divide between the two consonants: ac-/com-/mo-/date, in-/ter-/ro-/gate. In such examples as *fall-/ing* and *yell-/ing,* however, the rule about double consonants conflicts with the rule about suffixes; the rule about suffixes takes precedence.

11c. **Two or more words forming a compound adjective preceding a noun are hyphenated.**

E X A M P L E S

A broad-shouldered, long-legged boy; a rough-looking fellow; ready-made opinions; a twin-screw engine; in up-to-date condition; a well-traveled highway; a two-thirds majority; an old-fashioned sermon; a pitch-dark night; the Russo-Finnish border.

When a compound modifier consists of two or more words with a common beginning, the following style is used: *A three- or four-room addition, Anglo- and Franco-American, paid in five- and ten-dollar bills.*

The following are usually not hyphenated: compound modifiers that follow the noun; compounds in which an adverb ending in *-ly* is used.

E X A M P L E S

The man was well known for thievery. [We met a well-known poet.]

His information was up to date. [He planned an up-to-date revision of the book.]

It was a loosely worded statement. [His explanations were loosely worded.]

11d. **Compound numbers from twenty-one to ninety-nine are hyphenated.**

306

E X A M P L E S

Twenty-seven dollars, thirty-four inches

Fractions, when used as modifiers, are hyphenated. When one of the terms of the fraction is already a compound, however, no additional hyphen is used, as in *four twenty-fifths, twenty-one fortieths.* Such simple fractions as *one half, two thirds,* and so on, are often written without a hyphen, but *one-and-a-half* always follows the hyphenated form.

E X A M P L E S

The bill was finally passed by a two-thirds majority.

One half of the pie was already eaten.

11e. Hyphens are used with the following classes of compound words.

1. With prefixes *ex-* (in the sense of "former") and *self-:* ex-president, ex-minister, self-regard, self-help, self-pity.
2. When two functions that are usually distinct are united in one person or thing: cleaner-polisher, secretary-treasurer, publisher-editor, city-state.
3. With prefix *semi-* when second element begins with *i:* semi-independent, semi-invalid.
4. With suffix *-like* when first element ends with *ll:* bell-like; when first element is a proper noun: American-like.
5. With groups making or containing prepositional phrases: son-in-law, man-of-war, jack-in-the-pulpit.
6. To prevent confusion with similar words: re-form [to form again], reform [to change or amend]; re-count [to count anew], recount [to tell]; re-creation [a second creation], recreation [play, sport, diversion].
7. When the second element of a compound word is a proper noun: anti-American, pre-Renaissance, pro-Russian.

When in doubt about the correct form of a compound, consult *Webster's New Collegiate Dictionary, The American College Dictionary, Webster's New World Dictionary,* the *American Heritage Dictionary,* or *The Random House Dictionary.* See also, for a general

11

discussion of compound words, Bergen and Cornelia Evans, *A Dictionary of Contemporary American Usage,* Random House, 1957, pages 108–110.

EXERCISES

EXERCISE 1, SYLLABICATION. *Indicate which of the following words you should not divide at the end of a line. Show how you would divide the others. Give your reason in each case.*

1. agreed	6. sorely	11. brushed
2. precedence	7. speedy	12. elect
3. preeminent	8. unit	13. bankbook
4. through	9. across	14. squeezed
5. thorough	10. action	15. stringy

EXERCISE 2, COMPOUND WORDS. *With the aid of a dictionary determine which of the following should be written solid, which with a hyphen, and which are separate words.*

1. air raid	16. good bye
2. air raid shelter	17. half brother
3. all inclusive	18. half crazed lion
4. all right	19. half written theme
5. ante date	20. partly written paper
6. ante bellum	21. in as much as
7. anti climax	22. infra red
8. any body	23. north west
9. basket ball	24. post office
10. book store	25. score board
11. by law	26. text book
12. by pass	27. inter collegiate
13. post Renaissance	28. under graduate
14. dining room	29. week end trip
15. every thing	30. well made car

3 *Punctuation*

The purpose of punctuation is to help make clear the meaning of printed or written language.

To some degree punctuation symbolizes the pauses in oral speech, but it does so crudely and artificially. It is still useful to read a sentence aloud with attention to its meaning, and punctuate the pauses you hear in your own voice. But correct punctuation has also come to reflect the grammatical structures of sentences, as well as the particular conventions of the age. Therefore, a comma does not always represent a drop or pause in the speaking voice, and the various marks of punctuation do not consistently distinguish among the various subtle drops that our voices so naturally perform. Like most other conventional patterns of behavior, the conventions of punctuation have to be learned.

The practice of writers has been codified into a number of rules or principles of punctuation. These rules or principles govern a very large number of typical situations in writing. At times, however, certain marks are optional, depending on the writer's particular attitude toward what he is saying and on decisions of publishers. On the whole, nevertheless, a college student can have success if he follows codified usage. When in genuine doubt, he or she can usually resort to common sense.

Punctuation, then, is more than a series of rules: it offers one more way of clarifying expression. Even in the many situations where one has a choice—for example, to include a comma or leave it out—one's choice need not be arbitrary. The rhythm of one's prose style will be very largely controlled by the use or omission of punctuation marks where no rule clearly applies.

§ 12. END PUNCTUATION

The Period

12

12a. A period is used after a declarative or imperative sentence, or after an indirect question, but not after a direct question.

EXAMPLES

I had no idea where I had been or how I got there. [Declarative]

Always know where you are. [Imperative]

The woman asked where I had been. [Indirect question]

The woman asked, "Where have you been?" [Direct question, ending with a question mark]

Note the difference, in the last two examples, in the way the human voice is used. At the end of the indirect question there is a drop in voice level characteristic of all declarative sentences. But a rise in pitch at the end of a sentence—Where have you been?—is usually a sign of a question, to be symbolized by a question mark.

12b. Most of the common abbreviations require a period.

EXAMPLES

Mr., Mrs., Ms., Dr., St., Jr., a.m., B.C., Mass.

Increasingly, the period is not used with certain groups of letters or acronyms standing for organizations or government agencies. Note that the letters are written without spacing.

EXAMPLES

UN, USSR, CIA, TVA, FCC, NAACP, SALT, HEW, NOW

Usage is divided in regard to some of the older abbreviations consisting of the initial letters of words, though the tendency is toward omitting the period. Consult your dictionary when in doubt.

310

12. END PUNCTUATION

Y.M.C.A. *or* YMCA; r.p.m. *or* rpm; A.M.A. *or* AMA

12c. Spaced periods (ellipsis marks or suspension points, usually three within a sentence, four at the end of a declarative sentence to include the necessary closing period) are used to indicate the omission of words from a quoted passage, or pauses or hesitation in dialogue.

12

EXAMPLES

We the People of the United States, in order to . . . secure the Blessings of Liberty to ourselves and our Posterity, do . . . establish this Constitution for the United States of America.
                              —PREAMBLE TO THE U.S. CONSTITUTION
The souls of emperors and cobblers are cast in the same mould. . . . The same reason that makes us wrangle with a neighbor causes a war betwixt princes.

                              —MONTAIGNE

"Now let me think. . . . Yes. . . . I suppose so."

The Question Mark

12d. A question mark is used after a direct question but not after an indirect question.

Note the distinction in voice level discussed under §12a. Most of our problems in using the *question mark* are mechanical ones, involving other punctuation surrounding the mark in special cases.

EXAMPLES

What will I do if Miss Byrne is there? What will I say to her? she asked herself, but did not wait for an answer. [Quotation marks are sometimes omitted when unspoken thoughts are quoted.]

                              —MICHAEL MCLAVERTY, *School for Hope*

Was it not Plato himself who said that he would never write a treatise on philosophy, that the latter must be acquired by conversation, the flame leaping from speaker to speaker "until the soul itself caught

311

fire"? [Note relation of question mark to quotation marks when part of a phrase is quoted in a question.]

—Irwin Edman, "Fashions in Ideas"

12

After we landed we learned, with a tremendous surge of pride, that as the waters rose around them, those green troops, soldiers from far northwestern states mostly, stood in ranks on the canted decks singing a popular song of the war, "Where Do We Go from Here, Boys?" [A question mark ends the sentence if the last part is a quoted question.]

—Irvin S. Cobb

Instead of asking "What would a good education consist of?" many professors of education are asking "What do most college students want?"; instead of asking "What books are wisest and best and most beautiful?" they conduct polls to determine which the largest number of students have read with least pain. [Some writers would have put commas after each *asking*. Note that a question mark is used with a title if it is a question.]

—Joseph Wood Krutch, "Is Our Common Man Too Common?"

A single question mark is used after a double question—that is, a quoted question following a question. (See also §16.)

EXAMPLES

Who wrote "Where are the snows of yesteryear?"

Why does he not simply ask, "Where do I go now?"

A question mark within parentheses may be used to indicate doubt or uncertainty about the preceding figure or fact. This is a conventional practice in the case of a doubtful birth or death date.

EXAMPLE

Lucien Botha was born in 1779(?) and died in 1859.

But the use of a parenthetical question mark to indicate irony is the mark only of immature writing.

POOR

We had a wonderful(?) time at that party.

312

12. *END PUNCTUATION*

A question mark is often used after commands or requests phrased as questions if a formal effect is desired, but a period is used for a less formal effect. A convenient test, once again, is to read the sentence aloud, checking for the rise in pitch characteristic of the last syllable of a question.

FORMAL

May I ask the entire staff to reassemble here at four o'clock?

LESS FORMAL

Will the whole staff meet here again at four o'clock, please.

The Exclamation Point

12e. An exclamation point is usually used after an expression that indicates strong feeling or emotion.

The student's temptation often is to overuse the *exclamation point,* creating a breathless or overexcited style not unlike that produced by an overuse of italics. (See § 10d.) Words such as *yes, no, oh, well, alas, surely,* when beginning a sentence, are usually followed by a comma. Actually it is wise to avoid them in the opening position, except in dialogue. If *oh* introduces an expression of strong feeling, put the exclamation point at the end of the expression. Never use more than one exclamation point in a sentence.

EXAMPLES

"Good lord!" he gasped in amazement.

It is difficult to see how anyone in his right mind could have concluded *that!*

Oh, this is unpardonable!

The days wore on, and yet got nowhere. . . . Time had simply come to a standstill! He had never seen the like; this was worse than the deadest lay-up in Lofoten!

—O. E. RÖLVAAG, *Giants in the Earth*

313

13

EXERCISE

Exercise, End Punctuation in Dialogue. In the following dialogue, supply commas, periods, question marks, and exclamation points where they are necessary. Be careful to place punctuation correctly in relation to quotation marks.

1. "Did you know the ending would turn out that way" asked Dr Fisher
2. "No I didn't" she replied
3. The doctor asked her what other movies she had seen lately
4. "Oh not many" she said "Have you seen anything like this before"
5. "What makes you ask that" he replied
6. "Do you know who said 'Movies are getting better'" she asked
7. "Who was it that used to ask 'Why not try a good movie tonight'"
8. "Watch out" he shouted suddenly as they attempted to cross the street in front of the theatre
9. "Wasn't that Mr Wells in his MG Wow That was too close for comfort"
10. "I wonder" he observed "when the streets will ever be safe for pedestrians"

§ 13. THE COMMA

Of all the marks of punctuation, the *comma* has the widest variety of uses. Probably because the comma is used in so many situations, any attempt to codify the practice of writers and to state usage in terms of definite principles must give due weight to the exceptions. Yet, however important the differences of practice are, to the student the most important thing is that there is such a large area of agreement. Most of the uses of the comma can be stated in terms of principles that reflect what most writers are doing.

The student should always remember, however, that these

314

descriptions of usage must be interpreted with a little common sense. It is true, for instance, that writers place a comma after an introductory clause or phrase if they feel that this sentence element is not an integral part of the main clause—that is, if it is not closely restrictive—but no rule, only common sense, can tell a student when this clause is restrictive or nonrestrictive.

Generally, punctuation tends to be *close* (that is, with a liberal use of commas) in serious or formal writing, where precision is vital. It tends to be *open* (that is, using a minimum of punctuation) in informal description and narration and in journalistic writing.

Although the primary function of punctuation is to help make meaning clear, punctuation has another function, a rhetorical one. The comma—and to a certain extent the semicolon—may be used to indicate the degree of pause or emphasis or rhetorical balance or contrast of ideas. The important fact still remains, however, that before a writer can make punctuation an artistic resource he or she must first become familiar with the general practice of writers.

Because of its wide variety of uses, the comma may appear to some a subject of puzzling complexity, although at times it is hard to see why eager young people of eighteen, who speak familiarly of isotopes and learn to pilot jets, should be bowled over by so simple a thing as a comma. At any rate, it is possible to simplify a simple subject further by dividing all comma uses into two groups. In one group we have the *to separate* uses; in the other group we have the *to enclose* uses. A picture of the whole thing makes it still simpler and clearer.

A TABLE OF COMMA USES

Usually to Separate	*Usually to Enclose*
13a. main clauses	13h. nonrestrictive clauses
13b. elements in series	13i. parenthetical elements
13c. coordinate adjectives	13j. absolute phrases
13d. words that may be misread	13k. appositives
13e. introductory modifiers	13l. words in direct address
13f. transposed elements	13m. dialogue guides
13g. mild exclamations, etc.	13n. dates and addresses

13

13a. A comma is ordinarily used to separate coordinate clauses joined by *and, but, for, or, nor,* except when the clauses are short and closely related in meaning.

A writer is safe to apply this rule rather strictly in formal writing. At the same time it must be acknowledged that the use of a comma to separate main clauses has become almost optional. Journalistic writing discards the comma in this situation except to prevent misreading. At the formal level, the general practice is to omit the comma when the subject of the sentence does not change after the first clause. If there is any other clearly defined practice to help the beginning student, it is that the comma is obligatory before *for* (to prevent confusion with the preposition *for*) and recommended before *but.*

Marco Polo, the Italian explorer, visited the island of Sumatra in 1292, and in 1509 Portuguese traders established commercial stations there.

For the boundary between sea and land is the most fleeting and transitory feature of the earth, and the sea is forever repeating its encroachments upon the continents. [Note, as in this sentence, that the conjunction *for* may be used to begin independent sentences. *But* is another conjunction frequently used in this way.]

—Rachel Carson, *The Sea Around Us*

The brilliance of a nova at its peak is usually not sufficient to make it visible to the naked eye, but supernovae surpass in brilliance the brightest of ordinary stars and some of them can be observed in full daylight. [Note that no comma is used before *and* because the subjects of the last two clauses are felt to be closely related.]

In a sense, the processes of fission and fusion are similar, for they both are used to convert mass into energy in an amount given by Einstein's equation. [Note comma before *for.*]

—Donald J. Hughes, "Atoms, Energy, and Peace"

They [the buildings of architecture] may be sophisticated, worked out with the greatest intellectual subtlety, designed like the Parthenon by known architects of genius; or they may, like some old stone barn in Pennsylvania, be the naïve, natural legacy of half-understood tradition, put up by an anonymous builder. [Note the semicolon before *or*

316

in a compound sentence with a number of commas. See §14 for further discussion.]

—John E. Burchard, "Architecture and Building"

13

13b. Commas are used to separate words, phrases, or clauses in a series.

A *series* must have at least three members; usually the last is joined to the other by *and* or *or.* It is at this point, the point of the conjunction, that usage differs. Although the comma is generally used here in most formal writing, some writers do omit it. In informal writing there is a progressive tendency to discard the comma before the conjunction, except for clearness. In journalistic writing, the comma is regularly omitted.

Men, women, and children enjoyed the happy, carefree, and refreshing outing. [Nouns and adjectives in series] The boys stopped, looked, and then darted for cover. [Series of verbs]

In scarlet and blue and green and purple, three by three the sovereigns rode through the palace gates, with plumed helmets, gold braid, crimson sashes, and jeweled orders flashing in the sun. [Series of nouns]

—Barbara W. Tuchman, *The Guns of August*

So our girl in this free country has, in truth, little choice. Security is the goal, and as soon as possible. Marry the boy right away, get the house right away, have the brood right away. No time for search of self, no time for experiments in love and life, no time for interior growth, no time for the great world outside. [Series of predicates]

—Marya Mannes, *The Singular Women*

What is the nature of man's consciousness, his feelings, his hopes and aspirations, his personality, his learning, logic, and memory?

—Harold G. Wolff, "The Mind-Body Relationships"

Lying plays a decisive role in our daily lives, our politics, our love-affairs and our friendships, and since we attempt to deceive ourselves as well as others, our lies are brilliant and fertile, not like the gross inventions of other people. [Series with *and*]

—Octavio Paz, *Mexican Masks*

317

13

Here is an example from serious writing in which the author omits the comma:

To be courageous, these stories make clear, requires no exceptional qualifications, no magic formula, no special combinations of time, place and circumstance.

—John F. Kennedy, *Profiles in Courage*

In the following sentence notice not only the omission of the final comma in a series but also the use of the semicolon before *but* in a compound sentence.

An unstable society, with extremes of poverty and wealth, but with easy access to riches and a quick turnover in the composition of the aristocracy, might produce a brief, frenetic and opportunistic radicalism; but it was not likely to produce a radicalism which was serious, unbribable and consistent.

—Arthur M. Schlesinger, Jr., *The Age of Jackson*

13c. Commas are used to separate consecutive adjectives preceding the noun they modify when the adjectives are coordinate in meaning.

The comma is correct only when the adjectives are *coordinate*—that is, when each of the adjectives refers directly and independently to the same noun. When an adjective modifies the whole idea that follows it, it is not separated from it by a comma. If you can substitute *and* for the comma, the comma is correct. Note in the following examples that *and* would be a natural substitute for each comma used:

with slow, powerful strokes . . . these cold, treeless heights . . . the still, dimly lighted street . . . this bold, gleaming structure . . . his exuberant, energetic brother . . . their dull, inglorious lives . . . the muddy, tired, discouraged men

A safe practice is to omit the comma with numerals and with the common adjectives of size and age:

the little old lady . . . a dirty old man . . . the spreading chestnut tree . . . a large red-haired girl . . . four tiny black dots

318

More generally, a comma should not be used when one of two adjectives associated with a noun modifies the other adjective or the other adjective and the noun together.

13

EXAMPLES

Ground roast coffee ... dark brown earth ... pure spring water ...

13d. The comma is used to separate words and phrases that might be incorrectly joined in reading.

This rule applies to the following situations:
1. When the conjunctions *for* and *but* might be mistaken for prepositions.

The men all waited in anxious silence, for the messenger seemed to be in a desperate hurry. [Waited in anxious silence for the messenger?]

All the men slid down the ropes, but one sailor seemed to be caught in the rigging. [All slid down the ropes but one sailor?]

2. When a noun might be mistaken for the object of a verb, verbal, or preposition before it.

After washing, the men filed into the dining tent. [*Not* After washing the men]

Before starting to eat, Father bowed his head in prayer. [*Not* Before starting to eat Father]

Above, the sun burned a dull red; below, the sand radiated heat like a furnace. [*Not* Above the sun . . . below the sand]

When we left, the boys were still playing their endless game of pinochle. [*Not* When we left the boys]

13e. Ordinarily, a comma is used to set off a modifier that precedes a main clause, especially when the introductory element is long and not closely connected with the main clause in meaning, when it is not *restrictive*.

In punctuating modifiers that precede the main clause you should depend on your good sense as well as on rules. You should decide whether or not the sentence will be clearer with

13

the introductory modifier set off by a comma. Length of clause alone will not prescribe when to use a comma and when not to use it. Frequently very short clauses are set off for emphasis. In general, if the introductory element is not clearly restrictive, put a comma after it. The following distinctions will help you:

1. Use a comma when you begin with a fairly long (usually over five words) nonrestrictive adverbial clause:

When it came to the actual count, every measure against the Americans passed Parliament by large majorities.

—CATHERINE DRINKER BOWEN, *John Adams and the American Revolution*

Because the powerful beams that attract the insects are directed low over the river, they do not lead birds to their death as airport ceilometer lights, pointing straight up, sometimes do.

—EDWIN WAY TEALE, *Journey into Summer*

And if we are not all good stoics like Juárez and Cuauhtémoc, at least we can be resigned and patient and long-suffering.

—OCTAVIO PAZ, *Mexican Masks*

2. Use a comma to set off an introductory participial phrase modifying the subject or an introductory *absolute phrase* (see "Parts of Speech," page 165):

Stopping often to gaze back or to browse in ripe raspberries hanging beside the trail, we ascended to the top. [Phrase modifies *we*.]

—EDWIN WAY TEALE, *Journey into Summer*

The excitement being over, the students returned to the classroom. [Absolute phrase]

3. Set off short introductory prepositional phrases only when they are definitely nonrestrictive, such as *transitional phrases* (see "Parts of Speech," page 163).

NO COMMA

Up to this point we are on safe ground.

During the ceremony a dog strayed into the room.

In the spring the ground is covered with poppies.

320

13. *THE COMMA*

In addition, such experiences are educational.

Of the small islands, the nearest is heavily timbered.

In the first place, his idea is not new.

Long introductory prepositional phrases may be set off if the writer believes that a comma is an aid to clearness:

In addition to the picture information it sends out, a television station also transmits sound.

—Louis N. Ridenour, "Electronics and the Conquest of Space"

In the biological and physical as well as the sociological sciences, statistics have become, as they never were before, the most important tool of investigation.

—Joseph Wood Krutch

4. A short introductory clause is usually not followed by a comma. It may, however, be set off for greater emphasis or for clearness.

When he gives us a test he usually leaves the room. [Informal]

If the boy comes I shall tell him to look for you in the shop. [Informal]

13f. A comma, or commas, may be used to indicate transposed or contrasting sentence elements.

EXAMPLES

A boy, thin, ragged, and terribly frightened, had wedged himself behind the crate. [*Note:* A thin, ragged, and terribly frightened boy had. . .]

Inequality, by arousing jealousy and envy, provokes discontent. [*Not transposed:* Inequality provokes discontent by arousing jealousy and envy.]

He [Shakespeare] knew that Hamlet's dilemma, between the flesh and the spirit, was at the heart of every human being's private tragedy, and he made Hamlet so terrifyingly real, with his courtesy and his violence, his intelligence and his self-hatred, his inconsistencies and his terrors, that every generation since has been able to recognize in him its own image. [Note here how commas set off balanced elements.]

—Marchette Chute, *Shakespeare of London*

321

13

She insisted on blue, rather than white, candles. [Contrasting sentence elements]

13g. Commas are used to set off mild exclamations, sentence adverbs (i.e., which modify the entire sentence), and the responsives *yes* and *no* when they begin a sentence.

E X A M P L E S

Yes, he assigned another essay for Friday.

Evidently, you will not have it ready for him.

Unfortunately, I shall have to stay up all night to write it.

Mary said, "Well, what excuse can I give him?"

Oh, you will think of something to say before Friday.

13h. Commas are used to set off nonrestrictive clauses. They are not used to set off restrictive clauses.

If the distinction between restrictive and nonrestrictive clauses is not already clear to you, think of restrictive clauses as "identifying" or "pointing-out" clauses. A restrictive clause helps to locate or identify its antecedent. It says to the reader, "I mean this particular person or object, and no other." It is close to its antecedent in meaning, so close that it cannot be separated from it by a comma. A nonrestrictive clause does not point out or identify; it merely gives additional information about its antecedent.

R E S T R I C T I V E   C L A U S E S

The board decided in favor of another candidate *who has had more experience.* [Not just another candidate, but one with more experience]

The boy *who has a hobby* will never be lonely. [Not any boy, but that particular kind of boy]

Please bring me the book *that you see lying on the table.* [That particular book and no other]

N O N R E S T R I C T I V E   C L A U S E S

The board decided in favor of Mr. Rossi, *who has had more experience.* [The name identifies the person; the clause does not need to identify or point out.]

322

13. THE COMMA

Fenwick Jones, *who has a hobby,* will never be lonely. [The name identifies him.]

Please bring me Bellow's *Mr. Sammler's Planet, which you see lying on the table.* [The title identifies the book.]

Astronomy, *which is the study of heavenly bodies,* is a fascinating subject. [*Astronomy* identifies itself. It does not need a clause to tell which particular astronomy.]

My father, *who had not heard the question,* shook his head in silence. [A person has only one father. The clause cannot help identify him.]

Participial phrases may be either restrictive or nonrestrictive, depending on the meaning intended.

RESTRICTIVE

The boy *standing near the door* is waiting to register. [That particular boy]

A book *written by that author* is sure to be interesting. [Phrase points to a particular kind of book—one written by that author.]

NONRESTRICTIVE

Henry Black, standing there by the door, is waiting to register. [Name identifies him.]

Raising his rifle quickly, he fired at the moving object. [Nothing in the phrase helps to identify the person.]

13i. Commas are used to set off parenthetical elements (interrupters), or words, phrases, and clauses used to explain, to qualify, or to emphasize.

In a sense, several of the sentence elements discussed under other rules are "interrupters" in that they tend to break or interrupt the normal flow of a sentence, but strict classification is not here important. The parenthetical elements dealt with here may be classified as follows:

1. Conjunctive adverbs, such as *however, therefore, moreover, furthermore,* when they are used within the clause. In any style, an epidemic of *moreover*'s and *furthermore*'s is as bad as a plague of *and*'s and *but*'s.

323

13

An institution, *therefore,* may fail because its standards are too high.

In truth, *however,* it was probably not known until after the French Revolution.

And do not use a conjunctive adverb to force a connection. "She ate too many hot dogs; consequently, she was sick" is nauseous in more ways than one.

2. Directive and qualifying words and phrases. Some of the most common of these, such as *also, perhaps, indeed, too, at least,* may, in informal writing, be considered as close modifiers and therefore not set off by commas. Others are usually set off.

E X A M P L E S

All of this, *of course,* is theory.

My theory, *unluckily,* was disproved by the events that followed.

He would become, *in short,* a problem child of the worst kind.

3. Parenthetical phrases and clauses. Most of these are parenthetical comments, but some are adverbial clauses that interrupt the sentence flow.

E X A M P L E S

This, *I suppose,* is the essence of morality.

Our interpretation of his motives is, *I think,* totally unfair.

If you must take risks on the lake, see to it that, *whenever storm warnings are up,* you at least have a life preserver with you.

It should be noted here that three types of punctuation are used with parenthetical elements. Parentheses are used for the most distant interrupters, dashes for something a little less distant, and commas for interrupters most closely related to the rest of the sentence. For a further discussion see §§17 and 18.

E X A M P L E S

The Silent Generation (*loquacious enough among its contemporaries*) holds its tongue because it cannot both explore itself and explain itself.

—Thornton Wilder, "The Silent Generation"

In music, *especially slow music,* a given tone is held for an appreciable length of time. This means that reverberation adds to the power of a given tone resulting in a desirable (*to the bathroom tenor, at least*) expansion in volume.

—WILLIAM C. VERGARA, *Science in Everyday Things*

Finally—*and this is true both for storable and perishable products*—were there a good way of disposing of inventories there would be far less need to worry about production control.

—J. KENNETH GALBRAITH, "Why Be Secretary of Agriculture?"

13j. Commas are used to set off absolute phrases when they occur within the sentence.

EXAMPLES

A great dam came into view, *water boiling from its curved rank of spillways.*

—ANDREW H. BROWN, *National Geographic*

She stood there, *her damp face glowing with happiness,* and asked us all to be seated.

13k. Commas are used to set off appositives.

An *appositive,* or a word in apposition, is used to limit or qualify the meaning of another word, to stand for it, to add to its meaning, or to emphasize it. The name *appositive* refers to the fact that a word and its appositive stand side by side. Most appositives—with the exception of the types listed below—are to be set off by commas.

EXAMPLES

Mr. Perkins, the *foreman* of the plant, was hurt yesterday. [Appositive with modifiers]

Other animals, such as the giraffe, camel, and brown bear, use a different type of locomotion. [Appositive introduced by *such as*]

—WILLIAM C. VERGARA, *Science in Everyday Things*

As he neared Fourth Street, another man, *a new one,* sprang up suddenly before him, *a short, heavy-set fellow,* stepping out of the shadows

13

and striding directly toward him. [Notice how the use of appositives may add to sentence variety.]

—Robert M. Coates

Cooper, *an aristocrat in temper,* was a stickler for his social rights, *the rights to consideration, privacy, respect,* and he was often at war with himself, for his tastes and prejudices were by no means in harmony with his conscience and convictions.

—Van Wyck Brooks

But do *not* use commas with many common expressions in which the appositive and its substantive are so close that they are felt as a unit:

Jack the Ripper, Jack the Giant-killer, Henry the Eighth, my son Harold, William the Conqueror, the word *appositive,* the novelist Roth.

Participles and occasionally adjectives may be placed for greater emphasis or for variety after the words they modify. When so placed they are said to be in the appositive position and are therefore set off by commas. See also §13f.

EXAMPLES

During a pause in the game, one of the fans, *devotedly cynical,* shouted mock encouragement at the pitcher.

A growl, *low and distant like the roll of a train on a faraway bridge,* began to stir in his throat.

—Wolcott Gibbs

This style, *so elegant and so simple,* was to mark all of Irving's work, *the sign of his cheerful good nature and transparent good taste.* . . . [Adjectives in the appositive position and then a substantive appositive]

—Van Wyck Brooks

Appositives may also be enclosed in parentheses or set off by dashes to indicate a greater degree of separation, if such a distinction is desired. (See §§17 and 18.) Sometimes dashes are used because of the presence of several commas.

EXAMPLES

It follows that every policy of the West that contradicts these fears—every Marshall Plan, every extension of economic aid to backward areas, every increase in social economic opportunity, every act of justice and reconciliation—breaks with the Communists' fundamental gospel—the fatality of history—and restores, triumphantly and creatively, the freedom of the West. [Note here not only the two appositives set off by dashes but also the use of two adverbs, *triumphantly* and *creatively,* in an unusual position.]

—BARBARA WARD, *Policy for the West*

The city is always full of young worshipful beginners—young actors, young aspiring poets, ballerinas, painters, reporters, singers—each depending on his own brand of tonic to stay alive, each with his own stable of giants.

—E. B. WHITE, *Here Is New York*

Appositives are sometimes introduced by such words as *that is, namely, such as, for instance, for example,* and the like. In long, formal sentences these words may be preceded by a colon or a semicolon. In ordinary writing, both formal and informal, *namely, that is, for example,* and *for instance* are usually preceded and followed by commas. *Such as* is not followed by a comma.

EXAMPLES

Short prepositions, such as *in, on, to, for,* are not capitalized in titles.

We know that white light—light from the sun, for example—is really a mixture of light of all colors.

There is only one proper thing for a driver to do when the army mule dies, namely, cut the harness and pull the cart himself.

131. Commas are used to set off substantives used in direct address.

EXAMPLES

Professor Holmes, your lectures are a constant delight to your class. [To begin a sentence]

Read the poem, *my dear fellow,* and tell me if it means anything to you. [Within the sentence]

"Please change places with me, Helen," I requested. [With quotation marks]

13

13m. An explanatory clause such as *he said* (a dialogue guide), when it interrupts a sentence of dialogue, is set off by commas.

EXAMPLES

"For your next project," said the teacher, "you will write an essay about the Blarney Stone."

Sean McCarthy raised his hand and said, "Did you know that Cormack MacCarthy, one of my ancestors, built Blarney Castle in 1602?" [Dialogue guide begins sentence.]

"Most tourists," explained Eric Swensen, "do not know that the real Blarney Stone is impossible for them to reach."

"They are allowed to kiss a substitute stone," he added. "It works just as well." [Dialogue guide at end of one sentence and before the second sentence]

Also see §16 for placing of quotation marks in relation to commas.

13n. Commas are used to separate elements in dates and addresses that might otherwise be confused.

EXAMPLES

Ms. Joan Staley, 27463 West Chicago Street, Livonia, Michigan 48150

Mr. Thomas Larkin, 316 Northeast 54th Street, Kansas City, Missouri 64148 [It is unnecessary to set off the Zip Code by commas because it is already distinct from the name of the state preceding it.]

March 17, 1977 [The comma is necessary only to separate 17 from 1977. If the date is written European style, 17 March 1977, there is no need for a comma; nor is there in the absence of the day of the month, March 1977.]

Norman Mailer was born in Long Branch, New Jersey, and grew up in Brooklyn, New York.

—GEORGE McMICHAEL, *Anthology of American Literature*

CAUTION

Following her marriage in 1922 to a French engineering student, Kay Boyle made her home abroad, in France, England, Austria, and Ger-

328

many, before returning to America almost a quarter of a century later.
[No comma after the year]

—JAMES PICKERING, *Fiction 100*

13

EXERCISES

EXERCISE 1, NONRESTRICTIVE CLAUSES. *Punctuate each nonrestrictive clause in the following sentences.*

1. I remembered that this was the day when every student was to be on his best behavior.
2. Every year we have a homecoming day when everybody tries to impress parents and other visitors.
3. I awakened Toby Blair who was my roommate so that he would have time to dress more formally.
4. His everyday outfit which consists of white jeans and a sweater seemed hardly appropriate.
5. His father and mother of whom he was very proud were coming to visit us.
6. We found them a room at the Green Mountain Inn where most of the alumni liked to stay.
7. I did not think that my parents who were vacationing in Mexico would come for the reunion.
8. I am happy to have a roommate whose parents adopt me on occasion.
9. I know one boy who gets letters and checks from two sets of parents.
10. This weekend which we spent with Toby's parents was very happy for us.

EXERCISE 2, USING COMMAS AND SEMICOLONS. *Punctuate each of the following sentences. Decide whether to use a comma, a semicolon, or no mark at all. Be able to justify your decision.*

1. I have considered going into social work but my mother has tried to discourage me.
2. My mother is a practical person and she thinks that I am too young to know my mind.
3. I know something about the work for I have studied sociology and made trips to the state institutions.

13

4. During the summer I worked in the Red Cross office and I enjoyed the work.
5. A friend of mine is a social case worker and I have occasionally gone with her on her trips.
6. Her work is very interesting for it introduces her to all sorts of people.
7. She visits needy families but she does not actually take them baskets of food.
8. Sometimes she comes home very angry for she has no patience with drunken husbands.
9. She makes a careful study of each case and then she recommends the most suitable kind of assistance.
10. At times the Red Cross gives immediate help and then the happiness of the needy family is a welcome reward to the case worker.

EXERCISE 3, WORDS IN SERIES. *In the following sentences insert commas where they are necessary.*

1. Mark Twain was a journeyman printer a Mississippi River steamboat pilot and a famous writer and lecturer.
2. Few could compete with him in the ability to capture the lusty humor the spirit and the idiom of nineteenth-century America.
3. His humor his zest for life and his ability to see the ridiculous in everyday things endeared him to his readers.
4. Mark Twain was born in the Middle West lived in the Far West and died in New England.
5. He knew Bret Harte a poet short-story writer college professor and editor.
6. From his boyhood in Hannibal he found the materials for such characters as Tom Sawyer Huckleberry Finn and Becky Thatcher.
7. Mark Twain's best work reveals his genuine love of humanity his impatience with sham his irreverent lusty humor and his hatred of all pretense and deceit.
8. During his stay in San Francisco he associated with Bret Harte and Artemus Ward and other pioneers of the new literature of America.
9. He was attracted to Charles Farrar Browne, who was a humorist specializing in original spelling homely philosophy and shrewd comments on human nature.

330

10. As a tall imposing white-haired and white-garbed celebrity he was well known in his later years through his popular appearances on the lecture platform.

13

EXERCISE 4, INTRODUCTORY ELEMENTS. *In each of the following sentences decide whether the introductory phrase or clause is to be followed by a comma or not.*

1. If a blind poet had not written a long poem about it few modern readers would have heard about the Trojan War.
2. Because the wife of a Spartan king ran off with a young Trojan many good men perished before the walls of Troy.
3. Although the Homeric account may be the romantic version of the story the real cause of the war may have been political and economic rivalry.
4. After the sudden elopement of Helen and Paris the friends of King Menelaus of Sparta assembled to avenge the insult.
5. Having discovered a just cause to do what they liked to do even without cause the Greek heroes assembled at Aulis for the expedition.
6. Excited by hopes of an easy victory and thoughts of rich plunder the avengers gathered 100,000 men and 1,186 ships.
7. Unlike modern wars in which everybody loses ancient wars could often be profitable to the victors.
8. Ten long years having been frittered away before the walls of Troy both sides were willing to try any stratagem to win or call the war off.
9. Deciding to put their faith in trickery instead of bravery the Greeks built a large hollow horse and pretended that it was an offering to their gods.
10. Convinced by a Greek spy that the horse would make them invincible the Trojans dragged it into the city and with it enough armed Greeks to open the gates of the city to the invaders.

EXERCISE 5, DATES AND ADDRESSES. *Copy the following sentences. Insert commas where they are needed.*

1. Our friends used to live at 826 Elm Drive Harris Junction Illinois but they recently moved to 230 Warren Street Duluth Minnesota 55720.

13

2. Elinor Wylie was born in Rosemont Pennsylvania in 1887 and died in London England on December 16 1928.
3. Stephen Crane was born in Newark New Jersey on November 1 1871 and died twenty-nine years later on June 5 1900 at Badenweiler in the Black Forest.
4. Mary's new address is 722 East McMillan Street Rosemont Indiana 43130.
5. All inquiries should be addressed to 38 Oak Street Southwest Fargo Texas 71350.

EXERCISE 6, COMMAS AND RULES. *Copy the following sentences. Supply every missing comma and tell what rule of usage applies.*

1. If you have never heard of Phineas Barnum you have missed knowing what naïve curious gullible America will believe.
2. In 1842 Barnum opened the American Museum which housed an exhibit of wild animals freaks and curiosities.
3. Although many of his freaks were ordinary persons decked out to fool the public some we must admit to his credit were real celebrities.
4. Phineas Barnum an American showman was born in Bethel Connecticut.
5. Many of us still remember paying to gape at the tattooed lady the wild man of Borneo the sword swallower and the fire eater.
6. In 1871 having failed in a bid for Congress Barnum organized his famous circus publicized as "The Greatest Show on Earth."
7. Many years earlier he had publicized General Tom Thumb a dwarf whose real name was Charles Sherwood Stratton.
8. Stratton strange to say was a normal child of normal parents but at a very early age for reasons never known to medical science he seemed to stop growing.
9. Barnum who believed that you could fool all of the people all of the time depended on an extravagant flamboyant type of advertising new at that time but now general in the show business.
10. Barnum internationally famous as a showman was also interested in serious affairs; in 1850 for example he brought to this country Jenny Lind the famous Swedish soprano.

EXERCISE 7, ALL USES OF THE COMMA. *Punctuate the following sentences. Tell what rule or principle of usage applies to each comma that you use.*

1. At the desk sat a slender red-haired girl who gave us more cards to fill out.
2. As we watched the girl reached for the telephone dialed a number and asked for somebody named Monty.
3. Her soft pleading voice dripping with honey she spoke words that would have melted a traffic policeman's heart.
4. My companion Henry Biggs a graduate of M.I.T. knew her for they had worked at the same summer resort in Vermont.
5. Vermont with hills lakes and rolling rocky New England scenery is a famous vacation region.
6. As he confided to me in whispers they had picnicked swum hiked and ridden horseback together over the famous Long Trail but their bridle paths as he said never became a bridal path to the altar.
7. Monty an elusive sort of character if we might judge from the overheard conversation finally agreed to some tentative arrangement.
8. The crisis having been postponed for the time the girl turned her attention to us and to her work.
9. She accepted our cards and with a fluttery momentary smile tossed them into a box.
10. "If you should ask me which I hope you don't" said Biggs "I would tell you that our applications will never reach the boss."

14

§ 14. THE SEMICOLON

14a. A semicolon is used between the main clauses of a compound sentence when they are not joined by one of the coordinating conjunctions.

In weight, or length of pause, a *semicolon* is more than a comma and less than a period. The period separates sentences. The semicolon separates main clauses within a sentence. Its frequent use marks a dignified formal style, implying relatively long, balanced sentences, and for this reason an abundance of

14

semicolons in a light, informal paper should be viewed with suspicion. On the other hand the semicolon provides an excellent substitute for weak conjunctions between coordinate clauses, and it can often strengthen structures that are clearly parallel. It is in general an important device in making a firm, economical style.

Ordinarily a semicolon should not be used to cut off a phrase or a dependent clause from the main clause.

EXAMPLES OF INCORRECT USE

In these days, as writing grows increasingly brisk if not downright journalistic; one sometimes wonders what has happened to the good old semicolon.

She was habitually critical of me; because my manners, she said, were crude and my habits inconsiderate.

Notice, however, that substituting the semicolon for the subordinating conjunction, when the relationship between the clauses is implicit, can afford stylistic advantage.

EXAMPLE

She was habitually critical of me; my manners, she said, were crude and my habits inconsiderate.

OTHER EXAMPLES OF CONVENTIONAL USE

And there you have the whole secret of Beethoven. He could design patterns with the best of them; he could write music whose beauty will last you all your life; he could take the driest sticks of themes and work them up so interestingly that you find something new in them at the hundredth hearing: in short, you can say of him all that you can say of the greatest pattern composers; but his diagnostic, the thing that marks him out from all the others, is his disturbing quality, his power of unsettling us and imposing his giant moods on us.

—G. B. SHAW

The frontier has been a predominant influence on the shaping of the American character and culture, in the molding of American political life and institutions; the frontier is the principal, the recurring theme in the American symphony.

—CLYDE KLUCKHOHN

334

This does not mean, of course, that the people are happy; the society to whose traditions they are adjusted may be a miserable one, ridden with anxiety, sadism, and disease.

—DAVID RIESMAN

14

When the busman takes his proverbial holiday he takes a bus; when a sailor gets a holiday he hires a rowboat; when an anthologist has a holiday he thinks of another anthology.

—LOUIS UNTERMEYER

Often the verb in the second or third clause may be unstated, but understood to be the same as the verb in the first clause.

EXAMPLE

The humanist dismisses what he dislikes by calling it *romantic;* the liberal, by calling it *fascist;* the conservative, by calling it *communistic.*

—ROBERT GORHAM DAVIS

14b. A semicolon is used between the coordinate clauses of a compound sentence with one of the following conjunctive adverbs: *therefore, however, hence, accordingly, furthermore, nevertheless,* and *consequently.*

In modern prose, however, it is more common to find the conjunctive adverb placed within the second or third clause and enclosed in commas than to meet it as a conjunction at the beginning of its clause.

EXAMPLES

He had worked in the foreign service for two years without leave; hence he was tired almost beyond endurance.

He had worked in the foreign service for two years without leave; he was, consequently, tired almost beyond endurance.

From a running start Pedro launched his body into a vigorous racing dive; however, he was about thirty feet from the pool at the time.

14c. A semicolon is used in place of a comma when a more distinct pause than the comma would give is desirable.

335

In the following examples you will see uses of the semicolon that violate Rule 14a above. They should be studied as examples of unconventional placing, yet such uses of the semicolon are actually frequent in modern prose. Obviously such uses should be imitated with caution by the beginning writer.

EXAMPLES

No man was less of a literary aesthete than Benjamin Franklin; yet this tallow-chandler's son, who changed world history, regarded as "a principal means of my advancement" that pungent style which he acquired partly by working in youth over old *Spectators;* but mainly by being Benjamin Franklin.

—F. L. LUCAS

This, then, is what I mean by "form"; but what is meant by calling such forms "expressive of human feeling"?

—SUSANNE K. LANGER

We allow our ideas to take their own course and this course is determined by our hopes and fears, our spontaneous desires, their fulfillment or frustration; by our likes and dislikes, our loves and hates and resentments.

—JAMES HARVEY ROBINSON

EXERCISE

COMMAS VERSUS SEMICOLONS. *In the following sentences, determine appropriate punctuation to be used in the places marked by brackets. Would you use commas, semicolons, or no punctuation at all?*

1. His hair was white and stood up wildly on his head [ ] nevertheless I was struck by a singular neatness in his appearance.
2. It was due, I suppose [ ] to his lofty stature and immaculate dress [ ] no doubt he has a careful wife looking after him.
3. Like all distinguished men in political life [ ] he spoke with assurance, even with arrogance [ ] yet I could not help sensing a touch of anxiety in his behavior.

4. I walked up to him then [ ] and stretched out my hand [ ] but he evidently failed to recognize me.
5. When a man has the weight of nations on his shoulders [ ] he may be forgiven for overlooking individuals [ ] but I confess I was angry.
6. It is one thing to be dignified and detached [ ] it is quite another to be downright rude.
7. I had arrived early [ ] as was my habit [ ] I therefore felt privileged to take my leave without delay.
8. The affair was not the worst I have ever endured [ ] but it was nearly so [ ] at such times one wishes one could escape at any cost.
9. Once I had arrived at the entrance [ ] however [ ] there was no turning back.
10. When I go to a place like that [ ] I go gladly [ ] when I return [ ] I come home even more gladly.

§ 15. THE APOSTROPHE

15a. An apostrophe and -*s* are used to form the possessive of a noun, singular or plural, that does not end in -*s*.

EXAMPLES

A boy's will, women's hats, children's toys, a dog's life, the sun's rays, the earth's surface, Irene's husband, my mother-in-law's jewels.

When two or more names joined by *and* are represented as joint owners of something, in ordinary usage the last name alone takes the apostrophe.

EXAMPLES

Meier and Frank's store, Swenson and Carmody's Machine Shop, Nancy and Sally's mother, Larson, Jones, and Marshall's antique shop.

But when separate ownership is meant, the apostrophe follows each noun. Of course, when both nouns and pronouns are used, the pronouns take the possessive-case form.

15

EXAMPLES

Nancy's and Sally's clothes are strewn all over the bedroom.

Mr. Marshall's and Captain Ford's cars were badly damaged in the collision.

Mr. Danby said that his, his wife's, and his daughter's possessions were saved before the ship sank.

Usage sanctions such group possessives as *the Queen of England's hats,* but sometimes it is better to dodge an awkward construction by rewriting it. The double possessive or genitive is established usage, as in "some relatives of Mother's," "that old car of ours," "a friend of theirs," "that red coat of hers." [Note here that the *of*-phrase is used to indicate the possessive.] See §4e, "Pronouns."

15b. The apostrophe alone is used to form the possessive of a plural noun ending in -*s*.

EXAMPLES

Ladies' hats, three months' wages, girls' dresses, the Smiths' house, foxes' tails.

15c. The apostrophe with -*s* is used to form the possessive of singular nouns ending in -*s*, if the resultant form is not unpleasant or difficult to pronounce.

EXAMPLES

James's hat, Keats's poems, Jones's office; *but:* for goodness' sake, for conscience' sake, Demosthenes' orations.

15d. An apostrophe with -*s* is used to form the possessive of certain indefinite pronouns.

EXAMPLES

Anybody's game, somebody's hat, everybody's business, one's ideas, somebody's coat, another's turn.

The apostrophe should not be used with personal pronouns to form the possessive. See §4c, "Pronouns."

15. *THE APOSTROPHE*

EXAMPLES

If this coat isn't yours [not *your's*], it's probably hers [not *her's*].

The decision is ours [not *our's*].

The two dogs are theirs [not *their's*].

It's only a little dog; its [not *it's*] bark is worse than its [not *it's*] bite.

15e. An apostrophe is used to indicate the omission of letters or figures.

EXAMPLES

Hasn't, doesn't, weren't, o'clock, it's [it is], I'll, class of '75.

15f. An apostrophe and *-s* are used to form the plurals of figures, letters, and words referred to as words.

EXAMPLES

You have not dotted your *i*'s or crossed your *t*'s.

Your *m*'s, *n*'s, and *u*'s look alike.

He used too many *and*'s and *but*'s in his paper.

Be careful not to make your *3*'s look like *8*'s.

Note that only the figures, letters, and words are set in italics. The 's are set in roman type. Some publications omit the apostrophe in these situations, but there may be confusion in a sentence like this: In his handwriting the *i*s and *u*s are but a wavy line.

15g. The apostrophe is often omitted in names of organizations, associations, buildings, etc.

EXAMPLES

The Authors League, Farmers Market, Emporia Kansas State College, Home Economics Teachers Association, St. Elizabeths Hospital, Veterans Administration.

EXERCISES

EXERCISE 1, USE OF THE APOSTROPHE. *Copy the following sentences. Insert an apostrophe wherever it is correct.*

1. "Its almost ten oclock," said Toms cousin, "and hes not in sight yet."
2. "I shouldnt worry," replied Maries mother. "Theyre very busy now at Smith and Eberlys Department Store this season."
3. "Were hungry, Mom," said little Edie. "Arent you going to make us a sandwich?"
4. "Mind your *p*s and *q*s, young lady, and youll earn your *A*s and *B*s," remarked Marie apropos of nothing.
5. "If Dads not here pretty soon," said Tom, "hell be here in time for tomorrows breakfast."
6. "Its all in the days work. Once he took the Smiths pet pooch to the doctors and decided to sit up all night with it," said Marie.
7. "Youre joking, of course," replied Tom. "You know that its leg was broken."
8. "Well, for Petes sake," exclaimed Maries mother, "it was somebodys responsibility, wasnt it?"
9. "Mother, did you say 'for Keats sakes' or 'for Keatss sakes'?" asked Marie. "Theres a fine difference, you know."
10. "I think everybodys so hungry hes getting silly," said Tom. "Whos going to make some hamburgers for us?"

EXERCISE 2, POSSESSIVE FORMS. *Write the possessive singular and the possessive plural of each of the following. Example:* child, child's, children's.

1. boy
2. baby
3. Smith
4. mother-in-law
5. he
6. goose
7. it
8. woman
9. Williams
10. Allen
11. attorney
12. fox
13. wolf
14. Powers

16

§ 16. QUOTATION MARKS

16a. Double quotation marks are used to enclose a direct quotation in dialogue and in reproducing short passages from other writers.

EXAMPLES OF DIALOGUE

Jogging along in the hack along the Polifly Road they passed one of the brownstone farmhouses of the early settlers.

"Now, that's where I'd like to live," said Olga, the fat auntie.

"Is that so?"

"They're beautiful."

"You can have them," replied her sister Gurlie, Flossie's mother. "They're damp in summer and—cold in winter. And what are you going to do with the second floor? They never have room enough there to stand up in."

"They had to have it that way to keep warm."

"And they were always cold or too hot."

—W. C. WILLIAMS, *The Build-Up*

Note that in dialogue a new paragraph is used with every change in speaker.

The writer must be careful not to leave out one set of quotation marks. Quotation marks come in pairs, one set at the beginning and one set at the end of every quoted part.

WRONG

"I have no relish for the country, said Sydney Smith. It is a kind of healthy grave."

RIGHT

"I have no relish for the country," said Sydney Smith. "It is a kind of healthy grave."

341

A familiar error in citing passages from others is to begin a quotation that never ends. By failing to close the quotation with the appropriate second set of marks, the passage from the quoted author and the comment by the quoting writer can become thoroughly confused.

16

W R O N G
Sydney Smith once remarked, "I have no relish for the country. It is a kind of healthy grave. This remark has often fascinated his admirers.

If a quotation consists of several sentences, the quotation marks are placed at the beginning and at the end of the entire quotation, not at the beginning and end of each separate sentence in that section.

"You'd have had your stomach full of fighting, young man," added Colonel Williams, "if Squire Sedgwick had not taken them just as he did. Squire," he added, "my wife shall thank you that she's not a widow when we get back to Stockbridge. I honor your courage, sir. The credit of this day is yours."

—EDWARD BELLAMY, *The Duke of Stockbridge*

If a quotation consists of several paragraphs, quotation marks are placed before each paragraph but at the end of the last paragraph only. This convention applies to a continued speech by one speaker. If the speaker changes, his words are placed in a new paragraph or paragraphs. Short descriptive, narrative, or explanatory passages may be paragraphed with dialogue, especially if they are placed between sentences of dialogue spoken by the same person.

A quoted passage of several lines of prose or poetry—not a part of dialogue—may be indicated by indention. In typing it is often typed single-spaced; in print it may be set in smaller type than the rest of the text. No quotation marks are needed when indention is used.

No quotation marks are used with an indirect quotation.

D I R E C T
"Yes," I said to him, "it's all right."
"I am relieved to hear it," he replied.

342

INDIRECT

I told him it was all right.

He said he was relieved to hear it.

16b. Single quotation marks are used to enclose a quotation within a quotation.

EXAMPLES

"Finally," she said, "I just turned to him and shouted, 'Leave me alone, won't you?'" [Note the position of the quotation marks in relation to other marks.]

"If the good Lord should tell me that I had only five minutes to live," said Justice Oliver Wendell Holmes, "I would say to him, 'All right, Lord, but I'm sorry you can't make it ten.'"

—CATHERINE DRINKER BOWEN, *Yankee from Olympus*

16c. Quotation marks are used to enclose quoted titles of stories, poems, chapters, and other subdivisions of books, and, in newspaper style, the titles of books. (See §10.)

16d. Quotation marks are used to enclose words spoken of as words.

Italics are used for this purpose, however, when the style is formal, although writers are not consistent in this practice. In informal writing, quotation marks are usually more common. See §10c.

EXAMPLE

What I had to overcome was the traditional attitude toward such scare words as "socialization," "socialism," and "subsidization."

—HARRY S. TRUMAN, *Memoirs*

16e. Quotation marks are used to enclose words used in a special sense.

Often quotation marks are used to indicate to the reader that the writer, in repeating someone else's words, is opposed to their use, takes no stock in the manner in which they have been used, and is about to offer his own opposing views.

EXAMPLES

National greed has disguised itself in mandates to govern "inferior" races. [The writer does not think these races are inferior.]

How wrong-headed and time-wasting are the "refutations" of hedonism that spot and blot the pages of the history of ethics! [They are not refutations at all, according to the writer.]

—Wilmon S. Sheldon

The student is cautioned against the overuse of quotation marks in an apologetic or self-conscious way, enclosing slang or other expressions that he uneasily feels may be inappropriate. If they are inappropriate, he should find better ones. If they are appropriate, they need no apology.

16f. Quotation marks are often used to enclose the definitions or meanings of words spoken of as words.

EXAMPLE

Miscellaneous further illustrations of elevation are *pretty* from an early meaning "sly," through "clever," to something approaching "beautiful"; *nice* from an etymological meaning "ignorant," through its earliest English sense "foolish," and later ones like "particular," to its present broad and vague colloquial meaning of "pleasant" or "acceptable"; and *fond* from "foolish" to "affectionate."

—Stuart Robertson, *The Development of Modern English*

See also §10c.

16g. Commas and periods are always placed inside quotation marks.

This rule is a printers' convention. The period and the comma are the two marks that occupy the lower half of a line of print; all other marks—the colon, the semicolon, the question mark, and the exclamation point—stand the full height of the line. To have a comma or a period trail out beyond quotation marks looks bad. Remember the convention: periods and commas are *always* placed inside quotation marks. See §16b for examples.

16h. The question mark, the semicolon, and the exclamation point go inside quotation marks if they belong to the quoted part. They go outside if they do not belong to the quoted part.

16

EXAMPLES

Did you hear him say, "I won't go"? [The question mark belongs to the main clause, or the entire sentence. Hence it stands at the end. But notice that no period is used in addition to the end punctuation.]

"Well, I like that!" she exclaimed in anger.

"It is as much of a trade," says La Bruyère, "to make a book as it is to make a clock"; in short, literature is largely a matter of technique. [Note that the semicolon is not a part of the quotation. It belongs to the whole sentence.]

—IRVING BABBITT

16i. For dialogue guides (such as *he said*) with quoted dialogue, use the punctuation that the structure of the sentence calls for.

EXAMPLE

"The price is not a matter of profit," he said, stiffly; "it is a matter of principle." [Notice the semicolon to separate coordinate clauses in a compound sentence of dialogue. Most writers use a period and a following capital letter instead of a semicolon in this sort of construction. See § 16a for other examples of punctuating dialogue.]

The general practice is not to use a comma before a quoted part that is woven into the sentence or before a title. This is logical enough: note that the voice makes little or no pause before reading such quotations.

EXAMPLE

It was tariff policy which seemed to him [Cordell Hull] "at the very heart of this country's economic dilemma." He saw in the expansion of foreign trade not only the "path to recovery" but the means of escape from regimentation and the road to world peace.

—ARTHUR M. SCHLESINGER, JR., *Triumph of the New Deal*

17

It is doubtful if adolescents since the time of Byron have repeated any poems (without compulsion) as frequently or as enthusiastically as the youth of the 'twenties recited "My candle burns at both ends" and "Safe upon the solid rock . . ."

—OSCAR CARGILL, *Intellectual America*

EXERCISES

EXERCISE 1, COMPOSING A PARAGRAPH WITH QUOTATIONS. *Copy out a paragraph of formal prose that seems to you interesting, for any reason. Then write your own paragraph of comment, in which you quote three or four short phrases from the original, punctuating properly as you do so.*

EXERCISE 2, QUOTATION MARKS AND PARAGRAPHING. *Copy the following, punctuating and paragraphing correctly.*

The father caught his son's eye at last, and gave him a mild, responsive smile. I am getting on very well, he said. Have you drunk your tea? asked the son. Yes, and enjoyed it. Shall I give you some more? The old man considered, placidly. Well, I guess I will wait and see. He had, in speaking, the American tone. Are you cold? his son inquired. The father slowly rubbed his legs. Well, I don't know. I can't tell till I feel. Perhaps some one might feel for you, said the younger man, laughing. Oh, I hope some one will always feel for me! Don't you feel for me, Lord Warburton? Oh yes, immensely, said the gentleman addressed as Lord Warburton, promptly. I am bound to say you look wonderfully comfortable. Well, I suppose I am, in most respects. And the old man looked down at his green shawl, and smoothed it over his knees. The fact is, I have been comfortable so many years that I suppose I have got so used to it I don't know it. Yes, that's the bore of comfort, said Lord Warburton. We only know when we are uncomfortable.

§ 17. COLON AND DASH

The Colon

17a. The colon is used to separate an introductory statement from a list of particulars.

346

17. *COLON AND DASH*

The *colon* is a mark of emphatic separation and should not break grammatically related elements apart: should not divide a verb from its object, an object or subject from its appositives. Whatever precedes the colon, then, must constitute a grammatically complete clause or statement.

RUPTURED SENTENCE

In the kitchen drawer she kept: a hammer, a screwdriver, a pair of pliers, some assorted nails, and a pneumatic drill. [A hammer . . . drill are all objects of *kept*. No punctuation is necessary to announce them.]

COMPLETE CLAUSE INTRODUCING A LIST

In the kitchen drawer she kept a few household tools: a hammer, a screwdriver, a pair of pliers, some assorted nails, and a pneumatic drill.

Exception: a list set out in tabular form introduced by an incomplete clause.

If you can answer my questions, I should very much like to know:
1. how often you teach the course,
2. what textbook you usually use,
3. how many students normally enroll in the course,
4. what price of textbook you consider acceptable,
5. whether you feel the enclosed book might prove a useful substitute for the text you now use.

These clauses begin with a lower case letter and are closed with commas. If even one of the clauses contained internal commas, it would be necessary to close each with a semicolon to avoid confusion. As the clauses in this case are considered part of the sentence beginning with "If you can answer," the last one terminates with a period. When every clause in a list is a complete one, as those in the example are not, the usual practice is to treat each as an individual sentence beginning with a capital and ending with a period. *The art is to compose the list so that its punctuation may be consistent.*

17b. A colon introduces a long quotation.

EXAMPLE

Steinbeck gives a subtle suggestion of Spanish by using archaic constructions in English:

347

17

"Remember to be careful with the bullets—there are only ten. Do not fill thy stomach with jerky or it will make thee sick. Eat a little jerky and fill thy stomach with grass. When thou comest to the high mountains, if thou seest any of the dark watching men, go not near them nor try to speak to them. And forget not thy prayers."

—JOHN STEINBECK, *Flight*

(For purposes of illustration, the sample above is a somewhat shorter quotation than would ordinarily justify use of the colon.)

17c. The colon may be used to separate main clauses when the second amplifies, restates, or interprets the first.

EXAMPLES

Moreover, this author was somehow reassuring; he told the Province what it longed to hear: that its most fervent protests against Parliament were no new thing, no shocking innovation.

—CATHERINE DRINKER BOWEN, *John Adams and the American Revolution*

Modern science has not only purified this notion; it has also transformed it: a transformation that can be described by saying that modern science is *indifferent to nothing*.

—KARL JASPERS, *Is Science Evil?*

17d. In a formal business letter the colon rather than a comma is used after the salutation.

```
Dear Mr. Crushbum:

     The longline panty-girdle manufactured by your company,
Binding Foundations, Incorporated, contains several serious
defects. . . .
```

The Dash

17e. The dash is used to indicate a sudden, abrupt break in thought or structure.

EXAMPLES

My first sight of him—if a new boy may look at a monitor—was on my rather wretched second day at a Public School. . . . He seemed to me of a fabulous height—about five feet ten, I suppose; thin and bolt upright. He had a stick-up collar—"barmaids" had not yet come in—but not a very high one, and his neck was rather long.

—JOHN GALSWORTHY, "The Man Who Kept His Form"

17

"I wish—I wish you'd let him know—please do—it was an accident." [In dialogue to give the effect of hesitation]

"I don't know whether she would like—" [Speech abruptly broken off]

17f. The dash is used for an explanatory or parenthetical phrase or clause that breaks into the normal flow of the sentence.

Three kinds of marks may indicate parenthesis—*the comma, the dash,* and *marks of parenthesis.* The degree of separation indicated by these marks varies from the lightest, for which commas are used, to the most definite and the most formal, for which parentheses are used.

EXAMPLES

There may be lovelier country somewhere—in the Island Vale of Avalon, at a gamble—but when the sunlight lies upon it and the wind puts white clouds racing their shadows the Shenandoah Valley is as good as anything America can show.

—BRUCE CATTON, *A Stillness at Appomattox*

Like the British paratroopers to the east, the Americans—in humor, in sorrow, in terror and in pain—began the work they had come to Normandy to do.

—CORNELIUS RYAN, *The Longest Day*

17g. The dash is used to introduce or to set off a long, formal appositive or summary.

EXAMPLES

There is no other dog in the world to match the Afghan hound—for elegant beauty, for friendliness, and for blinding speed. [Introducing an appositive]

These obstacles—jagged triangles of steel, saw-toothed gatelike structures of iron, metal-tipped wooden stakes and concrete cones—were planted just below high- and low-tide water marks. [To set off long appositive]

—Cornelius Ryan, *The Longest Day*

The dash may occasionally be found before such words as *namely* and *that is* introducing an appositive. See also §13k.

EXAMPLE

Also you will find out about the queer fade-away, the slow curve, the fast in- and out-shoots that seemed to be timed almost as delicately as shrapnel, to burst, or rather break, just when they will do the most harm—namely, at the moment when the batter is swinging.

—Paul Gallico

A dash may be used before such words as *all* and *these* introducing a summary, or summarizing appositive, after a series. The occasions for this use of the dash are infrequent.

EXAMPLES

Cramming, dances, new clothes, blind dates—all these should be a part of your freshman year.

Regional survey and regional service—these are the chief ingredients for a reasonable citizenship. . . .

—Lewis Mumford

Caution: The dash must not be used indiscriminately for all other marks of punctuation. It should be saved for its special function, so that it will be intelligible when it is used.

§ 18. PARENTHESES AND BRACKETS

Parentheses

18a. **Parentheses are used to enclose material that is supplementary, explanatory, or interpretive.**

In theory, the general principle is that commas set off material that is fairly close to the main meaning of the sentence (see

§13i); dashes set off material more distant in meaning (§17g); and marks of parenthesis are used to indicate the most distant parenthetical relation. In practice, however, there is considerable variety among modern writers in the way parentheses are used. One traditional function is to enclose an explanation, a definition, or a set of examples to clarify a particular reference.

EXAMPLES

The book, *V-2*, by Von Braun's superior at Peenemunde (the German rocket-testing station), General Walter Dornberger, sustains this particular and astonishing complaint throughout its length. . . .

—MORRIS FREEDMAN

Many things may be legitimately inferred to exist (electrons, the expanding universe, the past, the other side of the moon) from what is observed.

—SIDNEY HOOK

A less conventional function of parentheses favored by contemporary novelists is to enclose remarks that come as from another voice than the speaker's—remarks that may inject a critical note as if one were whispering something facetious behind someone's back.

EXAMPLE

Ideally bald, sun-tanned, and clean shaven, he began rather impressively with that great brown dome of his, tortoise-shell glasses (masking an infantile absence of eyebrows), apish upper lip, thick neck, and strong-man torso in a tightish tweed coat, but ended, somewhat disappointingly, in a pair of spindly legs (now flanneled and crossed) and frail-looking, almost feminine feet. His sloppy socks were of scarlet wool with lilac lozenges; his conservative black oxfords had cost him about as much as all the rest of his clothing (flamboyant goon tie included).

—VLADIMIR NABOKOV

Sometimes parentheses may be used to introduce a comment by the author about what he is doing, drawing the reader's attention to some particular device of style.

351

EXAMPLE

Almost every high-school graduate "knows" (I put quotation marks around the word) that air is primarily a mixture of oxygen gas and nitrogen gas. . . .

—James B. Conant

Finally, journalists are prone to enclose whole parenthetical sentences inside other sentences, sometimes at awkward points in the structure.

EXAMPLE

The major surprise in the hop-skip-and-jump came when Vilhjalmur Eirnarsson of Iceland (his fellow undergraduates at Dartmouth called him Willie) sailed out 53 feet 4 inches for second place.

—John Kieran

18b. Parentheses do not obviate the need for other punctuation in the sentence.

An expression enclosed in parentheses may be part of a clause, and the clause, including the parenthetical remark, must close with the appropriate punctuation, which is set *outside* and *after* the parentheses.

EXAMPLES

Routine maintenance of an automobile can be carried out by numerous agencies (a dealership, a service station, or the owner), but when the car's guarantee is at stake only work done by the dealer will prove above question. [The comma necessary between independent clauses joined by a conjunction must follow . . . *owner*).]

What she referred to as "the statue's boots" were, in fact, greaves (armor for the shins). [The period follows . . . *shins*).]

Occasionally a parenthetical expression is a separate sentence adding information to the sentences preceding and following it. In such cases the parentheses *enclose* all punctuation, and the expression begins with a capital.

EXAMPLE

The British shows broadcast on American television are not representative of the British public's lust for highbrow social drama. (One of the most popular programs in England is *Kojak.*) They do demonstrate a typically British knack for adding a successful veneer of professional and technical refinement to a crude and ready-made commonplace, in this case the genre of soap opera.

Brackets

18c. **Brackets are used to enclose corrections, interpolations, and supplied omissions added to a quotation by the person quoting.**

Here is an example from a passage that has already been used (in §16i) for another purpose.

It was tariff policy which seemed to him [Cordell Hull] "at the very heart of this country's economic dilemma." [The reader would have no idea what person the author was talking about if we had not added the bracketed explanation.]

—ARTHUR M. SCHLESINGER, JR.

In this book you will find many examples of conventional use of brackets, like the one just above, where they set off comment about a quoted passage in such a way that the reader may not confuse the comment with the passage itself.

EXERCISES

EXERCISE 1, THE COLON AND THE SEMICOLON. *Copy out from any sample of formal modern prose five sentences in which colons are used. In which of these sentences could semicolons be used instead? What effect would such a substitution have on the meaning or the tone of each sentence?*

EXERCISE 2, THE COLON. *Write out three sentences of your own illustrating the use of the colon as a formal introduction, in the manner*

18

described in § *17a*. Then write out three others in which the colon is used to separate independent clauses (§ *17c*).

EXERCISE 3, PARENTHESES, BRACKETS, DASHES. *From one of your textbooks copy five sentences in which parentheses or brackets are used. Try substituting dashes for the parentheses and brackets. What is the effect on meaning and tone?*

EXERCISE 4, THE DASH. *Try writing a letter in which you use no punctuation at all except dashes and periods. What is the effect on tone: that is, what kind of voice do you hear uttering these words? What kind of person speaks in this way?*

4 *Spelling*

§ 19. THE SPELLING PROBLEM

As everyone knows, many words in English are not spelled the way they are pronounced. That is why spelling our language is so difficult.

Consider the problem of the foreign speaker who runs up against the various pronunciations of just one small group of letters: *-ough* in *cough, dough, rough, bough, through.* The exchange student from France, coming to America to improve his English accent, sees a headline on the front page of a newspaper: EXHIBITION PRONOUNCED SUCCESS. "Ah, this fantastic language!" he cries in utter discouragement, but without surprise.

There was a time, several centuries ago, when a writer gave little thought to using the right letters in his words. Some writers, Shakespeare for instance, appear to have spelled their own names in several different ways without a second thought. Our modern attitude toward standardized spelling, however, is very different. Almost everyone—not just your English instructor—takes spelling seriously, perhaps too seriously. One reason is that, unlike most matters of language, spelling is an area where there is usually a Right or Wrong, and it is tempting to make much of someone else's errors when you know they are really errors. There is even an economic importance in trying to learn to spell; employers everywhere assume that poor spelling is a sign of stupidity or illiteracy. They probably reason, rightly or not, that carelessness in spelling is a visible, measurable sign of carelessness in other, more important things. Spelling is something that shows. And because it does show, because it can be easily seen and easily judged, it has become one of the first tests of a person's education and fitness for a job.

What to Do About the Problem. Learning to spell requires memorizing the letters of virtually every word encountered in read-

9

ing so that it may be reproduced correctly in writing. Most of us, however, have something better to do with our lives, so it is fortunate that there are a few systematic approaches to the process and one invaluable resource. The aids do not let us out of the duty to practice words, to memorize a substantial list of essential ones, and to recognize when we need to investigate the spelling of an unfamiliar word rather than just have a shot at it, but they do give us a method to pursue.

A good beginning is *to learn a basic list of words* that may involve spelling problems. Such a list appears in the next few pages. As memories are fallible, misspellings of even familiar words occur in many writers' first drafts, but if work with the list does not engrave the word on the mind well enough for automatic use, it may yet fix the form in the subconscious so that a misspelling can be recognized after the act of composition. All written work should be proofread, and it is in this process that vague uneasiness at the shape of a word often signals the need for a recheck and correction.

Learn words, then, for two purposes: to spell them correctly and to recognize when they are spelled incorrectly. As for proofreading (best accomplished by having someone read aloud a carbon copy while you check the original), remember that there is no easier way to cite a writer for error than to pick out his or her bad spelling. The instructor who discovers numerous spelling errors in a paper would not be human if the frustration at correcting them did not adversely affect his or her appreciation of the entire work.

Knowing something of the analysis of words helps. To understand prefixes and suffixes and roots and stems increases vocabulary and contributes to the small set of rules applicable to spelling. Realize that *ante-* means "before" and *anti-* "against" and there is less probability that *antecedent* will be spelled as though it meant "something against going" rather than what it does mean, "something that goes before." Many English words are descendants of classical Greek and Latin words, to which they bear a more or less recognizable kinship. Other words have drifted into our usage from French, Italian, German (old and new), Spanish, American Indian, Sanskrit, Hebrew—from, in effect, practically the whole Atlas of languages alive and dead.

19

As the origin language of an English word is likely to follow a reasonably phonetic spelling, a spelling in which letters have consistent sound values, knowing what the original or root word is will suggest the spelling of most of its derivatives. Learning the meaning of a word as well as its derivation can aid the student in making that word part of his or her list of frequently used words.

Learning words in terms of their syllable divisions is another practical tool for mastering spelling. It forces concentration on the letters in the word and breaks down the number of letters to be learned at one time.

There are, too, some mechanical steps toward better spelling. The most effective one is the personal list of the writer. When a spelling error is pointed out, *write down the correction* (there is nothing like coordinating hand, eye, and brain to impress the memory) and compile a list of such corrected errors. Keep the list in rigid alphabetical order, make it out on 3 × 5 cards, or simply jot down additions as they arise, but keep the list active and file it where you can refer to it now and again. Some people treat the list like a parole sheet and note the number of offenses connected with it. The best system is the one *you* find easiest to follow consistently.

We mentioned an invaluable tool. Find a respectable dictionary and use it. Most dictionaries are well made, so don't be afraid of wearing yours out. Look words up in it whenever you are uncertain of their spellings or meanings, and when looking up a word take note of some of the incidental information given. A good desk dictionary gives not only the spelling of a word, its pronunciation, and all its standard modern meanings and uses, but its syllabification, its derivation, and its archaic and colloquial (informal) meanings. For some words the dictionary lists synonyms (words that mean almost the same thing) and antonyms (words with an opposite meaning) as well as giving alternative spellings when they are common enough to present a chance of confusion. The greater the detail with which a word is first investigated, the more likely the word and its spelling are to be remembered. Whatever you do, avoid the easy rationalization: "But how can I find the word in my dictionary if I don't know how to spell it?" You can come close enough.

357

19

For more on the use of the dictionary, see §21.

Finally, there are those spelling rules that seem general to apply. They are introduced after the list of commonly misspelled words.

19a. The following list of words often misspelled by college students is to be used as the instructor thinks necessary.[1]

1. abbreviate	30. answer	59. business*
2. absence	31. apartment	60. cafeteria
3. absorption	32. apology	61. calendar
4. absurd	33. apparatus	62. candidate
5. accidentally	34. apparently*	63. carburetor
6. accommodate*	35. appearance	64. career
7. accompanying	36. appropriate	65. category*
8. accomplish	37. arctic	66. certain
9. accumulate	38. argument*	67. changeable
10. accustom	39. arising	68. changing
11. achievement*	40. arrangement	69. characteristic
12. acknowledge	41. ascend	70. chosen*
13. acquaintance	42. association	71. commission
14. acquire*	43. athlete	72. committed
15. acquitted	44. athletics	73. committee
16. across	45. attendance	74. comparative*
17. additionally	46. audience	75. competitive
18. address	47. auxiliary	
19. aggravate	48. awkward	76. compulsory
20. all right	49. bachelor	77. conceivable
21. almost	50. balance	78. conference
22. although		79. conferred
23. altogether	51. barbarous	80. conqueror
24. always	52. becoming	81. conscience*
25. amateur	53. beginning*	82. conscientious*
	54. benefited*	83. conscious*
26. among*	55. biscuit	84. continuous
27. analysis	56. boundaries	85. convenient
28. analyze	57. brilliant	86. courteous
29. annual	58. bureau	87. criticism*

[1] Please pay particular attention to the words marked *. Vice President Thomas Clark Pollock of New York University has made a study of over 30,000 misspellings in the writing of college students. The words starred here are the words, or belong to the word-groups, that he found misspelled most often. The authors are grateful to Dr. Pollock for permission to use his findings.

88. criticize*
89. curiosity
90. cylinder
91. dealt
92. decision
93. definitely*
94. describe*
95. description*
96. despair
97. desperate
98. dictionary
99. dilapidated

100. disagree
101. disappear
102. disappoint
103. disastrous*
104. discipline
105. dissatisfied
106. dissipate
107. doctor
108. dormitory
109. eighth
110. eligible
111. eliminate
112. embarrass
113. eminent
114. enthusiastic
115. environment*
116. equipment
117. equivalent
118. erroneous
119. especially
120. exaggerated
121. exceptionally
122. exhaust
123. exhilarate
124. existence*
125. experience*

126. explanation*
127. extraordinary

128. extremely
129. familiar
130. fascinate*
131. February
132. foreign
133. frantically
134. fraternities
135. generally
136. government
137. grammar*
138. guard
139. guidance
140. height*
141. hindrance
142. humorous
143. illiterate
144. imaginary*
145. imagination*
146. immediately*
147. impromptu
148. incidentally
149. incredible
150. indefinitely

151. indispensable
152. inevitable
153. infinite
154. intellectual
155. intelligence*
156. intentionally
157. interesting*
158. irrelevant
159. irresistible
160. knowledge
161. laboratory
162. legitimate
163. lightning
164. literature
165. loneliness*
166. maintenance
167. maneuver
168. marriage

169. mathematics
170. miniature
171. mischievous
172. necessary*
173. nevertheless
174. noticeable*
175. nowadays

176. oblige
177. obstacle
178. occasion
179. occasionally*
180. occurred*
181. occurrence*
182. opportunity
183. optimistic
184. original*
185. outrageous
186. pamphlet
187. parallel
188. particularly
189. pastime
190. permissible
191. perseverance
192. perspiration
193. physically
194. picnicking
195. politics
196. practically
197. precedence
198. preference
199. preferred
200. prejudice*

201. preparation
202. prevalent*
203. privilege*
204. probably*
205. professor*
206. prominent*
207. pronunciation
208. prove

19

19

209. quantity
210. recognize
211. recommend
212. reference
213. referred *
214. regard
215. repetition*
216. representative
217. restaurant
218. rhythm*
219. rhythmical
220. ridiculous
221. sandwich
222. schedule
223. secretary

224. separate*
225. siege
226. similar*
227. simultaneous
228. soliloquy
229. sophomore
230. specifically
231. specimen
232. speech
233. strictly
234. surprise*
235. temperament
236. temperature

237. thorough*
238. throughout
239. tragedy
240. tries*
241. truly
242. Tuesday
243. unanimous
244. undoubtedly
245. unnecessarily
246. village
247. villain
248. weird
249. whether*
250. writing*

19b. The following spelling rules will help you to remember how certain words are spelled.

1. A word ending in silent -e generally drops the -e *before a suffix beginning with a vowel letter . . .*

DROP -*e*

admire	+ able	= admirable	desire	+ ous	= desirous
admire	+ ation	= admiration	dine	+ ing	= dining
allure	+ ing	= alluring	explore	+ ation	= exploration
arrange	+ ing	= arranging	fame	+ ous	= famous
arrive	+ ing	= arriving	imagine	+ able	= imaginable
believe	+ ing	= believing	imagine	+ ary	= imaginary
care	+ ing	= caring	love	+ able	= lovable
come	+ ing	= coming	lose	+ ing	= losing
deplore	+ able	= deplorable	move	+ able	= movable

but it retains the -e *before a suffix beginning with a consonant letter.* [There are some notable exceptions: judgment, abridgment, acknowledgment.]

RETAIN -*e*

arrange	+ ment	= arrangement
care	+ ful	= careful
force	+ ful	= forceful

360

hate	+ ful	= hateful
like	+ ness	= likeness
move	+ ment	= movement

But after c *or* g, *if the suffix begins with* a *or* o, *the* -e *is retained to indicate the soft sound of* c *or* g.

RETAIN -*e*

advantage	+ ous	= advantageous
change	+ able	= changeable
courage	+ ous	= courageous
notice	+ able	= noticeable
outrage	+ ous	= outrageous
peace	+ able	= peaceable
service	+ able	= serviceable

2. *In words with* ie *or* ei *when the sound is long* ee, *use* i *before* e *except after* c.

i BEFORE *e*

achieve	chief	pier	shriek
apiece	field	pierce	siege
belief	fierce	priest	thief
believe	frieze	relieve	wield
besiege	grief	reprieve	yield
brief	niece	retrieve	
cashier	piece	shield	

EXCEPT AFTER *C*

ceiling	conceive	deceive	receipt
conceit	deceit	perceive	receive

Exceptions: either, neither, financier, weird, species, seize, leisure.

These may be remembered by arranging the words in a sentence: "Neither financier seized either species of weird leisure."

The so-called seed words can be easily remembered. For those who cannot memorize, a careful reading of the list will suffice:

1. Only one word ends in -*sede:*   supersede
2. Three words end in -*ceed:*   exceed
   proceed
   succeed

361

3. The rest end in *-cede:*

accede
cede
concede
intercede
precede
recede
secede

3. Words consisting of one syllable or several syllables accented on the last and which end in a single consonant letter preceded by a single vowel double the final consonant before a suffix beginning with a vowel.

Now this looks like a formidable rule to unravel. Let us see what it involves. In the first place, it applies to short words such as *get, swim, drop, drip.* In the second place, it applies to longer words in which the accent is on the final syllable, such as *refer, begin, equip.* Examine the illustrations below to see what happens:

drop [word of one syllable] + ed [suffix beginning with a vowel] = dropped.
control [accented on the last syllable] + ed [suffix] = controlled.
benefit [not accented on last syllable] + ed [suffix] = benefited.
confer [accented on last syllable] + ed [suffix] = conferred.
confer [notice the shift in accent] + ence [suffix] = conference.
defer [accented on last syllable] + ed [suffix] = deferred.
defer [notice the shift in accent] + ence [suffix] = deference.

SUFFIX BEGINS WITH A VOWEL
One Syllable

brag	—bragging	man	—mannish
cram	—cramming	plan	—planning
drag	—dragging	snap	—snapped
din	—dinning	sin	—sinning
drop	—dropped	stop	—stopped
cut	—cutting	quit	—quitting
bid	—bidding	rob	—robbed
flag	—flagged	stab	—stabbed
get	—getting	whip	—whipped
clan	—clannish	glad	—gladdest

Accented on Last Syllable

admit′	—admitted	equip′	—equipped
begin′	—beginning	commit′	—committee
commit′	—committed	occur′	—occurrence
concur′	—concurring	submit′	—submitted
confer′	—conferring	compel′	—compelled

Not Accented on Last Syllable

prefer	—preference	benefit	—benefited
refer	—reference	profit	—profitable
happen	—happened	marvel	—marvelous

SUFFIX BEGINS WITH A CONSONANT

glad	—gladness	sin	—sinful
fat	—fatness	equip	—equipment
man	—manhood	profit	—profitless

4. *A noun ending in -y preceded by a consonant forms the plural in -ies; a verb ending in -y preceded by a consonant forms its present tense, third person singular, in -ies.*

ENDING IN *-y* PRECEDED BY A CONSONANT

baby, babies	sky, skies	fairy, fairies
marry, marries	copy, copies	fly, flies

ENDING IN *-y* PRECEDED BY A VOWEL

attorney, attorneys	valley, valleys	delay, delays
destroy, destroys	enjoy, enjoys	chimney, chimneys

Note: Some other rules for forming plurals are as follows:

5. *For most nouns, add* -s: boys, girls, houses, ideas, aches, pains.

6. *For nouns ending with a sound similar to* s, *add* -es: birches, foxes, boxes, classes.

7. *For nouns ending in* -f, -fe, -ff, *use* -s *or* -ves: chief, chiefs; staff, staffs, staves; wife, wives; sheriff, sheriffs; elf, elves.

8. *For nouns ending in* -o, *add* -s *or* -es: solo, solos; echo, echoes; potato, potatoes; motto, mottos, mottoes; tomato, tomatoes; alto, altos.

9. *Some nouns have irregular plurals:* foot, feet; mouse, mice; goose, geese; ox, oxen; woman, women; axis, axes; basis, bases; datum, data; locus, loci; formula, formulas, formulae.

But Mr. and Mrs. Berry are *not* "the Berries," but "the Berrys"; and Mr. and Mrs. Wolf are *not* "the Wolves," but "the Wolfs."

19

EXERCISES

Rewrite the following paragraphs, correcting the misspelled words.

EXERCISE 1.

It has often occured to me that any foreign environement begins to look familiar after sufficient experiance. In the beginning one may believe that a foriegn land is wierd or even barberous. But it is noticable that in the end one usally consedes the virtues of strangeness. What is outragous is to persist in repititions of embarassing criticisms that are definitly eroneous.

EXERCISE 2.

One chilly Febuary day, three sophmores were sitting in their dormitery discussing one of their most prominant proffessors. They sprawled on separate bunks in their room, occassionally engaging in arguement about the professor's appearance and achievments.

"I went to see his secretery last Tuesday," one boy remarked. "I think she's more intelactual than he is."

"I disagree," said another. "But why is he so predjudiced against fraternities?"

"Anyway," said the third, "I've always prefered a conference with the secretary. It's a priviledge to talk to her."

EXERCISE 3.

The most interesting knowlege is likely to seem irrevalent on its first occurence. Many have benefitted from explanations that at first seemed throughly and unnecessarily ridiculous. I recomend that you sieze consiously every ocasion for learning, even if your committment to grammer may be comparitively unenthusiastic.

§ 20. SIMILAR FORMS

Distinguish between words similar or identical in sound but different in meaning.

The list below is merely a check list for quick reference. If you need more than this list can give you, refer to your dictionary. You should also look at examples of similar forms in the "Guide to Usage."

20

accent. Emphasis or stress; to stress. [You accent the wrong syllable.]
ascent. Climbing; a way up. [The ascent of the cliff was difficult.]
assent. To agree; agreement. [He finally gave his assent to the plan.]

accept. To take something offered; to agree to; to approve; to believe. [He accepted the gift. I accept your interpretation.]
except. To leave out; to exclude. [All except the cook were rescued.]

admittance. Permission to enter a place. [The sign read, "No admittance."]
admission. Admitting to rights and privileges; the price of being allowed to enter. [No admission was charged.]

affect. To influence; to pretend; to assume. [His threats do not affect me.]
effect. To perform; make happen. [The attorney effected a reconciliation.]

all ready. Everyone is ready. [They were all ready.]
already. By this time. [They had already eaten breakfast.]

altar. Place of worship. [They knelt before the altar.]
alter. To change. [Do not alter any part of my criticism.]

ante. Before. [This piece is of ante-Victorian design.]
anti. Against; opposed to. [I poured some antifreeze into the radiator.]

breath. Air drawn into lungs. [We need a breath of fresh air.]
breathe. To take a breath. [We cannot breathe in this room.]

capital. Chief; important; leading city; resources. [London is the capital city of England. That's a capital story. Invest your capital.]
capitol. The state building. [We shall meet on the capitol grounds in Albany.]

censure. Blame; condemn; criticize severely. [They voted to censure the general.]

365

20

censor. To oversee morals and conduct; to examine and make changes. [Three women will censor all motion pictures.]

charted. Mapped or diagramed. [The Arctic is still not fully charted.]
chartered. Hired; granted certain rights. [We chartered a boat.]

choose. To pick out, select. [Will she choose me again?]
chose. Past tense of *choose*. [They chose a new secretary.]

cite. To quote or use as example. [Did he cite any authorities?]
site. Location. [This is a good site for our church.]
sight. Vision; to see. [His sight was keen. At last we sighted land.]

coarse. Rough; crude. [coarse food; coarse manners; coarse sand]
course. Direction; path; series; order. [a course of study; of course]

complement. That which completes. [a subjective complement]
compliment. Praise; a polite and flattering lie. [He paid her a compliment.]

consul. Government official appointed to look after foreign business interests.
council. A group; an assembly. [We shall call a council of the elders.]
counsel. Advice; one who advises; a lawyer. [Give her good counsel. The accused has a right to counsel.]

detract. Take away. [Her hair detracts from her beauty.]
distract. Draw away; disturb. [The noise distracts me. Do not distract my attention.]

eminent. Distinguished. [The eminent statesman spoke briefly.]
imminent. About to happen. [War seems imminent.]
immanent. Existing within. [God's will is immanent.]

fain. Eager; willingly; pleased. [I would fain stay with you.]
feign. Pretend. [She feigned complete surprise.]

formally. In a formal manner. [He was formally welcomed by the mayor.]
formerly. In the past. [Formerly, no one had greeted him.]

hoards. Stores; collections. [The police found hoards of stolen jewels.]
hordes. Crowds; groups of nomads. [the barbarian hordes; hordes of tourists]

imaginary. Existing in the imagination. [Her life is full of imaginary troubles.]
imaginative. Having imagination; able to imagine. [She is a very imaginative girl.]

implicit. Absolute, implied, [implicit obedience to orders; an implicit displeasure]

explicit. Distinctly stated; definite. [He gave us explicit directions.]

incredible. Unbelievable. [Your story is incredible.]

incredulous. Unwilling to believe. [He was incredulous when I told my story.]

irrelevant. Not to the point. [His question is irrelevant.]

irreverent. Lacking reverence or respect. [His action was irreverent.]

loose. Not fastened; careless; not confined. [Tie up your loose apron strings. There is too much loose talk here. Your dog is loose again.]

lose. To mislay; to fail to win; to waste. [She lost her keys again. We may lose this game yet. Put your loose cash away or you will lose it.]

principal. Chief; most important; chief person; chief teacher. [the principal of a school; the principal actor; the principal occupation; paying something on the principal as well as the interest]

principle. A truth; a belief; a scientific rule. [He is a man of high principles.]

regretful. Feeling full of regret. [He was very regretful about his bad behavior.]

regrettable. Expressing disappointment. [His behavior was regrettable.]

rend. To tear apart; to disturb. [The silence was rent by a frightening roar.]

render. Make; give; represent; play or sing. [You will render a service. The judge rendered his decision. She will render a selection.]

respectfully. With respect. [Speak to your teacher respectfully.]

respectively. Each in turn or in order. [His three sons, Igor, Dmitri, and Ivan, were 18, 21, and 25 respectively.]

stationary. Not movable; not changing. [a stationary engine; a stationary enrollment; a stationary income]

stationery. Writing materials. [Please let me have some stationery; I wish to write a few letters.]

straight. Not curved; upright; continuous; direct. [The road is straight. Come straight to the point.]

strait. Narrow; strict; restricting. [a strait jacket; a strait passage; the Straits of Magellan; the Straits of Gibraltar]

undoubtedly. Beyond a doubt. [She was undoubtedly correct.]

undoubtably. No such word.

20

21 | 5 *Words and Phrases*

§ 21. EXACTNESS AND THE USE OF THE DICTIONARY

Use words that convey your meaning exactly and idiomatically.

If a word always stood for only one thing or only one idea, communication would be simple indeed. But words have a way of acquiring many meanings through their use by different people at different times under different conditions. Some of the most common words, such as *get, give, hard, take, run, read, stand, shoot,* have dozens of meanings each. As an illustration of the complexity and multiplicity of meanings that a word can acquire, let us take the first in the list—*get.*

He got a reward. I'll get home early. Did you get him on the phone? Can you get Dallas on your set? Go get your coat. Can you get him to eat? Get going. Get the supplies to them. He got six months for that. He's got the habit. Drink will get him. Did you get the wig she was wearing? You'll get caught in the storm. Get it?

We speak of the *denotation,* or the exact, literal meaning of a word, and of the *connotation,* or associated meaning of a word. To be more exact we have to point out that literal meanings and associated meanings blend and merge, change with time and circumstance, and to some extent differ with every different person using these words. Consider a very common noun—*dog.* How did so many opposite associated meanings attach themselves to this poor animal?

Faithful as a dog. He dogged her footsteps. They showed dogged courage. He's a lucky dog. He's going to the dogs. It's a dog's life. It's dog eat dog with him.

21

Many words—and very important ones too—seem to live perpetually in a fog, because there is nothing tangible or visible for which they stand: nothing at which you can point your finger and say, "This is it. This is what I mean." When you say *dog* or *chair* or *book,* you can, if it is important enough, find some dog or chair or book to point to and say, "This is it." But when words stand for ideas, such as *temperance* or *democracy* or *security,* the problem is much harder. All you can do is qualify and define, or point to a person who is temperate, a state that is democratic, a social system that provides security. Such vagueness is not a very satisfactory condition for speakers and writers, but it is the best we have. When we do not choose our words carefully, when we do not define, or point to examples, we may be talking about one thing and our listeners or readers may be thinking another. And that is a worse condition.

To make the art of exact communication by words even more difficult, some people seem to use words in devious ways. Words have always been used by some people to conceal meaning, not to reveal it. Think of the way some politicians or their spokesmen distort meaning by using euphemisms: *inoperative,* we quickly learned, meant an outright lie when it was used by press secretaries and others during a recent political scandal. With other people, abstract words have only one real meaning—the meaning *they* have assigned. A difference of opinion over what a word means, however, does not always imply dishonesty or evil intent. Profoundly honest people may differ in their understanding of words, depending on differences in their background, their training, and their temperament. In the mind, the meaning of a word can change under the stress of emotion, or even under the stress of political campaigns and elections. Such words as *socialism, capitalism, extremism, recession,* and *bureaucracy* mean one thing to members of a political party when it is in office and another thing when it is out of office.

21a. Key words that may be understood in more than one sense should be carefully defined.

Most of the words that you use in your writing or speaking will do well enough without being defined. The least tricky

21

words are the names of specific persons or objects, such as *General Grant, laboratory,* the *White House,* a *Polaroid camera,* although, to be sure, each may arouse emotional reactions that color its meaning. More tricky are the words that refer to things or qualities that have been a part of the daily life of many generations, such as *dog, cat, war, generous, honest, selfish,* and so on. Usually the meaning of the word is defined well enough by the *context* (i.e., the sense of the words around it) in which it is used. Nothing of vast importance is lost through a lack of exact communication. But something of vast importance *is* at stake when people use such words as *radicals, reactionaries, liberals, realistic, democratic people, peace-loving, aggression, freedom of speech.* Terms such as these must be defined.

21b. Words used in an inexact sense should be checked and restudied with the help of a dictionary.

Most of us learn new words as we need them, without much help from vocabulary improvement schemes. All of us depend heavily and very often on the context, on approximations, for meanings. Here and there we miss the point—sometimes by a narrow margin, sometimes by a mile. Here and there someone catches us up.

The word you have missed—the one marked by your instructor—is a good word in its place, but it does not mean quite what you think it means. Perhaps it is a word that you have picked up recently and are trying out. Maybe it is a word that you did not quite hear when it was spoken or did not quite see when you read it. Now you confuse it with another word that sounds like it but means something else. And maybe you just guessed at its meaning because it made sense that way in its context—and you guessed wrong. See what your dictionary says about it. It would be naive to assert that a dictionary can solve all your problems of controlling the meanings of words. But here are a few examples to show how a dictionary can serve you:

The doctor decided to try an *explanatory* operation first. [That sounds reasonable, but is that what he actually decided to try?]

370

21. *EXACTNESS AND THE USE OF THE DICTIONARY*

The music served to *diverge* my thoughts to more pleasant things. [Here the writer was trying for a word that sounded like this one, and, in a vague way, meant something like it.]

She was listening *intensely* to the lecture. [The right word here is *intently.*]

21c. Vague, blanket words should be replaced with more precise words.

This statement refers primarily to such words as *deal, factor, stance, thrust, line, point of view, angle, proposition.* It refers also to any word that you have used, not because it expresses your idea precisely and cleanly, but because you were in a hurry and it was easier to use a vague word than to think of a more exact one.

INEXACT AND WORDY

Did you *get his deal* about wanting to go into something *along the line* of engineering?

BETTER

Can you understand that he wants to study a branch of engineering?

INEXACT

An exciting *factor* of our summer vacation was a trip to Japan.

BETTER

An exciting event of our summer vacation was a trip to Japan.

INEXACT

I never could decide what his *angle* was from the *point of view* of making high grades.

BETTER

I never could decide what his thoughts (ideas) were about making high grades.

Remember that although you may get away with using blanket words in speaking they are all too noticeable in writing.

21

21d. A writer should guard against the right word taking an unintended meaning in the context.

A serious writer, that is, should guard against unintentional humor. Bloopers (or malapropisms), either the natural or the synthetic variety, are of course the stock-in-trade of the gag writer or the television comedian. Here are some examples of unintentional slips:

BLOOPER

The writer made the poem more effective by the use of metaphors and illusions.

CORRECTION

The writer made the poem more effective by the use of metaphors and allusions.

BLOOPER

Finally, at midnight, I sat down to learn my history.

CORRECTION

Finally, at midnight, I sat down to study my history assignment.

BLOOPER

Every time he opens his mouth, some fool speaks.

CORRECTION

Every time he starts to speak, some fool interrupts him.

EXERCISES

EXERCISE 1, ASSOCIATED MEANINGS. *In the following groups of words, which words suggest an unfavorable attitude and which a favorable attitude?*

1. Teacher, tutor, professor, counselor.
2. Policeman, cop, pig, traffic officer.
3. Dainty, fragile, delicate, weak, flaccid, spineless.
4. Woman, female, chick, broad, girl.
5. Mixture, mess, jumble, patchwork, blend, alloy.

21

EXERCISE 2, EXACTNESS. *Point out every instance of inexact use of words in the following sentences and suggest a revision.*

1. The long arm of television permeates all of the civilized world.
2. In this poem the author tells about England's downfall from a leading country.
3. Judge Brand ordered the man to disabuse his wife and children.
4. The effect of the poem depends on what the reader divulges from it.
5. In order to solve their curiosity they must read the story to the end.
6. He quickly built a shelter to shed the rain off his precious equipment.
7. He describes in a realistic way about the things he has experienced in the slums.
8. My problems are more of an uncertainty, like being able to place a comma in this place or a semicolon in that place.
9. My hobby includes time, work, and expense.
10. As I am a seldom reader of poetry, I did not enjoy this book.

21e. Information found in a dictionary will help a student use words more exactly.

A dictionary lists the words of a language, in alphabetical order, and gives information about their meaning, their spelling, their use, their pronunciation, and their history; the degree of completeness of this information depends on the size and purpose of the dictionary. The information found in a dictionary is based on an extensive study of the language in action; for every word listed, a great mass of information has been collected, classified, filed, and studied by a trained staff and, where necessary, by consultants from special fields in which the word is used. All information in a reliable dictionary is based on a study of usage. *A dictionary reflects usage; it does not prescribe it.* It is an authority only insofar as it accurately reflects usage.

The various dictionaries of the English language fall into the following classes:

373

21

1. The monumentally complete ones, in which a word gets full historical treatment, with quotations illustrating its use from the time of its birth to the date of completion of the dictionary:

The New English Dictionary, in 10 vols. and a supplement, 1888–1928, reissued in corrected edition as *Oxford English Dictionary,* 12 vols., 1933 (also known as *N.E.D., O.E.D.,* the *Oxford,* and *Murray's*). In the *N.E.D.* there are 1,827,306 quotations of usage.

2. The one-volume unabridged dictionaries, which you find in schoolrooms and libraries for reference use. They are usually kept up to date by spot revisions and by "New Word Sections." The *New International,* however, has been entirely rewritten.

Webster's Third New International Dictionary. Springfield, Mass.: G. & C. Merriam Company, 1971.
Funk & Wagnalls New Standard Dictionary of the English Language. New York: Funk & Wagnalls Company, 1963.
The Random House Dictionary of the English Language. New York: Random House, 1966.

3. The one-volume, desk-size dictionaries, one of which almost every college student buys as a part of his working equipment. Each one of these listed here is well worth the cost; the choice is usually governed by the recommendation of the student's English instructor.

Webster's New World Dictionary, 2nd College Edition. Cleveland and New York: The World Publishing Company, 1974.
Webster's New Collegiate Dictionary. Springfield, Mass.: G. & C. Merriam Company, 1975.
The American College Dictionary. New York: Random House, 1973.
Standard College Dictionary, Text Edition. New York: Funk & Wagnalls Company, Inc., 1969. Text edition published by Harcourt Brace Jovanovich.
The American Heritage Dictionary of the English Language. New York and Boston: American Heritage and Houghton Mifflin, 1973.

The following kinds of information may be secured from a desk dictionary:

1. **The Meaning of a Word.** As you can see by examining the

374

various excerpts from dictionaries that are reprinted here, a dictionary uses several methods of clarifying the meaning of a word. First, it uses *phrases of definition*, and it often follows the definition with illustrative examples. Second, it uses *synonyms*, either immediately after the defining phrase or in a group below where the synonyms are compared and contrasted. Then, at times, it may present a special list of *idiomatic phrases* using the word. The dictionary also classifies the different meanings a word may have, numbers them, and, if a word has special technical uses, labels these uses and explains them. Some dictionaries list the oldest meanings first; others begin with the most commonly used meanings. It is important to know which method your dictionary uses. You should read *all* the definitions of a word before deciding to use the word in a certain sentence.

In the selection from *Webster's New World Dictionary,*[1] note that the most recent, the most commonly used sense of the word is given first. The thirteen different uses of *pull* as a transitive verb (*vt.*) are given in order, numbered, and, where necessary labeled, as: 6. [Colloq.]; 7. [Colloq.]; 9. [Dial.]. The definitions of *pull* as an intransitive verb and as a noun follow.

[1] From *Webster's New World Dictionary of the American Language,* Second College Edition. Copyright © 1974 by William Collins + World Publishing Company, Inc.

pull (pool) *vt.* [ME. *pullen* < OE. *pullian,* to pluck, snatch with the fingers: ? akin to MLowG. *pull,* a husk, shell] **1.** to exert force or influence on so as to cause to move toward or after the source of the force; drag, tug, draw, attract, etc. **2.** *a)* to draw out; pluck out; extract [to *pull* a tooth] *b)* to pick or uproot [to *pull* carrots] **3.** to draw apart; rip; tear [to *pull* a seam] ☆**4.** to stretch (taffy, etc.) back and forth repeatedly **5.** to stretch or strain to the point of injury [to *pull* a muscle] ☆**6.** [Colloq.] to put into effect; carry out; perform [to *pull* a raid] **7.** [Colloq.] to hold back; restrain [to *pull* one's punches] **8.** [Colloq.] ☆*a)* to take (a gun, knife, etc.) from concealment so as to threaten *b)* to take or force off or out; remove [to *pull* a wheel from a car] **9.** [Dial.] to draw the entrails from (a fowl) **10.** *Baseball, Golf* to hit (the ball) and make it curve to the left or, if left-handed, to the right **11.** *Horse Racing* to rein in or restrain (a horse) so as to keep it from winning **12.** *Printing* to take (a proof) on a hand press **13.** *Rowing a)* to work (an oar) by drawing it toward one *b)* to transport by rowing *c)* to be rowed normally by [a boat that *pulls* four oars] —*vi.* **1.** to exert force in or for dragging, tugging, or attracting something **2.** to take a deep draft of a drink or puff at a cigarette, etc. **3.** to be capable of being pulled **4.** to move or drive a vehicle (*away, ahead,*

21

around, out, etc.) —*n.* 1. the act, force, or result of pulling; specif., *a)* a dragging, tugging, attracting, etc. *b)* the act or an instance of rowing *c)* a drink *d)* a puff at a cigarette, etc. *e)* a difficult, continuous effort, as in climbing *f)* the force needed to move a weight, trigger, etc., measured in pounds *g) Baseball, Golf* the act or an instance of pulling a ball 2. something to be pulled, as the handle of a drawer, etc. ☆3. [Colloq.] *a)* influence or special advantage *b)* drawing power; appeal —**pull apart** to find fault with; criticize —**pull down** 1. to tear down, demolish, or overthrow 2. to degrade; humble 3. to reduce 4. [Colloq.] to get (a specified wage, grade, etc.) —☆**pull for** [Colloq.] to cheer on, or hope for the success of —**pull in** 1. to arrive 2. to draw in or hold back 3. [Slang] to arrest and take to police headquarters —**pull off** [Colloq.] to bring about, accomplish, or perform —**pull oneself together** to collect one's faculties; regain one's poise, courage, etc. —**pull** ☆1. to depart ☆2. to withdraw or retreat ☆3. to escape from a contract, responsibility, etc. 4. *Aeron.* to level out from a dive or landing approach —**pull over** to drive (a vehicle) to or toward the curb —**pull through** [Colloq.] to get through or over (an illness, difficulty, etc.) —**pull up** 1. to uproot 2. to bring or come to a stop 3. *a)* to drive (a vehicle) to a specified place *b)* to make (an aircraft) nose up sharply 4. to check or rebuke —**pull′er** *n.*
SYN.—**pull** is the broad, general term of this list, as defined in sense 1 of the *vt.* above; **draw** suggests a smoother, more even motion than **pull** [he *drew* his sword from its scabbard]; **drag** implies the slow pulling of something heavy, connoting great resistance in the thing pulled [he *dragged* the desk across the floor]; **tug** suggests strenuous, persistent effort in pulling but does not necessarily connote success in moving the object [he *tugged* at the rope to no avail]; **haul** implies sustained effort in transporting something heavy, often mechanically [to *haul* furniture in a truck]; **tow** implies pulling by means of a rope or cable [to *tow* a stalled automobile] —*ANT.* **push, shove**

Notice here and in the excerpt from *The Random House Dictionary of the English Language*[2] how carefully the various synonyms are illustrated and distinguished. These illustrations and discriminated synonyms are a valuable help to finding and using the exact word.

[2] Reprinted by permission of Random House, Inc., from *The American College Dictionary.* Copyright 1947, copyright © 1966, 1973.

crowd[1] (kroud), *n.* 1. a large number of persons gathered closely together; throng: *a crowd of angry people.* 2. any large number of persons. 3. the common people; the masses: *The crowd needs leadership.* 4. any group or set of persons: *They cater to a society crowd.* 5. a large number of things gathered or considered together. 6. *Sociol.* a temporary gathering of people responding to common stimuli and engaged in any of various forms of collective behavior. 7. audience; attendance: *Opening night drew a good crowd.* —*v.i.* 8. to gather in large numbers; throng; swarm. 9. to press forward; advance by pushing. —*v.t.* 10. to push; shove. 11. to press closely together; force into a confined space; cram: *to*

crowd clothes into a suitcase. **12.** to fill to excess; fill by pressing or thronging into. **13.** *Informal.* to place under pressure or stress by constant solicitation: *to crowd a debtor for payment; to crowd someone with embarrassing questions.* **14. crowd on sail,** *Naut.* to carry a press of sail. [ME *crowd(en)*, OE *crūden* to press, hurry; c. MD *crūden* to push (D *kruien*)]
—**Syn.** **1.** horde, herd. CROWD, MULTITUDE, THRONG are terms referring to large numbers of people. CROWD suggests a jostling, uncomfortable, and possibly disorderly company: *A crowd gathered to listen to the speech.* MULTITUDE emphasizes the great number of persons or things but suggests that there is space enough for all: *a multitude of people at the market on Saturdays.* SWARM as used of people is usually contemptuous, suggesting a moving, restless, often noisy, crowd: *A swarm of dirty children played in the street.* THRONG suggests a company that presses together or forward, often with some common aim: *The throng pushed forward to see the cause of the excitement.* **3.** proletariat, plebeians, people, populace. **8.** assemble, herd. **9.** shove, press. **11.** pack, squeeze, cramp.

2. **The Spelling of a Word.** If your instructor has marked *rythem* as misspelled, you may have trouble finding the correct spelling, *rhythm*, in the dictionary. The difficulty, however, is rare; ignorance of the first letter or two in a word is much less common than vagueness about those at about the middle or at the end. In by far the greater number of instances, the dictionary is the quickest and surest check for the spelling of a word. Some words have variant spellings. Where these are indicated, you will be safe in using the first one listed. In the following unit are some of the ways in which variant spellings are listed in dictionaries.

THE AMERICAN COLLEGE DICTIONARY

color: Also, *Brit.,* colour
theater: Also, *esp. Brit.,* theatre
check, n: Also, *Brit.,* cheque

STANDARD COLLEGE DICTIONARY

color: Also *Brit.* colour
theater: Also *esp. Brit.* theatre
glamour: Also *U.S.* glamor

WEBSTER'S NEW WORLD DICTIONARY

aesthete: Also spelled esthete
connection: connexion, British spelling

WEBSTER'S NEW COLLEGIATE DICTIONARY

pyjamas: *chiefly Brit var of* PAJAMAS
theater *or* theatre

3. **The Pronunciation of a Word.** The pronunciation of a word is usually indicated by respelling it with diacritical marks and symbols or respelling it in some form of a phonetic alpha-

21

bet. The method used is explained in detail at the front of every dictionary. A study of these explanations is worthwhile. A brief summary of the symbols used is given at the foot of every page or every two pages facing each other in the dictionary proper. Where two or more pronunciations are current, the dictionary will give both. Check the respelling, the variant accent, the pronunciation symbols, and the stress or accent points in the following from the *New Collegiate:*[3]

---

for·mi·cary \'fòr-mə-ˌker-ē\ *n, pl* **-car·ies** [ML *formicarium,* fr. L *formica*] : an ant nest
for·mi·da·ble \'fòr-məd-ə-bəl *also* fòr-'mid- *or* fər-'mid-\ *adj* [ME, fr. L *formidabilis,* fr. *formidare* to fear, fr. *formido* fear; akin to Gk *mormō* she-monster] **1 :** causing fear, dread, or apprehension <a ~ prospect> **2 :** having qualities that discourage approach or attack **3 :** tending to inspire awe or wonder — **for·mi·da·bil·i·ty** \ˌfòr-məd-ə-'bil-ət-ē; fòr-ˌmid-, fər-ˌ\ *n* — **for·mi·da·ble·ness** \'fòr-məd-ə-bəl-nəs; fòr-'mid-, fər-'\ *n* — **for·mi·da·bly** \-blē\ *adv*

Pronunciation symbols and the indication of accents may vary between dictionaries. Observe these symbols carefully in the dictionary you own and use.

4. **Labels: Subject, Geographical, Usage.** Every dictionary uses geographical and subject labels to show that a word in the sense indicated is characteristic of a region or language or that it has a special meaning in connection with a certain subject. To understand this more clearly, you might check the labels used with the following words: *pone, jollity, Erse, tot, trauma, suture, kirk, syne, cannikin.* You will find some of these words with a subject label in one dictionary and no label in another. A similar lack of agreement exists in connection with usage labels. *Webster's New World Dictionary* uses the following where in the judgment of its editors these labels are called for: *colloquial, slang, obsolete, archaic, poetic, dialect, British. Webster's New Collegiate* uses "status labels" instead of "usage labels." These are *obsolete, archaic, slang, substandard, nonstandard, dialect.* The "regional labels"—*dial Brit, New Eng, chiefly Scot,* and other similar ones—are classified under status labels. The *Standard College Dictionary* uses "restrictive labels," as follows: *illit., slang, dial., informal,* and other labels indicating regional or national divisions, such as *Southern U.S.,*

---

[3] By permission. From *Webster's New Collegiate Dictionary,* © 1975 by G. & C. Merriam Co., Publishers of the Merriam-Webster Dictionaries.

Brit., Scot. The American College Dictionary lists the following usage labels: *archaic, colloq., humorous, obs., slang, poetic, obsolesc., rare, Scot., Scot and N. Eng., South African, U.S.* Note that neither the *New Collegiate* nor the *Standard* uses *colloq.* All of the four still use *slang* as a label. Note the various usage labels in the following two excerpts, the first shown being from *The American Heritage Dictionary.* [4]

21

> **cool** (kōol) *adj.* **cooler, coolest. 1.** Moderately cold; neither warm nor very cold. **2.** Reducing discomfort in hot weather; allowing a feeling of coolness: *a cool blouse.* **3.** Not excited; calm; controlled. **4.** Showing dislike, disdain, or indifference; unenthusiastic; not cordial: *a cool greeting.* **5.** Calmly audacious or bold; impudent. **6.** Designating or characteristic of colors, such as blue and green, that produce the impression of coolness. **7.** *Slang.* Having a quiet, indifferent, and aloof attitude. **8.** *Slang.* Excellent; first-rate; superior. **9.** *Informal.* Without exaggeration; entire; full: *He lost a cool million.* —*v.* **cooled, cooling, cools.** —*tr.* **1.** To make less warm. **2.** To make less ardent, intense, or zealous. —*intr.* **1.** To become less warm. **2.** To become calm. —**cool it.** *Slang.* To calm down, slow down, or relax. —**cool one's heels.** *Informal.* To be kept waiting for a long time. —*n.* **1.** Anything that is cool or moderately cold: *the cool of early morning.* **2.** The state or quality of being cool. **3.** *Slang.* Composure: *recover one's cool.* [Middle English *col*, Old English *cōl*. See **gel-³** in Appendix.*] —**cool′ly** *adv.* —**cool′ness** *n.*
> **Synonyms:** *cool, composed, collected, unruffled, nonchalant, imperturbable, detached.* These adjectives apply to persons to indicate calmness, especially in time of stress. *Cool* has the widest application. Usually it implies merely a high degree of self-control, though it may also indicate aloofness. *Composed* and *collected* more strongly imply conscious display of self-discipline and absence of agitation. *Composed* also often suggests serenity or sedateness, and *collected,* mental concentration. *Unruffled* emphasizes calmness in the face of severe provocation that may have produced agitation in others present. *Nonchalant* describes a casual exterior manner that suggests, sometimes misleadingly, a lack of interest or concern. *Imperturbable* stresses unshakable calmness considered usually as an inherent trait rather than as a product of self-discipline. *Detached* implies aloofness and either lack of active concern or resistance to emotional involvement.

Now look for various usage labels in the excerpts from dictionaries reproduced on pages 375–377 (*Webster's New World* and the *Random House*), and then examine carefully the selection below, which is quoted from *Webster's New Collegiate Dictionary.* [5]

[4] © 1969, 1970, 1971, 1973, 1975, 1976, Houghton Mifflin Company. Reprinted by permission from *The American Heritage Dictionary of the English Language.*
[5] By permission. From *Webster's New Collegiate Dictionary,* © 1975 by G. & C. Merriam Co., Publishers of the Merriam-Webster Dictionaries.

21

¹**stiff** \'stif\ *adj* [ME *stif*, fr. OE *stif*; akin to MD *stijf* stiff, L *stipare* to press together, Gk *steibein* to tread on] **1 a :** not easily bent **:** RIGID **b :** lacking in suppleness <~ muscles> **c :** impeded in movement — used of a mechanism **d :** DRUNK **e :** incapable of normal alert response <scared ~> **2 a :** FIRM. RESOLUTE **b :** STUBBORN. UNYIELDING **c :** PROUD **d** (1) **:** marked by reserve or decorum (2) **:** lacking in ease or grace **:** STILTED **3 :** hard fought **:** PUGNACIOUS. SHARP **4 a** (1) **:** exerting great force <a ~ wind> (2) **:** FORCEFUL. VIGOROUS **b :** POTENT <a ~ dose> **5 :** of a dense or glutinous consistency **:** THICK **6 a :** HARSH. SEVERE <a ~ penalty> **b :** ARDUOUS. RUGGED <~ terrain> **7 :** not easily heeled over by an external force (as the wind) <a ~ ship> **8 :** EXPENSIVE. STEEP <paid a ~ price> — **stiff·ly** *adv*
syn STIFF. RIGID. INFLEXIBLE. TENSE. STARK *shared meaning element* **:** difficult or impossible to bend or enliven *ant* relaxed, supple
²**stiff** *adv* **:** in a stiff manner **:** STIFFLY
³**stiff** *n* **1 :** CORPSE **2 a :** BUM. TRAMP **b :** HAND. LABORER
stiff–arm \'stif-¸ärm\ *vb or n* **:** STRAIGHT-ARM

5. Derivation of a Word. As you know, our words have come from many languages, and some have undergone many changes in form and meaning. A daisy, for instance, was a "day's eye," a nasturtium was a "nose twister," our common dandelion was once a "lion's tooth." And would you believe that our word *emerald* had an ancestor that in Latin was once *smaragdus* and in Greek *smaragdos?* The Roman Emperor Nero once used a polished *smaragdus* as a lens in front of his near-sighted eye. So you see that the derivations of words are interesting in themselves, and they might enrich your understanding of words.

The following words have unusually interesting origins: *bedlam, boycott, broker, calico, curfew, dollar, exhume, lunacy, panic, sandwich, sinister, saxophone, tawdry, thug, vandal.*

6. Grammatical Information. A desk-size dictionary gives adequate information about plurals of nouns and the principal parts of verbs. Inflectional forms are usually given only when they are irregular or when they present difficulties of spelling or pronunciation. For example, no plurals are given for *book, chair, handkerchief* because it is assumed that these nouns, and all others like them, form their plurals in the regular way. But after *index* you find two plurals: *indexes, indices;* after *deer* you find the information that the plural is also *deer* (occasionally *deers*); after *ox* you find the plural is *oxen* (rarely *ox*). Similarly, no principal parts are given after regular verbs, especially when no special problems are involved: see *talk, walk.* But note that *study* is followed by *studied, studying* to show what happens to the ending in the formation of the past tense and the present participle and gerund. Then look up the verb *lie,* which has two main meanings, and note that the principal parts are necessary to distinguish between the two meanings: *lie* [recline], *lay, lain, lying; lie* [prevaricate], *lied, lying.* The last example also illustrates the fact that when the past tense and the past participle have the same form, it is given only once:

lie: He *lied.* I had *lied* about it. [lie, lied, lying]
bring: He *brought* it. I had *brought* it with me. [bring, brought, bringing]
ring: He *rang* the bell. I had *rung* it a minute earlier. [ring, rang, rung, ringing]

7. **Idiomatic Phrases.** Many of the simple, everyday verbs of the language, through many years of various uses and associations, have acquired special meanings in phrases that we call *idioms.* Notice the quotation from *Webster's New World Dictionary,* pages 375–376, to understand what is meant by an idiom: *pull apart* [to criticize], *pull down* [to degrade, to humble], *pull for* [to cheer on], *pull off* [to accomplish], *pull oneself together* [to regain poise], *pull over* [to drive to the curb], *pull through* [to get over an illness], *pull up* [to uproot, to come to a stop]. Anyone can see that these are not literal meanings of the verb. Here are a few more examples of idioms, from various dictionaries: *give ground, take amiss, take stock, take the floor, have it in for, have it out, run out of, do away with, do for, put one down, toe the mark.* See [§23] for a fuller discussion of idiomatic speech.

8. **Synonyms and Antonyms.** Pairs of words that have exactly the same meaning—literal and associated—are not too common in the English language, but words may have approximately the same meaning, or approximately the same meaning in certain uses. Examine the excerpts from dictionaries listed here and study the synonyms under *cool, crowd, pull, stiff.* Note that synonyms are used in illustrative phrases and then sometimes in a separate list where they are compared and contrasted. Antonyms are listed less commonly than synonyms.

21

EXERCISES

EXERCISE 1, DEFINITIONS. *Look up the meanings of each of the following words. List at least two very different meanings for each.*

intern	aggravate	irony	criticize
propaganda	fellow	nice	curious

EXERCISE 2, SPELLING. *Look up each of the following words. Decide whether both spellings are used in your locality, or whether one is more common than the other.*

adviser, advisor	glamorize, glamourize	sulfur, sulphur
although, altho	night, nite	theater, theatre

EXERCISE 3, PRONUNCIATION. *Look up the pronunciation of the following words. Notice where the accent is placed in each word. Where more than one pronunciation is listed, try pronouncing the word in each way. Which form do you use in your own conversation?*

acumen	data	Don Quixote	inquiry
adult	decade	exquisite	irreparable
aspirant	decadence	finance	lamentable
combatant	despicable	formidable	preferable
culinary	Don Juan	gondola	superfluous

EXERCISE 4, STATUS OR USAGE LABELS. *What usage or status label—if any—follows each of the following words?*

alarum	coulee	heap	loser
belike	enthuse	hokum	petrol
bozo	goober	joker	scram

EXERCISE 5, DERIVATION. *From what language did each of the following words come?*

banjo	lava	prairie	rodeo
chinook	mosquito	rebus	sapphire
ersatz	pongee	riata	soprano

§ 22. APPROPRIATENESS

Use words that are in keeping with the subject of your paper, with the occasion, and with the readers you are addressing.

22

Many of the papers that you write for your college courses are informal; some are formal. You should always remember that the terms *informal* and *formal* are relative—not absolute. Each covers a wide range. Obviously, you will probably never try to write with the formality of Oliver Wendell Holmes, or John Kennedy, or Winston Churchill addressing Parliament; you may, however, approach the style of a present-day historian or critic or essayist. Examples of each are to be found in Chapter 1, Section I, of this book.

When you write a serious discussion of a serious subject, you should use language that is dignified but not pretentious or affected. If your occasion is informal, you write in an informal, easy manner—remembering always that as there are degrees of formality so are there degrees of informality. The informality that runs to slang or vague terms has little place in your college work. We have mentioned before the analogy of varieties of writing with manners or dress. Every intelligent person has different styles of writing at his command just as he or she has clothes appropriate for different occasions. A man does not attend a formal dinner in sweater and slacks, or a football game in a tuxedo, unless he is determined to make a spectacular and probably unfavorable impression. There *are* rules and conventions in the use of language, just as there are conventions governing social behavior everywhere else—at a dinner table, at a football game, on a street corner, anywhere. A writer's good sense, wide awake to the situation around him, is his best rule of conduct.

Here are a few examples of failure in appropriateness (in the first two examples, the italicized words do not appear in the originals):

INAPPROPRIATE IN FORMAL WRITING

When Roosevelt took office on March 4, 1933, thousands of American banks *were going broke.* [The original has the more appropriate *verged on insolvency.*]

—WILLIAM MILLER, *A New History of the United States*

There is no doubt that a *whole batch* of new mathematical techniques will have to be *cooked up* before it will be possible to solve satisfactorily *a lot of* scientific problems that today can only be tackled empirically or experimentally. [The original has the more appropriate *variety . . . invented . . . innumerable.*]

—MARIO G. SALVADORI, "Mathematics, the Language of Science"

The State Department's difficulty was that it had failed to find any device for ensuring that the press would *keep mum* on the new international agreement. [Say *remain silent.*]

INAPPROPRIATE IN INFORMAL WRITING

I certainly hope you are having a good time at college this year *and realizing your potential for intellectual growth and development.* [Say *and getting a lot out of it.*]

He told me what to do and *I accomplished the operation.* [Say *I did it.*]

22a. In serious writing, inappropriate slang should be avoided.

Slang has often been defined as a kind of made-to-order language, characterized by extravagant or grotesque humor. This is by no means a complete or all-inclusive definition of slang, nor is an all-inclusive definition important in this book. Not even the editors of our excellent dictionaries agree on what is slang and what is not. *Webster's Third New International Dictionary* lists the following, among others, as examples of slang: rod [revolver, pistol], rap [to arrest, hold; to converse informally], bread [money], savvy [understanding, to understand], baloney [pretentious nonsense], threads [clothes]. In other dictionaries you may find other words listed as slang, words that the unabridged lists without any usage labels.

Slang is usually inappropriate in serious or formal writing, but some writers use it with telling effects. Writers who strain to avoid slang may still err by using stilted, general, vague, and pompously bookish words under the impression that a simple and direct style is not good enough for important ideas.

22b. A mixture of the colloquial and the formal styles is usually inappropriate in serious writing.

Most dictionaries—with the notable exception of *Webster's Third New International*—use *colloq.* as a usage label for certain words and phrases. The *New International* uses status labels, such as *slang, substandard, nonstandard,* but not *colloquial. Colloquial* means informal, or characteristic of a conversational style, as opposed to a formal, literary style. In the past, many people believed that *colloq.* implied a condemnation of a word or phrase, in spite of the fact that editors of dictionaries were careful to define the word correctly in the vocabularies and in the explanatory notes. Scholars, lexicographers, and linguists have pointed out that every educated person uses colloquial English, and, what is important to remember, he or she uses it correctly in appropriate situations.

EXERCISES

EXERCISE 1, APPROPRIATENESS. *Some of the following italicized expressions are appropriate in serious writing; some are not. With the help of your dictionary, decide which are more appropriate in colloquial than in formal situations.*

1. We are determined to *face up to* this monstrous foe with all our hearts.
2. Finally, after many years of service, the old buggy *gave out.*
3. The trusted servant, we discovered, had *made off* with our two cameras.
4. He was to board a plane at ten, but none of his friends was there to *see him off.*
5. The man was instructed to *sing out* if he saw any prowlers.
6. Within a year the young man *had run through* his inheritance.
7. At the end of the year he felt that it was not easy to *take off and leave* his new friends.
8. The principal was trying to find out who had *put him up to it.*

9. His arrogance was something no one was willing to *put up with*.
10. Nobody expected her to *carry on so* when she heard that her daughter had eloped.

EXERCISE 2, FORMAL AND INFORMAL EXPRESSIONS. *Give the formal equivalent of each of the italicized expressions.*

1. to *back down*
2. to *beat down the price*
3. to *go him one better*
4. *How come?*
5. He was *let out* when the company went broke.
6. You'll *get your cut!*
7. He *fed* the new girl *a line*.
8. That music really *moves* me.
9. Give him his *walking papers*.
10. *Stick around* for a while.

§ 23. IDIOMS

23a. Use idiomatic English.

An idiom is an expression peculiar to a given language. It cannot usually be translated word-for-word into another tongue, though its sense can often be rendered by an equivalent idiom native and natural to that tongue. Created out of the day-to-day living of ordinary people, idioms are often irrational, racy, and lively with images. Many of them have originated in someone's clever and original metaphor, which then became "dead" as it was repeated by other people. "You said a mouthful." "He was beside himself with worry." "Who slipped up?" "Water off a duck's back." As these examples suggest, idioms are often colloquial or slang, though not necessarily so.

Americans have been particularly fertile in producing an idiomatic language, and many volumes have been written on the subject of American word-making. For a useful collection and a guide to recent opinions about usage, see Roy H. Copperud's *American Usage: The Consensus* (New York: Van Nostrand Reinhold, 1970). Students interested in pursuing the history of a particular idiom should consult this work or the *New*

English Dictionary. See the further listing under "Dictionaries and Books of Synonyms" in Section I, Chapter 3.

Even more than other elements in the language, idioms change status constantly as they come into or go out of fashion, or as they become respectable in formal English or fall into disrepute. In fact such change has become so rapid and complex in our time that the editors of the latest unabridged *Webster's* have dropped most of their notations of *slang* and *colloq.* Even your desk dictionary, however, can be very useful in listing the various idioms formed from ordinary single words. Many idiomatic phrases have grown up around the verbs of everyday living—*go, do, catch, get, make, take,* and so on.

The student's difficulties in handling idioms are likely to be of two kinds. First, trouble occurs in sensing the status of a particular idiom for a particular purpose. He or she might, for instance, go so far as to write, in a formal essay, and with no humorous intention, "This flipped me!" In this case, of course, the writer has failed to recognize the highly colloquial and ephemeral quality of that expression. Or the student might say, in a serious descriptive essay, "It rained cats and dogs," thus failing to recognize that this particular idiom has long been a very tired cliché. (Clichés are treated more fully in § 26.) The best guard against errors of this kind is constant reading, writing, and listening, with an awareness of how different kinds of expressions are acceptable in different situations.

A second source of student difficulty with idioms might be called a failing of the ear—that is, the student may forget just how an idiom is said in English, and that there is seldom much rhyme or reason to the phrasing of idioms. The problem is most severe in the case of prepositions, as the subsection immediately following will show.

23b. Observe the idiomatic use of prepositions after certain verbs, participles, adjectives, and nouns.

The following list will not take the place of an unabridged dictionary. It will serve merely as a check list to put you on your guard. Consult the dictionary for more complete information.

387

23

abstain from
accede to
acquiesce in
acquit of
addicted to
adept in
adhere to
agree to (a thing)
agree with (a person)
agreeable to
angry at (a thing)
angry with (a person)
averse to
capable of
characteristic of
compare to (for illustration)
compare with (to examine qualities)
concern in (interest in)
concerned for (troubled)
concerned with (involved)
concur in (an opinion)
concur with (a person)
desire for
desirous of
desist from
devoid of
differ about
differ from (things)
differ with (a person)
different from
disagree with
disdain for
dissent from

distaste for
empty of
envious of
expert in
foreign to
guard against
hint at
identical with
independent of
infer from
initiate into
inseparable from
jealous of
obedient to
oblivious of
preparatory to
prerequisite to
prior to
proficient in
profit by
prohibit from
protest against
reason with
regret for
repugnant to
sensitive to
separate from
substitute for
superior to
sympathize with
tamper with
unmindful of
vie with

It is characteristic of English that an idiom may have several meanings, and that it may shift into a new part of speech. The professor *makes up* a roster of students, and the *makeup* of the class displeases him. A lady *makes up* her face, which is to say she applies *makeup*. I *make up* a fairy story, which then appears *made-up*. Idioms such as these, composed originally of a verb

plus an adverb, quickly become nouns in our language, as the
following short list will suggest:

blowup	run-in
carryover	runaround
cookout	runaway
countdown	turnover
drive-in	upkeep

This process of word formation is one of several such shifts
peculiarly in motion in our own time. Many nouns so formed
are obviously of recent origin: *cookout, countdown, drive-in.* The
student should not hesitate to make use of such new terms, in
spite of their predominantly informal quality. In the list above,
for example, almost every term is at least conceivably appropriate in almost any context.

EXERCISES

EXERCISE 1, IDIOMS. *In your desk dictionary find the idioms listed
under several of the following words. You will find idiomatic phrases
printed in boldface type, usually after the synonyms. Bring to class a number
of these for discussion. Try to decide why some are marked* colloq. *and some
are without a label.*

eat	go	head	mouth	stand
foot	hand	heart	pick	take
get	have	horse	run	word

EXERCISE 2, MISUSE OF IDIOMS. *Rewrite the following paragraph, correcting the misuses of idiom.*

He was superior than all of us, or so he thought, but his brag-
ging was no substitute of ability. He felt himself independent
from the rest of us, though he was usually agreeable with going
along with the majority. I was often angry at him, since he
differed from me so often.

24

EXERCISE 3, IDIOMATIC PREPOSITIONS. *Supply the idiomatic prepositions as required in the following sentences.*

1. Since I was so concerned (   ) my business at that time, she was concerned (   ) my health.
2. At that period we differed (   ) almost everything.
3. She especially differed (   ) me about money matters.
4. Finally we separated (   ) one another.
5. Neither of us, however, proved to be capable (   ) living alone.

§ 24. CONCRETENESS

In general, a concrete word with a clear image has more effect than an abstract one, a specific word evokes more response than a general one, and a homely word makes more friends than a bookish or pretentious one.

A *concrete* noun, such as *bridge, wall, needle, cloud, smoke, shoe,* or *apple,* names something that can be perceived through any of the senses. In other words, it names something you can touch, see, hear, taste, smell, or feel. *Abstract* words name ideas, or qualities, as *beauty, cleverness, elitism, truth, loyalty,* or *doubt.* Now of course you can seldom give a concrete equivalent of an abstract word, but you can—and should—spell out your concept of the abstraction you use. To say "My father is both stubborn and easygoing" is not enough if you want to present him dramatically; bring him out on the stage for us to see, and show him in the middle of an argument.

General words name classes or groups; *specific* words name the individual objects, actions, or qualities that compose the group. The terms are to some extent relative: *furniture* is a class of things; *chair* is more specific than *furniture,* more general than *armchair* or *rocking chair.*

Weapon is a general noun. When, for example, you write, "Mrs. Hanks assaulted her husband with a deadly weapon," what control do you have over what goes on in your reader's mind? What picture do your words call up? Did she stab him with a steak knife, club him with a baseball bat, slash him with a safety razor blade that she had slipped out of the medicine chest, or shoot him with .22 caliber pistol? You say the police found an ornament that she had dropped in the scuffle. It was probably a piece of jewelry—which is more specific than *ornament*—but it would have been more specific and more effective to say "a jade green earring."

The verb *move* is general; *stride, amble, creep, glide, lope* are all more specific ways of moving. The adjective *large* is general; when you try to make it more specific, you discover that different varieties of largeness are associated with different nouns. For instance, *bulky, towering, brawny, fat, spacious, hulking* are applicable to which of these—a building, a man, a room, a tree?

Homely words are those associated with the objects and activities of everyday living; *bookish* or *pretentious* words are those associated with excessive literary formality.

The following pairs of words and expressions will help to make the distinctions clearer:

24

ABSTRACT WORDS
the faithfulness of an animal; the harmony of music; a misfortune of battle; extreme intoxication.

CONCRETE WORDS
She served him like a dog; my mother hummed a lullaby; a shell fragment ripped open his right arm; he was lit up like a Christmas tree.

GENERAL WORDS
Furniture, clothing, cutlery, kitchen utensil, a crime, an industrial worker, a flower, an animal.

SPECIFIC WORDS
Sofa, raincoat, a carving knife, a frying pan, burglary, a welder, a rose, a lion.

BOOKISH OR PRETENTIOUS WORDS
Frigidity, inebriated, suspend, incarcerated, the matutinal meal, to delve.

HOMELY WORDS
Coldness, drunk, hang, jailed, breakfast, to dig.

391

24

These are by no means scientific classifications applicable to all words in the language. We are merely picking out handfuls of words as samples, and saying in effect: "Look at these. This type of word seems to do something more to your imagination and comprehension than that one." Abstract and general words are not bad words; they are necessary for the expression of abstract qualities and general ideas. Bookish words are natural in certain scholarly, formal contexts. But in the writing of the average student, abstract and general words are used too often where concrete and specific words would do a better job. Remember, disagreement over the meaning of an abstract term is frequent.

The following examples should help to make the idea clearer. You may assume that the "General and Ineffective" examples are not topic sentences.

GENERAL AND INEFFECTIVE

They would usually serve us a good breakfast in cheerful surroundings.

CONCRETE AND SPECIFIC

There would be a brisk fire crackling in the hearth, the old smoke-gold of morning and the smell of fog, the crisp cheerful voices of the people and their ruddy competent morning look, and the cheerful smells of breakfast, which was always liberal and good, the best meal that they had: kidneys and ham and eggs and sausages and toast and marmalade and tea.

—THOMAS WOLFE, *Of Time and the River*

GENERAL AND INEFFECTIVE

I took the spores from the puffball home, set up my microscope, and was startled when I saw the spores magnified.

CONCRETE AND SPECIFIC

At my desk, I draw the microscope out of its case, and though it is heavy, it slides out to me, when I grasp it by the middle, with an ease like a greeting. It is a matter of a moment to whisk the fungus spores on a glass slide, a moment more to find them in the lower magnification, and then with a triumphant click to swing the intense myopic gaze of the tinier lens upon them. From a speck as fine as a particle of wandering cigarette smoke, a spore leaps suddenly up at my eyes as a sphere of gold meshed with vitreous green bands that cut up this tiny world, this planetesimal of sealed-up life, into latitude and longitude.

—Donald Culross Peattie, *Green Laurels*

GENERAL AND INEFFECTIVE

The inconvenience of taking a bath in one of these old English homes is hard to realize.

24

CONCRETE AND SPECIFIC

I do not mind taking sectional baths with two pints of water in the country, where it seems unexceptional and goes along with fresh air, old clothes and being sleepy by nine o'clock in the evening. But segmented bathing in this weary, constricted, suburban household has nothing of rural simplicity about it, only skimpiness and inadequacy, and it makes you feel when you finish like a postage stamp that has been licked and then not used.

—Margaret Halsey, *With Malice Toward Some*

INEFFECTIVE

He removed his shoes and walked more comfortably in his bare feet.

MORE VIVID

He leaned down and untied the laces, slipped off first one shoe and then the other. And he worked his damp feet comfortably in the hot dry dust until little spurts of it came up between his toes, and until the skin on his feet tightened with dryness.

—John Steinbeck, *The Grapes of Wrath*

GENERAL AND INEFFECTIVE

The entryway was dirty and messy.

CONCRETE AND SPECIFIC

The space inclosed within the skewed and bent gate pickets was a snug harbor for the dust of many a gritty day. There were little grey drifts of it at the foot of each of the five steps that led up to the flagged floor level; secretions of grime covered the barred double doors on beyond the steps, until the original color was only to be guessed at; scraps of dodgers, pieces of newspaper and tattered handbills adhered to every carved projection at the feet of the columns, like dead leaves about tree boles in the woods.

—Irvin S. Cobb, "The Great Auk"

393

25

EXERCISES

EXERCISE 1, GENERAL AND SPECIFIC WORDS. *Find several specific words for each of the following general words.*

jewelry	animal	to move	road	to laugh
flower	ship	to speak	grass	to clean
entertainment	hat	to sing	bird	to hit

EXERCISE 2, ABSTRACT AND CONCRETE WORDS. *Construct sentences in which you give concrete examples of each of the following abstract terms.*

unselfishness	ignorance	fear
efficiency	stubbornness	laziness

EXERCISE 3, REVISING WITH SPECIFIC AND CONCRETE WORDS. *Rewrite the following sentences, making them more specific and concrete.*

1. On the porch a row of elderly women sat and rocked and watched the new guests come in.
2. An irritated and impatient policeman was trying to give directions to a driver.
3. The sounds at midnight are interesting to hear.
4. A little boy was happily playing in the alley.
5. The man leaned against the wall and fell asleep.

§ 25. CONCISENESS

Avoid using more words than are necessary for the adequate expression of your thought.

The stylistic fault of *wordiness* has been a concern of writers and rhetoricians for many centuries. Wordiness has been called by many names—verbosity, redundancy, prolixity, diffuseness, circumlocution, periphrasis. By any name, wordiness simply means the use of more words than you need in a particular situation. To achieve conciseness, you must ask whether every word you write is doing its work, carrying its proper load of meaning, and helping its neighbors with their loads.

Do not mistake brevity for conciseness. A sentence is not concise if it lacks the words necessary to adequate expression. Cutting out words in a good essay might also cut out of it those qualities that make it good—strength, variety, maturity, grace, wit, even accuracy.

Study the difference in effect produced by the following pairs of sentences. Notice that in each case the first sentence, although longer, is also stronger and richer.

25

1. The ant and the moth have cells for each of their young, but our little ones lie in festering heaps, in homes that consume them like graves; and night by night, from the corners of our streets, rises up the cry of the homeless—"I was a stranger, and ye took me not in."
2. Insects are more careful about their young than are human beings.

1. When we had done all this, there fell upon us the beneficent and deliberate evening; so that as we sat a little while together near the rakes, we saw the valley more solemn and dim around us and all the trees and hedgerows quite still, and held by a complete silence.

—HILAIRE BELLOC

2. When we had finished, it was evening; so that we sat a little while near the rakes and looked out upon the quiet valley.

Now study the following sets of sentences. Do you see what is meant by conciseness?

1. Whenever anyone called for someone to help him do some certain thing, Jim was always the first to volunteer and lend his help for the cause.
2. Whenever anyone called for help, Jim was always the first to volunteer.
1. This spirit of cooperation is essential and necessary for anyone to have in order to get along with other people, and this is a quality that Jim had.
2. Jim had the spirit of cooperation which is necessary if one wishes to get along with people.
1. Jim was one of those people of whom there are few in this world like him.
2. There are few people like Jim.

25

1. Lumbering is placed in the upper ten industries in the United States from the standpoint of importance.
2. Lumbering is one of the ten most important industries in the United States.

This section will concern itself with several kinds of wordiness to be avoided by the writer who hopes to be concise, direct, and to the point.

25a. Avoid careless repetition of the same word.

Careless repetition of a word weakens the effectiveness of a sentence and is often a symptom of wordiness. The fault may be corrected by using synonyms, by using pronouns, or by completely rewriting the sentence.

POOR

I have been asked to write on a controversial subject that has been the subject of controversy among historians for years. That subject, as you have probably guessed, is none other than how to account for the rise of Hitler's Germany. The rise of Hitler's Germany has fascinated me for a longer time than I can remember.

BETTER

I shall try to account for the rise of Hitler's Germany, a controversial subject that has fascinated me for some time.

The importance of avoiding awkward repetition must not distract the writer from the possibilities of *repetition for emphasis*—a tried and true device for securing certain kinds of attention from the reader. It is especially appropriate in persuasion and oratory, as the famous (and often parodied) selection from Winston Churchill below suggests, but it is used sparingly by most contemporary writers.

We shall go on to the end, *we shall fight* in France, *we shall fight* on the seas and oceans, *we shall fight* with *growing* confidence and *growing* strength in the air, *we shall defend* our Island, whatever the cost may be, *we shall fight* on the beaches, *we shall fight* on the landing grounds, *we shall fight* in the fields and in the streets, *we shall fight* in the hills; we

396

shall never surrender, and even if, which I do not for a moment be-lieve, this Island or a large part of it were subjugated and starving, then our Empire beyond the seas, armed and guarded by the British Fleet, would carry on the struggle, until, in God's good time, the New World, with all its power and might, steps forth to the rescue and the liberation of the old.

—WINSTON CHURCHILL, *Blood, Sweat, and Tears*

25

Note that Churchill's words are decidedly oratorical. The se-lection is not a piece of writing but a *speech* with punctuation and parenthetical interjections purposefully inserted to make an effective oral delivery. It is dangerous, unless the writer is exceptionally forceful, to adopt so measured a repetitious style in straightforward prose. Repetition in oral delivery ensures that the concept repeated is not forgotten by the listener. The writer need not clutch his reader by the figurative lapel quite so violently.

25b. Avoid repetition of words with the same meaning (tau-tology).

W O R D Y

The analysis was *thoroughly and wholly complete.*

All the requirements of *frank* and *honest candor* made his speech popular.

The *basic fundamental essentials* of a college education are *simply* and *briefly* these.

He woke up at six *a.m. this morning.*

Many clichés, particularly those picked up from legal jargon, are tautologies: *Null and void, goods and chattels, swear and affirm.*

25c. Avoid the double *that* before a clause (pleonasm, a gram-matical tautology).

W O R D Y

I was very glad that when I came into the house that I found every-thing in order. [Omit the second *that.*]

25d. Avoid roundabout expressions (circumlocution or pe-riphrasis).

397

WORDY

The reason why I was so upset was because she seemed so angry with me. [reason—why—because] [*Revise:* I was upset because she seemed so angry with me.]

25e. Avoid wordy use of intensives and other modifiers.

It is wise to question critically all modifiers (adjectives and adverbs), because it is often through these words that wordiness gets a foothold. The so-called intensives—*very, much,* and so on—are likely to weaken a sentence.

WORDY

They were absolutely so much astonished to find so very much still to do that they were absolutely speechless. [They were speechless with astonishment to find so much still to be done.]

She was completely and totally pleased by the very fine report that the children gave her. [She was pleased by the children's fine report.]

25f. Avoid repetition of similar sounds.

The awkward repetition of similar sounds in prose may seriously distract your reader from what you are trying to communicate. Consider the following warning on the subject and note the examples:

Bad prose is bad business, even if the badness be nothing worse than discord. Let the ear then have its way as the phrases are conned; rougher rhythms and inharmonious sounds will drag; as we read we resent something wrong, so that we hesitate, and look back to see where was the jar or the limp. *E.g.* "A more ac*commo*dating de*nomi*nation is *commonly* given to it." "*Gratitude* for his *rectitude*"; "an organisational centre of crystallisation"; "necessar*ily* tempor*ary*"; "ve*ry* near*ly* entire*ly*"; "so that it at once commenced"; "the native rulers were as a rule," etc. . . . "Of all I have kn*own* he could at least hold his *own*," is not only an untimely assonance but imparts the alien rhythm of verse.

—Sir T. Clifford Allbutt, *Notes on the Composition of Scientific Papers*

25g. Avoid officialese (also called "gobbledygook").

398

The language of official life, government and the military, is seldom concise. You will find there many examples of wordiness such as we have been illustrating. Note especially, in such writing, the overuse of passive verbs (see §6c) and a fondness for abstract nouns (§26a). A similar kind of stuffiness infects the report writing of committees—writing created, that is, by more than one author. And extracurricular student writing, strange to say, is not always free from the wordiness of hot air. See your own campus newspaper.

25

For an example of official style—by no means an extreme one—study this passage from the "Regulations and Information" section of the University of Missouri-Kansas City *Bulletin.*

Students enrolling in the University assume an obligation and are expected by the University to conduct themselves in a manner compatible with the University's functions and missions as an educational institution. For that purpose students are required to observe generally accepted standards of conduct. Obstruction of University teaching, research, administration, or other activities, indecent conduct or speech, failure to comply with requests of University officials in the performance of their duties, and violation of the laws of the city, state, or nation are examples of conduct which would contravene this standard.

It would not be too facetious to assert that a rendering of this paragraph in concise English might read:

Students at the University are expected to behave themselves.

25h. Avoid "fine writing."

"Fine writing" is not, as the phrase seems to indicate, good writing. It is flowery, artificial, overblown writing. In an effort to be literary, the writer loads his style with too many adjectives and adverbs, with big words, awkward repetitions of high-sounding phrases, and trite figures of speech. (See also §26c.) "Fine writing" is often the result of an overcomplicated sentence structure. Its effect is that of a voice that sounds pompous and stuffy, and no sensitive reader will listen to such a voice for very long.

399

25

Below is a parody of the prose style of Henry James which illustrates many of the faults of "fine writing."

Author Winner sat serenely contemplating his novel. His legs, not ill-formed for his years, yet concealing the faint cyanic marbling of incipient varicosity under grey socks of the finest lisle, were crossed. He was settled in the fine, solidly-built, cannily (yet never parsimoniously, never niggardly) bargained-for chair that had been his father's, a chair that Author Winner himself was only beginning to think that, in the fullness of time, hope he reasonably might that he would be able (be possessed of the breadth and the depth) to fill. Hitching up the trousers that had been made for his father (tailored from a fabric woven to endure, with a hundred and sixty threads to the inch), he felt a twinge of the sciatica that had been his father's and had come down to him through the jeans. Author Winner was grateful for any resemblance; his father had been a man of unusual qualities: loyal, helpful, friendly, courteous, kind, obedient, cheerful, thrifty, brave, clean and reverent; in the simplest of terms: a man of *dharma*.

—FELICIA LAMPORT, "By Henry James Cozened"

EXERCISES

EXERCISE 1, AWKWARD REPETITIONS. *In the following sentences, underline the awkward repetitions and examples of wordiness. Then rewrite the sentences, making them more concise by cutting or other revision.*

1. The several features of the situation were complex, and altogether the situation was complicated because of the many elementary elements involved.
2. It was perfectly clear that if she had come along with you as your companion that she would have been welcome.
3. I need hardly say to you all at this time and place that the very great economic loss is a serious source of loss to us all.
4. The chief significant reason why the economy failed was on account of an economic imbalance in the balance of trade.
5. I told him about the courses we were taking, French and history and so on and so forth, so he would get a good idea of the curriculum in which we take courses.

6. He had an arbitrary, set, inflexible rule for everything that he did, and for anything on which he had made up his mind it was very difficult to persuade him otherwise.
7. I really mean it, I certainly was relieved to make that discovery, to my real relief.
8. Unless a person is thoroughly and completely prepared, both mentally and psychologically, the chances of success in marriage are dim, doubtful, and obscure.
9. In regard to this matter of your new insurance policy, please be advised that your new policy is being taken up in a matter of approximately a week or thereabouts.
10. Without any doubt it is very true and unarguable that this great nation of ours is very ready to prepare to defend itself to the very last launching pad.

EXERCISE 2, OFFICIALESE. *Here is an example of officialese, not much exaggerated. Rewrite in plain English.*

It is desired by the administration at this particular time that students refrain and desist from the excessive noise and horse-play that has characterized their behavior in halls and corridors during recent occasions that I have observed. The magnitude of the noise involved has reached a degree where, in some cases of particularly recalcitrant offenders, the awarding of the degree in June may be jeopardized. All faculty personnel are enjoined to be alert to dispatch to this office any flagrant discrepancies of this sort that may come to their attention from time to time.

§ 26. VIVIDNESS AND METAPHOR

26a. Try to use words and phrases that give life and freshness to your style.

There are many ways to make a style vivid. Some of them were discussed in previous sections under the headings of "concreteness" and "conciseness." In this section we consider a few other devices available to the writer who wishes to create fresher, livelier language. First, you should be aware of the possibilities for freshness in the various parts of speech—nouns,

401

26

modifiers, verbs. Second, you should see the possibilities in figurative language, or metaphor. Then you must beware the dangers of metaphor, particularly since so much figurative language has been used before and has lost its freshness. Finally, you must recognize the related problem of overused language generally: the problem of triteness and clichés.

1. *Specific rather than general nouns will help to produce a vivid style.* (Go back to §24 to find out what is meant by *specific* and *general.*) When you write, "I heard a bird singing," your words may call up a definite sense image in the mind of your reader—or they may not—but you do not know what that image is. Have you pictured for your audience a canary or a robin or a song sparrow? If instead of "bird" you say "meadowlark" or "hermit thrush," your reader will at least make an effort to recall or imagine the song of a meadowlark or a hermit thrush. Whenever you use a specific noun, you make it easy for your reader's mind to create a specific image. You do more than suggest images by your words; you direct the picture-making that goes on in your reader's brain.

2. *Try to use strong, picture-making adjectives and adverbs.* (See also §25e.) No part of speech is more likely to turn blue and rot than a flat, uninspired adjective or adverb. You say, "That was a good lecture," when you mean that it was witty, or stimulating or instructive, or entertaining. You say "She is a nice girl," when you mean that she is friendly, or sympathetic, or generous, or loyal, or modest, or conventional. You can find many adjectives that are more accurate and more vivid than *nice, cool, heavy, big, easy, hard.* A book of synonyms will help you find them.

It is a good idea to be on guard against all weak, overused adverbs, such as *very, pretty, rather, little.* Often a weak verb-adverb group can be replaced more effectively by a single strong verb. Note the following examples:

He ran quickly. [He fled, sprinted, trotted, rushed, surged, dashed.]
He was breathing rapidly. [He was panting, blowing, wheezing, puffing, gasping.]
She cut through it. [She pierced it, sliced it, tore it, split it, ripped it.]

He threw it down violently. [He hurled it, flung it, heaved it, pitched it.]

3. *Try replacing general or colorless verbs with more specific and descriptive verbs.* Here are some examples.

He moved toward the door. [He crept, sneaked, crawled, strolled, sidled, inched, drifted, flitted toward the door.]

He spoke several words. [He whispered, roared, shouted, hissed, mumbled, muttered several words.]

We put it on the truck. [We tossed, lifted, pitched, threw it on the truck.]

She got on the horse. [She scrambled, leaped, jumped, vaulted on the horse.]

26b. Figurative language can be used to add freshness to your style.

Some college freshmen feel that figurative language is a bit insincere, a little phony perhaps, good enough for poetry but out of place in honest prose. The truth is that all writing, from the deeply serious or reverent to the lightest, is often metaphorical. Our daily talk is salted with figures of speech. We meet metaphors in our reading and take them as they come, hardly realizing what they are. Churchill speaking before Parliament ["the life of the world may move forward into *broad, sunlit uplands*"], a historian, Oscar Handlin ["mariners *hugged* the margins of the continent"], a nuclear scientist, J. Robert Oppenheimer ["broken the *iron circle* of his frustration"], a scholar and naturalist, Joseph Wood Krutch, describing a tarantula ["Plainly, he is a discontinued model—still running but very difficult, one imagines, to get spare parts for"]—all use figurative language.

Although all figurative language is usually called metaphorical, some elementary distinctions are useful. A *metaphor* is a figure that likens one thing to another by saying that one thing *is* another, not literally of course: "Life's but a walking shadow, a poor player" ... "all the world's a stage" ... "a critic is a

403

legless man who teaches running" . . . "a camel is a greyhound designed by a committee"—these are metaphors. When the likeness is actually expressed by the use of *as* or *like,* the metaphor becomes a *simile.* "All the world is *like* a stage" . . . "insubstantial *as* a dream" . . . "the water lay gray and wrinkled *like* an elephant's skin"—these are similes. Figurative language, it is true, can be overdone, especially by a writer groping for a gaudy style.

Figures of speech are best observed in context, where they look at home, as in the following selections. Seen alone as specimens they too often remind us of brightly colored butterflies pinned to a board. In the following, observe also the vivid nouns, verbs, and adjectives:

Many of us, if we have happy childhoods, are tempted to believe that life is a pony, beribboned and curried, which has been given to us as a present. With the passing of years we, sooner or later, come to learn that, instead of being a pony, life is a mule which unfortunately has more than four legs. To the best of my knowledge, no one who lives long enough fails to be kicked, usually again and again, by that mule. Why this should surprise us or unnerve us, I as an older person have long since ceased to understand.

—JOHN MASON BROWN, "Prize Day Address," at Groton School for Boys

Then the creeping murderer, the octopus, steals out, slowly, softly, moving like a gray mist, pretending now to be a bit of weed, now a rock, now a lump of decaying meat while its evil goat eyes watch coldly. It oozes and flows toward a feeding crab, and as it comes close its yellow eyes burn and its body turns rosy with the pulsing color of anticipation and rage. Then suddenly it runs lightly on the tips of its arms, as ferociously as a charging cat. It leaps savagely on the crab, there is a puff of black fluid, and the struggling mass is obscured in the sepia cloud while the octopus murders the crab. On the exposed rocks out of water, the barnacles bubble behind their closed doors and the limpets dry out.

—JOHN STEINBECK, *Cannery Row*

He gave his speech out of that bolt of cloth he had been weaving for all his life, that springless rhetoric so suited to the organ pipes of his sweet voice, for it enabled him to hold any note on any word, and he could cut from the sorrows of a sigh to the injunctions of a wheeze. He was a holy Harry Truman. Let us not quote him except where we must, for the ideas in his speech have already entered the boundless deep of yesterday's Fourth of July, and ". . . once again we give our testament to America . . . each and every one of us in our own way should once again reaffirm to ourselves and our posterity that we love this nation, we love America!"

—NORMAN MAILER, *Miami and the Siege of Chicago*

26

26c. Metaphors and other phrases that have become trite should be avoided.

Trite expressions, whether they were once metaphors or not, are also called *hackneyed phrases* or *chichés*. At one time they may have been apt or witty and appropriate, but now, because they have been used so often, they are stale and flat. They put off the reader. The following list may help to put you on your guard:

aching void	conspicuous by his absence
acid test	course of true love
after all has been said	devouring element
all in all	discreet silence
all work and no play	doomed to disappointment
among those present	drastic action
ardent admirers	dull, sickening thud
as luck would have it	dyed in the wool
at a loss for words	each and every one
at one fell swoop	easier said than done
avoid like the plague	equal to the occasion
beat a hasty retreat	face the music
beggars description	fair sex
better half	familiar landmark
better late than never	favor with a selection
blissfully ignorant	festive occasion
blushing bride	few and far between
bolt from the blue	goes without saying
breathless silence	gridiron warriors
budding genius	grim reaper
busy as a bee	holy bonds of matrimony
by leaps and bounds	in all its glory
caught like rats in a trap	in the last analysis
checkered career	irony of fate
clear as crystal	justice to the occasion

405

26

last but not least
leaves speechless
long-felt want
meets the eye
method in his madness
monarch of all he surveys
mother nature
motley crowd
needless to say
nipped in the bud
none the worse for wear
no sooner said than done
partake of refreshments
play with fire
pleasing prospect
pot luck
powers that be
presided at the piano
proud possessor
psychological moment
reigns supreme
rendered a selection
replete with interest
riot of color
ripe old age

sadder but wiser
seven deadly sins
shadow of the goal posts
silence reigned supreme
specimen of humanity
sumptuous repast
sweat of his brow
sweet girl graduate
table groaned
tempest in a teapot
tired but happy
troubled waters
untold wealth
vale of tears
venture a suggestion
[make a] virtue of necessity
water over the dam
wee small hours
wends his way
where ignorance is bliss
with a vengeance
with bated breath
words fail to express
worked like a horse
wrought havoc

EXERCISES

EXERCISE 1, WRITING FOR VIVIDNESS. *Rewrite the following paragraph. Pay special attention to the verbs, adjectives, and adverbs, and try to make use of metaphors or similes where they can be made appropriate.*

The boy walked home from school very slowly. It was April, and he observed as he went the various signs of the spring season. As he approached his own house, he paused to speak to his neighbor, who was puttering about on his lawn. Finally he turned and walked indoors, for he was hungry.

EXERCISE 2, CLICHÉS AND TRITE PHRASES. *Now rewrite this passage again, this time using as many clichés and trite phrases as you can.*

406

§ 27. REFERENCE OF PRONOUNS

27

27a. The antecedent of a pronoun in a sentence should be immediately clear to the reader.

As a rule, pronouns should have definite antecedents and should be placed as near their antecedents as possible. The hedging in this last sentence, represented by the phrase "as a rule," refers to two or three special situations. First, there are a number of idiomatic phrases in which a pronoun has no visible antecedent, such as *it rained last night; it's the climate; it is time to go home.* There is no lack of clearness in these sentences. Second, the pronoun *you,* in the sense of *one,* or a *person,* has wide currency in informal written and spoken English, and occasionally in good formal writing. Third, the pronouns *which, this, that* may refer to an idea or fact expressed by a whole clause or a sentence, or by a part of a clause, if the reference is unmistakably clear. These last, however, present a greater risk than the previous two idioms. Even when the reference *is* unmistakably clear, *which, this,* or *that* may be weaker than some more specific noun. It is not enough to answer the case against them; a case must be made for them.

In good writing, the meaning of a sentence should be clear on the first reading. If the reader has to hesitate, if he has to search for the substantive (i.e., a noun or anything that functions as a noun) to which the pronoun refers, or if he has to puzzle over which of two possible antecedents it does refer to, the sentence is inept. And we may add here that even if you can find a bucketful of muddled sentences in the writing of great scientists, great educators, or great public servants, those sentences still are muddled and not as good as they could have been.

INDEFINITE

She saw a play at the elegant new Plymouth Theatre, but later she was not able to remember it very well. [What could she not remember, the play or the theatre?]

27

CLEAR

At the elegant new Plymouth Theatre she saw a play that she later was not able to remember very well.

OR

She saw a play at the elegant new Plymouth Theatre, but later she was not able to remember the building very well.

INDEFINITE

Since my grandfather was a doctor, it is not surprising that I have chosen *that* for a career. [The antecedent of *that* is only vaguely implied.]

CLEAR

Since my grandfather was a doctor, it is not surprising that I have chosen medicine for my career.

It is usually awkward to have a pronoun refer to an antecedent in a subordinate position, such as the object of a preposition. The reader will instinctively associate a pronoun with the most prominent substantive in the clause he has just read. The result is confusion—possibly a momentary confusion but still an undesirable one.

CONFUSING

Men have lounged and crouched around their fires; they have been the companions of their dreams and meditations. [The reader will hesitate when he comes to ''they have,'' because he will assume that the subject of the sentence is still ''men.'']

CLEAR

Men have lounged and crouched around their fires, which have been the companions of their dreams and meditations.

OR

Men have lounged and crouched around their fires—the companions of their dreams and meditations.

As long as they occur close together in the same sentence, a pronoun and its "antecedent" may change places, the pronoun coming first.

408

27. *REFERENCE OF PRONOUNS*

E X A M P L E

Although she was an attractive woman who could have made herself beautiful, Maria disdained to wear makeup or have her hair styled.

27b. The reference of a pronoun should not be ambiguous.

A M B I G U O U S

The title of the book was so dramatic that *it* was a great help in remembering *it*. [Does the first *it* refer to the title, or to the drama of the title? Does the second *it* refer to the book, or to the title of the book?]

C L E A R

I remembered that book easily because of its dramatic title.

A M B I G U O U S

The players and umpires know one another well and sometimes they call them by their first names.

C L E A R

Players who know umpires well sometimes call them by their first names.

A M B I G U O U S

Mr. Beamis told his brother that he did not yet know the situation thoroughly.

C L E A R

As Mr. Beamis admitted to his brother, he did not yet know the situation thoroughly.

O R

Mr. Beamis charged his brother with not knowing the situation thoroughly.

It is clumsy to resort to a parenthetic repetition of the antecedent after a pronoun.

A W K W A R D

Mr. Beamis told his brother that he (Mr. Beamis) did not yet know the situation thoroughly.

409

27

27c. In formal writing, the indefinite reference is less common than in informal writing and in speech.

We are here referring to two particular situations: (1) the use of the indefinite *you* to mean *one, a person* and the indefinite *they* to mean *people,* and (2) the use of *this, that,* and *which* to refer to a clause, sentence, or a general idea.

1. The indefinite *you* and *they* are common in speech and in many forms of informal writing; they are less appropriate in formal writing. The student should guard against making their use a habit, especially in papers of explanation.

F O R M A L
First the seed is scattered evenly over the ground; then the soil is raked lightly and firmed with a roller. [Note the passive voice here.]

I N F O R M A L
First you scatter the seed; then you rake it in and firm the soil with a roller. [Or "First scatter the seed; then rake it in and firm the soil with a roller." *You* is understood.]

F O R M A L
When a soldier salutes, he must stand up straight and bring his right hand up smartly to the visor of his cap.

I N F O R M A L
When saluting, you must stand up straight and bring your right hand up smartly to the visor of your cap.

F O R M A L
In the army, a soldier does not ask; he obeys.

I N F O R M A L
In the army, you do not ask; you do what you are told.

2. A pronoun may have a clause or a sentence for its antecedent; it may even refer to a thought expressed by a part of the preceding sentence. As long as the reference is unmistakable, the sentence is clear. But the careless writer may fall into the habit of stringing together a series of *this-, that-,* and *which-* clauses without troubling himself about either clearness or ex-

410

actness. When the writer suspects the clearness or definiteness of an antecedent, he can sometimes summarize the idea of the clause referred to by an expression such as *this truth, this condition, a circumstance which,* and so forth. If the result is still unsatisfactory, he should rewrite the sentence.

Notice that the references are clear in the following sentences.

CLEAR

I have finished my work at last. That should satisfy the boss.

He recommended that I write to the secretary, which I did without delay.

If you have decided to speak out on this issue, it should be done quickly.

Now notice the vague references in the following sentences.

VAGUE

The antismoking campaign in England, which had such little effect, has cost a good deal of money and energy, and this leads to pessimism about our own campaign.

CLEAR

The costly and energetic antismoking campaign in England has had little effect, a result that leads to pessimism about our own campaign.

VAGUE

The fish are kept alive and fresh in glass tanks, and it also attracts people which helps the business considerably. [What do *it* and *which* refer to?]

CLEAR

The fish are kept alive and fresh in glass tanks. The display of live fish helps business by attracting people to the place.

27d. The careless use of *same, such, above,* and *said* as reference words often produces an awkward sentence.

These words are used as reference words in legal or technical writing; in ordinary writing they should be avoided, not be-

411

27

cause they are incorrect but because they usually lead to awkwardness of expression. Use one of the common pronouns (*it, them, this*) or the name of the thing to which you refer.

P O O R

I stood there holding the monkey wrench and oil can in my hands. The foreman ordered me to return the same to the engine room.

B E T T E R

I stood there holding the monkey wrench and oil can in my hands. The foreman ordered me to return the tools to the engine room.

P O O R

The significance of said decision is not yet fully comprehended.

B E T T E R

The significance of this decision is not yet fully comprehended.

P O O R

Please return same to me by bearer.

B E T T E R

Please return it [or name the object] to me by the bearer of this note.

P O O R

The above is a complete refutation of their arguments.

B E T T E R

The facts mentioned completely refute their arguments.

27e. **A pronoun should agree with its antecedent in number, gender, and person.**

For a discussion of the agreement of pronouns, see §4i.

P O O R

Every student is required to bring their books.

B E T T E R

Every student is required to bring his (or her) books.

412

POOR

A team that loses most of its games may owe its failure to the fact that they do not have a good coach. [You must be consistent. If you begin by considering *team* as singular, you must continue to refer to it as one unit.]

BETTER

A team that loses most of its games may owe its failure to its lack of a good coach. [Or, more simply, ''may owe its failure to poor coaching.'']

27f. It is usually considered awkward to begin an essay with a reference to the title.

It is better to repeat the words of your title, in your first sentence, than it is to refer to your title with a pronoun. For example, if your title is "Coming About in a Small Boat," do not begin your paper, "This is difficult for the beginning sailor to learn." Say instead, "The beginning sailor will have some difficulty learning how to come about in a small boat." (The writer would do well, in fact, to lead up to a reference to his subject with a more intriguing opening altogether. This one is flat. When taking an essay test, however, in which the question must be incorporated in the answer, and where there is little time for stylistic nicety, the first sentence of the response might well rephrase the question as a beginning for the argument.)

EXERCISE

EXERCISE, FAULTY REFERENCE. *In each of the following sentences underline the pronoun or pronouns with faulty reference. Rewrite each sentence so as to correct the error.*

1. The baggage was loaded onto a small handcart which was the only way to get it through the crowded station.
2. I worked for the college physics department last year, washing equipment for them and cleaning their laboratories.
3. He told me all about it, and very well too. It was something I would like to have done myself.

4. The history of this community goes back to the seventeenth century which makes a visit well worth while.
5. The obligations of an army sergeant are that of any leader in a small group.
6. While a person would suppose that she wanted nothing else in life, you could be very wrong about this.
7. The wealth of the country is controlled by a few who live in the city, which is usual in such societies.
8. Every player must learn his signals which will make an efficient and coordinated team.
9. He laughed at what I had said. This was amazing.
10. Everybody knows the reason why the economy is in such poor shape. It is a source of dismay to us all.

§ 28. PROPER ARRANGEMENT

The parts of a sentence should be so arranged that the meaning of the sentence is clear at the first reading.

Since English is not a highly inflected language (i.e., not one in which words change form to reflect grammatical relations), the meaning of an English sentence depends largely on the arrangement of the words in it. The reader naturally assumes that the parts of a sentence that are placed next to each other are logically related to each other. You must therefore be careful to arrange words in a sentence in such a way that its meaning will be clear on the first reading. The rule that will guide you may be stated in two parts: (1) place all modifiers, whether words, phrases, or clauses, as close as possible to the words they modify; (2) avoid placing these elements near other words they might be taken to modify.

28a. In formal writing, place adverbs logically.

Let us use *only* as an illustration of what happens when idiom contradicts logic. Logically, an adverb should be placed near the word it modifies; idiomatically, it is often placed elsewhere. For instance, would you say, "We have room for only two

414

more," or, "We only have room for two more"? The person with a logical mind says that "only" modifies "two"; the person who prefers the second form answers that idiom does not pay much attention to logic. Both forms are used. The second is used generally in speech, in a great deal of informal writing, and often in formal writing. The first is used by writers and speakers who are disturbed by the logic of the second. No statistical study of the incidence of each form in formal writing has been made.

28

The same explanation applies to *not*. Compare "Not everyone can be first" and "Everyone cannot be first." Logic sanctions the first form; idiom sanctions the second form—at least in speech and informal writing.

Only slightly less controversial is the placing of several other adverbs, such as *hardly, just, almost, nearly, merely, scarcely.*

COMMON IN SPEECH

He *only* worked half a day.

Everyone is *not* honest.

The child *hardly* ate any food.

She *just* took one apple.

He *almost* weeded the whole garden.

MORE LOGICAL AND PREFERRED BY MANY

He worked *only* half a day.

Not everyone is honest.

The child ate *hardly* any food.

She took *just* one apple.

He weeded *almost* the whole garden.

28b. **Avoid ambiguous placement of phrases.**

There is no exact position in a sentence that phrases must always occupy; the best rule to follow is to keep them away from words they must *not* be understood to modify. The result of such misplacement is often unintentionally humorous.

MISPLACED

He began to lose his desire to reach the summit *after a time.*

415

28

BETTER

After a time he began to lose his desire to reach the summit.

MISPLACED

I was dressed and ready to start climbing *within an hour.* [Does the phrase refer to *being dressed* or to *starting to climb*?]

BETTER

Within an hour I was dressed and ready to start climbing. [*Or*] I was dressed *within an hour* and ready to start climbing.

28c. Avoid ambiguous placement of clauses.

Clauses, like phrases, may be placed wherever they seem to fit in a sentence—except near words they can be mistaken to modify.

AMBIGUOUS OR LUDICROUS

I hid the ring in my pocket *that I intended to give to her.*

BETTER

The ring *that I intended to give to her* I hid in my pocket. [*Or*] I hid in my pocket the ring *that I intended to give to her.*

28d. Avoid squinting modifiers.

Modifiers so placed in a sentence that they may be understood with either the preceding or the following words are called *squinting modifiers.* As a rule, it is better not to try to cure the fault by means of punctuation.

SQUINTING

I firmly decided *the next day* to start studying.

CLEAR

I firmly decided to start studying *the next day.*

SQUINTING

After we had stopped at a service station *with the help of the attendant* we found our position on the map.

416

CLEAR

After we had stopped at a service station, the attendant helped us to locate our position on the map.

SQUINTING

The girl who had sat down *quickly* opened her textbook.

CLEAR

The girl who had sat down opened her textbook *quickly*.

28e. Use the split infinitive only to avoid awkwardness.

Placing an adverbial modifier between the sign *to* and the verb of an infinitive results in what is traditionally known as a "split infinitive" ("to quickly walk" *splits* the infinitive *to walk;* "to walk quickly" is a better arrangement). The split infinitive is no longer considered one of the capital crimes of composition—if it ever was. It is not true that the parts of an infinitive are inseparable. But since a split infinitive still causes many persons (especially composition instructors) discomfort, it is better not to split infinitives too rashly or promiscuously. A good rule to follow is this: place the adverbial modifier between *to* and the verb of an infinitive only when such an arrangement is necessary to avoid an awkward phrase. Here are some examples: "to even wish," "to seriously cripple," "to further confirm," "to utterly forget," "to further complicate," "to first consider." Remember that these are exceptions to the rule.

28f. Avoid the awkward separation of any words that normally belong near each other.

Words that usually belong near each other are subject and verb, verb and object, the parts of a verb phrase, noun and adjective modifier, and noun and appositive.

AWKWARD

Justice Holmes, in a brilliantly written interpretation of the Fourteenth Amendment, dissented. [Subject and verb split by long phrase]

28

BETTER

Justice Holmes dissented in a brilliantly written interpretation of the Fourteenth Amendment.

AWKWARD

Finally, we caught, after sitting in our rowboat for four hours, a small salmon. [Verb and object split]

BETTER

Finally, after sitting in our rowboat for four hours, we caught a small salmon.

AWKWARD

After it got dark, the girls bedded down beside a stream, wet, tired, and discouraged.

BETTER

After it got dark, the wet, tired, and discouraged girls bedded down beside a stream. [*Or*] After it got dark, the girls—wet, tired, and discouraged—bedded down beside a stream.

EXERCISES

EXERCISE 1, ELIMINATING SPLIT INFINITIVES. *Improve each of the following sentences by eliminating an awkward split infinitive.*

1. I hope to some day in the near future visit Paris again.
2. You should now begin to methodically and carefully budget your time for study.
3. If you care to remain in college, you must plan to quickly change your habits.
4. Your first concern should be to not carelessly waste your time.
5. If you really care to materially improve your grades, you should promise to immediately give up your trips to the city.

EXERCISE 2, CORRECTING MISPLACED ELEMENTS. *Point out the misplaced element in each of the following sentences. Then show how the sentence can be improved. Do not use punctuation as a means of correcting an error in arrangement.*

29

1. We decided at nine o'clock to call him at his home.
2. Taking too many vitamin pills frequently causes bad effects.
3. Her dropped parcels were collected before any had been stepped on by the bus driver.
4. The fullback returned to the team after two days' absence on Friday.
5. Father, not wishing to prolong the argument far into the night, agreed.
6. To be misunderstood often is the fate of an original poet.
7. The departing train brought thoughts of distant friends to the poor girl rumbling over the high bridge.
8. Our teacher has many theories about things that are different.
9. The sheriff was stabbed while sleeping by an unknown person.
10. He needs someone to show him how to put his affairs in order badly.

§ 29. DANGLING OR MISRELATED MODIFIERS

29a. Awkward dangling modifiers should be avoided.

At present there is considerable difference of opinion among educated people over the use of what is traditionally known as the "dangling modifier." Some say that it should be called the "misrelated modifier," for instead of dangling it actually attaches itself too easily to the wrong word. When it does, especially when it results in confusion or in unintentional humor, it is bad. When it calls attention to itself and away from the intended meaning of the sentence, it is bad. One might add that it is wrong because so many educated persons have been taught to regard it as a careless way of writing.

Here are some examples of dangling participles, the most common error in this category. Notice that the phrasing often results in unintentionally ludicrous meanings.

Walking along the quiet street, the houses looked old and comfortable.

While waiting for the coffee to warm, the cereal boiled away.

419

29

Strewn on the floor in clumsy piles, he glanced idly through the remains of his books.

I had a summer job that year, thereby enabling me to return to school. [This is more awkward than plain wrong. Who or what enabled me to return to school?]

In addition to participles, infinitives are sometimes left dangling. The problem here is that there is no visible subject of the infinitive in the sentence.

To see this view properly, the sun must be shining. [Does the sun see the view?]

To succeed as a businessman, the basic facts of economics are apparently not always necessary.

In each of these sentences, it does not matter whether the phrase dangles because it is not attached where it should be or is misrelated because it attaches itself where it should not be. Each sentence is awkward or misleading, to say the least.

A dangler may be corrected in three ways: (1) by changing the phrase to a clause, (2) by providing a noun or pronoun to which the dangler can properly attach itself, or (3) by reordering the sentence.

EXAMPLES

As I walked along the quiet street, the houses looked old and comfortable.

While I waited for the coffee to warm, the cereal boiled away.

He glanced idly through the remains of his books, which were strewn on the floor in clumsy piles.

The money I made on a summer job that year enabled me to return to school.

To appreciate this view properly, one should see it when the sun is shining.

In order to succeed as a businessman, it is apparently not always necessary to know the basic facts of economics.

Note that the absolute phrase does not dangle. In the absolute phrase the word that the participle attaches itself to is in the phrase itself.

420

E X A M P L E S

The day's work being over, we returned to town.

The guests having arrived, Mother went to the door.

Three more girls, their wet hair plastered down over their eyes, stumbled into the classroom.

29

It may be helpful to think of the participle as a kind of preposition in such sentences as these:

Considering the size of the house, it seemed remarkably cheap.

Judging by his voting record, he is a responsible congressman.

A slight shift in phraseology, however, produces a dangler, even though the meaning is essentially unchanged:

Viewing his voting record, he is a responsible congressman. [The sentence suggests that the congressman is responsible, and he is viewing his voting record.]

Certain idiomatic phrases, especially those that express a general action and those that serve as directive and transitional links, are always acceptable in either formal or informal situations. These are phrases like *generally speaking, looking at it from another point of view, taking everything into consideration, provided that, failing,* and others that are similar.

E X A M P L E S

Failing agreement, the meeting was adjourned.

Generally speaking, the worse a pun is, the better it is.

29b. **A sentence with any sort of expression, such as a phrase or an appositive, that is not easily understood with the rest of the sentence is awkward and usually misleading.**

I L L O G I C A L

A gentleman farmer, his wardrobe ranges from faultlessly tailored suits to four-buckle rubber boots. [The expression *a gentleman farmer* seems to be in apposition with *wardrobe.*]

421

29

REVISED

As he is a gentleman farmer, his wardrobe ranges from faultlessly tailored suits to four-buckle rubber boots.

ILLOGICAL

After five years in a city school, a country school presents many problems in adjustment. [One naturally associates the opening phrase with *a country school.*]

REVISED

A person who has spent five years in a city school encounters many problems in adjustment when he goes to a country school.

The dangling or misrelated modifier, it can be seen from the examples offered, is a stylistic mistake. If it causes confusion, even momentary confusion, or if it is associated with an unintentionally humorous image, it is undesirable.

EXERCISE

EXERCISE, CORRECTING DANGLERS. *Some of the following sentences are correct, while some contain objectionable danglers. Pick out the faulty sentences and correct them.*

1. Buying her ticket at the box office, she walked into the opera house.
2. While waiting to be seated, the usher approached her.
3. He delayed taking her ticket, thus causing a small traffic jam.
4. Seated at last, she glanced through her program.
5. The opera, based vaguely on Shakespeare, was the famous *Falstaff.*
6. One of Italy's most beloved composers, the music was by Verdi.
7. The curtain having gone up at last, she sat back in her seat feeling thoroughly relaxed.
8. While sitting there quietly, the stage exploded with excitement.
9. To see an opera at its best, the scenery too must be appreciated.

422

10. Rising at the intermission, she strolled into the outer lobby.
11. She heard a familiar voice, thereby meeting an old friend.
12. Being an old opera lover, they got along famously.
13. When young, the opera had seemed too complicated.
14. Now, however, having matured, she enjoyed almost all performances.
15. Returning home in a taxi, the music of Verdi still seemed to sing in her ears.

30

§ 30. EMPHASIS IN THE SENTENCE

The relative importance of ideas in a sentence may be shown by various devices of structure. The principle used is known as *emphasis*.

Emphasis is a word that may be understood in more than one sense. A speaker may emphasize his words by shouting or screaming them; a writer may emphasize words by indicating that they be printed in italics or capitals. Some writers and speakers have used these methods. But that is not the sense in which we use the word here. By *emphasis* we mean using rhetorical devices that show the relative importance or prominence of ideas and details in a sentence or paragraph. Some of these devices we have discussed elsewhere in connection with other qualities of good writing—clarity, directness, order, coherence, conciseness, directness. Two or three others will be pointed out here and in the following sections.

It may be useful to restate the various devices by which the relative importance of ideas can be shown:

1. By placing the important idea by itself in a short sentence.
2. By placing the idea in a main clause of a complex sentence.
3. By changing the usual order of a sentence. [Sympathy I did not want!]
4. By using parallel structure. [See § 32.]
5. By using the order of climax.

423

6. By repeating key words. [See §25a.]
7. By using the active instead of the passive voice.
8. By giving an important idea fuller treatment.
9. By placing important words in prominent positions.
10. By using periodic structure.

30

30a. Placing important words in the important positions in the sentence will help to show the relative importance of ideas.

The most conspicuous positions in a sentence of some length are the beginning and the end. These are the positions that should be used for ideas that deserve attention and emphasis. The less important details, the modifiers, the qualifying comments should be tucked away inside the sentence.

WEAK

The student who cheats in an examination is cheating only himself ultimately.

BETTER

The student who cheats in an examination is ultimately cheating only himself.

WEAK

Public speaking should be taught in freshman English, I think.

BETTER

Public speaking, I think, should be taught in freshman English.

No writer can consistently rearrange his sentences to begin and end them with important ideas. Many sentences are so short that the reader's mind comprehends them as units. In many others the word order is determined by the nature of the English language. A writer may occasionally construct a sentence such as this—as Stephen Leacock once did—"Him they elected president," but in sentences such as the following no problems of emphasis can arise: "He is a good man." "Her son was killed in Vietnam." "The day's work is done." "The President saluted the flag."

424

30b. Occasionally you may express a thought more effectively by changing a sentence from the loose to the periodic form.

A *periodic sentence* is one in which the main idea is held until the end; a *loose sentence* is one in which the main idea is followed by details and modifiers. The effect of a periodic sentence is one of suspense—that is, the reader is asked to wait for the main idea until he has comprehended the details upon which the main idea is based or by which it is limited or changed. Not all sentences in English are periodic; a large majority of them, in fact, are loose. It is precisely for this reason that an occasional periodic sentence is emphatic.

30

LOOSE

In recent years many factories were established in the city, especially plants engaged in the manufacture of brass products.

PERIODIC

In recent years many factories, especially plants engaged in the manufacture of brass products, were established in the city.

LOOSE

Stop talking if you have nothing more to say.

PERIODIC

If you have nothing more to say, stop talking.

LOOSE

It is of course impractical to legislate for those who will behave themselves while completely ignoring those who will not.

PERIODIC

To legislate for those who will behave themselves while completely ignoring those who will not is, of course, impractical.

The periodic effect, one of suspense, of waiting, is not limited to sentences in which the dependent clauses all come before the main clause. Note the following two sentences:

Metaphors are so vital a part of our speech, so common and used so unconsciously, that they become, as William Empson has indicated,

425

the normal mode of development of a language. And it is the incalculable reach of the image—the establishment of a kinship between unrelated objects, the combination of exactness and ambiguity—which is its charm and power.

—Louis Untermeyer, "Play in Poetry"

30

Then note the way a writer creates suspense by using a summarizing main clause with *all* or *such:*

To transfer admiration from the thing possessed to its possessor; to conceive that the mere possession of material wealth makes of its possessor a proper object of worship; to feel abject before another who is wealthier—such emotions do not so much as enter the American mind.

—Hilaire Belloc

30c. Use the active instead of the passive voice where the active is more direct and natural.

The use of the passive voice is not in itself a grammatical or stylistic fault; it is the *overuse* of it that is a fault. The passive voice has several proper and necessary uses: (1) when the object or receiver of the action of the verb is more important than the doer; (2) when the doer of the action is not known; (3) when the writer wishes to place the emphasis on the receiver instead of on the doer.

To the satisfaction of everyone, Grabowski was chosen best player of the tournament.
Several priceless old manuscripts were destroyed.
The wounded prisoner was dragged into the trench.

Then note the difference in the following sentences when the active voice replaces the passive:

PASSIVE
A good time was had by all.
Then a driver's test was taken by me.
A period of weightlessness is endured by the astronaut.

426

ACTIVE

Everyone had a good time.

Then I took a driver's test.

The astronaut endures a period of weightlessness.

30

EXERCISES

EXERCISE 1, EMPHASIS. *Using the principle of emphasis by position, improve the following sentences.*

1. A fool can ask more questions than a wise man can answer, according to the Italian proverb.
2. Long sentences in a short theme are like large rooms in a small house, the professor explained.
3. Generally speaking it is well not to speak generally, as someone has said.
4. Generally speaking, one good teacher is worth a dozen good books.
5. When in danger or in doubt, run in circles, scream and shout, the sergeant advised.

EXERCISE 2, LOOSE AND PERIODIC SENTENCES. *Change the following loose sentences to periodic sentences.*

1. Stress has a harmful effect on our ability to learn, it was discovered by these experiments.
2. For this experiment two control groups were selected who had the same ability to memorize.
3. One group was told that its scores were poor after they had completed about half the test.
4. Their performance at once deteriorated when the testing was resumed.
5. But their ability improved considerably after they had been praised for their improved performance.

EXERCISE 3, ACTIVE OR PASSIVE VERBS. *Improve the following sentences by changing the verb from the passive to the active.*

1. The skidding car was brought safely to a stop by the alert driver.

427

31

2. The policeman's warning was accepted by her with humility.
3. I thought that she would be nervous and tearful, but a very different reaction was observed by me.
4. As she informed me, a set of new tires had been bought by her husband a few days ago.
5. But the need for new tires, she said, was vetoed by her.
6. Instead, the new tires were returned to the dealer and a new guitar was purchased with the money by her.
7. "Do you think now that a new guitar is worth your life?" was asked by the officer.
8. The workings of a careless person's mind cannot be understood by more cautious people.
9. After a few minutes the trip to our destination was resumed by us.
10. Glancing up at the rear-view mirror, it was observed that the woman's car was now following us.

§ 31. SHIFT IN POINT OF VIEW

Any unnecessary and illogical shift in point of view should be avoided.

In §40, we consider problems of consistency in point of view that involve fairly large matters of style. There we take up the *position* in time and space chosen by the writer, his *tone* toward his reader (including his consistent use of formal or colloquial language), and his *attitude* toward his subject. Here we consider some smaller, largely grammatical dangers—but they are just as important as the larger questions in the completion of a polished essay.

Three common grammatical shifts in point of view are (1) from active to passive voice, (2) from past to present tense, and (3) from *one* to *you* and similar shifts of person. These and other shifts are described below. Writing is both clearer and more pleasing if you maintain your point of view, unless, of course, you have some logical reason for changing to another.

31a. Unnecessary shifts from active to passive voice are undesirable.

S H I F T

You wrap the bundle carefully in paper; it is then tied securely.

We were acquainted with his brother, and his eighty-year-old father
was also well known to us.

B E T T E R

You wrap the bundle carefully in paper and tie it securely.

We knew both his brother and his eighty-year-old father.

31b. Needless shifts in tense—from past to present or from
present to past—are usually objectionable.

See also §6.

S H I F T

I *go* right on into the room and then *looked* around me to see what he
would be doing with all that furniture. [Such shifts in tense must be
watched for especially in narrative accounts.]

B E T T E R

I *went* right on into the room and then *looked* around me to see what he
might be doing with all that furniture. [Or *might have done* with all that
furniture]

S H I F T

After *planning* the trip I *had thought* I *deserved* a little credit for its success.

B E T T E R

After *having planned* the trip, I *thought* I *deserved* a little credit for its
success. [All verbs in past tense]

31c. Needless shifts in number or person should be avoided.

S H I F T

If one really wishes to sample fine cooking, try that restaurant on the
corner.

31

CORRECT IN FORMAL CONTEXT

If one really wishes to sample superior cooking, he [or *he or she*] should try the restaurant on the corner.

CORRECT IN INFORMAL STYLE

If you really want to try some good eating, try that restaurant on the corner.

See also §27e for a discussion of number in pronouns.

31d. A writer should guard against mixing two distinctly separate constructions in a sentence.

A *mixed construction* is usually the result of hasty and careless writing. The writer begins one construction, and immediately, without troubling himself to look back on what he has written, continues with another construction.

MIXED

In our basement we found a small wood stove, which upon removing the front, made it resemble a fireplace. [*Which* refers to *stove.* The stove cannot remove its own front, nor can the stove make itself resemble anything.]

CLEAR

In our basement we found a small wood stove, which we made into a fireplace by removing its front.

In our basement we found a small wood stove. By removing its front, we made it resemble a fireplace.

MIXED

She did not say a word, but took me to the back yard in what seemed to me a bit hurriedly. [The writer has forgotten his original intention. He could say either *took me in what seemed a hurried manner* or *took me a bit hurriedly.*]

Occasionally a writer will run an independent clause into a sentence in such a way that it appears to stand as the subject of a verb.

430

31. *SHIFT IN POINT OF VIEW*

MIXED

We were tired of traveling is the main reason we came here.

I was all alone was what truly frightened me.

CLEAR

We came here mainly because we were tired of traveling.

What truly frightened me was that I was all alone.

31e. Mixed figures of speech are inappropriate in serious writing.

In the teaching of writing, warnings against scrambled metaphors may have been given an undeserved and an unfortunate prominence. A *mixed metaphor* is often a sign of mental vitality. It is surely a lesser literary crime than page after page of dull and uninspired prose. If you scramble two incongruous images, you probably need little more than a hint to show you that your metaphors are inappropriate. It is unthinkingly comic to speak of "watering the spark of originality," or "blazing a trail over the sea of knowledge," or "being blinded by a thirst for revenge." Even Shakespeare spoke of taking up arms against a sea of troubles.

The following samples illustrate more clearly what is meant by "mixed imagery."

Many high-school athletes think they can ride on their high-school laurels right into a position on the college team. [How can one ride on a laurel?]

The future of jazz was at its lowest ebb. [Even were the future not transported to the past, a rare feat in itself, how could a future ebb?]

Instead of narrowly pursuing the mechanics of grammar, the clever teacher will often digress into anecdotes which will make the class fairly rock with laughter. [Can "mechanics" be pursued, either narrowly or broadly?]

A college education enables the graduate to meet the snares and pitfalls of life with a broader point of view.

EXERCISES

31

EXERCISE 1, ILLOGICAL SHIFTS. *In each of the following sentences specify the type or types of illogical shift that you find—in tense, voice, number, or person. Then make the necessary corrections.*

1. The submarine *Seashark* goes down in April of 1973, and many scientists participated in the investigation that followed.
2. They conducted research from several ships; also a survey of the ocean bottom was made.
3. One would suppose the task would have been easy, since all you have to do is find the hull on the ocean floor.
4. The scientific group had its hands full, however, for they could discover no trace of the missing craft.
5. The Navy called off its search in September; they had done all they could.
6. New efforts have been undertaken by private scientific organizations and universities have continued research into the mishap.
7. Until late 1974, no one knows just where the ship is lying— you would have been amazed to learn how the discovery was finally made.
8. A bathysphere is ordered; it has been at work for some time on the scene.
9. No doubt many scientists on the project would prefer to return to shore as a laboratory researcher.
10. In the process, however, the ocean floor in the area has been fully investigated, which had been useful for future oceanographers.

EXERCISE 2, MIXED CONSTRUCTIONS. *Here are ten badly confused sentences. Rewrite them. Do not be afraid to break them up if they can be improved in that manner.*

1. You could view that painting as a complex pattern of colors or as an amateur who knows very little about art.
2. They had a magnificent wedding which I regret to say they never asked me to come.
3. The table was made of inlaid wood and a source of admiration to all who saw it.

4. Everybody considered her a beauty that she was an ornament to the community.
5. The dean said he believed in a straightforward, middle-of-the-road, thoroughly well-rounded plan of education which everyone ought to have the opportunity.
6. Industriousness has always been a bad point with me due to my time has always been so preoccupied with fun.
7. He looked bravely into the eye of the future with a brisk and unfaltering step.
8. The reason things are at such a low ebb is because of the inevitable swing of the economic pendulum.
9. Sometimes you see a student reading comfortably in the library and looks as if he has fallen asleep as indeed he has.
10. Anyone who writes sentences like these that thinks he can write English ought to know better.

32

§ 32. PARALLEL STRUCTURE

32a. Parallel structure expresses similar ideas in the same grammatical and rhetorical patterns.

Parallel structure is primarily a rhetorical device that writers use to give their sentences force, clearness, grace, and rhythm. In its more elementary uses it gives sentences greater clarity and smoothness. For a more complete discussion of rhetorical uses of parallelism and balance, turn to Section II, Chapter 2. Here are two examples from the works of writers to whom style is important:

Then she would fill the page
with recommendations and suggestions,
with criticisms of the minutest details of organisation,
with elaborate calculations of contingencies,
with exhaustive analyses and statistical statements piled up in breathless eagerness one on the top of the other.
And then her pen, in the virulence of its volubility, would rush on
to the discussion of individuals,
to the denunciation of an incompetent surgeon or the ridicule of a self-sufficient nurse.

—LYTTON STRACHEY, *Eminent Victorians*

433

32

The city [New York] at last perfectly illustrates both
|| the universal dilemma and
|| the general solution,
this riddle in steel and stone is at once
|| the perfect target and
|| the perfect demonstration || of nonviolence,
|| of racial brotherhood,
this lofty target || scraping the skies and
|| meeting the destroying planes halfway,
|| home of || all people and
|| all nations,
|| capital of everything,
housing the deliberations by which || the planes are to be stayed
|| and their errand forestalled.

—E. B. WHITE, *Here Is New York*

In its simpler and more elementary form, parallel structure is a balancing of noun with noun, an infinitive with another infinitive, a phrase with another phrase, and a clause with another clause. Used at this level, the device will cure many a deformed or wandering sentence:

AWKWARD

Sororities teach a girl to be a friend and courteous. [Noun paralleled with adjective]

PARALLEL IN FORM

Sororities teach a girl to be || *friendly* and
|| *courteous.*
[Adjective || adjective]

AWKWARD

Our English teacher asked us to close our books, to take pen and paper, and that we were to write a short theme. [Two infinitives and a clause]

PARALLEL IN FORM

Our English teacher asked us || *to close our books,*
|| *to take pen and paper,* and
|| *to write a short theme.*
[Infinitive || infinitive || infinitive]

434

32. *PARALLEL STRUCTURE*

AWKWARD

Few of the leaders anticipated the bitterness of the strike or how long it would last. [A noun and a clause]

PARALLEL IN FORM

Few of the leaders anticipated || *the bitterness* or
the duration of the strike.
[Noun||noun]

35b. Avoid the *and who* and the *and which* constructions.

The "and who" or "and which" fault, as it is called, consists of using *and who* or *and which* in a sentence that does not have a preceding *who* or *which* clause.

FAULTY

He is a man of wide experience *and who* is also very popular with the farmers.

PARALLEL

He is a man of || wide experience and
great popularity among the farmers.

FAULTY

I am interested in electronics, because it is a new field *and which* offers interesting opportunities to one who knows science.

PARALLEL

I am interested in electronics, || which is a new field and
which offers interesting
opportunities . . .

32c. Avoid the false parallel.

Straining for parallelism where it is not natural is a fault that occurs rarely in college writing. The false parallel, however, is not the result of too much care for form; it is purely accidental.

ILLOGICAL

I finally realized that my daydreaming was not making me happy, intelligent, or friends. [The three words seem to depend on *making*

435

me, but two of them are adjectives and one is a noun. They are not logically parallel.]

32

REVISED

I finally realized that my daydreaming was not making me happy and intelligent or bringing me friends.

Parallel forms may be used with the correlative conjunctions *both—and, either—or, neither—nor, not only—but also.* Care should be taken in placing these correlatives so that the intended meaning of the sentence is not obscured.

EXERCISES

EXERCISE 1, PARALLEL FORM. *In the following sentences under-line the parts that should be expressed in parallel form. Then revise each sentence.*

1. Professor Macy is a middle-aged woman, short, stocky, blue eyes, and partly gray-haired.
2. Her lectures are witty, interesting and she outlines them carefully.
3. She told us that we should read our text and to write a short review of it.
4. The book is interesting and I can learn from it.
5. Ms. Macy said she would give us a quiz on the first chapter and for us to review it carefully.

EXERCISE 2, FALSE PARALLELS. *In the following sentences correct the faulty use of correlatives.*

1. My summer's work proved not only interesting but I also learned much from it.
2. I wondered whether I should continue with it or should I return to college.
3. My boss was not only pleasant but he was also generous.
4. A college education was both necessary and I could afford it.
5. Not only was I getting older fast, but I also planned to be married soon.

§ 33. COMPARISONS

33a. In standard formal English, comparisons should be logical and complete.

Written English, especially formal written English, requires a logic and a precision in expressing comparisons that is often lacking in loose, informal speech. In informal speech certain elliptical or illogical comparisons have become idiomatic. Some of these shortened comparisons, or illogical comparisons, are becoming more and more common in *both formal and informal* writing; as in other cases of divided usage, the choice made by the student should be based on an understanding of the facts of usage.

1. In informal writing do not omit than *or as* in a double comparison.

USUALLY INAPPROPRIATE IN FORMAL USAGE
The bus is about as fast if not faster than the train.
Football coaches earn as much if not more than college presidents.
California is now as populous, if not more populous than New York.

LOGICAL BUT AWKWARD
The bus is about as fast as, if not faster than, the train.
Football coaches earn as much as, if not more than, college presidents.
California is now as populous as, if not more populous than, New York.

The last three examples illustrate what is often called the *suspended construction*. Some writers use it; others object to it because of its awkwardness. It can be easily avoided.

LOGICAL AND SMOOTH
The bus is about as fast as the train, if not faster.
Football coaches earn as much as college presidents, if not more.
California is now as populous as New York, if not more so.

33

2. Avoid ambiguity in making comparisons.

AMBIGUOUS

I saw more of him than Jones. ["more than Jones did" or "more than I saw of Jones"?]

CLEAR

I saw more of him than I saw of Jones. [Or *more of him than Jones did*]

AMBIGUOUS

Our country helped France more than England.

CLEAR

Our country helped France more than England did. [Or *more than our country helped England*]

3. Do not omit other *after* than *or as* in comparing two members of the same group or class.

MISLEADING

Ms. Jenkins is more literate than any woman in the class. [If Ms. Jenkins is not a member of the class, the sentence is clear. If she *is* in the class, she cannot be more literate than herself.]

CLEAR

Ms. Jenkins is more literate than any other woman in the class.

BETTER

Ms. Jenkins is the most literate woman in the class.

4. Finish your comparisons so that you will not seem to be comparing something that you do not intend to compare.

MISLEADING

The salary of an English teacher is lower than a lawyer. [Are you comparing salaries, or are you comparing salary and lawyer?]

CLEAR

The salary of an English teacher is lower than that of a lawyer. [The *that* here completes the comparison and also avoids needless repetition of *salary*.]

MISLEADING

The duties and responsibilities of a traffic officer are more complex than a game warden.

33

CLEAR

The duties and responsibilities of a traffic officer are more complex than those of a game warden. [Name the second term of the comparison.]

33b. **In standard English, comparisons are completed except when the missing term of the comparison can be easily supplied by the reader.**

NOT CLEAR

It is easier to remain silent when attacks are made upon the things one loves. [Easier than what?]

CLEAR

It is easier to remain silent when attacks are made upon the things one loves than to risk criticism by defending them.

NOT CLEAR

Students who live in a dormitory do better work. [Better than students who live where?]

CLEAR

Students who live in dormitories do better work than those who room in apartments. [Or *who live in fraternity houses*].

There are, however, many idiomatic expressions in which an unfinished comparison is easily understood, such as "It is always better to tell the truth"; "we thought it wiser to agree." No misunderstanding is possible in statements like these. The uncompleted superlative is also used, especially in speech, and its sense is not that of a comparison but of an intensive, as in: "She is the *most* unselfish woman," "he is a *most* peculiar man."

EXERCISE

EXERCISE, COMPARISONS. *Revise the comparisons in the following sentences. Use the forms appropriate in standard written English.*

1. The snails of South America known as apple snails are as interesting if not more interesting than the allied *Pila* of the Old World.
2. Their shells are like apples, greener and rounder than other snails.
3. They are one of, if not the most amphibious kind of snail known to science.
4. Equipped with both gills and lungs, they are better swimmers than any snails.
5. When one compares the two types, the apple snail is clearly the best adapted to its environment.
6. The English periwinkle is as common if not more common than most other snails.
7. The lungs of the periwinkle are more developed than most other such sea animals.
8. Here the development of the lungs has reached a point higher than any place on earth.
9. Some snails can live as long if not longer than six months out of water.
10. Snails are the most fascinating animals; they are so attractive and varied in appearance.

§ 34. WORDS LEFT OUT

Words necessary for clearness should not be left out.

Two kinds of omissions need to be considered here. One is the result of carelessness. Its cure is careful proofreading. The second results from carrying speech habits into writing. We often speak in a more clipped or telegraphic manner than is permissible in writing, especially in serious and dignified writing on serious subjects.

The following are some of the omissions that need to be guarded against.

440

34. *WORDS LEFT OUT*

34a. Do not omit *that*.

MISLEADING

I soon observed nearly all the women, especially the young and pretty ones, were carrying strange little baskets. [Did he "observe the women, especially the young and pretty ones," or did he observe *that* the women were carrying baskets?]

He told me his story in its original version had been rejected by thirteen publishers. [Supply *that*. "He told me *that* his story . . ." The confusion is undesirable even if it is momentary.]

(Be careful, however, about needless repetition of *that,* as in: "He told me that there were numerous obscene magazines in that store, and that that troubled him." A useful correction would be: "He told me that there were numerous obscene magazines in Weston's [name the store], a situation which troubled him.")

34b. Do not omit part of a verb or of a verb phrase.

MISLEADING

The patient was given an anesthetic and the instruments made ready. [It is better to say *were made ready,* because *patient* is singular, and the verb *was,* which follows it, cannot be understood with *instruments made ready.* We need a plural verb.]

His ideas were progressive and adopted without debate. [Repeat *were.* The two verbs are not parallel. The first *were* is used as a main verb—*ideas were*—but the second *were* is an auxiliary verb—*were adopted. Progressive* is not part of the verb phrase.]

34c. Do not omit words required by the use of a noun or a verb in a double capacity.

AWKWARD

He never has and never will deceive a customer. [Supply *deceived* after *never has.* Although this sort of construction is common in speech, many people object to it in written English.]

This boy is one of the best, if not the best fullback I have ever watched. [Say *one of the best fullbacks.*]

441

34d. Do not omit necessary prepositions in idiomatic expressions.

INCOMPLETE

Spring term the course will be repeated for all new students. [Say *During the spring term. . . .*]

We must show our faith and devotion to our country. [Say *faith in. Faith to* is not idiomatic.]

Customers have neither respect nor faith in a merchant who cheats. [Say *respect for. Respect in* is not idiomatic.]

For a more complex sentence in which idiomatic prepositions are used with precise care, examine this sentence from John Galsworthy's "Some Platitudes Concerning Drama":

This third method requires a certain detachment; it requires a sympathy with, a love of, and a curiosity as to, things for their own sake; it requires a far view, together with patient industry, for no immediately practical results.

34e. Do not omit function words that indicate balanced and parallel constructions.

WEAK

He said that Communism had never had many adherents in the United States and there were fewer party members today than at any time since the Russian revolution.

STRENGTHENED

He said *that* Communism had never had many adherents in the United States and *that* there were fewer party members today than at any time since the Russian revolution.

WEAK

We thanked her for her kindness, which we had not always reciprocated, the stimulation we found in her classroom, and the long hours she had spent helping us with extracurricular activities.

STRENGTHENED

We thanked her *for* her kindness, which we had not always reciprocated, *for* the stimulation we found in her classroom, and *for* the long hours she had spent helping us with extracurricular activities.

EXERCISE

EXERCISE, MISSING WORDS. *Supply the missing words in the following sentences. Rearrange the wording wherever necessary.*

1. This student, I feel sure, never has and never will write a passing theme.
2. We visited one of the oldest, if not the oldest church in Vermont.
3. We noticed many churches were almost surrounded by graveyards.
4. He needed better evidence to prove his demands were justified.
5. Sundays more men studied their lessons than women.

§ 35. VARIETY

Variety in the length and the structure of sentences usually makes writing more effective.

A writer may avoid monotony of sentence structure by avoiding the following:
1. Beginning a series of sentences with the same word or the same subject.
2. Beginning a series of sentences with participial phrases.
3. Using the same sentence pattern in a group of sentences.
4. Beginning each of a series of sentences with the same kind of subordinate clause.

Here are some elementary examples of monotony. Notice the consistent shortness of the sentences, the unvaried vocabulary, and the needless repetition of sentence structure.

SHORT SENTENCES, ALL BEGINNING
WITH THE SUBJECT

Mrs. Helmer is a fine woman. She has always been most kind to me. I have appreciated her efforts in my behalf. She helped me find a summer job. I met a number of interesting people through her. She has always been a good friend of mine.

443

35

Waking up in the morning, I dressed quickly. Hurrying into the kitchen, I saw my mother at the stove. Pouring me a cup of coffee, she advised me not to delay. Gulping my coffee quickly, I began to collect my thoughts for the day ahead.

Few students should be guilty of such monotonous writing. Some common techniques for introducing variety include the following:

1. Mixing simple sentences with complex or compound sentences.
2. Putting a short sentence in the midst of several long ones.
3. Occasionally beginning a sentence with modifiers instead of with the subject.
4. Occasionally beginning with a conjunction instead of with the subject.

In the selection that follows, note how richness and variety are achieved by weaving various details, in phrases, clauses, and appositives, into the sentences themselves.

The week before, at home, some academic friends had been over and as we talked and drank we looked at a television showing of Tod Browning's 1931 version of *Dracula.* Dwight Frye's appearance on the screen had us suddenly squealing and shrieking, and it was obvious that old vampire movies were part of our common experience. We talked about the famous ones, Murnau's *Nosferatu* and Dreyer's *Vampyr,* and we began to get fairly involved in the lore of the genre— the strategy of the bite, the special earth for the coffins, the stake through the heart versus the rays of the sun as disposal methods, the cross as vampire repellent, et al. We had begun to surprise each other by the affectionate, nostalgic tone of our mock erudition when the youngest person present, an instructor in English, said, in a clear, firm tone, "*The Beast with Five Fingers* is the greatest horror picture I've ever seen." Stunned that so bright a young man could display such shocking taste, preferring a Warner Brothers forties mediocrity to the classics, I gasped, "But why?" And he answered, "Because it's completely irrational. It doesn't make any sense, and that's the true terror."

—PAULINE KAEL, *Zeitgeist and Poltergeist; Or, Are Movies Going to Pieces?*

§ 36. AWKWARDNESS AND OBSCURITY

Sentences that are confused, awkward, illogical, or obscure should be rewritten.

An awkward and confused sentence may occasionally be a sign of slovenly thinking, but it is probably more often a result of haste and carelessness in writing and revision. A confused sentence may have several faults:

36

1. The central thought may be lost in a tangle of modifiers.
2. The thoughts may not be arranged properly.
3. The words used may be inexact, ambiguous, or inappropriate.
4. Several constructions may be telescoped into one.

See also §31

CONFUSED

If more emphasis was stressed in college on extempore speaking, the graduating student would be better prepared to face people of social prominence and college professors.

REVISED

Colleges should stress courses in extempore speaking in order to give their graduates more confidence and social ease.

CONFUSED

The word *laureate* comes from the Greeks when they used laurels to crown certain people.

REVISED

The word *laureate* comes from the language of the ancient Greeks, who used a laurel crown as a mark of special honor.

EXERCISE

EXERCISE, AWKWARD AND OBSCURE SENTENCES. *Revise the following sentences.*

1. Some allergic people live in pollen-proof rooms created by air-conditioning, not including air-cooling, to escape paroxysms of sneezing caused by chilling.

36

2. The hay fever patient should be wary of squirting insecticides about the yard or house, for squirting pyrethrum, the ground-up flower of the chrysanthemum, which is a member of the composite family, also is contained in these.

3. A student spends two or three terms in college to become accustomed with the rules needed for comprehensive learning.

4. Proper use of the English language is very essential in any type of work, whether a business woman or a profession.

5. Many people have sacrificed wonderful professions because of simple misconceptions of their judgment.

6. There are some girls who really cannot afford to live in a sorority house but who would rather have it known that she belongs to a sorority and do without other things like food and clothes.

7. Having never attended college before gives me the opportunity to develop to the fullest extent my study habits and idle time.

8. Still half asleep and unconscious of what I was doing, I applied the makeup on the left-hand side of the table, which happened to be the kind used for evening wear.

9. Privacy hindered my studying while in high school because living in a house where there are many children it is very hard to secure privacy.

10. The subject of classifying what I think is an ideal roommate should be written to an unlimited length if one was to take every point in doing so.

§ 37. ADEQUATE PARAGRAPH DEVELOPMENT

37a. Effective presentation of ideas requires paragraphs of suitable length.

Rarely do college students write paragraphs that are too long; the chief difficulty is finding enough to say so that their paragraphs will not resemble a series of slightly expanded sentences.

If three or four paragraphs appear on every page of a theme, the paragraphs are probably too short. A five-hundred-word essay split into ten or twelve paragraphs contains paragraphs that are too short. The paragraphs of a newspaper story are short, it is true; so are the paragraphs of a business letter. But we are not speaking of those special types of writing when we say "expository" writing. In expository writing it is customary to develop ideas more fully or to group ideas into larger units than in news stories or in letters. In expository writing a series of very short paragraphs is an indication of malnutrition; paragraphs need to be fed details to make them effective.

The following examples illustrate some common weaknesses in paragraph development. See also Section II, Chapter 3, especially the section "Problems of Internal Organization."

UNDEVELOPED PARAGRAPH

Advertisements in magazines and on television these days are a lot better than they are given credit for. Some of them are quite funny. I think advertising is more interesting than a lot of other things going on nowadays. [This is vague, repetitious, undeveloped. Note especially some of the undefined words and phrases: *a lot better* (how are they better?), *more interesting* (in what way?), *a lot of other things* (what sort of things?).]

447

37

REWRITTEN PARAGRAPH

The growth of humor in the writing of advertisements is a pleasant phenomenon of recent years. In magazines and on television many writers of ads have been exploiting a sense of the absurd, almost as if they were making fun of themselves. A well-known airline now produces commercials featuring Peter Sellers, in various continental guises, as a barker for the company's sophisticated service. Sellers' exaggeratedly condescending tone makes you laugh at the same time you are seduced by the snob appeal of his message. In a somewhat different approach one desperate American car-maker has modified an old folk tale in its magazine and TV ads. These commercials depict a long line of hum-drum cars following its unique and racy coupe to the dealership of "P. Piper." Altogether this kind of fun-making is a healthy development in a profession that often appears to take salesmanship all too solemnly.

UNDEVELOPED PARAGRAPH

I like to travel all right, but it is the people you meet rather than the things you see that I appreciate. When I visit a new place I am really happy to find some new faces and names that I can make friends with. [This paragraph has reduced informality to not much more than chattering. Again it is vague and unconvincing. Note how, in the revision, the writer has exploited the unintended rhyme—new places, new faces—to enliven his first sentence. Then he proceeds with some relatively concrete, memorable examples.]

REWRITTEN PARAGRAPH

When I go traveling, it is new faces, not new places, that I go to see. The Grand Canyon is certainly an awesome sight, but what I remember most vividly from my visit there is the figure of a priest I met in a hotel lobby. Lean, ascetic, with flashing black eyes, he spoke to me of his order and its commitment to teaching. And at Yellowstone Park, where I was duly impressed by Old Faithful, an elderly woman with bright silver hair and the manner of an actress took one look and sniffed. "Another dull show in the provinces," she concluded scornfully. Sightseeing is all very well, but I suspect our own human depths may be more mysterious and fascinating than any canyon. Thoreau put it better, at a time when maps still contained large, unexplored blank spaces. "What does Africa, what does the West stand for?" he asked. "Is not our own interior white on the chart?"

Some sketchy paragraphs are the result of a failure to think in larger units. The writer fails to decide on the central idea, and then does not see that those miniature paragraphs are merely parts of the topic idea.

37

SKETCHY PARAGRAPHS

Dad and Mother marveled at the way my sister Lois and I got along; they still do in fact. They are proud of the family unity we show.

When Lois married, I was as thrilled and happy as she, I am sure. I think I knew better than anyone else what a wonderful wife she would be. Her marriage is an example to me.

Although my sister never attended college, she has encouraged me greatly. I am working to live up to the high standards she set for me, and I am constantly hoping that some day I can in some way repay her.

[Try combining under a topic sentence like this: *My sister Lois has been a companion and an example to me.*]

The buzzard usually glides over wooded areas in search of food because a domestic animal is more likely to meet a mishap in the forest than out in a plain pasture. Also one will find buzzards around the sloughs in the summer because the water is drying up and the buzzard will feed on the dead fish.

The buzzard lives in a nest on top of high cliffs and in tree tops.

It is against the law to shoot buzzards because they scavenge the animals that have died in the woods through accident.

[Try combining these three paragraphs under a topic sentence that makes a statement about the feeding and nesting habits of buzzards.]

I suppose any mother is happy and proud when her daughters surprise her by cooking a meal. I know that my mother always is. This is one way in which we like to make her happy.

Mother always remembers kindness, whether it be in thoughts or actions, and always forgets the unkindness of others. She appreciates having us cook for her.

[Try constructing a topic sentence about Mother's appreciation of a kind act.]

37b. Concrete details help to make a paragraph interesting and effective.

37

The tendency of beginners is to write in generalizations and abstractions: "The closing hour at the cafe is always a scene of great confusion." What actually is going on? Why not make us see—hear and smell, too—the various details of that confusion? Just what did you see that justified your conclusion that the closing hour at the cafe is a scene of confusion? In criticism, the statement "I like this poem" is of course practically meaningless. Why do you like it? Because it irritates you? or because it soothes you? In presentation of character—"My father is an honest man." How is he honest? What does he do that shows honesty? Drag him out on the stage and let us watch him being honest. In discussions of college problems—"Dormitory rules are more liberal, and thus more demanding, than parental rules"—give us examples, many of them. Let us see college men and women in situations that require choice; let us see how they behave and what they think in relation to questions of social morality. Give us action and proof. Give us the evidence that you have observed.

Here are some examples to show how details can be used.

BEFORE

Holding a little boy by the hand, a fat old woman waddled slowly up the staircase.

AFTER

Her carpet slippers flapping against the stone steps, the huge woman made her way laboriously up the staircase. Her dark shapelessness almost hid the little boy beside her, whose thin white arm stretched taut as she pulled him along.

BEFORE

The closing hour at the cafe where I work is always a scene of great confusion. The juke-box is playing, the customers are shouting their orders, everyone is impatient and in a hurry.

AFTER

The raucous blast of a Beatles number from the jukebox and the bellows of customers impatient for their final orders of hamburgers and french fries turn closing hour at the cafe where I work into a fair approximation of the last moments aboard the *Titanic*.

450

Notice that the writer's "scene of great confusion" has now become more vivid for the reader through the addition of a few concrete details. Remember that concrete writing does not call for overwhelming the reader with descriptive minutiae. It ought to be the art of making each statement specific and unmistakably pertinent.

38

§ 38. UNITY IN THE PARAGRAPH

38a. Effective paragraphs of exposition observe the principle of unity.

A paragraph of *exposition* is a unit of structure. It deals with one idea, or with one phase of a larger idea. Its unity may be destroyed by:

1. digressions from the main thought or topic idea, usually expressed by the topic sentence,
2. the addition of irrelevant details,
3. afterthoughts that should have been disposed of earlier in the composition.

There are two methods of correcting a paragraph's lack of unity. If the problem is one of extraneous detail, the irrelevant matter may simply be deleted. When a paragraph errs in confounding two or more major ideas, however, nothing will improve it but the isolation and development of one of the ideas in a complete rewriting. See § 37 and Section II, Chapter 3, for help in building up and presenting an idea in paragraph form.

The following are paragraphs that violate unity. Study them and the criticisms that show the error and the method of revision:

PARAGRAPH 1

Well-built and comfortable houses can be built for a small amount of money. [Topic sentence] Any family with small means may build a well-equipped home a short distance from the city limits for less than they could live on in a run-down apartment. Materials for building are also important. Houses are more and more being built with steel frames. The windows are usually steel sashes. The outside may be almost any type—brick, stone, wood, or stucco.

451

CRITICISM

This paragraph breaks in half after the second sentence, since the writer seems to have forgotten his original idea, that families of small means can build inexpensive houses. The material here should be developed more fully in two paragraphs.

PARAGRAPH 2

Little is known about McGuffey's early theories of education because he failed to write down his sermons and lectures. It is known, however, that he felt the need of a systematic education and textbooks. He liked to do his teaching outdoors. He would seat his children on logs. He had a log for each subject. The best students would sit at the head of a log and the poorest at the foot. He would often question his students until they could see the truth or falsity of their reasoning. By these methods he encouraged the competitive spirit among his students, and taught them to think logically and speak clearly. He established the tastes of four fifths of the nation's school children in regard to literature, morality, social development, and—next to the Bible— their religion.

CRITICISM

This paragraph has an understood topic sentence. The paragraph deals with what little we know about McGuffey's early theories of education, which we infer from what he did. Hence the last sentence violates unity, for although it is about McGuffey's teaching, it is not about his early theories or methods. If the facts in the last sentence are important or pertinent, they should be put into a paragraph dealing with his lifetime influence upon American youth.

38b.   The topic sentence is a useful device for securing unity in a paragraph of exposition.

When your instructor refers you to this section, you should underline the topic sentence of your paragraph or write a topic sentence if it is implied in your paragraph. It is quite probable that your instructor is trying to make you see that your paragraph lacks unity, or a close-knit structure, faults that your attention to a topic sentence would help to correct.

Not all expository paragraphs, of course, begin with a topic sentence. In some paragraphs the summary is left to be made by the reader; the paragraph details do relate to one central idea

452

but are not conveniently tied together by a topic sentence. In other paragraphs it seems as if all that holds the ideas together is a mutual friendship, or a common interest in the same subject. The most common, the most typical, and, to the student, the most useful paragraph of exposition, however, has a topic sentence, usually expressed somewhere near the beginning, either after the transitional phrases or combined with them.

38

What has been said here and in Section II, Chapter 3, about the topic sentence applies primarily to fully developed paragraphs of exposition, not to special paragraphs such as transitions or summaries, nor to paragraphs of narration, description, or dialogue.

Here are some examples of different methods of using a topic sentence. They merit careful study. The first example shows topic sentences beginning two consecutive paragraphs:

The wings of both male and female monarchs [butterflies] have another characteristic which has interested naturalists for generations. [Topic sentence] This is their striking, contrasting pattern which makes them easily seen. These brilliant wings are more than adornments. They are warnings to insect-eating birds to keep away. The exact opposite of protective coloring, their purpose seems to be to attract attention, to let the birds know they are the wings of a monarch. For these insects have an evil-tasting blood which nauseates the bird that tries to eat them. By warning inexperienced birds away, the wings of the insect protect it from attack. Otherwise, in learning that the monarch is not good to eat, birds would kill or injure numbers of the insects. Its "aggressive coloration" is an advertisement; and, for the monarch, it pays to advertise.

A notable and oft-cited instance of "mimicry" among insects which already has been mentioned is connected with the flaunting wings of the monarch. [Topic sentence] A butterfly of a different family, the viceroy, an insect with entirely different history and habits, rides about on wings that have almost exactly the same pattern as those of the monarch. Its eggs, its caterpillar, its chrysalis are different. Its body contains no nauseating fluids. Yet, because it looks like a monarch, it, too, is immune from the attacks of birds. As the New England entomologist Clarence Weed once put it: The viceroy is a sheep in wolf's clothing. The advertising of the monarch aids it, too. It thrives through mistaken identity.

—Edwin Way Teale, *The Strange Lives of Familiar Insects*

Here is an example of a paragraph of exposition that uses *narration* as its method of explaining something. The topic sentence at the end clearly indicates that the purpose of the paragraph is not to tell a story but to explain how something was done.

One day in June at Wolf Camp in the Gobi Desert, Walter Granger and I were prospecting for fossils on the gray white sediments below the tents. A tiny piece of bone caught my eye. It was not more than an inch long, but I knelt down and with a whisk broom began to brush away the loose gravel. More and more of the bone was exposed, and it kept getting bigger as I went deeper. It was solid, too, and that meant that it belonged to a large piece. I called Walter. Under his expert hands a flat stone was exposed right over the bone, and he moved the block with the greatest care. It was like lifting a trap door, for under it lay a mastodon's molar tooth firmly set in bone. Granger followed it down while I looked on seething with excitement. The enormous spoon-shaped lower jaw of a rare shovel-tusked mastodon slowly took shape under his brush. Near its lower end a second tip of bone just showed in the sediment. As that was exposed, still another came to view. This went on bit by bit until we had excavated the skull, jaws, and parts of the skeletons of a big mother shovel-tusker and her baby. For two million years they had been lying there covered with unknown tons of sediment which had gradually worn away by the action of weather until that first telltale point of bone which I had seen had been exposed. That is the way fossils are found. [Topic sentence]

—Roy Chapman Andrews, *This Amazing Planet*

Quite often the topic sentence takes the form of a question. The paragraph then is the answer to that question. In the preceding paragraph, the author could very easily have written: "How are fossils found?" or "Are fossils found by plan or by accident?" The paragraph would have followed the question. Occasionally the question is a question merely in form, as in the following example.

Why does the American public refuse to let King Kong rest in peace? It is true, I'll admit, that *Kong* outdid every monster movie before or since in sheer carnage. Producers Cooper and Schoedsack crammed into it dinosaurs, headhunters, riots, aerial battles, bullets, bombs, bloodletting. Heroine Fay Wray, whose function is mainly to scream, shuts her mouth for hardly one uninterrupted minute from first reel to last. It is also true that *Kong* is larded with good healthy sadism, for those whose joy it is to see the frantic girl dangled from cliffs and harried by pterodactyls. But it seems to me that the abiding appeal of the giant ape rests on other foundations.

—X. J. KENNEDY, Who Killed King Kong?

39

Finally we have a paragraph in which the topic idea is loosely expressed in the first two sentences, the first one being a transitional sentence.

What happened to woman in painting happened to her in poetry as well. Her beauty was celebrated in terms of the riches which clustered around her: her hair was gold wires, her brow ivory, her lips ruby, her teeth gates of pearl, her breasts alabaster veined with lapis lazuli, her eyes as black as jet. The fragility of her loveliness was emphasized by the inevitable comparisons with the rose, and she was urged to employ her beauty in love-making before it withered on the stem. She was for consumption; other sorts of imagery spoke of her in terms of cherry and cream, lips as sweet as honey and skin white as milk, breasts like cream uncrudded, hard as apples. Some celebrations yearned over her finery as well, her lawn more transparent than morning mist, her lace as delicate as gossamer, the baubles that she toyed with and the favors that she gave. Even now we find the thriller hero describing his classy dame's elegant suits, cheeky hats, well-chosen accessories and foot-wear; the imagery no longer dwells on jewels and flowers but the consumer emphasis is the same. The mousy secretary blossoms into the feminine stereotype when she reddens her lips, lets down her hair, and puts on something frilly.

—GERMAINE GREER, "The Stereotype," from The Female Eunuch

§ 39. COHERENCE IN PARAGRAPHS

39a. A skillful arrangement of details helps to produce an effective paragraph.

A discussion of coherence in an *opening* paragraph appears in Section II, Chapter 3, under "Kinds of Introductory Paragraphs." In that section three common ways of beginning an essay with an effective paragraph are analyzed:

455

39

1. A statement of the thesis to be argued.
2. Narration of an anecdote related to the argument to follow.
3. Definition of a key term important to the thesis.

Paragraphs in the body of a paper must maintain coherence too, and a few suggestions for their development are worth consideration.

1. Try presenting your material in "deductive order," that is, "from the general to the particular." Most paragraphs of exposition follow this order. State your general idea first in a topic sentence, and then present the reasons, details, examples, illustrations, and so on, that make your general statement understandable and convincing.

2. Try the "order of enumeration." In your topic sentence state that your idea may be seen from two points of view, that it has three important aspects, that you are going to use four illustrations, that you have two excellent reasons for believing it, and so on. There are numerous uses for this method, and its declaration of an order contributes to a clear, compact, and well-organized paragraph.

The following topic sentences from the works of professional writers demonstrate how this method is used:

All social organization is of two forms.

There were also three less desirable results of the Peace Conference.

There are two uses of knowledge.

Among the leading purposes of law today we may list three.

Remember, however, that this sort of beginning gives a formal tone to your writing. Use the device occasionally, when the material of your paragraph is adapted to classification and enumeration.

3. Try the "time order." If details can be arranged in the order of their occurrence, there is no particular advantage to be gained by trying any other arrangement. The order of time (often called the "chronological" order) or occurrence produces a clear and orderly paragraph. It is inherently simple, perhaps elementary—but it has the unquestioned virtue of

456

being almost foolproof. It may be used with material that at first glance does not arrange itself in the order of time.

4. Try using the "inductive order." It may be that your paragraph idea should not be stated bluntly in the first sentence. The reader may not be ready for it. Prepare him for it by using your details, your examples and instances, to guide his thoughts, so that when you are ready to use your summarizing topic sentence he will also be ready to accept it. This process is the reverse of "the general to the particular," for the generalization concludes the paragraph.

If the problem of coherence is in your concluding paragraph, especially in its relation to your beginning, review the section on "Beginnings and Endings" in Section I, Chapter 2. In that section, eight possible beginning-and-ending combinations are listed, with examples.

39b. Paragraphs are made more effective by the skillful use of connectives and transitions.

Section II, Chapter 3 ("Problems of Internal Organization"), lists four main ways of linking ideas—by using conjunctions and transitional words and phrases, by using pronouns, by repeating key words, and by expressing related ideas in parallel structure.

1. **Transitional Expressions.** The following is a brief list of transitional words and phrases. You must not think that this list is complete. The natural, spontaneous phrases of transition that occur to you as you write are by no means necessarily incorrect or unliterary.

on the other hand	conversely	finally
in the second place	of course	after all
on the contrary	in conclusion	indeed
at the same time	to sum up	next
in particular	moreover	similarly
in spite of this	in addition	again
in like manner	for example	and truly
and so again	for instance	meanwhile
as I have said	furthermore	
in contrast to this	accordingly	

39

39

EXAMPLES OF TRANSITIONS

In like manner, all kinds of deficient and impolitic usages are referred to the national love of trade; though, *oddly enough,* it would be a weighty charge against a foreigner that he regarded the Americans as a trading people.

—CHARLES DICKENS

I am not blaming or excusing anyone here. . . . I find, *for instance,* that prejudice, essentially, is worse on the prejudiced than on their targets.

—LOUIS ADAMIC

There were then very few regular troops in the kingdom. A town, *therefore,* which could send forth, at an hour's notice, twenty thousand men. . . .

—THOMAS BABINGTON MACAULAY

Their [the immigrants'] children, *however,* follow the general increase which is found in the American population. *Furthermore,* the form of the body of immigrants' children undergoes certain changes. . . .

—FRANZ BOAS

2. Pronouns Referring to Antecedents in the Preceding Sentences. The technique of using pronouns for transition is a standard practice, but often runs the risks of vagueness of reference. See §27 for illustrations of vagueness.

EXAMPLES

In the summer, Father had his usual two or three weeks of vacation. *These* were spent usually at our cabin in the mountains.

I know a writer of newspaper editorials. *Himself* a liberal, *he* has to grind out a thousand words daily which reflect the ultra conservative policy of the paper for which *he* works. *He* keeps a record like a batting chart. . . .

—STUART CHASE

If the use of a pronoun in one sentence that refers to an antecedent in a preceding sentence is risky, the use of a pronoun in one paragraph with its antecedent in the preceding paragraph is even more likely to involve dangerous confusion. The wisest course is to rely on the use of pronouns from paragraph to para-

458

graph only when the antecedent is emphatically central to both paragraphs—as in a discussion of the work of one author, who may be referred to as he or she after one identification.

3. Key Words Repeated. In the two following passages, the words *civilization* and *understanding* are repeated to hold the arguments together.

40

EXAMPLES

Nothing in the way of civilization is inborn, as are the forms and workings of our bodies. Everything that goes to make up civilization must be acquired anew in infancy and childhood, by each and all of us.

—James Harvey Robinson

In some of my early writings I spoke of the twofold problem of understanding—there was the problem of understanding the world around us, and there was the problem of understanding the process of understanding, that is, the problem of understanding the nature of the intellectual tools with which we attempt to understand the world around us.

—P. W. Bridgman

4. Parallel Structure. In the example, the repeated subject-verb phrasing relates each clause to all the others.

EXAMPLE

While I talk and the flies buzz, a sea gull catches a fish at the mouth of the Amazon, a tree falls in the Adirondack wilderness, a man sneezes in Germany, a horse dies in Tartary, and twins are born in France.

—William James

§ 40. POINT OF VIEW

Maintain a consistent point of view.

In §31 we discussed some dangers, largely grammatical, involving shifts in point of view. Here we consider some larger questions of consistency. To maintain a consistent point of view is to be sensitive to all the principles this handbook has out-

459

lined. Sentence structure, vocabulary, even mechanics and spelling—all these have a direct bearing on the central problem of a writer: that of producing a consistent, controlled prose style.

40

40a. Maintain a consistent point of view in time and space.

One way to understand the phrase "point of view" is to think of it quite literally as a *point* from which one *views* one's subject.

Having chosen a particular "point" from which the material is to be "viewed," you owe it to your reader to maintain your position, and to skip around only for a very good reason. This injunction applies to points in *time* as well as in *space*. At its simplest, it means that a paragraph in the present tense should be followed by a paragraph in the past tense only if the break in point of view is deliberate and desirable. Similarly, if a scene is to be described from the vantage point of one particular spot, or through the eyes of one particular person, then an abrupt removal to another spot or another person, simply to suit the author's whim or convenience, is sure to disturb a careful reader.

Here are some passages from a brief anecdote, written by a college student, that will help us to define some of these difficulties.

The small gray Chevrolet pulled up to the side of the road and halted as the hitchhiker dropped his solicitous thumb and moved to the car. He looked inquiringly at the driver, his companion, and the back seat, and opened the door.

"Going to Baker?"

The driver, decked out in blue denims and with a short peaked cap covering a head of silver hair brushed down on the sides, gave a nod and replied, "Sure am. Hop in back."

The stranger got in and found the back seat already taken by a large German police dog, stretched out full length on the seat. His surprised grunt came just as the farmer's companion, apparently his wife, turned around and rasped, "Don't worry about him, son, he's pretty friendly. Get down, Boss."

The object of her order gave a perturbed gesture with his front paws and jumped to the floor as the new rider took over the back seat. He glanced at the backs of his two benefactors.

460

The *point* from which we are asked to *view* this scene is, of course, the physical position occupied by the hitchhiker. Notice how we follow him about, and when he is in the car, we too see the car from the back seat where he is situated. This is logical and proper enough. The woman in the front seat is "apparently" the farmer's wife; we know no more about her than the hitchhiker does. But note too that we are not so placed as to know what's going on in the hitchhiker's mind. The speaker refers to him as "the stranger" and "the new rider." We are observing the situation from outside any one person's consciousness, and this too is part of our point of view. The writer has placed us in a certain position of distance from "the stranger" and must be careful to maintain that distance unless there is a good reason for changing it.

The story goes on:

The dog was resting, head on his paws, with his eyes fixed on the new rider. He was a massive beast, and the result of good care showed in a well-filled body that rested firm under a sleek gray coat. The stranger passed his eyes from the dog's rump along the line of his back to his head, and noticing the canine gaze still upon him, glanced briefly at the long angular jaws.

The gaze prompts a sudden thought, and half to himself he comments, "That dog must have been raised in the Arctic."

Here a change in point of view has taken place—a change that is probably too abrupt, though it is not absolutely drastic. We have moved closer to "the stranger": first, we are aware that he notices "the canine gaze"; then, with a curious and awkward change of tense, we are told that the gaze prompts a "sudden thought." A few sentences later, however, as the author describes a conversation taking place in the car, we find this sentence:

"Just what breed of dog is this?" came from the back seat.

Can you see what has happened? We have suddenly been catapulted, in our point of view, from the back seat to the front seat, right over the headrests! The scene that we saw from one point in space, we now see—for no good reason—from quite another

461

point. And a few sentences later, the writer slips even further from his original place next to the hitchhiker as he tells us:

> The woman was intent on continuing the discussion, but then the idea of some new plan faded from her mind and she turned full around to face the front and the road unwinding ahead of them.

As you can easily see, we have now come almost full circle, for when we know what is going on inside the woman's mind, we have been moved thoroughly about inside that automobile. (Only the farmer has remained inscrutable!) In the hands of a skilled professional writer, such shifts might be purposeful and desirable, but for most beginning writers a shift in point of view is perilous. Although the problem is most obviously demanding in fiction, as in this example, it is crucial in all writing and must be watched carefully.

40b. Maintain a consistent *tone* toward your reader.

When a writer selects language to express what he has to say, he inevitably creates as he does so a particular speaking "voice," a kind of personality through which he projects his meaning. (We are not now speaking of voice in the grammatical sense, of course, as in active or passive voice.) This dramatic identity, this mouthpiece must suggest by its language a certain relation with the reader—informal or formal, intimate, friendly, even hostile. It is this relation with the reader (and the material) that we call *tone*, and it is an indispensable part of a point of view.

By leafing through the columns of any daily newspaper, you can discover a number of different voices that make their appeals with many different tones. Some of them, as in the more formal news articles or editorials, may hold you at arm's length, or they may chide you as from the editor's seat on a local TV news program.

It has been announced that a government delegation will depart from Hong Kong tomorrow for technical discussions on a new Communist proposal to increase the amount of water which the British Colony receives from the mainland.

462

The nominee for the Vice Presidency on both the Republican and the Democratic tickets should be selected solely because he is the best-qualified person available to step into the Presidency, if fate should call him there. Considerations of religion or sex or race or family or place of residence should not enter into this choice. Ability to carry on the duties of the Presidency of the United States with distinction is the proper, and the only proper, criterion.

40

Note the relatively long sentences, the elaborate structures, and the passive verbs in these passages—all devices for promoting a formal tone. On the other hand, in other columns of the daily paper, you may be addressed in an excessively friendly way by other voices as they assume an intimacy with you that may be quite surprising. This is most obvious in the advertisements, of course: an ad for soap may cry out at you, in black print, "Dry skin? Not me, sweetheart!" Or a shipping line may assume it knows just what you want:

Why just get there when you can *cruise* there? Our ships offer you far more than just transportation. They slow down your pace and help you relax and revel in lazy, sunny days at sea.

Sometimes, in other passages, the voice that addresses you may be so extremely detached and formal as hardly to exist at all, except as something dry, crisp, and impersonal:

Pursuant to the provisions of the amended Certificate of Incorporation, notice is hereby given that the Board of Directors will dispose of said property on Wednesday, 16 May, at ten o'clock in the forenoon.

These examples will suggest the enormous range of possibilities in manipulating tone. Success in consistency, of course, depends on not changing personalities from paragraph to paragraph as you write.

40c. Maintain a consistent *attitude* toward your subject matter.

A familiar use of the phrase "point of view" occurs in a question like "What is his point of view on that?"—meaning, What

40

is his attitude, his value judgment, his opinion? This aspect of the problem is also part of the character or voice you are creating with your language. Consistency in attitude is simply a matter of taking a stand and sticking to it, without wavering or contradictory statements. If you have expressed disapproval of United States foreign policy in your first paragraph, do not praise it in your fourth unless the intervening sentences demonstrate and defend the change in attitude. The part of speech to watch with particular care in expressing attitude is, of course, the adjective. A great many adjectives state by definition a speaker's approval of the modified noun; examples are *attractive, beautiful, industrious, virtuous, warm-hearted.* Such adjectives are called *honorific;* they almost always commit their users to a favorable view of the subject. On the other hand, many adjectives act by definition in just the opposite way: *unattractive, ugly, lazy, evil, cold-hearted.* Such adjectives are called *pejorative,* and they are very difficult to use without suggesting disapproval. Between these extremes, there are infinite subtle variations of approval and disapproval to be controlled by the skilled writer.

EXERCISES

EXERCISE 1, POINT OF VIEW. *Look through the pages of a large national magazine that offers a varied table of contents. Find the opening paragraphs of a piece of fiction, and define carefully the time and place of the narrator's point of view. Show what shifts in position there may be, and try to decide why such shifts are there.*

EXERCISE 2, TONE. *In the same magazine find half a dozen paragraphs from various pages to show different speaking voices in action with markedly different tones. Show what kind of person the reader is expected to be, as he responds to the language in each case.*

EXERCISE 3, INTIMATE TONE. *Select an advertisement from the magazine that employs a particularly intimate tone. Point out the grammatical and rhetorical devices by which this tone was created. What happens to the advertisement if you try rewriting it in formal style? What happens when you satirize its intimate tone?*

EXERCISE 4, DISTANT TONE. *Find a voice in the magazine that is particularly distant or detached from the reader. Rewrite the passage to bring the speaker closer to the reader.*

EXERCISE 5, WORDS THAT EXPRESS ATTITUDES. *In all the passages you have chosen, show what words have been used to express attitudes toward what is being talked about. Rewrite two or three of the passages, reversing or drastically changing the attitude by replacing the modifiers and other language as necessary.*

40

A GUIDE TO USAGE

§ 41. GLOSSARY

This section is to be consulted for information about current usage.

Correctness and incorrectness in English usage are relative terms. We usually prefer to speak of the appropriateness of an expression in a given context, rather than of its correctness. An expression is appropriate in a certain situation, on a certain occasion, in a certain locality, among certain people; it may be inappropriate in another situation, on another occasion, in another locality, among other people.

But saying this much hardly solves your difficulties in deciding what is or is not appropriate in various situations. You have a right to expect some firm assistance on such questions from an English handbook, in spite of the relativity in usage that we all recognize. Your questions will no doubt arise in a number of cases where the current status of an expression is debatable, and the list that follows is intended to help you respond intelligently to some of these cases, as well as to those many other cases of confusing or troublesome usage where no argument exists.

In considering this matter of status, important in perhaps half the items in our guide, we will speak of three classifications of language, conscious as we do so of the artificial nature of such constructions. First, there are all those words and expressions that are part of Standard Literary English, and as a matter of fact these account for most of the words in the language. Very many words in Standard English are appropriate on any occasion, formal or informal, anywhere. Second, we label certain expressions Colloquial or Informal, which simply means that these expressions are perfectly natural in most conversations, and perhaps in some informal writing, but are usually not ap-

41

propriate in formal expository writing. An example is the expression *I guess:* "I guess his analysis was correct." Most problems of usage arise from a failure to recognize and avoid the Colloquial-Informal in the writing of serious essays. (The fact remains, of course, that many fine writers of serious prose are able to modify their formality of style by the deliberate, occasional use of informal language. Their skill depends, naturally, on a high sensitivity to the current status of words, so that just the right mixture can be concocted.) Finally, there is a small body of language that simply has to be called Illiterate. For example, to use the phrase *could of* for *could have* ("I could of come if I'd wanted to") is conceivable in writing only if you are quoting someone who uses language of that sort.

As we have said, there are some expressions whose current status is a matter of argument, and their number is probably increasing in our fast-changing society. For example, no one can tell just when it will become widely acceptable to use such words as *put-down* or *hassle* in formal prose—if it ever will. Similar fluid and unpredictable conditions in words have reached a point where, as noted earlier, the editors of *Webster's Third New International Dictionary* (1971) have simply omitted such labels as *colloq.* in many of their dubious entries. This does not of course mean that these editors believe the status of all language is the same, but simply that the status of current English words has become so complicated and various that strict labels would be misleading.

You can learn much that is both useful and entertaining by following some of these controversies, or by examining the recent history of some fast-changing expressions. The books listed below, arranged in chronological order, will help you pursue a study of any doubtful expressions you choose. (Our own guide contains only a small fraction of the words included in a full dictionary of usage.) It is important to recognize, however, that popular usage, in conversation or in informal writing, is *not* the same as usage in formal expository prose. For our purposes in this handbook, the differences matter. Although colloquial expressions may often be included in serious formal writing, they are usually effective only when the writer is clearly aware of the shifts in tone that he or she is introducing. The books below, and our guide to usage, should help you become aware of the available choices, so that you can be genuinely discriminating in your acts of composition. (For further examples, see §20, "Similar Forms.")

41

H. W. FOWLER, *A Dictionary of Modern English Usage.* 2nd ed., revised by Sir Ernest Gowers. New York: Oxford University Press, 1965.

BERGEN EVANS and CORNELIA EVANS, *A Dictionary of Contemporary American Usage.* New York: Random House, 1957.

MARGARET M. BRYANT, *Current American Usage.* New York: Funk & Wagnalls, 1962.

WILSON FOLLETT et al., *Modern American Usage: A Guide.* New York: Hill and Wang, 1966.

ROY H. COPPERUD, *American Usage: The Consensus.* New York: Van Nostrand Reinhold, 1970.

EDWIN NEWMAN, *Strictly Speaking: Will America Be the Death of English?* Indianapolis: Bobbs-Merrill, 1974.

a, an Use *a* before a word beginning with any consonant sound except silent *h*. EXAMPLES: *a book, a tree, a European, a union, a house.* Use *an* before a word beginning with a vowel sound. EXAMPLES: *an American, an onion, an hour, an honorable man.*

above Used awkwardly as a transition: "As we pointed out *above*. . . ." A better transition would be *Therefore* or *Consequently.*

accelerate, exhilarate Sometimes confused because of resemblance in sound. To *accelerate* is to quicken or speed up. To *exhilarate* is to arouse joy, to give pleasure. EXAMPLE: *An exhilarating experience can accelerate the heartbeat.*

accept, except Often confused because of resemblance in sound. *Accept* means to receive, to agree to; *except* means to exclude or make an exception. EXAMPLES: *He accepted the invitation. She was excepted from the list of guests.*

acquiesce Use *acquiesce in; to* and *with* are vague.

A.D., B.C. Should be placed *before* the date: "A.D. 1540." B.C. *follows* the date: "85 B.C."

ad This clipped form and others like it (such as *math, exam, auto*) are appropriate in informal speech, but in formal writing the words usually appear in full.

adapt, adept, adopt To *adapt* is to change something for a purpose. *Adept* (adjective or noun) means skillful, or one skilled. To *adopt* is to take possession of. EXAMPLES: *He adapted the motor to another current. He was adept at fixing electric appliances. She was an adopted child.*

471

41

adverse, averse *Adverse* means antagonistic or unfavorable; *averse* means disinclined. EXAMPLES: *He was a victim of adverse fortune. The company president was averse to his suggestion.*

affect, effect A familiar confusion. To *affect* is to influence. To *effect* means to bring about. *Effect* as a noun means result, what has been brought about. EXAMPLES: *The strike will affect the industry. The effect of the strike will be severe. The labor board will try to effect a settlement.*

aggravate *Aggravate* means to intensify, to increase. Colloquially it means to irritate, to annoy. COLLOQUIAL: *The speaker's mannerisms aggravated everyone.* FORMAL: *The speaker's mannerisms annoyed everyone.*

agree to, agree with You *agree that* something is true. You *agree to* a proposal. You *agree with* a person. One thing *agrees with* (corresponds with) another.

aggression Use the singular *aggression.* Avoid the plural as a general statement of your feelings: "I got rid of my *aggressions* by kicking the chair." *Hostility* or *frustration* would be more precise in this context.

ain't Colloquial. Avoid its use in your writing.

all right See *alright.*

allude, refer *Allude* means to refer to a person or thing indirectly or by suggestion. EXAMPLE: *When the teacher spoke of "budding Swifts," every student wondered to whom he was alluding.* To *refer* to something means to mention it specifically. EXAMPLE: *I shall now take time to refer to the question of smoking on the campus.*

allusion, illusion An *allusion* is an indirect reference. (See *allude.*) An *illusion* is a deceptive appearance or false notion. The two words have nothing in common except a resemblance in sound.

already, all ready *Already,* an adverb, means by this time, before this time. *All ready,* two words, means entirely ready or that everyone is ready. EXAMPLES: *The war had already started. The men were all ready to go.*

alright The correct spelling is *all right. Alright* is a colloquial expression.

alternately, alternatively *Alternately* means to follow one another by turns; *alternatively* means to choose between two things. EXAMPLES: *The contestants answered questions alternately. She decided alternatively not to go with him.*

altogether, all together *Altogether* (one word) is an adverb meaning entirely, completely, on the whole. *All together* means in a group. EXAMPLES: *He was altogether too generous. They were all together again at last.*

alumnus, alumna, alumni, alumnae A male graduate is an *alumnus,* a female an *alumna;* male graduates are *alumni,* females *alumnae.* In

472

current usage *alumni* frequently serves to describe graduates of coeducational colleges.

A.M., P.M., a.m., p.m. Should not be used for *in the morning, in the afternoon.* Correct only with the name of the hour.

among, between *Among* is used with three or more things or persons, as: "They divided the property *among* six relatives"; "talk this over *among* yourselves." *Between* usually refers to two things or persons, as: "Let nothing stand *between* you and me"; "much must be done *between* sunrise and breakfast." *Between* can sometimes refer to more than two things in such expressions as: "*between* the leaves of a book"; or "the agreement *between* France, West Germany, and England."

amoral, immoral *Amoral* describes acts not subject to moral or ethical judgments; *immoral* means consciously violating moral principles. EXAMPLES: *Because he lacks a sense of right and wrong, his actions must be considered amoral. The sadistic games of the camp guards were immoral.*

amount, number *Amount* refers to quantity; *number* refers to things that can be counted. EXAMPLES: *the number of pages, the amount of steel.*

analyzation No such word. The writer means *analysis.*

and etc. *Etc.,* for *et cetera,* means "and so forth." *And etc.* is obviously redundant. In any case it is better for most purposes not to use the abbreviation.

angry at, angry with *Angry at* is used when a thing or situation is concerned; *angry with* when a person is involved.

ante-, anti- Both are prefixes, but *ante-* means before, *anti-,* against.

any place, anyplace These are colloquial forms for *anywhere,* like *no place* for *nowhere, every place* for *everywhere,* and *some place* for *somewhere.*

anyways, anywheres Colloquial forms of *anyway* and *anywhere,* to be avoided in formal prose.

a piece, apiece *A piece* is a noun; *apiece* is an adverb. EXAMPLE: *All those present are to have a piece of pie apiece.*

apprehend, comprehend To *apprehend* something is to perceive its *meaning;* to *comprehend* a system or a theory is to understand it completely. EXAMPLES: *I think I apprehend the sense of that word. I don't think I will ever comprehend the meaning of love.*

apt, likely, liable *Apt* suggests a habitual or inherent tendency. *Likely* suggests a probability. *Liable* suggests a chance, a risk of some sort, or a danger. But in American speech all three are often used to mean a probability and nothing more. EXAMPLES: *She is apt to be irritable because she is not well. A cheerful boy is likely to succeed. You are liable to break your neck if you climb that rock.*

41

41

as (1) Highly colloquial when used in place of *that* or *whether*. EXAMPLE: *I cannot say as I care much for that.* (2) *As* in the sense of *because* is frowned upon by some writers, but is widely current in speech and writing nevertheless, especially in clauses at the beginnings of sentences. EXAMPLE: *As I was free that day, I went along with him.*

as—as, so—as In negative statements some careful writers prefer *so—as* to *as—as*. At present, *as—as* seems to be established in both speech and writing for both positive and negative statements. For negative statements in a very formal style, *so—as* is probably preferable. EXAMPLES: *Your promise is as good as your bond.* FORMAL: *A vast army is not so important as a well-equipped air force.* INFORMAL: *A vast army is not as important as a well-equipped air force.*

aspect A clichéd word with no concrete basis when used as a synonym for *consideration*, as in: "There are many *aspects* of this problem." Use more precise words, such as *parts* or *sides*. (*Facet*, like *aspect*, has been overused without any hint of its literal meaning.)

assume, presume *Assume* connotes taking something for granted, while *presume* implies a more forceful or defensive attitude. EXAMPLES: *Let us assume that the statement is true. You presume too much in your claim.*

at Redundant, in both speech and writing, in such sentences as: "Where are we *at* now?" "Where does he live *at?*"

at this point in time, at the present moment The writer means *now*. Testimony in the recent Watergate hearings has engendered such silly redundancies as "within this time frame" and "time bracket." Be sure that these redundancies do not creep into *your* prose.

avocation, vocation A *vocation* is one's principal life work. An *avocation* is not. EXAMPLE: *His vocation was medicine; his avocation was collecting stamps.*

awake, wake, waken For the most part these verbs are interchangeable. *Awake* is widely favored for *becoming awake:* "I *awoke* at noon." *Wake* is better suited for transitive constructions: "I *waked* him at noon." For passive constructions, *waken* is probably best: "I was *wakened* at noon."

award, reward You are given an *award* in a formal and specific sense, while *reward*, though it may be a specific amount of money or a gift, may also be used in an unofficial or general context. EXAMPLES: *Elizabeth Taylor won the acting award. Faye Dunaway didn't win the award, but her reward was the consolation of her friends.*

awful, awfully Colloquially these words, and others like *frightful, terribly, shocking, disgusting*, are used as mild intensives. Often they mean little more than *very*. In formal writing, *awful* and *awfully* should be saved for their precise meaning, to describe something truly awe inspiring. EXAMPLE: *He accepted the awful responsibility of carrying on the war.*

bad, badly In formal and informal writing *bad* should not be used as an adverb meaning severely ("My feet hurt *bad*"), or as a predicate adjective meaning impressive or well-dressed ("In his new suit he looked *bad*"). *Badly* may be used to mean "very much" only in the negative sense: "Her face was *badly* burned."

balance When used for the *remainder, the rest,* it is usually considered colloquial. COLLOQUIAL USES: *The balance of the crew will be released. We listened to records the balance of the evening.* FORMAL: *The rest of the crew will be released.*

bank on In the sense of *rely upon* it is a colloquial idiom.

basically, essentially These adverbs should be avoided in such sentences as: "*Basically,* the Administration has a plan to end the war." "This is *essentially* what the president means." They add nothing to the meaning of the sentence.

because Often used in informal speech, and sometimes in literary English, as a substitute for *that* in constructions like "the reason was *because.* . . ." *That* is still preferable in formal written prose.

being This participle is frequently used redundantly in student writing: "The players were unhappy, with the better ones *being* ready to quit the team." Notice that *being* provides a too easy means of adding afterthoughts to the main clause. It can be dropped without any loss of coherence.

being as, being that Dialectal for *since, because.* EXAMPLE: *Since* (not *being as*) *it is long past midnight, we should abandon the search.*

beside, besides According to present usage, *beside* is used as a preposition meaning at the side of, as in: "Please sit down *beside* me." *Besides* is ordinarily used as an adverb, meaning in addition to, as in: "There were no casualties *besides* the one reported earlier."

between See *among.*

between you and I The writer means *between you and me. Between,* a preposition, requires the objective pronoun *me.*

broke Colloquial when used as an adjective to mean poverty-stricken or short of cash.

bunch Colloquial when used to mean several, a group. EXAMPLES: *We saw a group* (not *a bunch*) *of men near the gate. Several* (not *a bunch*) *of them belonged to another union.*

but however, but yet These expressions are redundant. *However, yet, nevertheless, probably* should stand alone.

but what, but that Formerly considered colloquial. *But that* now appears to be standard literary English in sentences like: "I don't doubt

41

but that he is disappointed." *But what* should not be used to refer to persons. Most careful writers still prefer a simple *that* to both these expressions. EXAMPLE: *There is no doubt that* (not *but what* or *but that*) *the president wishes to avoid war.*

can, may In formal usage, *may* implies permission or possibility, *can* implies ability. In informal usage, *can* is very often used in the sense of *may*. INFORMAL: *Mother, can I go now? Can't we stay up until midnight? No, you can't.* FORMAL: *Sir, may I go now? The delegate can speak three languages.*

cannot help but, can't help but These forms are widely used in speech and by some writers in formal prose.

can't hardly A double negative, objectionable in conversation, unthinkable in formal writing.

case, instance *In the case, instance of* is a circumlocution. Note that *for* can be substituted for *in the case of* in the following sentence: "Who is to blame *in the case of* John's failure?"

cause and reason *Cause* is what produces an effect; *reason* is what man produces to account for the effect, or to justify it. EXAMPLES: *His reasons for going were excellent. The cause of his departure remained a mystery.*

cause of To say that the *cause of* something was *on account of* is a muddled construction. EXAMPLES: *The cause of my late theme was my having* (not *on account of I had*) *too much work to do. The cause of my late theme was the fact that I had too much work to do.* Both of these sentences, however, are awkward. It may be better to avoid the *cause-of* construction entirely and simply say, "My theme is late because I had too much to do."

censor, censure A *censor* (who is censorious) is one who supervises public morals, expurgates literature, and so on. *Censure* is adverse judgment, condemnation.

center around *Center* means a point, not a circle. *Center on* makes more sense, but even this expression is a circumlocution: "The question *centers on* a failure of communication." ("The question *is.* . . .")

climactic, climatic *Climactic* has to do with climax, as: "The play had reached a *climactic* moment." *Climatic* has to do with climate, as: "*Climatic* conditions in Bermuda are ideal."

close proximity Redundant.

compare to, compare with, contrast *Compare to* means to represent as similar. *Compare with* means to examine the differences and similarities of two things. To *contrast* two things is to examine the differences between them. EXAMPLES: *One may compare some men to wolves. One may compare the novels of Dreiser with those of Zola. The novels of Dreiser can be contrasted to those of James.*

476

comprise, compose *Comprise* means include; *compose* means make up. *Comprise* is used mistakenly in: "The university is *comprised* of faculty, staff, and administrators." The sentence should read: "The faculty, staff, and administrators *compose* (or *constitute*) the university."

41

concept, idea *Concept* means a generalized or abstract notion which characterizes elements of a class. *Idea* is a broader term and generally more suitable than *concept* or *conception*. Note that *concept* would be too narrow a word in the following sentence: "My *idea* received little comment from the manager."

contact Widely used in the sense of *communicate with, meet, interview,* but it should be used sparingly, if at all, in preference to the more exact expressions.

contemptible, contemptuous *Contemptible* is used to describe something or someone deserving contempt, while *contemptuous* means expressing contempt. EXAMPLES: *She told him his behavior was contemptible. He was contemptuous of my argument.*

continual, continuous Any event that recurs at intervals is *continual; continuous* means uninterrupted. EXAMPLES: *We were bothered by the continual dripping of the faucet. When I tried to repair the faucet, I was greeted by a continuous stream of water.*

contractions Less appropriate in formal writing, where they are occasionally found, than in speech and informal writing, where they are entirely at home. EXAMPLES: *I'd like to go, but I'm tired. Can't he explain it to you, or doesn't he care?*

convince, persuade The following sentences illustrate the differing connotations of these two words: "I *convinced* her that she was wrong." "I *persuaded* her to join our group." *Convince* means winning agreement; *persuade* means moving to action.

could of Illiterate for *could have.*

couple Colloquial for *two, a few, several.* COLLOQUIAL: *A couple of men left the theater.* FORMAL: *Two* (or *several*) *men left the theater.* Standard for a man and woman married, betrothed, or otherwise appearing as partners.

credible, credulous An event, fact, argument is *credible* when it is believable; you are said to be *credulous* if you are easily convinced, or gullible.

criteria The plural form of *criterion.*

cunning A colloquialism to describe attractive children and small animals. Not to be used in formal writing.

cute See *cunning.*

data, strata, phenomena These are the plurals of *datum, stratum,* and

477

41

phenomenon. At present these words seem to be in a transitional stage, inasmuch as some good writers and speakers use them as singular forms while others believe strongly that only the correct Latin forms should be used. There is no doubt, however, that a mixture of forms is undesirable, as: "Although the *data* collected at the laboratory are vouched for by several scientists, much of it has to be restudied."

date Inappropriately colloquial when referring to an appointment with the dean, but perfectly acceptable when referring to Saturday night at the movies.

deal Used figuratively in phrases like "square *deal,*" "new *deal.*" Informal in the sense of a commercial transaction or political bargain. COLLOQUIAL: *Good deal!* But with the indefinite article it is literary English, as: "a good *deal* of trouble."

decimate To reduce by one tenth, not to destroy entirely.

deduce, deduct *Deduce* is used to mean infer; *deduct* means to take away. EXAMPLES: *We deduced a certain dislike in his actions. The company deducted ten dollars from her pay.*

denotation, connotation Use *denotation* when referring to a word's specific meaning; use *connotation* when speaking of a word's implications.

deprecate, depreciate *Deprecate* means to express regret over, or disapproval of, while *depreciate* means to lessen the value of.

device, devise A *device* is an instrument for performing some action. To *devise* something is to invent it, to contrive or plan it.

dichotomy A splitting into parts or pairs. The word is now overused, especially in contexts where *difference* or *split* is more appropriate.

differ from, differ with One thing *differs from* another. One person *differs with* another when he disputes or quarrels with him. One may also *differ from* a person when he disagrees with him.

different from, different than Both forms have been used by good writers. At present, *different from* seems to be preferred when a single word follows it, as in: "His suggestion is *different from* mine." When a clause follows, many speakers and writers use *than* to avoid a roundabout construction, as in: "This group of engineers will use a very *different* method of extracting the ore *than* the old Quebec miners used."

discreet, discrete A *discreet* person is tactful or judicious; a *discrete* matter is distinct or separate from another.

dissimulate, simulate To *simulate* is to pretend; to *dissimulate* is to hide by pretense. EXAMPLES: *He simulated drunkenness by weaving around the floor. He dissimulated his drunkenness by an effort to speak rationally.*

478

dissociate, disassociate These words mean the same thing, but *dissociate* is more common in modern usage.

double negative An expression in which two or more negatives are used to make the negative more emphatic is of course illiterate. EXAMPLES: *Nobody never tells me nothing. We ain't seen nobody.* Another type of concealed double negative appears in a very small number of expressions like *can't hardly, didn't hardly, wouldn't scarcely.* These expressions are not appropriate in writing, though they are widely heard in speech. A third type of deliberate double negative is entirely correct, and common in formal writing. EXAMPLES: *The brief rest was not unwelcome. These people were not uneducated.* (Notice that these expressions are more cautious and moderate than the corollary affirmative statements: *The brief rest was welcome. These people were educated.*)

dove The most generally used form is *dived,* though *dove* has been widely used in speech and occasionally in writing.

dubious, doubtful The result of an action or the truth of a statement may be *dubious,* while the person who questions either is *doubtful.*

due to, owing to *Due to* was originally an adjective, and no one questions its use in sentences like these: "His lameness was *due to* an accident." "The spring floods, *due to* prolonged rains, did much damage to the stockyards." The adverbial use of *due to* is also common, as: "*Due to* an accident, we arrived late." If a more formal tone is desired, the expression *owing to* may be substituted for *due to. Due to the fact that* is a common, and deplorable, substitute for a simple *because.*

each other, one another The first refers to two people only, at least in formal discourse. The second refers to more than two. EXAMPLES: *The two senators started hitting each other. The whole senate started hitting one another.*

effect See *affect.*

e.g., i.e. Although these abbreviations are often used interchangeably, *e.g.* means "for example" and *i.e.* means "that is." They should be used only in parenthetical expressions and in footnotes.

elicit, illicit You *elicit* a *reaction* or *response* from someone; a person may commit an *illicit* act. EXAMPLES: *His proposal elicited support. Society labels certain acts illicit.*

emigrate, immigrate Use of these words depends on point of view. You *emigrate* when you leave America for Canada; from Canada's standpoint you have *immigrated* there, and are called an *immigrant.*

end up Unacceptable colloquialism for *end* or *conclude.*

enthuse U.S. colloquial for "to be enthusiastic" or "to show enthusi-

41

asm." Many people dislike it thoroughly. FORMAL: *She never showed any enthusiasm* (not *enthused*) *about grand opera.*

equally as good This may be wordy, but many educated people use the expression. It means "equally good," or "just as good." EXAMPLE: *My composition was just as good* (not *equally as good*) *as his.*

escalate A currently attractive but inaccurate substitute for *increase. Escalate* means specifically to increase in intensity or size by calculated stages.

et al. Proper in footnotes and bibliographical lists, *et al.* means "and other people."

etc. See *and etc. Etc.* is to be avoided at the end of a series when the reader cannot grasp the reference. EXAMPLE: *All his friends—John, Al, Len, etc.—were invited.*

euphemism, euphuism A *euphemism* is a mild or roundabout word which is substituted for another word thought to be too harsh or blunt ("passed away" for "died"). *Euphuism* is an artificially elegant style of writing that was popular in Renaissance England.

everyone, every one EXAMPLES: *Everyone has arrived by now. Every one of those dishes must be washed thoroughly.*

exam See *ad.*

except See *accept.*

exception that proves the rule A confusing cliché that should be avoided in formal and informal writing.

exhilarate See *accelerate.*

expect Colloquial in the sense of *suppose.*

facet See *aspect.*

fact that This expression can be easily deleted, thereby achieving economy and directness. "I was shocked by *the fact that* you behaved so childishly" should be rewritten: "I was shocked by your childish behavior."

fallacy The word has a specific meaning in logic: a formal mistake in reasoning or in the conclusion of an argument. It should not be used when *mistake* or *error* is meant in the general sense.

farther, further The fine distinction between these two words, and between the superlative forms, *farthest, furthest,* is that both can be used to speak of distance, but that *further* and *furthest* have an additional meaning of "additional." STANDARD USAGE: *They could go no farther. The Johansen party penetrated furthest into the jungle. The senator promised further revelations soon.*

faze American slang or colloquial for *disconcert, worry, disturb, bother, daunt.* It has no connection with *phase.* COLLOQUIAL: *He wasn't fazed by the amount of work he had to do.*

feel A spineless substitute for *think* or *believe,* in such examples as "I *feel*

480

that the United Nations is doing more harm than good." Don't feel it—just say it.

fewer, less Use *fewer* when referring to numbers. Use *less* when referring to quantity or degree. (See also *amount, number.*) EXAMPLES: *There will be fewer* (not *less*) *men on the campus next year. Most women are earning less than they did last year.*

finalize Many are irritated by this and other recent coinages from business and officialese. Use cautiously if at all. Also see *contact*.

fine See *nice*. A vague word of approval, entirely proper in conversation, but in exact writing a more exact word should be used.

first and foremost A cliché—avoid it like the plague (another cliché).

fix Colloquial in the sense of *predicament*, as: "The headmaster was in a predicament (not *fix*)." Also colloquial in the sense of *arrange* or *prepare*. COLLOQUIAL: *Give me a few minutes more to fix my hair.*

flaunt, flout You may *flaunt* your intelligence or your sexual prowess, but you *flout* rules and conventions when you *ignore* them.

flunk Colloquial for *fail*.

folks Colloquial for *relatives, family*.

former, latter Use only when referring to two items which your reader will clearly recognize. To avoid needless confusion, simply repeat the items. EXAMPLE: *Doctors and lawyers are fighting vigorously over malpractice insurance rates; lawyers* (not *the latter*) *have an advantage because of their expert knowledge.*

formulate Use only when you mean *state systematically*. EXAMPLE: *She formulated a new approach to teaching preschool children*. Otherwise, use *form*.

fun Not to be used as an adjective: "a *fun* thing to do." This is a transitory colloquialism.

funny Colloquial for *strange, queer, odd*.

gap Such expressions as *generation gap* or *credibility gap* are clichés—avoid them.

get *Get* has a large number of uses, both formal and informal. In formal or literary contexts, it means obtain, receive, procure, acquire. In informal and conversational usage, it has a large number of meanings, figurative, idiomatic, and otherwise. In speech *have got* in the sense of *have* is very common. The form *have got* in the sense of *must* or *have to* is felt to be more emphatic. *Got* and *gotten* are both past participles found in speech and in writing.

graduate The passive *was graduated* is no longer required in formal usage. "She *graduated* from Wisconsin" is proper in formal and informal writing.

guess The expression *I guess* is too colloquial for most formal prose. Write *I suppose,* or *I presume,* or *I assume*.

41

had better, had best, had rather Correct idiomatic forms, as are *would better, would best, would rather.*

had ought, hadn't ought Colloquial. It is easy to substitute *ought, should, should have, shouldn't have,* all forms appropriate in both speech and writing.

hanged, hung People are *hanged;* objects are *hung.* EXAMPLES: *The murderer was hanged. The clothes were hung on the line.*

hangup Colloquial for *problem, inhibition, perversion.* Precisely because it is too often used to mean any one or all of these states, *hangup* should be avoided in your writing.

hardly, scarcely See *double negative.*

hassle Colloquial for *problem, conflict, annoyance, fuss.*

have got See *get.*

healthy, healthful Strictly, *healthy* means being in a state of health; *healthful* means serving to promote health. People are healthy, but good food is healthful.

hear, listen *Hear* means auditing any sound; *listen* means focusing your hearing. EXAMPLE: *She listened for his voice but heard only the birds' song.*

hopefully When used in the sense of *it is hoped* (i.e., "*Hopefully* we can agree on a price"), the word is inappropriate.

humaneness, humanity Both words may be used to mean possessing compassion or sympathy, but *humanity* is also used to describe human kind. There is no such word as *humanness.*

identify, relate These words should not be used without the reflexive pronoun. EXAMPLES: *I identify myself with Othello's fate. He cannot relate himself to any institution.* In most cases other constructions are more exact: "I feel a strong identity with Othello's fate."

if, whether Both *if* and *whether* are used to introduce a noun clause in indirect questions after verbs like *doubt, ask, wonder. Whether* is more likely to be used if an alternative introduced by *or* is stated. There is still some feeling among teachers and writers that *whether* is more formal, but both words are used and have been used for many years to introduce noun clauses. EXAMPLES: *I doubt if they can come. He wondered whether or not he should warn the settlers. Ask him if he has any food left.*

ignorant, stupid *Ignorant* means lacking knowledge of, while *stupid* means unable to comprehend. EXAMPLES: *She was ignorant of the facts in the case. Running into other cars is a stupid habit.*

imply, infer *Imply* means to indicate or suggest without stating; *infer* means to derive or conclude a meaning. EXAMPLES: *The professor* implied that her answer was wrong. *She inferred a different meaning from his words.*

important *More important,* not *importantly,* is the correct adverbial usage of the word.

in, into In theory, the distinction between these words is that *in* denotes location inside something, whereas *into* denotes motion from outside to inside something. In practice, however, *in* is also used in the sense of *into.* EXAMPLES: *Throw that in the waste basket. Please jump in the lake.* "Are you *into* painting?" is a colloquialism.

in back of, back of Both forms, still considered by many to belong to informal speech, have been used in writing for some time. The more formal word is *behind.*

in conclusion, in summary Use of such expressions as introductions to the final paragraph of your essay is awkward and mechanical. Simply state your conclusion (your reader can *see* that you have reached your last paragraph) without this rhetorical throat-clearing.

in terms of, in connection with Officialese. These phrases should be avoided, as they add nothing to the import of sentences. EXAMPLE: (*In terms of sheer power,*) *Hank Aaron is the best home run hitter in baseball.*

in the worst way Colloquial for *extremely.*

in this day and age Cliché. Use *now.*

ingenious, ingenuous An *ingenious* person is inventive, or clever; an *ingenuous* person is unaffected, or artless. EXAMPLES: *The general's plan showed ingenious thinking. Tom is so ingenuous he didn't realize that he was being tricked.*

insightful A recently invented adjective, which has quickly become overworked: "an *insightful* person," "an *insightful* comment." It is probably better to declare that "She *showed insight*" or that hers was "a *perceptive* remark."

irony, ironic Use *irony* or *ironic* only when there is a *dramatic* discrepancy between what is said and what is meant, or between what is supposed to happen and what does happen. It is a *coincidence* if two people with the same car models have an accident. It is *ironic* if both are members of the National Safety Council.

irregardless The writer means *regardless.*

is when, is where These expressions when used in definitions appear awkward and juvenile.

its, it's *Its* is the possessive form of *it. It's* is the contraction of *it is.* The two forms should not be confused.

kind, sort In colloquial usage, these words are often felt to be plural in constructions like this: "These *kind* of dogs are usually hard to

41

train." In more formal situations, both in speech and in writing, most people prefer the singular, as: "I do not like this *sort* of entertainment." "That *kind* of man is not to be trusted."

kind of, sort of Colloquial when used to modify a verb or an adjective. Use *somewhat, somehow, a little, in some degree, rather, for some reason* in formal contexts.

lay, lie The principal parts of *lay* are as follows: "Now I *lay* it down"; "I *laid* it down"; "I have *laid* it down." The principal parts of *lie* are these: "I *lie* down"; "I *lay* down yesterday morning"; "the dog *had lain* in the shade all day." The participles of *lie* and *lay* are *lying* and *laying*. STANDARD: *He had laid* (not *lain*) *his bundle on the table. It had lain* (not *laid*) *there all morning. The dog was lying* (not *laying*) *in the road.*

lead, led The past tense of *lead* (pronounced *leed*) is *led* (pronounced like the metal *lead*).

leave, let It is just as correct to say *leave him alone* as *let him alone*. But *leave* cannot be used for *allow* in such a sentence as "I begged my mother to *leave* me do it."

lend, loan Generally speaking, *lend* should be used as a verb, *loan* as a noun. EXAMPLES: *I lent him ten dollars. We signed many forms to get the loan.*

less Often used in place of *fewer* with collective nouns: "*less* clothes, *less* people." But say *fewer hats, fewer persons.*

liable, likely See *apt.*

lie See *lay.*

like, as, as if In written English, *as* and *as if* introduce clauses; *like* generally governs a noun or pronoun. In speech the substitution of *like* for *as* is widespread. It is probable that the use of *like* as a conjunction will eventually gain acceptance in formal writing. It has not done so yet. INFORMAL: *I wish you would do it like I said you should.* FORMAL: *The war, just as he had predicted, lasted more than five years. Few men could sway an audience as he did.*

line Often vague and redundant, as: "Have you anything interesting in the *line* of fiction?" "He wrote epics and other works along that *line*." BETTER: *Have you any interesting novels? He wrote epics and other narrative poems.*

locate In the sense of *settle,* it is appropriate only in informal use.

lots, lots of Widely used colloquially for *many, much, a large number, a large amount, a great deal.* COLLOQUIAL: *He has a lot to learn. There are lots of exceptions to this rule.*

mad Colloquially *mad* is used in the sense of *angry.* In formal usage it means insane.

majority Inaccurate when used with measures of quantity, time, dis-

484

tance. The appropriate word is *most*. EXAMPLE: *Most of the day* (not *the majority of the day*) *we stood in line and waited.*

material, materiel *Material* means any kind of substance, while *materiel* refers specifically to arms or other military equipment.

media The plural of *medium*. This word is now overworked as a shorthand label for newspapers, radio, and television. Be specific; write "the newspaper reporter," not "the *media* representative."

might of Illiterate for *might have*.

mighty Colloquial for *very*. Unacceptable in most writing.

militate, mitigate *Militate* means to have influence (used with *against*); *mitigate* means to make less severe. EXAMPLES: *Conditions militate against a peaceful solution. The extra pay mitigates the tedium of the work.*

most, almost *Most*, in formal written English, is the superlative form of *much* or *many*. EXAMPLES: *Much food, more food, most food, many men, more men, most men. Almost* is an adverb meaning nearly. In colloquial use *most* is often substituted for *almost*. FORMAL: *Almost* (not *Most*) *all of our friends have returned from college.* In conversational usage, *most* is frequently used to qualify *all, everyone, everybody, anyone, anybody, always.*

much, many *Much* should not be used in place of *many* with most plural nouns. EXAMPLES: *There was too much food. There were too many courses.*

nauseous, nauseated Something that causes nausea is *nauseous;* a person experiencing nausea is *nauseated.* EXAMPLES: *The fish had a nauseous odor. He became nauseated after eating it.*

neat When used as a general honorific ("That's *neat!*"), it is another overused and transitory colloquialism, like *the greatest,* or *fun* (adjective). To be avoided in writing.

neither, nor; either, or *Neither* should be followed by *nor* and *either* by *or*. Both *neither* and *either* may be used with more than two alternatives, as: "*Either* past, present, *or* future . . . ."

nice Strictly used, *nice* means discriminating. When used as a vague word of mild approval, it is to be avoided in serious writing.

no good, no-good Colloquial when used for *worthless, useless, of no value.*

no one Not *noone*.

now An adverb, not an adjective, as in "This is the *now* generation." Be on guard against letting such jargon creep into your writing.

nowhere near, nowheres near The first is common in both speech and writing; the second is common in colloquial speech. In formal writing it is better to use *not nearly*. EXAMPLE: *That was not nearly* (not *nowhere near*) *as much as he had expected.*

O, oh *O* is used with another word, a substantive, usually in direct

41

address, often in poetry. It is always capitalized and is not followed by any mark of punctuation. *Oh* is an exclamation, not capitalized except when it begins a sentence, and is followed by either a comma or an exclamation point.

obviate *Obviate* means to dispose of or provide for, as in "The arms agreement *obviated* the risk of war." It does not mean to make obvious.

occur, take place *Occur* is a broader term than *take place,* which is properly used to refer to planned activities. EXAMPLES: *The accident occurred on the corner. The trial will take place on June 10th.*

off of The *of* is unnecessary. EXAMPLE: *He took the book off* (not *off of*) *the shelf.*

oftentimes The writer means *often.*

O.K. Colloquial.

on account of The writer means *because of.*

one another See *each other.*

oral, verbal *Oral* refers to spoken language; *verbal* refers to all words, spoken or written.

orient, orientate Modern usage generally prefers *orient* to *orientate,* as in: "We waited until we became *oriented* to the campus rules."

out loud Somewhat less formal than *aloud, loudly, audibly.*

outside of Colloquial for *except, besides.* EXAMPLE: *There was no witness to the robbery except* (not *outside of*) *the mailman.*

over with Colloquial in the sense of *finished, ended.*

pack Colloquial in the sense of "He *packs* a wicked punch."

party Except in legal and telephone usage, *party* is colloquial and semihumorous when it means a person.

past history *Past* is redundant here.

per cent Used after numbers. The sign % is not used except after figures in tabulations or in technical writing. *Per cent* is not an exact synonym for *percentage.*

persecute, prosecute To *persecute* is to harass or treat oppressively; to *prosecute* is to bring suit against, with a legal connotation.

personal, personally Students are understandably disposed to hedge their bets, with expressions like *in my personal opinion, personally I believe, my view is,* and so on. In essays on literary interpretation, expressions such as *I get the feeling that . . .* are common. In many cases such qualification weakens the force of what is being said. If you are wrong in what you say, then you are wrong, whether you say it's your personal opinion or not.

plenty Colloquial when used as an adverb in such expressions as *plenty good, plenty good enough, plenty rich,* and so on, or as an adjective before a noun. COLLOQUIAL: *He was plenty rich. The room is plenty large.*

486

There is plenty wood for another fire. FORMAL: *He was very rich. The room is large enough. There is plenty of wood for another fire. Ten dollars is plenty.*

41

plus *Plus* should not be used in place of *moreover* or *in addition.* "I worked overtime; moreover (not *plus*), I had to wait weeks for my paycheck."

P.M. See *A.M., a.m.*

poorly Colloquial for *in poor health, not well, unwell.*

practicable, practical *Practicable* means something possible, feasible, usable. *Practical* means useful, not theoretical, experienced. *Practical* may apply to persons, things, ideas; *practicable* may not apply to persons.

predominate, predominant *Predominate* is a verb, *predominant* an adjective. Be sure to keep these words distinct in your writing. EXAMPLES: *Threatening weather conditions predominate today. He has the predominant army on his side.*

prescribe, proscribe Prescribe means to set down or give directions; *proscribe* means to prohibit.

proceed, precede *Proceed* means to go on with; *precede* means to go before. EXAMPLES: *After a short interruption, she proceeded with her analysis. His wife preceded him to the stage.*

prophecy, prophesy Don't confuse these words. *Prophecy* is a noun ("The *prophecy* came true"), *prophesy* a verb ("He claimed he could *prophesy* the outcome").

proposition, proposal *Proposal* implies a direct and explicit act of proposing; *proposition* implies a statement or principle for discussion. The loose use of *proposition* to mean an idea, a thing, a task, a business enterprise, a problem is disliked by many people. EXAMPLES: *It is a poor practice* (not *proposition*) *to study until three in the morning. Moving the settlers out of the district was an impractical plan* (not *proposition*).

quiet, quite Two words carelessly confused. *Quiet* has to do with stillness or calmness. In formal standard usage, *quite* means entirely, completely. "You are *quite* right." In informal usage it may also be used to mean very, to a considerable degree. "The dog seems *quite* friendly."

quite a few, quite a bit Overused in student writing.

raise, rise Two verbs often confused. The principal parts of *raise:* "I *raise* my hand"; "he *raised* the window"; "they *have raised* the flag." The principal parts of *rise:* "I *rise* in the morning"; "they *rose* before I did"; "they *had risen* at sunset."

rap Colloquial for *sentence* or *judgment,* as in "a bum *rap*." Recently the word has been used as a verb and noun to mean discuss or debate: "We *rapped* about drug abuse." It is colloquial in this use too.

487

41

ravage, ravish These words are often confused but they mean different things. EXAMPLES: *The city was ravaged (destroyed) by fire. She was ravished (raped) by her abductor. Ravish* also means to carry away or transport with joy or pleasure.

real *Real* as an adverb, in the sense of *very* ("It was a *real* exciting game") is colloquial. Its formal equivalent is *really.* Both, however, are vague and weak intensifiers, of little use in promoting meaning. See *awful, so, such.*

reason is because See *because.*

refer See *allude.*

relation, relationship These words are used synonymously, though *relationship* means specifically the state of being related. EXAMPLE: *Something has changed the relationship* (not *relation* or *relations*) *between John and his father.*

relevant This word should be used with *to,* then a noun: *"relevant to* her beliefs"; *"relevant to* the funds available." Such sentences as "This book is not *relevant"* are vague and misleading. The book is *certainly* relevant to someone's interests, if only to the author's.

same, such Appropriate in legal documents. In ordinary speech and writing it is better to use *it, this, that.* EXAMPLE: *When you have repaired the watch, please ship it* (not *same*) *to me.*

scene Colloquial when used in such sentences as "This is a bad *scene."*

see where For *see that,* as: "I *see* where the team lost another game." Permissible only in colloquial speech.

sensibility, sensitivity *Sensibility* means the ability to perceive or feel; *sensitivity* means ready susceptibility to outside influences. EXAMPLES: *The music critic possesses a mature sensibility. The plant's reaction revealed its sensitivity to light.*

sensual, sensuous *Sensual* usually means lewd or unchaste; *sensuous* means pertaining to the senses. A *sensuous* person is one who puts value in experiences of the senses, but he or she need not be *sensual* in the process.

set, sit Two verbs often confused. Learn the principal parts: "I *set* it down"; "I *have set* it down"; "now he *sits* down"; "I *sat* down"; "they *have sat* down." But of course one may speak of "a *setting* hen," and the sun *sets,* not *sits.* "You may *set* the cup on the shelf and then *sit* down." "I *sat* on the stool after I had *set* the cup down."

shape Colloquial for *condition.* COLLOQUIAL: *The athlete was in excellent shape.* FORMAL: *The equipment was in very good condition* (not *shape*).

simulate See *dissimulate.*

situation, position Both words are abused in officialese: "Regarding the present *situation* . . ."; "With respect to the president's *position* on . . . ." If you must use these words, try to restrict their connotations as much as possible. EXAMPLE: *Her position on the team was right field.*

so As a conjunction between main clauses, *so* is much overused in student writing. Usually the primary fault is too little subordination instead of too much use of *so*. EXAMPLES: *The bridge was blown up during the night, and so the attack was delayed. The attack was delayed because the bridge had been blown up during the night. The Russians were not ready, so they waited until August to declare war on Japan. Since the Russians were not ready, they waited until August to declare war on Japan.*

In clauses of purpose, the standard subordinating conjunction is *so that*, as in: "They flew low *so that* they could observe the results of the bombing." But *so* is also used, especially in spoken English.

So as a "feminine intensive" can be easily overworked in speech—and it often is. It has a long literary tradition, however. EXAMPLES: *She is so kind and so charming. The work is so hard.*

social, societal *Social* describes society or its organization, persons living in it, or the public. *Societal* should be reserved for describing large social groups, their customs and activities. EXAMPLES: *Excessive drinking is a major social problem. Doctors and lawyers hold opposing societal views.*

sort of See *kind of.*

state Used frequently when *say* is more precise. *State* is appropriate when you mean an official declaration.

strata See *data.*

such As an intensive, it is used like *awful* or *so*. Also see *real. Such* introducing a clause of result is followed by *that*. EXAMPLE: *There was such an explosion that it could be felt for miles.* When introducing a relative clause, *such* is followed by *as*. EXAMPLE: *Such improvements as are necessary will be made immediately.*

sure Colloquial for *certainly, surely, indeed.*

swell Another hardy colloquialism, in the sense of *excellent, very good, admirable, enjoyable.* Avoid in writing.

tactics, strategy *Tactics* means specific actions, while *strategy* means an overall plan. EXAMPLES: *Her tactics included holding long meetings and evading questions. Her strategy was to avoid confrontation.*

temerity, timorousness *Temerity* means rashness; *timorousness* means fearfulness. Be sure not to confuse these two words.

that there, this here Illiterate forms.

their, they're *Their* is a possessive pronoun. *They're* means "they are." EXAMPLE: *They're happy because their team won.*

thorough, through An elementary spelling problem.

489

41

to, too, two Another elementary spelling problem. EXAMPLE: *He too should make two trips to the dictionary to learn how to spell. It's not too hard.* Do not use *too* as a substitute for *very.*

type of The phrase is excess baggage and should be avoided. EXAMPLES: *He is a moody type of person* (*a moody person*). *It is a racing-type bicycle* (*a racing bicycle*).

use, utilize In most cases *utilize* is officialese for *use.* *Utilize* means specifically to put to use. Note the awkwardness in the following sentence: "To these natives the *utilization* of knives and forks is foreign."

verbal See *oral.*

very, very much Many educated persons object to *very* instead of *very much* or *very greatly* as a modifier of a verb or a participle in a verb phrase. Other persons point out examples of its use in the works of reputable writers. See the note under *very* in *Webster's Third New International.* EXAMPLES: *They were very pleased. They were very much pleased. They seemed very disturbed. They seemed very greatly disturbed.*

viable Now overworked in officialese: "a *viable* alternative." Use *workable* or *practicable* in its place.

vocation See *avocation.*

wait on Regional for wait for, stay for. Standard in the sense of attend, perform services for, as: "It was the other girl who waited on me."

want in, want out, want off, etc. Dialectal forms of *want to come in, want to go out, want to get off,* etc.

way, ways *Way* is colloquial for *condition.* *Ways* is dialectal for *distance, way.* FORMAL: *When we saw him, he was in bad health* (not *in a bad way*). *We walked a long distance* (not *ways*) *before we rested.*

where at The *at* is unnecessary. EXAMPLE: *Where is he now?* (not *Where is he at now?*) A sentence such as "I don't know *where* you're *at* intellectually" is both colloquial and redundant. You may get away with it in speaking but not in writing.

which and that, who and that *Which* refers to things; *who* refers to people. *That* can refer to either things or people, usually in restrictive clauses. EXAMPLES: *The pictures, which were gaudy and overdecorated, made me wince. The pictures that I bought yesterday were genuine; the others were fake. Who* can also be used in a restrictive clause, as: "I want to see all the people *who* care to see me." With *that,* the same clause is still restrictive: "I want to see all the people *that* care to see me."

while Frequently overused as a conjunction. Usually *but, and,* or *whereas* would be more precise. It is standard in the sense of *at the same time as* or *although.* It is colloquial in the sense of *whereas.*

490

who, whom *Who* should be used for subjects, *whom* for objects of prepositions, direct or indirect objects, subjects and objects of infinitives.

-wise This suffix has been so absurdly overused that it has become largely a joke. "He is a competent administrator *economy-wise,* but *politics-wise* he is a failure." Avoid. Educated people have taken to using the term almost entirely facetiously. "That's the way it goes, *cookie-crumblewise.*"

41

Index

to Quoted Passages

494

Index

497

501

503

Rend, render, defined, 367
Repetition:
 effective use of, 197–199
 for emphasis, 396–397
 of key words, for coherence,
  459
 sentence structure, 443–444
 similar sounds, 398
 wordiness, 394–400
Research paper, 81–130
 bibliography for, 97–101
 choosing a subject, 94–95
 deciding on a general field, 94
 footnotes for, 108–113
 importance of, 81–82
 limiting the subject, 96–97
 outline of, 103, 106, 116
 reading and taking notes, 101–
  103
 sample research paper, 116–130
 subjects for, 94–97
 use of note cards, 103–106
 value of, 94
 writing of, 106–109
Respectfully, respectively, defined, 367
Restrictive clauses, punctuation
  with, 173
Retained object, defined and diagramed, 162
Reverend, Honorable, before names,
  296
Revision of manuscript, 71–72,
  288–291
 specimens of, 288–289
Rhetorical patterns in sentences,
  178–200
Rhythm in prose, 199–200
Roman numerals in footnotes, explained, 112
Run-together sentences, 237–241
 corrected by:
  coordinate conjunction, 238
  subordination, 238
  using period, 239
  using semicolon, 238–239
 legitimate comma junctions,
  239–240

516

S

Said, as reference word, 411–412
Salutation or greeting, in letters,
  134–135
Same, as reference word, 411–412
Same, such, as reference words, 488
See where, for *see that,* 488
Seem, verb, adjective complement
  with, 269
Selecting a subject, 32
-self pronouns, 254
Semicolon, uses of, 333–336
 between main clauses, 333–335
 characteristic of a formal style,
  333
 to show balance or contrast, 333
 when not correct, 334
 with conjunctive adverbs, 335
 with internal punctuation, 335–
  336
 with quotation marks, 344
Sensual, sensuous, differentiated, 488
Sentence outlines, 76–77, 116
Sentences:
 awkward and obscure, 445
 awkward repetition in, 396–398
 balance in, 433–436
 choppy style in, 179–180
 clear reference in, 181, 407–409
 comparisons in, 437–439
 conciseness of expression in,
  394–396
 dangling modifiers in, 419–422
 defined and diagramed, 158–175
 effectiveness in, 178–200
 emphasis in, 423–424
 excessive details in, 394–396
 logical completeness in, 233–236
 long and short, for variety, 188–
  190
 loose and periodic, 425–426
 misplaced modifiers in, 414–418
 misrelated modifiers in, 419–422
 mixed constructions in, 430
 mixed imagery in, 431
 overloaded, 398–400

519

KEY TO THE HANDBOOK